Arctic Ocean

Bering Sea

Sea of Okhotsk

RUSSIA

Sea of Japan

JAPAN

MONGOLIA

NORTH KOREA

SOUTH KOREA

CHINA

Yellow Sea

0   800 kms

The
CIS
Handbook

The CIS Handbook

Edited by

Patrick Heenan and Monique Lamontagne

Advisers

Ronald J. Hill
University of Dublin (Trinity College)

Bogdan Szajkowski
University of Exeter

FITZROY DEARBORN PUBLISHERS

LONDON • CHICAGO

Regional Handbooks of Economic Development
Prospects onto the 21st Century

The China Handbook
The India Handbook
The Japan Handbook
The CIS Handbook
The Central and Eastern Europe Handbook

Forthcoming

The Southeast Asia Handbook

FITZROY DEARBORN PUBLISHERS
919 North Michigan Avenue
Chicago, Illinois 60611
USA
or
310 Regent Street
London W1R 5AJ
UK

British Library Cataloguing in Publication Data
Russia/CIS handbook. – (Regional handbooks of economic
development: prospects onto the 21st century)
   1. Russia (Federation) – Economic policy – 1991–
   2. Former Soviet Republics – Economic policy
   I. Heenan, Patrick
   330.9′47′086

ISBN 1-57958-088-2

Library of Congress Cataloging in Publication Data is available.

First published in the USA and UK 1999
Typeset by Florence Production Ltd, Stoodleigh, Devon
Printed in Great Britain by The Bath Press

Contents

International Relations

Appendices

Editors' Note

Of all the books published so far in the series *Regional Handbooks of Economic Development*, this has been perhaps the most difficult to give a title to. As several contributors make clear, the CIS has proved to be ineffective in most of its activities, and largely irrelevant to the daily lives of the citizens of its member states. Nevertheless, any study of the development of these 12 successor states of the Soviet Union and their prospects requires at least some consideration of the CIS, the only organization that brings them all together now or is likely to do so in the coming years.

This is not to say that the CIS fully defines the region, which has some well-known alternative names. However, most of these include one or another variation on the words "Soviet" or "Communist" and therefore carry their own risks of misrepresentation. The Soviet Union, created and controlled by the Communist Party, endured for 69 years; many more years will have to pass before it is no longer a living memory or a source of continuing controversy. Not surprisingly, much of what happens in the successor states cannot be understood without reference to the Soviet period, and the distinctive institutions and attitudes that were formed during it. Yet it has gone, presumably for good. Its former citizens are now rebuilding their societies, using unstable compounds of the Soviet legacy itself, the still older legacy of the nationalist, religious and other ideologies that the Communist Party never completely suppressed, and the newer ideas and practices flooding in from the West and elsewhere.

Still other names for the region might include some explicit reference to Russia, which is overwhelmingly the largest country of the 12, in area and in population. Yet even those who can accept the idea of a "Greater China" (at least as a cultural unit) would hesitate to suggest that the CIS region is no more than a "Greater Russia." The presence of large Russian minorities in each of the other 11 states, and the persistence of Russian as a *lingua franca* for the region, may arouse fears of a revival of past imperialism, whether Soviet or pre-Soviet. Even so, the chances are greater than ever before that mutual respect and cooperation may prevail, fulfilling one of the many ideals that fueled the revolutions of 1917, only to be betrayed as Communism degenerated.

Meanwhile, the peoples of all 12 countries in the CIS look beyond the region for political support, economic interaction, and cultural exchange: to NATO, the EU, and central and eastern Europe (whether including Yugoslavia or excluding it); to the Islamic world; or to China. Yet all 12 find that they are regarded as, at best, welcome guests, and, at worst, suspect strangers. In any case, history has imposed a common identity on these former provinces of a great land empire, and part of that identity rests on a determination not to fall into the hands of any other empire. The CIS countries, like those of central and eastern Europe, are often called "transition economies," but their transition started from distinctive foundations, and is taking them towards distinctive futures.

No single book can hope to provide a complete account of even one of these 12 countries, let alone of the whole CIS. (Nor does this book attempt to examine Estonia, Latvia or Lithuania in any detail, since these three Baltic states were never recognized in international law as Soviet republics, and have not joined the CIS. Instead, they are included in a companion volume, _The Central and Eastern Europe Handbook._) Our goal here has been to discuss a defined range of facts and issues, as concisely, accessibly, and evenhandedly as possible. The book is aimed at students, scholars and the general public alike.

We would like to thank all those who have helped in the making of this book. Our contributors have been patient and cooperative throughout; their contributions include not just the chapters in their names, but large parts of the appendices. Our academic advisers both did useful work, recommending contributors and helping to shape the structure of the book, and we are grateful to Dr Graham Field and to many others who took an interest in the project. Finally, Roda Morrison has once again supplied valuable editorial support at every stage.

Linguistic Conventions

The Soviet Union and its successor states are referred to by their generally accepted names in English. For eight of these states, these names closely resemble their names in their own main languages, although there are differences in spelling, such as Kazakhstan (Qazaqstan), and/or in vowel sounds, such as Uzbekistan (Uzbekiston). There are, however, two cases of significant difference: Armenia (Hayastan) and Georgia (Sak'art'velo). The following cities, and the regions that are named for them, are also referred to by names that have become customary in English: Baku (Baki), Minsk (Miensk), Moscow (Moskva), Nakhichevan (Naxçıvan), St Petersburg (Sankt-Peterburg), Samarkand (Samarqand), and Tashkent (Toshkent). Most names of subnational units, such as Nagorno-Karabakh (Artsakh or Karabagh to its Armenian inhabitants), Crimea (Krym) or Siberia (Sibirya), are also given in the accepted English forms. Other place names – including Kyiv, which is still probably better known in the West by its Russian name, Kiev – are rendered in the most appropriate language.

Readers should note that the word "region" is unavoidably used with three different meanings: the CIS territory as a whole; the major subnational unit in most CIS countries (although the Russian term _oblast_ and its equivalents also appear); and an unofficially defined socioeconomic area (such as "western Ukraine").

The ethnic group often still referred to as "Gypsies," reflecting a nonexistent connection with Egypt, are referred to here by their preferred name, "Roma."

Currency Symbols

AD	dram (Armenia)	R	Russian ruble
AM	Azerbaijani manat	TR	Tajik ruble
BR	Belarusian rubel	TM	Turkmen manat
GL	lari (Georgia)	UH	hrivna (Ukraine)
KS	som (Kyrgyzstan)	US$	US dollar
KT	tenge (Kazakhstan)	UzS	sum (Uzbekistan)
ML	Moldovan leu (plural, lei)		

Abbreviations

The following abbreviations are used throughout this book:

CIS	Commonwealth of Independent States
Comecon	Council for Mutual Economic Assistance (1949–91)
CSCE / OSCE	Conference on Security and Cooperation in Europe (1975–94)/ Organization for Security and Cooperation in Europe (since 1995)
EU	European Union

GATT	General Agreement on Tariffs and Trade
GDP / GNP	Gross Domestic Product / Gross National Product
IMF	International Monetary Fund
NATO	North Atlantic Treaty Organization
OECD	Organization for Economic Cooperation and Development
UK	United Kingdom (when used as an adjective)
UN	United Nations
US	United States (when used as an adjective)

In other cases, the meaning of each abbreviation or acronym is stated at its first appearance within each chapter.

History
and
Context

Chapter One

The Soviet Economy, 1945–91

Robert C. Stuart

After the Bolshevik revolution of 1917, and a 10-year period of change and interrupted development (War Communism and the New Economic Policy), the administrative command economy was introduced in the Soviet Union by Josef Stalin, beginning in 1928 (see Gregory and Stuart; Davies; Davies, Harrison, and Wheatcroft; and Nove 1986 and 1992). Under a leadership guided by "Marxist-Leninist" principles, the means of production were nationalized, agriculture was collectivized, and finally, national economic planning was introduced. The systemic changes of the 1930s, and the policy directives of the Soviet regime guided by the Communist Party of the Soviet Union, fundamentally changed the nature of resource allocation in the Soviet Union (see Konn). These organizational arrangements and economic policies established during the 1930s remained, with only limited change, until the demise of the Soviet Union as a political entity in 1991.

The Soviet experience during the 1930s was one of the most tumultuous periods in modern economic history. Change, especially in agriculture, was often introduced with brutal force, backed by the reign of Stalinist terror (see Lewin). At the same time, patterns of resource allocation were fundamentally changed, such that, on the eve of World War II, a system and its outcomes that would last through the 1980s were basically in place. The Soviet leadership attempted to harness agriculture to support a program of rapid industrialization, sharply moving resources away from the consumer and service sectors towards industry, and especially heavy industry. The arrangements put in place by Stalin fundamentally changed the nature of resource allocation in the Soviet Union, sharply altering both the sources and the uses of national income, reducing the importance of foreign trade, and generating rapid rates of economic growth during the 1930s (see Table 1.1).

Although controversy surrounds much of the Soviet economic experience of the 1930s, few would disagree that fundamental change occurred, establishing a command economy about to enter a major military conflict. Although there was a significant shift towards military production in the latter part of the 1930s, ultimately the cost of World War II to the Soviet Union was massive. Whether measured by the losses of personnel, the destruction of the capital stock, or the human suffering of the population, a substantial part of the economic achievement of the 1930s was lost, a fact that led to a continuation of Stalinist oppression until the dictator's death in March 1953.

The Soviet Union lacked a systematic means for the replacement of its political leaders. Accordingly, the death of Stalin was followed by a leadership struggle and, by the mid-1950s, the emergence of Nikita Khrushchev as the leader of the Soviet Union. In many respects, the Khrushchev era ushered in important changes, often characterized as a "thaw" or relaxation when compared to the Stalin era. However, while important changes were attempted in the Soviet economic system during the Khrushchev era, fundamentally the system and the associated policies put in place by Stalin remained. The Khrushchev era ended when he was ousted in the fall of 1964, and was followed by the leadership of Leonid

Brezhnev (1964–82). If Khrushchev was flamboyant and experimental, Brezhnev was quite the opposite, staid and traditional. Although Brezhnev was in power for many years, it was a period of limited change, failed economic reforms, and ultimately much lethargy. For a limited period in the 1980s, the Soviet Union was led by Yuri Andropov (1982–83) and Konstantin Chernenko (1983–85), to be superseded by Mikhail Gorbachev, the last Soviet leader, in 1985. What was the nature of the Soviet economic system inherited by these Soviet leaders?

The Soviet Economy: The Emergence of Planning

Most economies are in fact mixed systems, in the sense that they rely upon a combination of market mechanisms and administrative measures or directives for the purpose of allocating resources towards the achievement of economic and social objectives. The classic Soviet-type economy was fundamentally a hierarchical administrative structure, with state and Party power at the upper levels, sectoral ministries at the intermediate level, and state-owned enterprises and farms at the local level (see Gregory and Stuart). Within these organizational arrangements, decisions on the allocation of resources were carried out largely, though not exclusively, through the national economic plan, with important decisions made at the upper levels, and lesser decisions made at lower levels of the hierarchy. It was this system, put in place in the 1930s, that would be sustained, in spite of continuing attempts at reform, through the end of the 1980s.

Planning and Resource Allocation

The basic decisions of any economy – namely, what to produce, how to produce, who gets the production (distribution of the product), and, finally, how to achieve and sustain economic growth – were, in the Soviet case, decided largely by the state. Soviet arrangements to answer these questions were often described as a system of planners' preferences, as contrasted to consumer sovereignty in market economies.

Fundamental to any system of planning is the preparation of the plan, the implementation of the plan, and, finally, feedback to modify the plan through time. Although it would be simplistic to believe that the Soviet economy was a rigidly and fully centralized system, and that all allocation decisions were made within the formalities of the central plan, nevertheless the fundamental allocation of resources was based on Party directives, conveyed through the State Planning Commission (Gosplan), which sent the five-year plan (and annual sub-plans) to ministries, and ultimately to producing enterprises.

Plan formulation in the Soviet Union, though time-consuming and complex, focused mainly on the key products and activities of the economy, such as steel or chemicals. The essence of the plan was a system of balances, essentially relating inputs and outputs, or sources and uses, and attempting to maximize output, and thus the growth of the economy. For example, the state targeted the output of steel and the inputs (land, labor, and capital) necessary for producing the steel. The plan directives told firms what to produce (how much steel) and how to produce the steel (the mix of inputs), with state institutions responsible for the coordination of the process (delivery of inputs) and the distribution of the product to an intermediate or final user. While planning was in theory complex and difficult, as we shall see below, many simplifications distorted the system, allowing it to function in the real world, albeit at low levels of efficiency.

Implementing the Plan: Ministries and Firms

While the national economic plan was formally developed by Gosplan and its agencies, the plan directives were disaggregated through the ministries and presented to the individual enterprises for fulfillment. Soviet enterprises were state-owned and budget-financed, in the sense that enterprise revenues flowed into the state budget, while enterprises' expenses, for example wage payments for labor, were allocated from the state budget. Although enterprise managers played a role in the formulation and, especially, the execution of the plan, the managerial milieu was complex. Targets were often poorly specified and difficult to achieve in a setting of shortages (inadequate supplies of inputs), where managerial rewards were closely tied to the achievement of overoptimistic plan targets. As we shall note below when assessing the performance of the Soviet economy, understanding the managerial milieu is fundamental to understanding why plans were often not fulfilled, quality and product mix were often ignored, and cost reduction was not a major objective of enterprises. It was for these reasons that the management system was a target of reform throughout the postwar years.

Money and Prices in the Soviet Economy

In market economies, we are accustomed to the presence of markets in both factors and products, in which the interaction of supply and demand creates prices. Thus, in these markets the exchange of both factors and products takes place along with roughly equivalent monetary flows, derived from the sale and purchase of both factors and products. The resulting prices formed in these markets are crucial to the process of resource allocation, both for factors of production and for products. The Soviet economy was very different, since there were no product or factor markets, allocation being achieved through administrative directives. There were, however, roles for both money and prices.

The State Bank (Gosbank) was responsible for the money supply, a state secret during most of the Soviet period, which was intended to bear a close resemblance to the requirements of the economy, specifically the value of output. Prices were set by the state based not upon supply and demand, but rather upon cost and associated markups, including profit and the turnover tax; the latter a major element of state revenues. Factor prices (wages) were also set by the state and capital, allocated administratively through the state banking system to state enterprises, carried only a limited charge originally intended not as a price for a scarce factor, but rather as a charge to cover administrative costs.

Conceptually, the creation of a balance between the monetary and real sides of the Soviet economy was feasible, with various mechanisms for adjustment such as the rates for the turnover tax, levels of wages, and extraction by the state of enterprise profits. The system functioned rather differently in the 1950s than it did in the 1980s, but, on balance, money played only a very limited role in the Soviet economy, a fact that would significantly complicate the process of transition to markets in the 1990s.

Inputs: Labor and Capital

We have emphasized that factor markets did not exist in the Soviet economy. In fact, however, the degree of state influence and the role of the national economic plan in factor allocation varied. The state's demand for labor was derived from norms or coefficients relating targeted output (steel in our example above) to the labor required to make the steel. Although administrative mechanisms were used for the allocation of labor, market-type mechanisms, such as significant wage differentials, were also used. Thus, the primary form of household accumulation was wage income, and the labor supply decision was vested largely in the household. While consumer goods were sold in state stores, at retail prices set by the state, shortages prevailed, limiting the growth of consumption and leading to significant household accumulation of rubles, an especially important process in the absence of financial markets. Thus, while the state did not directly "plan" the economic activities of the household, nevertheless the household functioned within major constraints.

The magnitude of accumulation (investment) was determined by the state, since the state controlled output and the major input (wages of labor) to be used in production. Moreover, as we have emphasized, the allocation of capital to sectors of the economy, and to particular enterprises within these sectors, was also controlled by the state. Specifically, capital allocations to enterprises were determined by administrative means through the state banking system, in the absence of capital markets and interest rates. In this setting, it is not surprising that managers aggressively sought capital, or that Soviet industry was capital-intensive. It is also understandable that under such a system of capital allocation, state priorities could be emphasized, with heavy industry favored and light industry (consumer goods) not favored. Thus major determinants of economic growth, namely the magnitude of investment and its allocation to growth-enhancing activities, were determined directly by the state, not by consumers in a market-place. These systemic arrangements and asso-ciated polices led to patterns of resource use (as in Table 1.1) that were very different from those that would be expected in a market setting, and that have proved very difficult to change during the transition era of the 1990s.

Special Sectors: Agriculture and Foreign Trade

In the typical development experience, both agriculture and foreign trade play important and varying roles. The differences in the Soviet case are worth examining, since developments in both sectors are important for our under-standing of the Soviet economic experience.

The empirical evidence clearly indicates that agriculture was an important sector of the Russian economy during the decades before the revolution. During the 1920s, there was con-siderable debate on the role that agriculture would play in the Soviet economic experience. Through the creation of both state and collec-tive farms, Stalin attempted to use agriculture as a means to force rapid accumulation, and hence rapid economic growth, in the 1930s. While the details of that story can be found else-where (see Lewin), the organizational arrange-ments and the policies in agriculture under the Soviet leadership were, to put it mildly, very controversial. Although agriculture became the focus of much attention throughout the postwar era, in fact production did not keep pace with domestic demand, the net result being growing imports and major subsidies to an agricultural sector plagued with inefficiency (see Gray).

Like agriculture, trade is often envisioned as a mechanism that can play a leading role in the process of economic development (see Holzman). Again like agriculture, trade played an important role in the Russian economy

before the revolution, not only through the effects of both imports and exports, but also because of the inflow of foreign capital, which is so significant in enhancing economic growth in relatively backward countries. Beginning in 1928, the arrangements and policies of Soviet foreign trade were changed fundamentally. The conduct of foreign trade was centralized in state institutions, the ruble was not a convertible currency, and foreign investment as a means to promote economic growth effectively came to an end (see Holzman). While the state could dictate elements of the trading outcome, by reducing imports of consumer goods, trading with "friendly" coun-tries, and the like, one could argue that, from an economic perspective, the Soviet leadership effectively isolated the Soviet Union from the world economy, and indeed from the potential benefits that could be derived from active participation in it. During the early years, Stalin effectively controlled foreign trade, selling grain and raw materials while importing machinery and equipment, and sharply curtailing the import of consumer goods. While the Soviet system facilitated such changes, the nature of the Soviet foreign trade structure arguably reduced the importance of trade in the economy, and thus limited the extent to which the Soviet Union could benefit from comparative advantage and specialization in world markets. Postwar efforts to integrate the Soviet Union with the satellite economies of central and eastern Europe also failed.

The Soviet Economy: Theory and Reality

Thus far, we have outlined the basics of the Soviet economic system, emphasizing how this system differed from the market system with which we are familiar. As we pursue the evolu-tion of these systemic arrangements and their performance through the 1980s, it is important to appreciate that change arose in part because, as with most economic systems, theory and reality differed. These differences mattered, as both Soviet institutions, and the policies guiding those institutions, were challenged by the continuing reality of lagging economic performance.

Although even a simple description of Soviet reality could be lengthy, the basics are noteworthy. First, while output was in theory planned, in fact only important products in critical industries were planned at the center. The fact that the output of lesser items would be planned at lower levels or even in localities meant that there was considerable diversity in production and distribution arrangements. Although a second or underground economy arose, this economy was of a limited (though expanding) scope.

Second, while the creation of a national economic plan can be elegant in theory, in fact even the basic information requirements of such a plan were well beyond Soviet reality, especially in an era when computers were in their infancy. A major outcome of information problems was the simplification of plan preparation, for example, often using inaccurate and outdated norms, leading to plan mistakes. Output targets were based upon inaccurate and dated calculations regarding input requirements, and with limited changes from year to year. Factories were asked to make products for which there were no inputs, while surpluses of these inputs languished at other factories. Although there was barter, there were no markets to coordinate these activities.

Third, in a system based on priorities where planning and implementation mistakes were common, the concept of "buffer" or "low priority" activities arose. In this context, it is not surprising that the Soviet Union produced an excess of unneeded steel (a priority) while consumer goods were in persistent shortage. What is more striking is the fact that over time the system lacked a mechanism to make seemingly obvious adjustments. Although a state-owned retail store might sell a product to a consumer at a state-set price, and realize a profit, this profit was simply a part of state revenue, from which there was no feedback to influence production. Shortages and surpluses persisted with no mechanism of adjustment.

Fourth, although Soviet organizational arrangements could be characterized in a theoretically elegant way, for example as the chart of a complex hierarchical organization, in fact many of the difficulties of the Soviet economic experience arose from problems familiar to anyone who has experienced the culture of a large complex organization. In contemporary terminology, the Soviet economic system was a classic example of a large complex organization in which a variety of agency (principal-agent) problems arose. The problems of information and incentive compatibility were evident in continuing Soviet attempts to reform the system, beginning with Nikita Khrushchev in the 1950s and ending with Mikhail Gorbachev in the 1980s.

Finally, as we assess Soviet economic policies as they evolved in the postwar period, it is useful to consider the Soviet system within its own declared framework of intentions, namely the development of a "socialist" and ultimately a "communist" economic system, based upon Marxist-Leninist principles. While scholars of Marx might well argue that the Soviet Union, judged critically against the norms of such systems, was not socialist at all, nevertheless these principles can be useful to enhance our understanding of Soviet economic behavior.

From Khrushchev to Gorbachev

The Soviet economic system described above was largely still in place, albeit heavily damaged, at the end of World War II. Although one might have anticipated change in response to both the trauma of the 1930s and the impact of World War II, the last years of the Stalin era, in the late 1940s and early 1950s, witnessed a return to the policies and methods of terror used earlier. However, after Stalin's death and the emergence of Nikita Khrushchev as Soviet leader, a new era began.

The Khrushchev Era: Relaxation and Rebuff

The 1950s were in many respects good years for the Soviet economy. From the perspective of economic performance, the evidence seemed positive. Although controversy justifiably surrounded official estimates of an average rate of economic growth of more than 10% a year during the 1950s, even the most conservative alternative estimates suggested an average annual rate of more than 5%. These were heady times for the prevailing Soviet leadership, since the slowdown in growth, and the troubling forces underlying this slowdown, would not become evident until the 1960s and later.

In a setting of apparently healthy economic growth, Nikita Khrushchev was a vibrant and ideologically committed leader. Although he denounced Stalin, in the famous "secret speech" in February 1956, with the launching of Sputnik in the following year Khrushchev challenged the West to an economic race in which he proudly declared: "we will bury you." This, however, was a claim that the West took seriously, as when, for example, US President John F. Kennedy promised to "get the economy moving again" in the 1960s.

If Khrushchev was an important figure in the emergence of the Cold War, under the Soviet policy of "peaceful coexistence," he was busy at home, and few aspects of the economy missed his attention. Khrushchev was responsible for major, if sometimes quietly implemented, changes in agriculture. There was a major emphasis on expanding inputs, for example through a continuation of the Virgin Lands program for the significant expansion of the area of cultivated land, and the high priority placed upon the expansion of the chemical industry for the production of chemical fertilizers. Organizational change did not escape his attention. Beginning earlier and continuing through the 1950s, there was a major campaign to consolidate farms, sharply increasing their size and forming the beginnings of what would be termed "agroindustrial integration." On both state and collective farms, arrangements were changed to improve decision-making and to enhance incentives.

There were also important changes in the urban-industrial sector. Most attempted reforms in Soviet industry focused in one way or another on making things work better – improvement of the planning system, improvement of the management system, generally approached through organizational change. Beginning in the late 1950s, considerable attention was paid to the ideas of the Soviet economist Evsei Liberman, who proposed that managerial bonuses be closely tied to the profitability of enterprises, in order to make managers more likely to fulfill plans, and to do so cognizant of quality, cost reduction, and product assortment. In the end, this reform languished, to be resurrected in a different form under the subsequent leadership of Leonid Brezhnev. Another important reform was the attempt to change the basic direction of Soviet planning, away from a product or industry basis to a regional basis.

Although these changes were not as fundamental as those implemented earlier by Stalin, they were nevertheless viewed as controversial, and led to the ending of the Khrushchev era. Indeed, these early postwar attempts to reform the Soviet industrial system demonstrated features of Soviet reform that would guarantee failure through the end of the Gorbachev era. Reforms tended to be based upon simplistic notions of organizational change, and little attention was given to the problems of implementation in the face of strong and contrary vested interests. Most Soviet reforms were partial in nature: for example, the notion that the Liberman reform could function effectively, given the nature of Soviet price-setting arrangements, was naïve, yet little attention was paid to the critical issue of price reform.

While Stalin was characterized in Soviet writings as fostering a "cult of personality," Khrushchev was described as a "harebrained schemer" and a promoter of "subjectivism" – characterizations which in large part were due to the controversy surrounding many of his attempted changes. His plan to reorganize industry was scrapped, and his campaigns in agriculture, such as those directed towards the elimination of crop rotation were viewed as scientifically inappropriate, even in an era when scientific leadership in agriculture came from the biologist Trofim Lysenko, who was later comprehensively discredited. Although changes made during the Khrushchev era were important, fundamentally the Soviet system of earlier years remained in place.

The Brezhnev Era: Stagnation

The Brezhnev era was, in a sense, a return to routine. A number of the changes from the Khrushchev era, for example the attempted shift to regional planning, were abolished. Beginning in 1965, there was a series of major reform attempts, all of which failed, in the sense that they had little if any positive impact on Soviet economic performance. The reform of 1965, usually identified as the Kosygin Reform – named for the Prime Minister, Aleksei Kosygin – bore a close resemblance to the earlier Liberman proposals. The Kosygin reform attempted to reduce and simplify the targets to be achieved by enterprise managers.

Beginning in the early 1970s, there was another series of reforms focusing on a number of critical areas in the operation of the Soviet economy. Attention continued to be given to management problems, and in addition, labor issues and price formation received attention. The last major reform initiative of the Brezhnev era came in 1979 with the announcement of a program to improve the economic mechanism, a series of changes intended to improve the planning system and to change the role of the enterprise in this system.

The Brezhnev era was subsequently characterized as an era of stagnation, with failed attempts at reform accompanying, not arresting, the continuing decline in economic performance. The task of recognizing the real state of the economy in this era would fall to subsequent leaders.

After Brezhnev

Leonid Brezhnev died in November 1982. It was well known that he had been in very poor health for some time, and had provided little or no leadership for the ailing economy. Although Yuri Andropov had administrative experience as head of the KGB, the Soviet security service, it was evident during his short term in office that, in spite of his efforts to modify the managerial system, his overall posture was conservative. Little if anything was accomplished during the short leadership of the ailing Konstantin Chernenko. Thus, as Mikhail Gorbachev assumed the leadership of the Soviet Union in the spring of 1985, a relatively young Soviet leader emerged, about to introduce a new era of *perestroika* (reconstruction).

The Gorbachev Era: Radical Reform and Collapse

There is little doubt that, by the early 1980s, there was growing recognition that the Soviet economy was in trouble. The growth performance of the economy (to be discussed below) presented a troubling picture. The numerous economic reforms beginning with Nikita Khrushchev in the 1950s seemingly had little effect on the performance of the economy, which was fundamentally in disequilibrium. Households accumulated rubles for which no goods or services were available, while the state continued to direct resources to industry, and especially to the military. If there had been earlier enthusiasm for the building of a new society, that enthusiasm had evaporated, and even the presence of a growing underground economy could not placate consumers who had long been promised a better life. Against this background, Mikhail Gorbachev faced seemingly insurmountable obstacles (see Wilczynski).

While Gorbachev became the subject of early criticism in the West because he lacked a comprehensive program of economic reform, a series of important legislative acts emerged, beginning in 1986, in combination with a series of policy themes that quickly took center stage, both in the Soviet Union and in the West (see Desai). When they are compared to earlier Soviet attempts at reform, it is evident why Gorbachev's proposals for radical reform were viewed as being fundamentally different.

Perestroika was to be a restructuring of the economic system, and, unlike in earlier reforms, political change would be included too, through *glasnost* (openness) and *demokratizatsia* (democratization). However, like earlier reforms, optimistic predictions were made concerning outcomes, especially accelerating economic growth (*uskorenie*), with the "human factor" being a major force to increase productivity and enhance growth.

One could argue that *perestroika* was not a comprehensive reform program, but rather a series of legislative acts, albeit important ones, promulgated in an ad hoc fashion over time. As new legislation was forthcoming, it was often difficult to know precisely what set of rules governed the operation of any particular part of the Soviet economy. However, the legislation was important, and the evidence suggests that there was improvement in economic performance during the early years of *perestroika*, a pattern that would change sharply in 1989 (see Figure 1.3). Thus, from 1986 through 1988, the growth rate of output and the growth rate of productivity both increased steadily, but both declined sharply from then onward.

One major theme of the Gorbachev era was the opening of the economy to full participation in the global economy. Beginning in 1986, Gorbachev introduced at least three major changes in the foreign trade sector. First, the monopoly of the Ministry of Foreign Trade, established by Stalin, was brought to an end, and enterprises were permitted access to foreign exchange, enabling them to engage directly in foreign trading arrangements. Second, beginning in 1987, Soviet enterprises were permitted to enter into joint ventures with foreign firms. Finally, the Soviet Union began to pursue engagement in major world trading arrangements and organizations such as the General Agreement on Tariffs and Trade (GATT), the World Bank, and the IMF.

While these new directions represented fundamental change in both the institutions and the policies of the Soviet Union with regard to foreign trade, they nevertheless failed, for a variety of reasons. The Soviet Union had effectively been isolated for many years, and new arrangements were difficult to implement. Many restrictions, such as those on ownership arrangements for joint ventures (limited equity, managerial participation, and repatriation of profits for foreigners) effectively limited their attractiveness to potential western partners. In effect, even radical economic reform failed, in part for reasons that were quite traditional in the Soviet setting: it was still partial reform, implemented in a piecemeal fashion through appeals to an uncompliant population.

Another major example of change under Gorbachev was yet another attempt to modify the system of planning and management, with the introduction of the Enterprise Law in 1987. If it had been fully implemented this Law could have led to fundamental changes for Soviet industrial enterprises. For example, Gorbachev envisioned an end to plan targets and their replacement with state orders, the implication being that the state would purchase from those enterprises with lower costs, better quality, and so on. Fundamentally, the Enterprise Law was intended to replace much of the command system (directives) with economic incentives, contracts, and the like. The Law was complex and profound, but in the end it failed. It was a set of changes proposed, once again, in isolation from necessary concomitant changes, such as price reform. The market-type mechanisms that were to replace command mechanisms were simply not in place.

The Gorbachev reform was certainly more radical than earlier attempts, both in the depth of the proposals and in the sectors, such as foreign trade, that became the subject of attention. However, one could argue that it was yet another case of attempting to ignite the "Russian spirit," the human factor, which had been done without success so many times in the Soviet period. Like earlier reforms, *perestroika* represented, in many respects, a very limited program for change, once again suggesting how difficult it is to construct mixed systems as social experiments. Much of the old order collapsed, and yet there was nothing to take its place; and, as problems arose during *perestroika*, Gorbachev reverted to the established Soviet tradition of reversing changes.

The Soviet Economy: System, Performance, and Collapse

Although many of the difficulties of the Soviet economy have become evident in this story, it remains to be asked: why did the Soviet economy collapse?

Fundamentally, economies grow because they save from current output, and invest to create more future output. During the early stages of economic development, it is critical to develop institutions and policies appropriate to bringing inputs, such as capital, into the production process. Over time, it is equally critical to develop ways in which available inputs can be used more effectively, that is, with increasing efficiency. While the nature of the institutions appropriate to such tasks is a subject of major complexity, we have emphasized that the Soviet Union chose institutions and policies fundamentally different from those typical of the market experience. Soviet institutions and policies served to replace consumer sovereignty with state control, shifting resources away from the expansion of consumers' well-being towards the growth of output, especially industrial output. This system in effect used force to shift resources to those activities that were able to generate high initial rates of economic growth, albeit doing so at a high cost, notably in the restricted growth of consumption. The Soviet system practiced what is often termed "extensive" economic growth, or growth achieved through the expansion of inputs, and failed to evolve towards "intensive" growth, or growth achieved broadly through the better use of inputs (greater efficiency). The failure to evolve, that is to change, can be directly related to the fundamental characteristics of the economic system examined here.

The postwar economic record of the Soviet Union is quite clear, even though there are understandable debates about measurement issues (see Easterly and Fischer), and about the underlying systemic and policy issues. First, the average annual rate of growth of output in the Soviet Union declined steadily, with inevitable variations, from the 1950s through the 1980s (see Figure 1.1). While one could observe an average annual rate of economic growth of roughly 6–8% in the 1950s (as discussed above), this rate had fallen to, at best, 2–4% by the early 1980s. The downward drift is evident, although with differences, in the official Soviet series, the unofficial Soviet series, and the estimates computed by the US Central Intelligence Agency.

Second, the rate of growth of inputs (land, labor, and capital) generally remained high compared to other developing economies, but it also declined throughout the postwar years, for understandable reasons. The extensive margin of land cultivation had been achieved in the Khrushchev era, if not earlier. In spite of the large land area of the Soviet Union, major capital investment would have been required to expand the area under cultivation. The labor force, in part because of a significant

reduction in the net annual expansion of the eligible population, could not continue to expand significantly, especially given that there were already very high rates of participation. Finally, as we have emphasized, while the restriction of the growth of consumption facilitated very high levels of investment judged by international standards, these levels could not be increased by further limitations on consumption for a population long accustomed to empty promises about the abundance of Communism. These forces were of growing importance in and beyond the 1960s.

The net result of these forces was a very troubling economic profile, which was recognized by Gorbachev as *perestroika* was introduced. Put simply, the growth of inputs declined less than the growth of output, the result being precisely the reverse of what was needed in a modernizing industrial economy, namely a steady and sharp decline in factor productivity (see Figure 1.2). The rate of growth of productivity of both capital and labor declined, although the latter remained positive, as did the rate of growth of total factor productivity (labor and capital weighted by their respective shares in the production process).

It is clear that the Soviet Union relied on extensive growth, and was seemingly unable to move towards intensive growth. Why might this have been the case? While the precise causes of the Soviet growth dilemma are not easy to characterize, we must focus on the nature of the economic system, its organizational arrangements, and its policies. Basically, the Soviet Union was attempting to sustain economic growth by substituting capital for labor, and yet its capital productivity was negative and falling. Put differently, the substitution of an input with productivity that is falling more rapidly, for inputs with productivity that is falling less rapidly, implies a decline in the rate of economic growth. The focus of any explanation, therefore, must be on the use of inputs, and especially capital, in the Soviet economy. Beyond the mechanics of the growth equation, there are several important explanations for the decline.

First, it is evident that, while markets are far from perfect, they nevertheless generate valuable information for decision-making purposes, along with appropriate incentives to stimulate effort in the pursuit of economic objectives. The Soviet experience with planning suggests that, while some state objectives could be achieved at considerable cost, the system was incapable of rationally allocating resources over time. The differences between the information mechanisms of the market economy and those of the Soviet economy form a subject beyond the scope of this chapter, but, as an example, the absence of scarcity-based prices in the Soviet Union denied decision-makers information critical to decisions about the use of scarce resources.

Second, if planning could achieve crude objectives at high cost, the system became increasingly ineffective in an economy growing more complex over time. Repeated attempts to reform the economic system and to make it more efficient failed, in large part due to the limited nature of the attempts at reform, and to the vested interests of those who benefited from the status quo.

Third, the most fundamental element in enhancing efficiency is technological change, originating in the scientific establishment and contributing to economic growth through application in the field. The Soviet system placed great emphasis upon the achievements of its scientific establishment, and they were significant in some priority industries, but they were not spread widely in the economy. Put differently, Soviet managers were rewarded for expanding output, and little attention was paid to reducing costs through technological change.

Fourth, no economic system can be sustained over time in the absence of a significant work ethic among its peoples. If the allure of Communist abundance could motivate Soviet citizens in the 1930s, it was clear that the human factor was all but gone by the time Gorbachev emerged as the last Soviet leader. Although it is difficult to characterize with precision the relationship between workers' efforts and their standards of living, it is evident that the allure of Soviet abundance declined over time, especially for later generations that had little interest in the promises of the 1930s.

Finally, a major tenet of socialist economic thought, namely replacing private gain with public benefit, clearly failed in the Soviet Union. Soviet leaders took great pride in their ability to provide what could loosely be termed public goods. For example, medical care and education were generally provided without charge to their users. However, the availability of these benefits, of the quality provided in the Soviet Union, did not translate into encouraging workers' efforts at the factory. A measure of equality was achieved, but at a sustained low level of economic well-being, a level increasingly unattractive to the Soviet population.

For some, the apparent economic strength of the Soviet Union, in space, in industry, and in the military, and its record of challenging the West over so many years, seem to stand in stark contrast to a story of declining economic performance and, ultimately, economic and political collapse. In fact, the contrast is much less marked than might at first seem to be the case. As we have noted, the Soviet economic and political systems replaced consumer sovereignty with state control, pursuing a strategy that brought resources into selected areas of the productive process, but paid little attention to efficiency. In a setting without change, the inability to sustain input growth inevitably led to economic decline. Our focus therefore should not be on how an inefficient system could put human beings in space, but rather, on how Soviet leaders could ignore economic realities for so long.

Further Reading

Davies, R. W., *Soviet Economic Development from Lenin to Khrushchev*, Cambridge and New York: Cambridge University Press, 1998

A brief and very readable tour through the basic issues pertaining to the early years of the administrative command system

Davies, R. W., Mark Harrison, and S. G. Wheatcroft, editors, *The Economic Transformation of the Soviet Union, 1913–1945*, Cambridge and New York: Cambridge University Press, 1994

An excellent collection of essays dealing with major sectors of the Soviet economy, including references and data

Desai, Padma, *Perestroika in Perspective*, Princeton, NJ: Princeton University Press, 1990

An excellent treatment of important economic issues pertaining to *perestroika*

Easterly, William, and Stanley Fischer, "The Soviet Economic Decline," in *The World Bank Economic Review*, Volume 9, number 3, September 1995

An excellent analysis of the decline in Soviet growth, including useful comparisons to other countries

Gray, Kenneth R., editor, *Soviet Agriculture: Comparative Perspectives*, Ames: Iowa State University Press, 1990

An excellent collection of articles on various aspects of Soviet agriculture

Gregory, Paul R., and Robert C. Stuart, *Russian and Soviet Economic Performance and Structure*, sixth edition, Reading, MA and Harlow: Addison-Wesley, 1998

A standard text covering the Russian economic experience from 1860 through 1998

Holzman, Franklyn D., *International Trade under Communism: Politics and Economics*, New York: Basic Books, 1976

A very readable study of international trade in the command economy, by a pioneer in the field

Konn, Tania, editor, *Soviet Studies Guide*, London: Bowker Saur, 1992

A very useful guide to information on the Soviet Union

Lewin, Moshe, *Russian Peasants and Soviet Power*, London: Allen and Unwin, and Evanston, IL: Northwestern University Press, 1968

An excellent discussion of the process of collectivization

Nove, Alec, *The Soviet Economic System*, London and Boston: Allen and Unwin, 1986

A classic text by a pioneer analyst of the Soviet economy

Nove, Alec, *An Economic History of the USSR 1917–1991*, London and New York: Penguin, 1992

A readable and authoritative economic history of the USSR by a pioneer in the field

Wilczynski, J., editor, *The Gorbachev Encyclopedia*, Salt Lake City, UT: Charles Schlacks, Jr., 1993

An excellent reference source on all aspects of *perestroika*

Robert C. Stuart is Professor of Economics at Rutgers University, New Jersey, and Editor of *Comparative Economic Studies*.

Table 1.1   The Soviet Economy: The Impact of System and Policy, 1928–38

	1928	*1938*[1]
Indices of Industrial Production (1928 = 100)		
Soviet official figures	100	446
Western estimates	100	279
Contributions to Net National Product (%)		
Agriculture	49	31
Extraction and manufacturing industries	28	45
Service industries	23	24
End uses of GNP (%)		
Consumption	80	53
Investment	13	26
Government	3	26
Foreign Trade (% of GNP)		
Exports plus Imports	6	1

1 Except the first two figures in the column, which are for 1937

Sources: Gregory, Paul R., and Robert C. Stuart, *Russian and Soviet Economic Performance and Structure*, sixth edition, Reading, MA and Harlow: Addison-Wesley, 1998; Davies, R. W., Mark Harrison, and S. G. Wheatcroft, editors, *The Economic Transformation of the Soviet Union, 1913–1945*, Cambridge and New York: Cambridge University Press, 1994

Figure 1.1   Estimates of Average Annual Growth in the GDP of the Soviet Union, in selected periods, 1951–85 (%)

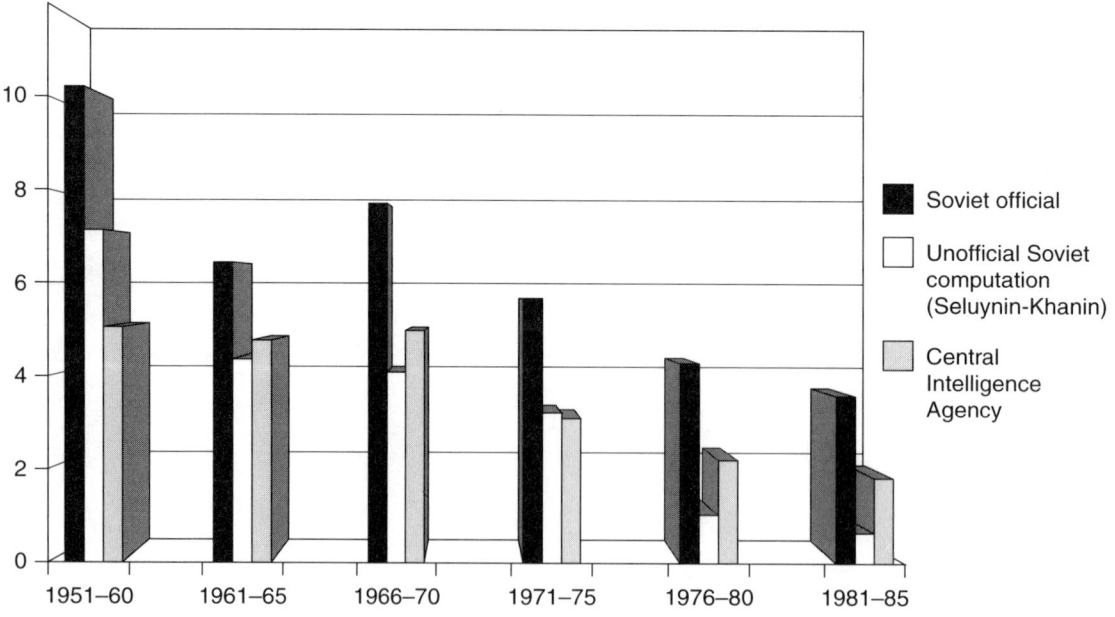

Sources: Central Intelligence Agency, *Revisiting Soviet Economic Performance Under Glasnost: Implications for CIA Estimates*, Washington, DC: CIA, 1998; Central Intelligence Agency, *Handbook of Economic Statistics*, Washington, DC: CIA, various years

Figure 1.2   Changes in Total Factor Productivity, and in the Productivity of Labor and Capital, in the Soviet Union, in selected periods, 1961–85 (%)

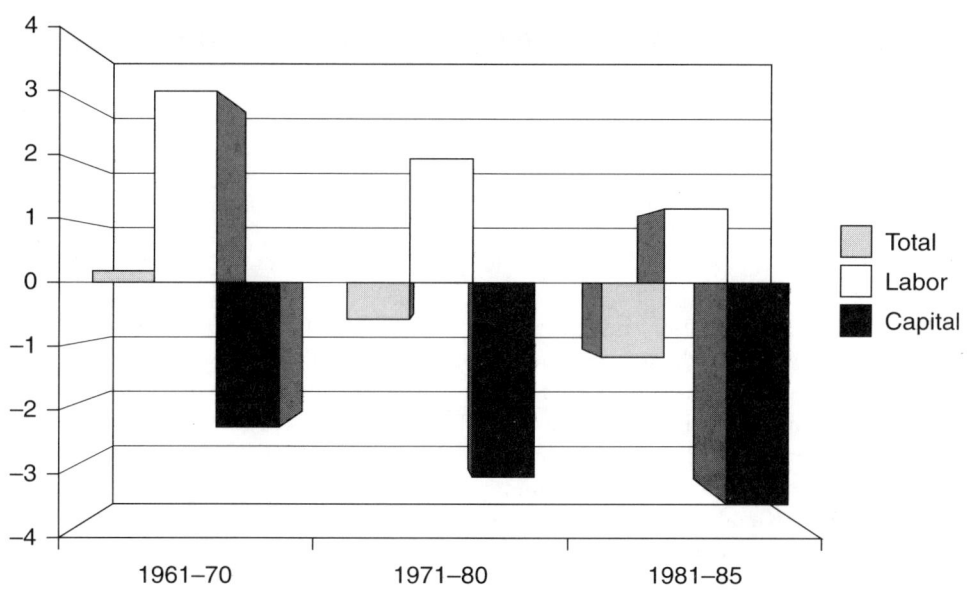

Note: Labor productivity here refers to the number of hours worked per member of the labor force.

Source: Central Intelligence Agency, *Handbook of Economic Statistics 1991*, Washington, DC: CIA, 1991

Figure 1.3   Changes in GNP, and in Combined Factor Productivity (Labor and Capital), in the Soviet Union, 1986–90 (%)

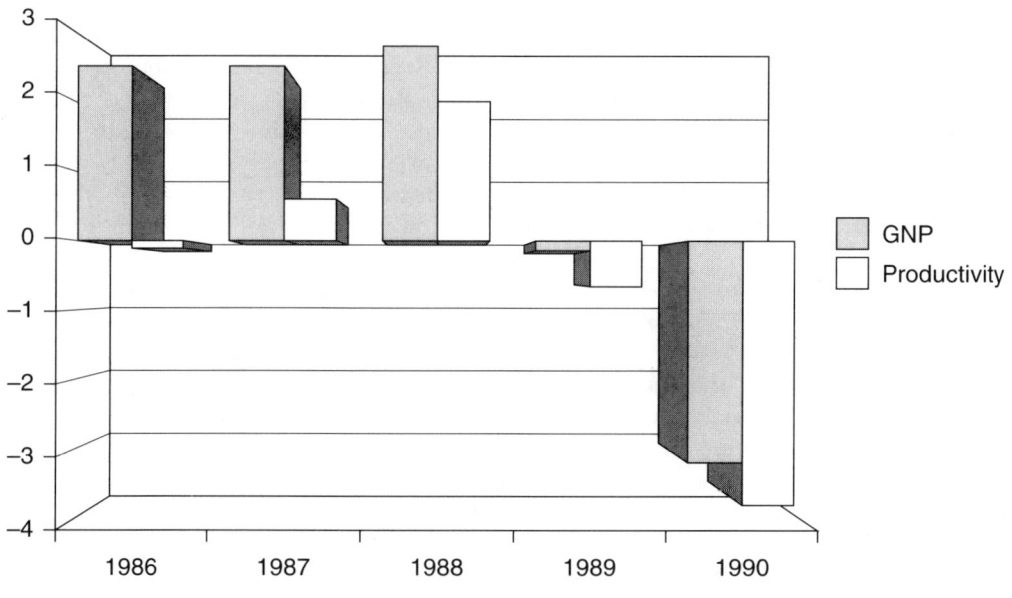

Source: Central Intelligence Agency, *Handbook of Economic Statistics 1991*, Washington, DC: CIA, 1991

Chapter Two

The CIS as an International Institution

Neil Robinson

The CIS is a regional international institution made up of successor states to the former Soviet Union. It was founded in December 1991 by the newly independent states of Russia, Belarus, and Ukraine. The three founders were quickly joined by eight other Soviet successor states, Armenia, Azerbaijan, Kazakhstan, Kyrgyzstan, Moldova, Tajikistan, Turkmenistan, and Uzbekistan. Georgia initially refused membership of the CIS, and only joined in 1993, when Russia essentially forced it into the institution (as described below). The three Baltic states, Latvia, Lithuania, and Estonia, have not participated in the new organization at all.

The member states of the CIS share common problems, as well as the basic post-Communist tasks of dealing with the collapse of a planned economy and rebuilding political institutions. At the time the CIS was created, they had many things in common that might have supported dealing with these problems collectively:

- a shared language, Russian, which had been the main language of administration in the Soviet Union;
- economic ties among enterprises in what had been a single economic space;
- a common currency, the ruble;
- overlapping populations and cultures, with around 25 million Russians living in the newly independent states, and members of ethnic groups from the new states in Russia;
- almost identical structures in areas such as social services or local government; and
- shared standards on such matters as educational provision and legal rules.

Russia and the other successor states needed one another. For example, only a very few Soviet successor states are not dependent on Russia for energy supplies. These are mostly the new states in Central Asia, although their independence in the production of natural gas and crude oil is tempered either by their importation of electric power (as in Kyrgyzstan), or by their reliance on Russia and other states for processing facilities. Just after independence, Belarus and Moldova received 100% of their gas supplies from Russia, while Ukraine received 56% and Georgia 27% of theirs. Ukraine took 89% of its oil from Russia, Belarus 91%, Georgia 82%, and Uzbekistan 55% (Dawisha and Parrott p. 175). Where the newly independent states need Russian energy, Russia needs production facilities on their territory. For example, a report submitted to the Russian Federal Assembly in 1996 found that Russia possesses 80% of the Soviet defense industry, but without CIS cooperation it can produce only 17% of Soviet military production.

However, despite the close links that existed among the Soviet successor states in 1991, when the CIS was founded, the institution has not developed a clear identity or purpose independent of Russian foreign policy. It is therefore something of an anomaly among regional international institutions, particularly when compared to the international regional organization that is geographically closest to it, the EU. The CIS was born into the world of new possibilities for regional international institutions that was created by the end of the Cold War. Unfortunately, the unique circumstances of its birth as the successor to a totalitarian "empire," the Soviet Union, have meant that it has not been able to develop and be effective, either as an integrative organization, or as a regime that monitors and regulates the behavior of its members.

The potential problems that might be caused by the failure of the CIS to develop a clear identity or purpose of its own cannot be understated. The stability and longevity of Russian democracy are closely linked to its relations to the newly independent states that are members of the CIS, and vice versa. If peaceful cooperation and mutual respect between Russia and the other members of the CIS cannot be ensured, the prospects for democracy and economic progress across the region are diminished, since conflict and/or unchecked Russian hegemony in the post-Soviet space could destabilize what are very often (at best) weak democracies. A regional international institution is potentially the best means of ensuring peaceful cooperation and mutual respect among the Soviet successor states, and the CIS, as the extant regional organization, is hence the best bet for creating an international environment that can support democratic development in its member states. Its success or failure may therefore be of global importance.

Types of Regional International Institution

Two types of regional international institution have been developed over the past 50 years. First, there are organizations such as the EU (formerly the European Community), through which states come together to manage economic policy collectively, in order to reduce economic costs and improve the living standards of their citizens. Such organizations may develop policy cooperation in other areas – such as social policy – and eventually may create political integration, the pooling of sovereignty among states in supranational institutions such as the EU's Council of Ministers, its European Parliament or its European Central Bank. Second, there are organizations such as the OSCE, formerly the CSCE, through which states meet to agree to certain principles and standards, for example on the observance of human rights, and which

then monitor the observance of these principles. Integration is not the outcome of such institutions. Their competence may change, but institutionally they remain monitors of the behavior of their members, and are shaped principally by the interactions of their members and the agreements that they reach.

The end of the Cold War changed the context in which both these types of institution operate. During the Cold War, the European Community, the CSCE, and other international institutions were unable to develop fully or achieve their full potential. In the case of the European Community, development was limited because member states guaranteed their security by alliance with the United States and through NATO. In the context of the Cold War, it was neither desirable nor possible to replace this security regime with one based on the European Community, which therefore developed as an economic institution, rather than as a political and security regime. Other institutions, such as the CSCE, were constrained by their inability to monitor the behavior of Communist member states and ensure their compliance with international agreements, and by the fact that any decisions made within them were influenced by the dominant conflict in world politics, the conflict between the United States and the Soviet Union.

The end of the bipolar conflict between the Soviet bloc and the "West" changed this. The creation of regimes committed to democracy in the former Soviet bloc weakened the conventional military threat across the globe, and instituted a search for forums to guarantee security from new threats, such as organized crime, and to promote economic development, in a world where political and economic frontiers were being eroded by the globalization of capitalism. Regional institutions were an obvious means of achieving these ends, since they could ensure cooperation among small groups of states with a common geography. As the Cold War drew to a close, new institutions for regional cooperation were created, such as the Asia-Pacific Economic Cooperation (formed in 1989 by 19 states), the North American Free Trade Agreement (signed in 1992 by the United States, Canada, and Mexico) or the Central European Free Trade Association (founded in 1992 by Czechoslovakia, Poland, and Hungary). Meanwhile, some existing institutions underwent an expansion of their roles. For example, the European Community was relaunched as the EU under the Treaty of Maastricht, signed in December 1991. Similarly, the CSCE expanded its activities to help manage new problems, such as the disintegration of Yugoslavia, and began to monitor security problems more effectively with the help of new, more open and democratic regimes in central and eastern Europe. The competencies of the CSCE were extended with the signing of the Charter of Paris for a New Europe in November 1990; and the change of name from CSCE to OSCE, effective from January 1, 1995, signaled its achievement of a more permanent status and increased institutional freedom from the superpower politics of the past.

However, the success of regional international institutions and the hopes vested in them are not just a function of the end of the Cold War. Institutions such as the EU and the OSCE develop and generate hopes for their future growth because they are effective. Indeed, there were high hopes for these institutions at the start of the 1990s because those features that make them effective correspond to changes brought about by the end of the Cold War. Oran R. Young has defined a broad range of factors that influence how well international institutions function (Young pp. 176–193), as follows:

- how easy it is to monitor compliance with their rules, since, if breaking the rules is easy and does not lead to sanctions, an international institution will be ineffective;
- the "robustness," the ability to cope with change, of its decision-making processes – an institution will not be effective if its decision-making processes cannot adapt to deal with change, because it will become redundant as its members are forced to deal with change outside the frameworks provided by the institution;
- the capacity of states to implement the policies adopted by the international institutions of which they are a part – in other words, an international institution is only as good as its members;
- a relatively even distribution of power among member states, since where power is concentrated too greatly in one member state, an international institution will be ineffective, because the powerful state will force its wishes on other states, and they will have little incentive to respect the institution;
- the degree to which member states are dependent on one another, since the more that states need agreement on a range of issues, the more likely they are to strive to enhance the effectiveness of an institution that deals with an issue, or set of issues, that they have in common; and
- their having an intellectual foundation – if the ideas that led to the creation of an institution are discredited or no longer believed in it will lose effectiveness, and may cease to exist.

It is not necessary for all these factors to be present for an international organization to be effective. For example, if an international institution is founded on a strongly held set of common ideas, can monitor its members efficiently, can adapt to change, and comprises states that can enforce its policies, then it may be effective even if its members have few or no other common concerns (and are therefore not interdependent). However, one negative factor can also erode an institution. As we shall see in the case of the CIS, uneven distribution of power between member states can weaken incentives to cooperate, even where member states are very interdependent.

Regional international institutions should have some advantages over other types of international institution, in that certain of the factors that lead to successful, effective international institutions are produced more easily at a "regional" level than at the global level. A common geography naturally produces some measure of interdependence, since neighboring states generally trade with one another, cannot escape each other's pollution, have to worry about each other's military forces, and so on. Shared ideas that can underpin an international institution may also emerge in a region, as in western Europe, where the desire to avoid another war inspired the setting up of the EU's forebear, the European Economic Community, under the Treaty of Rome, signed in 1957. Such regional developments were among the factors that created high hopes for regional international institutions at the end of the Cold War, and stimulated their further development. The expansion of the EU into central and eastern Europe, for example, has been seen as a way of securing peaceful development in the region, by setting entry targets for post-Communist states. As a result, the rules of the EU as an international institution, and its ability to monitor compliance with them, are having an effect even before the institution actually expands.

The End of the Soviet Union and the Belovezha Agreement

The CIS should have shared some of the advantages that regional organizations have as international institutions. We have already mentioned some of the things that CIS member states had in common, such as the economic links among enterprises in what had been a single economic space. These might have facilitated the effectiveness of the CIS because they required the CIS states to cooperate with one another. However, the weight of history was working against these factors. The CIS was not founded with goodwill and a strong sense of common purpose, and has struggled to overcome the circumstances of its birth. Its creation was a necessary accident, an event that had to happen to sort out the mess of the Soviet Union and allow the successor states to disengage from one another, but its participants did not uniformly desire it.

The formation of the CIS took this unhappy form because it came at the end of a protracted power struggle between the republics of the Soviet Union, on the one hand, and the central Soviet state on the other. The form that this struggle took was different from republic to republic, as the resources that the independence movements and political elites in each republic possessed varied dramatically. At one end of the spectrum, mass independence movements emerged in Latvia, Lithuania, and Estonia, enabling nationalist governments to come to power in the republican elections of 1990 (these three countries are examined further in *The Central and Eastern Europe Handbook*). At the other end of the spectrum, in Soviet Central Asia – the republics of Kazakhstan, Uzbekistan, Tajikistan, Turkmenistan, and Kyrgyzstan – there was little effective popular political mobilization. Instead, Communist Party elites used the political liberalization brought about by Mikhail Gorbachev's *perestroika* (restructuring) to secure a degree of freedom from the central Soviet state, and to increase their personal power. These republics had no traditions of national independence to fall back on, since they had not been states before their incorporation into the Russian empire in the 19th century. Before their colonization, the area had been made up of loose tribal federations and semifeudal city states. Formed as republics within the Soviet Union, each of these new states not only had a high degree of ethnic diversity, but shared ethnic populations with one another, and with neighboring states such as China and Afghanistan. Unlike the nationalists in the Baltic states, the political goal of the leaders of these states, such as Nursultan Nazarbayev of Kazakhstan, was not full independence from the Soviet Union, but a more advantageous position within the Union for themselves and their administrations.

The other Soviet republics – Russia, Ukraine, Belarus, Moldova, Georgia, Azerbaijan, and Armenia – fell between these two extremes. These republics had popular democratic movements seeking independence, but each had weaknesses. The Belarusian Popular Front was not well-established. Rukh, in Ukraine, was not truly national in influence, since it was strong in western Ukraine but weak in the more Russified South and East. The Azeri and Armenian independence movements were propelled to prominence by the conflict between Azeri and Armenian communities in the disputed region of Nagorno-Karabakh, and did not develop social support, organizations or political programs. Where pro-independence governments came to power in these republics, after the elections of 1990, they did not have matters all their own way, since they could not command the full popular support that their counterparts in the Baltic states enjoyed. Georgia, for example, was split by calls for independence by some of its regions, and soon lapsed into a state of civil war, while the Russian government under Boris Yeltsin struggled against pro-Union conservatives to hold on to power in 1990 and the first six months of 1991. Other governments, which were dominated by members of the old Communist elites – for example in Belarus and Ukraine – drifted towards nationalist politics only as the Soviet Union crumbled, and their members realized that they needed to secure their place in the post-Soviet order.

The very different types of independence movements and republican governments ensured that there was no consensus on what should replace the Soviet Union. None of the independence movements was powerful enough to force an end to the Soviet state, and there was confusion among the majority of the Soviet population about what kind of state they wanted to live in. In a referendum conducted throughout the Soviet Union in March 1991 – except in the Baltic states, Georgia, Moldova, and Armenia, 76% of those taking part (around 60% of those eligible to take part) voted in favor of a renewed Union. However, they also supported local nationalists and democrats against the central Soviet state. There was thus no stable basis on which to renegotiate the treaty that had established the Soviet Union in 1922.

Gorbachev's best effort was to secure agreement with the leaders of nine of the republics, at Novo-Ogarevo in April 1991. The concessions that Gorbachev made in this agreement angered Soviet conservatives, who had previously been in alliance with him. Two days before the new Union treaty was scheduled to be signed, in August 1991, a hard-line coup destroyed the balance of power that had produced the Novo-Ogarevo agreement. Gorbachev's response to the coup was to press for the signature of the new treaty and then, when that failed, to urge its renegotiation and the creation of a new state.

However, there was no need for the republics to participate in this process. After the failure of the coup, the independence of the Baltic states was recognized by Russia, as well as by the western powers (which in any case had never formally recognized their loss of independence in 1940). This became a model for nationalists to follow in Ukraine and other republics. It also served as a warning to members of the old Communist elites, such as Leonid Kravchuk in Ukraine, that they could no longer mediate between nationalists and the Soviet center to maintain their positions: they would have to find new political strategies. Adopting nationalist policies was the most obvious way to stay in power. Kravchuk began to campaign for the Ukrainian presidency as a nationalist, and supported calls for independence in a referendum that was held on the same day as the presidential election, December 1, 1991 (see Kuzio and Wilson).

Meanwhile, the Russian leadership under Yeltsin was divided over the future of the Soviet Union. The Prime Minister, Ivan Silayev, and some other members of the government were committed to maintaining common political structures to manage the economy; others, including Yeltsin and many of his key advisers, were determined that there should be complete Russian control over the economy and other important areas of policy. Silayev quit the government in September 1991, and Yeltsin became Prime Minister in November in order to begin the drive for economic reform. Nazarbayev and other leaders in Central Asia fretted that they would be left to fend for themselves as heads of new nation-states, but were unable to force Russia or any other republic into a new Union.

Yeltsin's determination to rule Russia and Kravchuk's jump to nationalism killed the Soviet Union. At the beginning of December Kravchuk was elected President of Ukraine, and a large majority in the referendum supported independence. For Yeltsin, as well as for Stanislau Shushkevich, the new leader of Belarus, the difficulty was that a unilateral move toward independence by Ukraine would have left Belarus isolated; complicated Yeltsin's domestic position, because of concerns about ethnic Russians in Ukraine and Russian nationalist hostility to its independence; and left no institutional mechanisms to solve pressing common problems. These problems were numerous, since the republics, having been parts of one state for nearly 70 years, were highly interdependent. It was not at all clear, for example, whether the republican borders would be recognized as state borders; what citizenship rights people from ethnic groups living outside their home territories should have; what was to happen to Soviet debts; who was to inherit the Soviet Union's military arsenal; how separate national economies were to be managed while they used a common currency; what trade and customs barriers would be installed between the new states; or how conflicts in some of the republics could be settled, such as the conflict in Moldova, where Russian separatists refused to acknowledge Moldovan rule.

On December 8, Yeltsin, Kravchuk, and Shushkevich met at Belovezha in Belarus. Yeltsin and Shushkevich sought an agreement on a new structure to replace the Soviet Union and enable the management of common problems. Kravchuk, wearing his new nationalist colors, sought recognition of Ukrainian independence, and did not want it compromised in any way by a new institution. Both sides got what they wanted – an accommodation of their different concerns – rather than a comprehensive and thorough replacement of the mechanisms of the Soviet state. The three leaders signed an agreement that declared the Soviet Union dead, and established the CIS, yet the organization that was formed was minimal. The agreement on the CIS, and the declarations on its formation and economic policy, were all very vague (see Brzezinski and Sullivan). Most of their positive content concerned the fate of the Soviet Union, and promised such things as respect for international agreements signed by the Soviet Union. The only other practical matter settled by the Belovezha documents was the recognition of existing republican borders as the borders of the new states. Only one supranational CIS institution was established by the agreement on the CIS, a united military command. However, a mechanism for "implementing interrepublican economic agreements" was promised in the declaration on economic policy, and other institutions were obviously intended, since the agreement

announced that they would be based in Minsk, the capital of Belarus. The working procedures for the CIS were left vague. Article 9 of the CIS agreement states merely that "disputes over the interpretation and application of the norms of this agreement are to be resolved through negotiations between appropriate bodies, and, when necessary, at the level of heads of government and state." Article 10 allowed the signatories to quit the CIS or opt out of any of its provisions after giving one year's notice, and decreed that the agreement could be changed only by common consent. The bulk of the Belovezha documents were made up of abstract promises to coordinate activities among the signatories, secure living standards, and so on.

In addition to ending the Soviet Union, the other immediate effect of the Belovezha agreements was to anger the five republican leaders of Central Asia. They met at Ashgabat on December 13, 1991, expressed their "surprise" at developments, and demanded that they be considered as joint founders of the new organization, and that it take into account the "historic and socioeconomic realities of Central Asia." The five leaders, who had not been in favor of independence, were worried about the viability of their economies and states if Russia concentrated on its relations with western Europe, the United States, Ukraine, and Belarus. They feared that other powers, such as Iran or China, would be drawn into the resulting strategic vacuum, or that instability would be imported from Afghanistan (as was to occur in Tajikistan). They therefore pressed for membership of the CIS. On December 21, their five states, along with Moldova, Armenia, and Azerbaijan, were admitted to the new organization, at a meeting at Almaty (Alma Ata), then the capital of Kazakhstan. Georgia, divided by civil war and ruled by a radical nationalist, refused to join.

The enlargement of the CIS made its identity significantly more complicated. Its member states each had very different reasons for joining it, which meant that there was no common CIS interest, no central idea, no intellectual foundation for the organization. All that the 11 states had in common was the desire to end the Soviet Union, and once that had been achieved there was little to bind them together. One of the factors identified above as influencing the effectiveness of international institutions was thus missing from the CIS from the start. In addition, the political systems of all the CIS states were weak, and it would be difficult for them to implement policies that were decided on domestically, let alone internationally through the CIS. Matters were made worse, however, by the fact that both Moldova and Azerbaijan were so fragmented internally that they could not ratify the agreements their leaders had made to join the CIS. Other states, such as Belarus, also had difficulty adopting CIS acts that their leaders agreed to. During the first three years of its existence, more than 400 documents were adopted at CIS meetings, but fewer than 200 were ratified by national parliaments (Brzezinski and Sullivan p. 718). The effectiveness of the CIS was thus significantly hampered by the weakness of its member states. Moldova and Azerbaijan did not become fully active members of the CIS until after 1993, when Georgia also joined.

Early Developments

At the end of December 1991, the enlarged CIS agreed to establish a Council of Heads of State (CHS) and a Council of Heads of Government (CHG). The CHS was to meet at least twice a year, the CHG at least once every three months. Their chairs were to rotate among the member states. Each state was to have one vote in each of the Councils, and decisions would be made by common consent. However, states could declare that they had no interest in an issue, and CIS decisions would not apply to them. The CHS and CHG were both intergovernmental rather than supranational bodies. Indeed, most of the institutional development of the CIS, in its first year of existence and since, has been through intergovernmental commissions and committees, such as the CIS Committee on Nuclear Policy. These bodies differ little from any other meeting of diplomats anywhere else in the world, except that they have a "CIS" prefix attached to them. The record on reaching agreements though these committees is varied, and they have no real independent institutional

position or powers of the sort developed, for example, by the Commission of the EU.

The lack of rapid institutionalization, the opt-outs permitted to member states, the weakness of member states, and the lack of a common idea all had serious implications for the development of the CIS during its first year. Collective action to solve mutual problems could have eased the initial stages of reform, reduced the political costs of change, and underwritten more successful changes. Instead, while agreement could be reached on issues to do with the ending of the Soviet Union, such as the division of responsibility for its debts in March 1992, it was impossible to agree on the construction of new practical links among the states. States opted out of, or could not participate in, the most important early CIS agreements. For example, in March 1992, when the Interparliamentary Assembly was created in an attempt to increase the effectiveness of the CIS's monitoring and harmonization of domestic policies, Ukraine, Turkmenistan, Moldova, and Azerbaijan would not or could not agree to participate. President Yeltsin and successive Russian governments have also been reluctant to take the Assembly seriously, partly because of their own conflicts with the Russian legislatures from which Assembly members are drawn.

Another constraint on collective action was the fact that many of the CIS member states appeared not to believe in it. Military cooperation is a case in point. A peacekeeping agreement, providing for CIS troops to intervene in conflicts in the post-Soviet space, was drawn up at the same time as the Interparliamentary Assembly was created: Ukraine, Turkmenistan, Azerbaijan, and Belarus did not sign it. In any case, even though the 11 member states had all agreed on unified military structures in the Belovezha agreement, they rapidly ordered the construction of national armed forces. The process started in January 1992, when Kravchuk decreed control over all ex-Soviet armed forces on Ukrainian territory, and declared the Black Sea Fleet to be Ukrainian. In May, Russia set up its own Ministry of Defense and Armed Forces, and joined with Armenia, Uzbekistan, Kazakhstan, Kyrgyzstan, and Tajikistan to sign the CIS Treaty on

Collective Security. Azerbaijan and Moldova could not sign it, while Ukraine had no intention of being bound into a security agreement with Russia. By the middle of 1993, the idea of a common defense policy had little meaning for the CIS as a whole, although in 1995 all the CIS states except Tajikistan and Azerbaijan reached broad agreement on air defenses.

The CIS Charter and After

Despite this poor start, further attempts were made at consolidating the CIS by extending the basic agreements signed at Belovezha. A Charter of the CIS was worked on throughout 1992, and signed by seven member states in January 1993. Like the original CIS documents, it was full of grand promises of coordination and cooperation on such matters as economic and military policy, the resolution of conflicts and the protection of the environment, copyright and investment, education, science and technology, sport, culture, and health care. It incorporated the main points of the agreement that had created the CHG and CHS, and also established seven more bodies. The Council of Foreign Ministers, the Council of Defense Ministers, the Joint Armed Forces High Command, and the Council of Commanders of Border Troops were intergovernmental, and were concerned with specific functions. However, the Coordinating and Consultative Committee, the Commission on Human Rights, and the Economic Court appeared to be supranational organizations, since they were to be made up of permanent representatives from each of the CIS member states. The Coordinating and Consultative Committee was also to have a Secretariat, which was to prepare documents and proposals for discussion at the CHG and CHS, and "promote" the "implementation of accords in specific areas of economic mutual relations," which implied some sort of monitoring function (Brzezinski and Sullivan pp. 508–9).

As usual, not all the CIS states ratified or signed the Charter. Turkmenistan, Belarus, Moldova, and Azerbaijan did not ratify it until 1994, and Ukraine and Tajikistan have yet to do so. The Coordinating and Consultative Committee, and its Secretariat, have not

developed as institutions, and the Committee has become a forum for Deputy Prime Ministers – in other words, yet another intergovernmental body. Supplementary agreements have been signed on the Economic Court, but their influence has been small. In August 1995, some of its members complained about their limited jurisdiction, and other bodies have been established that overlap their competence. Even the intergovernmental bodies established in the Charter have not always been effective, because of poor attendance. In March 1994, for example, Ukraine, Belarus, Moldova, Turkmenistan, Uzbekistan, and Armenia all sent officials rather than politicians to the Council of Foreign Ministers. This substitution of ministers by officials has been a regular occurrence across all CIS meetings. Sometimes, as at the meeting of the Council of Defense Ministers in January 1997, when there were no representatives from Turkmenistan and Moldova, not even officials have turned up.

Most of the development of the CIS since the adoption of the Charter has been intergovernmental, based on meetings of ministers or officials. In March 1995, for example, the heads of secret services in CIS states agreed to form a joint coordinating body to help combat organized crime and terrorism. However, the creation of these bodies, and even of the more supranational Interstate Economic Council (see below), has not made the CIS an effective coordinator of policy. Although the CHS, for example, is supposed to meet at least twice a year, its meetings have been delayed and postponed almost from the start, and Yeltsin's recent illnesses have played havoc with its schedule. In addition, while the chair of the CHS is supposed to rotate among the leaders of the member states, Yeltsin has chaired most of its meetings.

Self-interest versus Integration

The failure of collective action, and the slow, uneven pace of institutionalization, have encouraged states to act in their own interest. In particular, Russia has tended to deal with other states either bilaterally or in small multilateral groupings. The pursuit of self-interest and the growth of bilateralism have highlighted another weakness of the CIS, the uneven distribution of power among member states. Russia is far more powerful than any other member: it has the largest population, the lion's share of ex-Soviet military capability, (potentially) the largest economy, and the largest presence in the international system (especially as it inherited the Soviet Union's permanent seat on the UN Security Council). Russia's power enabled it to take decisions without considering their effects on other CIS states, and to use the dependence of other CIS states to force them to comply with its wishes. As a result, other member states had little incentive either to respect the CIS, or to support moves for collective action, since any such action would be dominated by Russia.

The most significant results of action for self-interest have been the collapse of the ruble, the common currency inherited from the Soviet Union, and the slow progress made on economic cooperation. The fate of the ruble was determined by one of the factors that had brought about the creation of the CIS, the desire of the Russian leadership to control the Russian economy. It embarked on rapid marketization and anti-inflationary "shock therapy" in January 1992, independently of the other CIS states, which soon found themselves in dire straits. Rising prices in Russia turned the terms of trade heavily in its favor, and sucked money out of the other successor states, which responded by extending unsecured loans to enterprises on their territories. This in turn further fueled inflation in Russia. CIS agreements, such as the February 1992 agreement on trade regulation and economic cooperation, sat uneasily with the liberalized economic environment that the Russian reformists under Yegor Gaidar were trying to create. Meanwhile, the Russian state itself became divided, as the central bank and the legislatures supported traditional policies that funded the economies of the other successor states, through the transfer of huge credits. In 1992, the IMF estimated that the Russian central bank was financing 91% of Tajikistan's GDP; 49–70% of the GDPs of Uzbekistan, Turkmenistan, Georgia, and Armenia; 20–25% of the GDP of Azerbaijan, Ukraine,

Kazakhstan, and Kyrgyzstan; and 10% of the GDPs of Moldova and Belarus (Aslund p. 123). Efforts were made to coordinate CIS fiscal policies, as with the creation of an Interbank Coordinating Council on Mutual Settlements, in October 1992. However, these fell short of the creation of a true interstate bank, the solution favored by Russia but feared by Ukraine and other states. They did not want to give Russia an opportunity to control the other national central banks by wielding a vote that would have been overwhelming, in line with its majority capitalization of such a bank. In the absence of collective economic action, bilateral economic agreements were made to ensure that established trading relationships were maintained, foreshadowing later agreements on customs and tariffs among a limited number of CIS states.

The ruble staggered on as a common currency until July 1993, when Russia recalled all previously issued rubles from circulation, and refused to issue more credits to CIS states. The aim was to force those states that had not already introduced their own currencies to agree to coordinate their monetary policy with Russia's, under threat of inflation caused by the flooding of their economies with pre-1993 rubles. In September 1993, Belarus, Kazakhstan, Armenia, Uzbekistan, and Tajikistan reached an agreement with Russia on a new ruble zone, with coordinated monetary, customs and banking policies. However, Russia's demands were too much for most of the states, and after 1994 only Tajikistan, which had collapsed into civil war and anarchy, and was stabilized by the presence of Russian troops, still remained in the ruble zone (Rubin p. 156). In theory, the Treaty on Monetary Union between Russia and Belarus, signed in 1994, gave Russia's central bank control over the currency in Belarus, but in practice Russia has been unwilling to take responsibility for the Belarusian economy (Webber p. 291). Once again, the economic integration of the CIS was stalled because of fears of Russian domination.

This pattern has repeated itself. The Coordinating and Consultative Committee produced a Treaty on Economic Union very soon after its formation in 1993, as part of the response to the collapse of the ruble zone. As with the initial formation of the CIS, this was preceded by an agreement signed in July by Ukraine, Russia, and Belarus. Yet Ukraine did not join the Economic Union as a full member; nor did Turkmenistan. President Kravchuk of Ukraine insisted on associate membership, and although his successor, Leonid Kuchma, was seen as more amenable to improving relations with the CIS and with Russia, he was no more willing than Kravchuk to dilute Ukrainian sovereignty, or to allow Russia to dominate its economy any more than it already did. This weakened the Economic Union considerably, since it could not develop institutionally. In December 1993, an Interstate Economic Council was established, but at first it was ineffective. A year after the Economic Union was set up, an attempt was made to reform the Council. Voting would have been based on each member state's capitalization. Russia would provide 50% of the funding and thus have 50% of the votes, but decisions on trade and financial matters would require a majority of 75%, and strategic questions, such as the establishment of a monetary union, would be by consensus, so that states could opt out. Nevertheless, Ukraine and several other states added an amendment to the proposed agreement, stating that its provisions could not override national legislation. Not surprisingly, the Council has not developed into a motor for integration, as it has no executive powers and no means of ensuring the adoption of common policies. Integration has thus remained no more than an aspiration for the CIS as a whole, and the heads of state have periodically paid lip service to it by adopting still more documents, such as the "Concept for Integrated Economic Development" approved by eight of the 12 CIS states in January 1997.

Military Affairs

Bilateralism in military affairs developed even more quickly than in economics, and took two forms. First, squabbles over the division of Soviet military power were conducted on a bilateral basis, most notably between Russia and Ukraine. The main issue between them was the division of the Black Sea Fleet, which Ukraine laid claim to, but which mostly insisted on swearing loyalty to Russia. No outside force or institution significantly influenced the discussions on the fleet, the fate of which was ultimately settled in summit meetings between Yeltsin and Kravchuk. Russia has signed other bilateral military agreements with many of the other CIS states, most notably with Belarus, which granted Russia the use of military bases and the right to station troops on its territory in a series of agreements in 1993 and 1995.

Second, peacekeeping activities undertaken nominally by the CIS have in fact been little more than military actions taken by Russia. Although the other CIS states formed their own armed forces, Russia alone has had the capability, need, and desire to intervene in the conflicts that sprang up as the Soviet Union crumbled. Russia inherited the bulk of the Soviet Union's effective combat forces; it has felt compelled to protect ethnic Russians in the former Soviet space; and it wants to prevent China, Iran, Turkey, and other states from developing their influence in its "backyard." It has therefore been the Russian army, rather than any "CIS" force, that has been involved in the conflict over Transnistria in Moldova, a conflict provoked in part by the old Soviet security apparatus, including the army (see Chapter 9). The Russian army has also been involved in border clashes and political chaos in Tajikistan, as well as in regional wars inside Georgia (see Kreikemeyer and Zagorski, and also Chapters 8 and 13).

The onesidedness of "peacekeeping" operations has led to the CIS being labeled a front for Russian security interests. Indeed, Russia has been accused of provoking and supporting some of the conflicts that it has later been involved in as a peacekeeper, for example in Abkhazia and South Ossetia, both inside Georgia. The "Key Tenets of the Concept of the Foreign Policy of the Russian Federation," developed over 1992 and published in 1993, made it clear that Russia saw itself as having a unique role in the CIS as a peacekeeper and peacemaker, for historical and cultural reasons. Peacekeeping operations by organizations other than the CIS, such as the UN or the OSCE, would be welcome only as long as they did not involve the stationing of foreign troops on the territory of the CIS (Aron p. 29). To help ensure that no foreign troops are stationed in the CIS, Russia has pressed the UN to recognize its unique role as a peacekeeper in the former Soviet Union, and pressed for more use of regional institutions like the CIS in peacekeeping. In 1993, Russia agreed to stop the war in Georgia, and save the Georgian government from collapse, only when it agreed to join the CIS. Attempts to internationalize peacekeeping in the CIS, such as the appeal by President Eduard Shevardnadze of Georgia, in January 1998, for an international effort to enforce peace in Abkhazia, have been rejected by Russia.

Smaller Groupings within the CIS Region

Agreements made among smaller numbers of ex-Soviet states have proliferated, creating a range of alternatives to the CIS in the post-Soviet space. In 1993, Kazakhstan, Kyrgyzstan, and Uzbekistan created a Central Asian Union, and have held regular tripartite meetings ever since. In 1994, the Union formed an interstate council (to which Russia and Tajikistan were admitted as observers in 1996), as well as a Central Asian Bank for Cooperation and Development, and President Nazarbayev of Kazakhstan has also called for the creation of a "Eurasian Union" to replace the CIS. A Customs Union was created by Russia, Kazakhstan, and Belarus in 1995; and in 1996 and 1998, Russia signed treaties with Belarus, now led by a pro-Russian President, Alyaksandr Lukashenka, creating a new "Community of Sovereign Republics," with an executive committee and a joint parliamentary assembly. It was also in 1996 that Russia, Belarus, Kazakhstan, and Kyrgyzstan created a series of interstate councils to promote quadripartite integration.

None of these alternatives to the CIS has been any more successful at integrating any of the CIS member states, but they offer both a source of hope and a potential problem for the CIS as a whole. Hope springs from the possibility that one of these groupings may become a source of integration, and serve to kickstart the CIS itself, as states see the benefits of collective action. On the other hand, bilateral, trilateral or quadrilateral links among CIS member states could pull them further apart, dividing them into smaller regional groups based on religious affiliations (the Islamic states of Central Asia) or perceived ethnic links (the mainly Slav states of Russia, Belarus, and Ukraine), and so weaken the CIS even further.

Conclusion

The failure of the CIS to promote integration, and the inability of its members to agree common policies, have made the institution a peculiar creature. As we have seen, it has been accused of being a front for Russian interests, and it is true that the CIS legitimizes Russian military involvement in other CIS states, and also that it is dominated by Russian politicians, and hence very often by Russian proposals. However, the CIS is not a very effective vehicle for Russian domination of the former Soviet space, apart from its peacekeeping functions. Russia may dominate the CIS as an institution, but it has had little success in getting other states to agree to its proposals through the CIS, or in having any agreements enforced by it. The poor performance of the institution's various bodies – which number 80 in all – was recognized by all the CIS leaders at their summit in March 1997, when they declared a moratorium on the establishment of any new CIS bodies. Where Russia has an influence in the other CIS states, it is because of its general economic and military dominance in the region, and because of its specific control over energy resources, not because of the CIS. Indeed, Russia's power can be said to have worked against the CIS, since the use of its power has demonstrated the dangers of Russian hegemony to other CIS states. Russian pressure on other CIS states has prevented them from forging links with non-CIS states – for example, it has sought to block the development of relations between the five states of Central Asia and their neighbors – but this has not promoted better relations within the CIS. It is hard to see what real value the CIS has brought to Russia, or how it has helped it to harmonize its relations with other member states.

The failure of the CIS to develop strong institutions or to be effective as a forum for agreeing policy is not surprising. There was a lack of consensus about what it was to do when it was founded; Russia dominates the region, and so deters collective action, from fear of a loss of sovereignty; the member states cannot honor commitments made to one another by their leaders because of internal political fragmentation; and the ability of members to opt out of policies makes their harmonization and monitoring impossible. The CIS has always lacked many of the features that can be identified as creating successful international institutions, and it does not appear to possess the means to create such features for itself.

Further Reading

Arbatov, Alexei, Abram Chayes, Antonia Handler Chayes, and Lara Olson, editors, *Managing Conflict in the Former Soviet Union: Russian and American Perspectives*, Cambridge, MA: MIT Press, 1997

The papers in this collection provide detailed analyses of regional conflicts in the CIS countries.

Aron, Leon, "The Emergent Priorities of Russian Foreign Policy," in Leon Aron and Kenneth M. Jensen, editors, *The Emergence of Russian Foreign Policy*, Washington, DC: United States Institute of Peace Press, 1994

Aslund, Anders, *How Russia Became a Market Economy*, Washington, DC: Brookings Institution, 1995

An account of the transition process by a prominent advocate of rapid liberalization

Brzezinski, Zbigniew, and Paige Sullivan, editors, *Russia and the Commonwealth of Independent States: Documents, Data, and Analysis*, Armonk, NY: M. E. Sharpe, 1996

A collection of documents that is the best single factual source on the CIS and its development up to 1995

Dawisha, Karen, and Bruce Parrott, *Russia and the New States of Eurasia: The Politics of Upheaval*, Cambridge and New York: Cambridge University Press, 1994

Kreikemeyer, Anna, and Andrei V. Zagorski, "The Commonwealth of Independent States (CIS)," in Lena Jonson and Clive Archer, editors, *Peacekeeping and the Role of Russia in Eurasia*, Boulder, CO: Westview Press, 1996

Kuzio, Taras, and Andrew Wilson, *Ukraine: Perestroika to Independence*, second edition, New York: St Martin's Press, and London: Macmillan, 1998

Rubin, Barnett R., "Russian Hegemony and State Breakdown in the Periphery: Causes and Consequences of the Civil War in Tajikistan," in Barnett R. Rubin and Jack Snyder, editors, *Post-Soviet Political Order. Conflict and State Building*, London and New York: Routledge, 1998

Russell, Wynne, "Russian relations with the 'Near Abroad,'" in Peter Shearman, editor, *Russian Foreign Policy since 1990*, Boulder, CO: Westview Press, 1995

A good general overview of Russian relations with other CIS states

Webber, Mark, *The International Politics of Russia and the Successor States*, Manchester: Manchester University Press, 1996

A good introduction to the foreign relations of Russia and other former Soviet states, including sections on the formation and development of the CIS, and on economic relations among CIS states

Young, Oran R., "The Effectiveness of International Institutions: Hard Cases and Critical Variables," in James N. Rosenau and Ernst-Otto Czempiel, editors, *Governance without Government: Order and Change in World Politics*, Cambridge and New York: Cambridge University Press, 1992

Dr Neil Robinson is a Lecturer in Government at the University of Essex in England.

Chapter Three

Aspects of Economic Development in the CIS

Gennady Polonsky

The 12 member states of the CIS together cover most of the Eurasian continent. Their industrial potential is around 10% of the world's total, and their natural resources constitute around 25% of all known natural resources. Their aggregate territory covers 16.3% of the world's land area, and almost 300 million people, or 5% of the world's population, live there. These populations enjoy very high rates of literacy, and among them are around 25% of the world's pool of scientific workers. The scientific and intellectual potential of the CIS, as expressed in the form of intellectual property rights, has been estimated to be worth around US$500 billion, while their transport infrastructure – railroads, highways, airports, sea and river ports, natural gas and oil pipelines – is relatively well-developed (see Chistyakov and Shul'ga). The CIS is also the world's fourth largest producer of electrical energy: in 1996, 1.25 trillion kilowatt hours were produced on its territory, around 10% of total world output. However, energy consumption is around 1.5 times higher than in more advanced countries.

Since December 1991, these 12 countries have had a unique opportunity to shape their own economies and to try to exploit their enormous potential. All 12 have repeatedly confirmed that their goal is to create developed democratic market economies. However, all 12 have found themselves facing a severe decline in output, macroeconomic instability, and, consequently, drastically falling living standards, rising unemployment, high inflation, and a range of associated economic and social

problems. In addition, the transitional routes that each country chose, and the eventual speed of reform, have varied substantially. Indeed, according to Boris Berezovsky, writing in 1998 when he was Executive Secretary of the CIS, the disintegration of the Soviet Union occurred precisely because the Soviet republics could not agree on a common model for transformation, and started their own uncoordinated movements towards free market economies. In his view, it was an "asymmetrical reaction to a symmetrical shock" that, more than any other factor, brought about the breakup of the Union (Berezovsky p. 5).

In 1994, the European Bank for Reconstruction and Development (EBRD) conducted an extensive study of the progress in transition in all 27 post-Communist countries, rating them on a scale from 1, where reform was negligible or absent, to 4, where reform was comprehensive, based on six categories of economic reform. Within the CIS, Kyrgyzstan and Russia were singled out as the leaders, with 2.83 points and 2.67 points, respectively. Moldova (2.17 points), Uzbekistan (2.00), and Armenia (1.83), along with Belarus, Kazakhstan, and Tajikistan (1.67 each) were put in the middle of the range. Among the least advanced on the path to the market economy were Azerbaijan, Georgia, and Ukraine (1.33 each), with Turkmenistan (1.17) at the bottom of the league table. In contrast, the Czech Republic, the country given the highest rating, received 3.50 points. These ratings reflected the fact that Russia and Kyrgyzstan had rushed ahead with "shock therapy," while the other countries had decided to adopt more gradual approaches, using the state, or the presidential powers of their leaders, as the main engine for economic transition.

Thus, in spite of their enormous potential, these countries are rapidly losing their competitive advantage, lagging behind other countries with much more modest economic endowments. This is confirmed by the fact that the share of the CIS in the world's aggregate GDP fell from 4.1% in 1993 to around 2% in 1996, and is still falling (see Table 3.1). The aggregate GDP of the CIS in 1996 was just 60% of what it had been in 1992, and 55% of the equivalent figure for 1989, when these 12 countries were still Soviet republics. By 1997, the total volume of industrial production in the CIS countries was at around the level it had reached in 1972; by 1998, the aggregate GDP of the CIS stood at the same level as in 1977 (see Ziyadulaev).

The rate of economic decline has varied from country to country, but all have shared one common feature: a drastic fall in GDP (see Table 3.2). The worst affected countries have been Georgia, where GDP in 1996 was less than 40% of GDP in 1992, Azerbaijan (42%), Ukraine (47.1%), Tajikistan (48.1%), and, above all, Russia (62.2%). Mutual indebtedness and barter relations make the CIS countries highly interdependent. This is illustrated by the catastrophic decline in GDP observed in Turkmenistan in 1997, when it fell by one third compared to 1996. This was the result of a decline in the price of natural gas, shortages of raw cotton, and the government's decision to stop supplying natural gas to Armenia and Ukraine because of their constant default on payments. This decision in turn created severe difficulties in the economies of those two countries, and further falls in their GDPs. Ukraine's debt to Turkmenistan was more than US$1 billion, with the total debt of CIS countries reached US$2 billion (see Ziyadulaev).

It is important to note that this decline continued in 1997 and 1998, despite some changes in economic policy in most CIS countries, often in response to the recommendations of the IMF and the World Bank. Thus, in April 1999 the EBRD estimated that the GDP of Russia had fallen by 3.5% in 1998, while the

aggregate GDP of the 12 CIS countries hads fallen by 1.3%, ending the year at around 55% of the level reached in 1989 (see EBRD). Against this background of declining output, especially in industry, due to the disintegration of the former system of state orders and the general impoverishment of the population, the structure of the CIS economies has changed substantially. The relative size of the industrial sector (mining and manufacturing) has fallen, while there has been some growth in the services sector. On average, services accounted for around 50% of GDP across the CIS in 1998.

Investment Activities

The disintegration of the Soviet Union, and the drastic decline in GDP that followed, have had an extremely negative impact on investment activities in the CIS. For example, from 1992 to 1996 investment in the Russian economy fell by 100% overall and by 400% in the industrial sector. In 1997, the average total investment in fixed capital among CIS countries was at around 27% of the level in 1990 (see Table 3.3). The decline in fixed capital investment between 1990 and 1997 ranged from 5% to 14% in Georgia, Kazakhstan, and Moldova, and from 20% to 25% in Russia and Ukraine, but it stood at 34% in Belarus, 49% in Kyrgyzstan, 59% in Uzbekistan, and as much as 93% in Azerbaijan. In Kazakhstan, investment was at around the same level as in 1955, in Moldova and Ukraine it was at around the level reached in 1958 (see Ziyadulaev).

Such sharp declines in investment have led to the physical degradation of key assets. The wear and tear on most of the industrial equipment in Russia is indicated by a rate of depreciation at about 50–60 percent, which is bringing the economy to a point close to physical collapse (see Komarov). Despite the decline up to 1997, indicated above, Azerbaijan is the only country in the CIS where investment activity has in fact increased in recent years; even there it has risen only slightly, and almost exclusively in its growing oil industry.

In Belarus, the decline in investment has been much worse even than the decline in

GDP. Compared to 1990, investment had fallen sevenfold by 1998, while foreign direct investment has proved negligible: in 1997, for example, it amounted to slightly more than US$400 million. In the same year, the Ministry of Economics prepared a "National Project" for attracting investment into the economy, which included such proposals as equalizing the requirements for domestic and foreign investors, changing the investment climate, and providing risk insurance. One of the major themes of the National Project was an increase in cooperation with Russia, Kazakhstan, and Kyrgyzstan through the setting up of joint ventures, financial-industrial groups, and transnational corporations.

Ukraine has not escaped a drastic decline in investment either. However, at the moment it probably has the most developed institutional system for attracting foreign direct investment, centered on the Foreign Direct Investment Support Center established within the Ministry of Economy. A vast amount of legislation has been implemented, backed up with bilateral agreements signed with 25 countries, which are aimed at securing foreign investment and setting rules for double taxation. In spite of these measures, the amount of foreign investment has been extremely small. It reached only slightly more than US$650 million in 1995, which was considerably less than the US$40 billion estimated as necessary for the restructuring of the national economy, and during the first quarter of 1997 Ukraine attracted only US$350 million dollars-worth of foreign investment. By then, there were around 3,000 officially registered joint ventures.

In Kazakhstan, President Nursultan Nazarbayev has declared that the aim of the country's investment policy is to provide assistance to "priority industries" and export-oriented enterprises. According to official estimates, the annual investment requirement stands at US$1.5 billion. It is expected that the majority of investors will be from the West. Kazakhstan has created a very favorable investment climate, in which recently enacted legislation plays an important role, and it is expected that from 1999 to 2004 Kazakhstan will be able to increase investment by 82%, of which 32% will be found internally.

These forecasts may prove to be overoptimistic, but they reflect the widespread belief that foreign direct investment will be crucial in helping the CIS countries to recover from their investment crises and to restructure their national economies. By 1998, however, the proportion of foreign investment within total investment was generally still very low. In Belarus, for example, it was around 7%, in Moldova 6%, in Russia 2%, and in Ukraine just 0.7%. Those countries that displayed more impressive shares of western investment capital – Kyrgyzstan at 68%, Azerbaijan at 58%, Armenia at 42%, Georgia at 29%, and Uzbekistan at 16% – could only do so because the total amount of investment, from any source, was extremely small in all these cases.

The decline in investment is especially striking in civil construction. Only in Russia and Ukraine has the share of housing expenditure in total fixed capital investment increased at any point in the 1990s, and in the other 10 CIS countries this kind of expenditure has decreased substantially, leading to catastrophic declines in the rate of commissioning of new houses and apartments (see Table 3.4).

Agriculture

Agriculture in all 12 CIS countries has undergone a substantial transformation, from a situation in which state and collective farms accounted for most agricultural production, to one in which cooperative and private farms are increasingly central, although the rate of transition has varied from product to product. For example, between 1991 and 1997 the private sector's output of potatoes increased from 72% of total CIS output to 89%, while its output of vegetables rose from 45% to 64% of the total, of meat from 31% to 53%, of milk from 30% to 49%, and of eggs from 28% to 39% (see Ziyadulaev). There are also, as might be expected, considerable variations from country to country; and it should be noted that most of the private sector in agriculture comprises cooperative farms, rather than individual or family holdings. By the beginning of 1997, there were about 786,000 private farms across the CIS, renting or owning 35 million hectares of land, and there was a positive trend in the growth of such farms. However, their contribution to overall agricultural production is still quite modest: in 1998, it varied across the region from around 1.5% to 10%.

In any case, the changes in ownership in agriculture resemble the changes in the ownership of industry: formal reorganization has not necessarily brought in any fresh capital or personal commitment from the new owners. Not surprisingly, 75% of all farms make heavy losses. The average farm income at the end of 1997 was just R225,000 (around US$40), around half the level of workers' incomes in industry (see Bulatov). The major problem that has to be resolved is that working on the land is simply not profitable. Under the present system of taxation in Russia, for example, around 70–75% of farm incomes is taken in various kinds of taxes. In addition, in Russia, as in most of the other 11 countries, there has been virtually no support for agriculture from the government or the state budget. The funds allocated to agriculture were initially largely devoted to the rapidly disappearing and inefficient collective farms, and little or nothing was given to private farmers.

The crucial question of the sale of land to private individuals had not been resolved at the time of writing. For example, on several occasions the State Duma, the lower house of the Russian Federal Assembly, in which the Communists and allied groups are strongly represented, has blocked President Yeltsin's proposals to start the process of land privatization. These opponents have frequently predicted that foreigners would buy Russia out, or "new Russians" would purchase the most attractive plots of land, ruining an agricultural sector that has already been damaged by the abolition of the system of state and collective farms. In February 1998, when Dimitrii Ayatskov, the Governor of the Saratov *oblast* (region), decided to go ahead with auctions of some plots to the highest bidders – a measure that was so successful that the revenues from the auctions were three times more than anticipated – one member of the Duma suggested (in a conversation with this author) that Ayatskov should be executed as a traitor to the Motherland. Yet one cannot seriously consider

privatizing agriculture without privatizing the land, and in the meantime the farmers who have use of the land cannot exert full control over it. Similar attitudes prevail in most of the other CIS countries.

The seriousness of the situation within agriculture can be illustrated by the following facts. On average, from 1996 to 1997 the production of meat in the CIS declined by 9%, that of milk by 6% and that of eggs by 0.3%. Only in Armenia, where the cooperative form of ownership is dominant and more than 95 per cent of all agricultural output is produced privately, has agricultural output per capita increased. In all the other CIS countries there has been a considerable decline, reaching as high as 50% in Kazakhstan (see Table 3.5). This largely reflects the severe decline in investment in agriculture, in the case of Azerbaijan from 15% per cent of total investment in 1991 to 3% in 1995, in Belarus from 26% to 9%, in Kazakhstan from 28% to 2%, in Russia from 18% to 3%, and in Ukraine from 22% to 8% (see Komarov).

Retail Trade and Consumer Goods

The most obvious trend in retail trade, as in other sectors of the CIS economies, has been toward changes in ownership. In Russia and Armenia all retail enterprises are now privately owned; in Kyrgyzstan 90% are, and in Belarus around 70% are. However, these changes have had little impact because of the dependence of these enterprises on the flow of goods from the manufacturing sector. This has been badly damaged by the severing of traditional ties among enterprises, due to the disintegration of the Soviet Union; the general lack of investment and the problem of accumulating or maintaining minimum working capital; the high cost of energy; and the notoriously high levels of corruption in most CIS countries. Thus, for example, for the CIS as a whole the output of fabric and of shoes in 1997 was around 20% and 10%, respectively, of the output achieved in 1991, and in some countries the production of these and other basic consumer goods had all but ceased. In 1997, Georgia produced only slightly more than

1% of its 1991 output of fabric, while Armenia produced 2.2 per cent, and Kazakhstan and Ukraine produced around 9%; similarly, Georgia produced just 0.3% of its 1991 output of shoes, while Azerbaijan produced 3.3%, Kazakhstan and Kyrgyzstan 4.5%, and Tajikistan and Ukraine 7%. The average over-all output of fabric declined from 43.4 square meters per capita in 1990 to 8.5 square meters in 1996, while that of shoes fell from 2.9 pairs to 0.3 pairs (see Goscomstat).

The fall in production has been accompanied by underutilization of existing capacity. For example, in Belarus in 1997, capacity utilization in the production of television sets and paper was respectively 13% and 18%; in Ukraine in the same year, the utilization of equipment for the production of shoes was around 14% (see Komarov). At the same time, imports from the West, Turkey and East Asia account for around 50% of the market for consumer goods in the CIS. In Russia, for example, before the devaluation of the ruble in August 1998, western textile goods and shoes accounted for 50–60% of the market.

The Labor Force and Education

The Soviet economy employed a very high proportion of the labor force: David Lane has suggested it was "probably the highest yet known in human history" (Lane p. 32). In the late 1980s, labor participation rates were around 97.6% for men and 92.7% for women. Mostly for ideological reasons, there were no unemployment statistics, but according to some estimates frictional unemployment was in the range 1.3–1.5% and was mostly concentrated in Central Asia, where agricultural work was subject to seasonal fluctuations (see Lane). Such a low level of unemployment indicated enormous inefficiency in the utilization of labor.

Labor mobility was also at an extremely low level. Among the major reasons were the lack of incentives to change one's job or residence, as monetary benefits were almost the same across the Soviet Union; the absence of a housing market, which made it all but impossible to find an apartment or house in another city or republic, except by agreeing on an exchange with a person or family resident there; and the system of registration, known as *propiska*, under which an individual could not be registered unless he or she had found a job, but to get a job one had to be registered. Leaving one's job also meant loss of social benefits and welfare facilities: housing, child-care, access to recreation facilities, and so on. All changes of employment had to be recorded in an individual labor record book (the *trudovaja knizhka*), and the more often a person changed jobs the less reliable he or she was perceived to be.

Labor mobility has increased substantially since 1991. However, unfortunately, the main reason for this increase was not economic: it was largely prompted by the military conflicts within some of the CIS countries and the associated rise in nationalism, forcing people to leave their homes. For example, even before the Soviet Union was dissolved, warfare erupted between Armenia and Azerbaijan in 1988 over Nagorno-Karabakh, a region within Azerbaijan that has an Armenian majority population. In 1990, there were massacres of Armenians in Baku, the capital of Azerbaijan, and according to the Russian General Aleksandr Lebed, who was in charge of restoring law and order there: "people were running for their lives from medieval cruelty, in an hour losing everything that was the essence of human life . . ." (Lebed p. 242).

In addition, the collapse of the Soviet Union has left millions of Russians, and large numbers of other ethnic minorities, outside their countries of ethnic origin and, in many cases, subject to varying degrees of discrimination. As Jonathan Carr has put it:

"Millions of Russians were left marooned in the former Soviet republics when the USSR ceased to exist . . . they have been subject to a constant onslaught of official legislation and even physical intimidation by nationalizing 'host governments'. Since 1991, strict residency and language requirements have been imposed to assess citizenship and, worse still, laws governing employment and workplace conditions made it impossible for non-natives to work" (Carr p. 12).

Around half of the 20 million Russians outside Russia itself are located in Ukraine, 6 million are in Kazakhstan, and Belarus, Latvia, Uzbekistan, and Kyrgyzstan are home to around 1 million each.

Economic reforms have brought about a new phenomenon – unemployment – yet, as in the past, there are no reliable statistics. According to the official figures issued in the CIS countries, unemployment is not a major problem, which is somewhat puzzling, considering the decline in GDP discussed above. For example, according to official statistics, unemployment in 1996 was just 3.4% in Russia, 1.4% in Georgia and in Moldova, 1.5% in Ukraine, and 0.3% in Uzbekistan (see Table 3.6). One explanation of these astonishing figures is that enterprise directors tend not to make people redundant, sometimes because they have a strong sense of social responsibility toward their workers, but also because they fear social unrest, as one large enterprise can often be the only employer in a city or district. Another explanation could be that salaries are so low, and are paid so irregularly, that people do not bother to quit their jobs: instead, they remain registered as employees while actually working and earning their incomes elsewhere. In any case, the extremely low level of unemployment compensation in all the CIS countries does not encourage people to register as unemployed. It is therefore appropriate to estimate the real levels of unemployment in the CIS at around 10 times the official figures. The worst-hit countries are four of the five states in Central Asia (excluding Uzbekistan), where unemployment was probably around 19% of the labor force in 1998, and Armenia, where it was probably around 21% (see *Inter*).

Unemployment has affected all the sectors of every economy in the CIS, but perhaps the most alarming development is that unemployment is growing rapidly in the area of research and development, where total numbers employed fell between 1991 and 1997 by 55% in Armenia, Belarus, and Moldova; by almost 60% in Tajikistan and Uzbekistan, 41% in Russia, 39% in Ukraine, 35–37% in Georgia, Kazakhstan, and Kyrgyzstan, and 20% in Azerbaijan (see Kabaev). Nor are these lost skills being replaced. The difficulty of finding jobs, the low level of funding for research and development, and the low rates of pay (if pay is even received) have all reduced university students' interest in continuing their studies. All over the CIS, students prefer not to continue their education after completing first degree courses, and try to find work instead. As a result, much smaller numbers of students are moving on into postgraduate studies toward doctorates or other specialist qualifications. The number of students taking doctoral courses declined between 1991 and 1997 by 45% in Kazakhstan, 29% in Moldova, 28% in Uzbekistan, 21–22% in Russia and Tajikistan, 16% in Ukraine, and 12% in Belarus (see Kabaev).

Integration and Trade

The similar problems faced by all the former Soviet republics, as well as their common history, have compelled them to seek possible ways of pooling their resources and establishing some form of economic cooperation. Such integration – often referred to, for obvious reasons, as reintegration – is one of the major topics for discussion at all levels and among a wide range of institutions in the newly independent states. The issue is raised regularly at meetings of the CIS Council of Heads of State, its International Expert Committee, and its Interparliamentary Assembly (see also Chapter 2). In the literature on CIS and economic integration, one often comes across the statement that reintegration of the former Soviet republics should be easier than it would otherwise be, because of the legacy of the Communist division of labor and centrally planned economic coordination. In fact, the situation is the reverse: building new relations and new structures would be easier if it was not first necessary to clean the Augean stables left behind by the Soviet regime, and to find ways of overcoming the persistence of ingrained Soviet patterns of thought and work.

Thus, in spite of the numerous agreements and institutions associated with the CIS, very little has actually been achieved. Prominent figures in the CIS itself have acknowledged this. For example, in March 1997 President Yeltsin of Russia declared at the CIS Council of Heads of State that "the mechanics of the CIS work very badly. Our Commonwealth is hurt by a chronic gap between decisions and their implementation" (as quoted in *Nezavisimaya Gazeta*, November 13, 1998). According to Boris Berezovsky (already cited above), "it is obvious that the CIS is in a deepest crisis. Instead of seven years of integration we have in fact had seven years of disintegration" (Berezovsky p. 1). It is not surprising that many observers, considering the condition in which CIS countries find themselves, believe that it is unlikely that there will be any real integration in the near future (see Shishkov).

The major argument for this conclusion is that, in contrast to the advanced market economies that belong to the EU, the level of economic and institutional development in the CIS countries does not allow the establishment of secure and stable economic relations. The failure of attempts by less developed countries elsewhere in the world to establish lasting forms of economic integration is often cited in support of this argument. Another obstacle on the way to integration is the substantial range of differences in economic development among the member states of the CIS. Russia, Ukraine, Belarus, Armenia, and northern Kazakhstan are relatively developed industrial economies, with growing output from services; the other CIS economies are still largely dominated by agricultural activities. Thus, for example, Russia's GDP per capita is 10.5 times larger than Azerbaijan's, 4.5 times larger than Armenia's, almost five times larger than Uzbekistan's, and 4.6 times larger than Georgia's (see Chistyakov and Shul'ga). Meanwhile, the volume of trade among CIS countries is falling, not only in absolute figures but also in proportion to their outputs. Between 1992 and 1997 the level of mutual exports as a proportion of GDP fell by 400%, while the share of other CIS countries in Russian exports fell by 300%.

Within the framework of the general decline in trade among CIS countries, some of those countries are changing their trade priorities. In the export trade of Belarus, Ukraine, Moldova, and Kazakhstan, the Russian share has an obvious tendency to grow, in line with the decline of export shares for all the other

countries in the region. Russian exporters in their turn are shifting their attention increasingly towards the markets of Europe and Kazakhstan, and increasingly neglecting Transcaucasia and Central Asia. By 1997, the share of Russian trade with the rest of the CIS in the total volume of its export-import operations was about 18%, the lowest level of intra-CIS trade in any of the 12 countries. Among the most dependent on the CIS were such countries as Kyrgyzstan (78% of its trade), Moldova (68%), Belarus and Turkmenistan (67% each), and Georgia (65%) (see Goscomstat).

Among the smaller, subregional international bodies created since 1992 (see Chapter 2), the most promising and economically sound is probably the Customs Union established in 1995 by Russia, Kazakhstan, Ukraine, and Belarus. At a meeting of the heads of these states in April 1998, it was confirmed that Tajikistan would also join the Customs Union in 1999, once it had adjusted its legislation. However, at this level as across the CIS as a whole, integration is relatively ineffective (see Mikhailov). None of these five countries is ready to open its borders to completely free trade with its partners, or to establish and observe consistent rules on common external tariffs on imports from third countries.

Against this background, Boris Berezovsky has argued that there are a number of major obstacles that prevent the CIS from moving toward real and effective integration (Berezovsky pp. 6–8). The CIS countries have not decided on the final aim of integration and, not knowing where they want to get to, they cannot identify the most appropriate ways of getting there; they are not ready to make the individual sacrifices necessary to open the way to integration; they have not created the forms and structures necessary for integration; and they have not created appropriate and effective institutions that would allow for the implementation of agreed decisions. According to Leonid Mikhailov, an adviser to the CIS Committee for Integration, it is unlikely that any of these obstacles, as identified by Berezovsky and others, will be overcome during the next 10–15 years (see Mikhailov).

Integration is made even more complex and difficult an issue because of the different geopolitical aspirations of the leaderships in the various CIS countries. Russia and Ukraine do not see eye to eye on Ukraine's ambition to join NATO (see Chapter 15). Azerbaijan is unhappy over Russian military support for Armenia, while Russia is concerned about Azerbaijan's offer to have a US military base relocated from Ingirlic in Turkey to the Apsheron Peninsula. There are major problems over the extraction and transportation of Caspian oil and natural gas, where the interests of the United States, Azerbaijan, Turkmenistan, Iran, Armenia, Turkey, and Russia are interlinked and also in competition (see Chapter 10). Many politicians in other CIS countries perceive the promotion of cults of personality and the revival of Islam in Central Asia as potential threats to stability.

Finally, the most severe economic and financial crisis since the collapse of Communism, which hit Russia in August 1998, has affected the countries of the CIS in different ways. According to Karl Johansson, area manager for Ernst and Young: "Ukraine and Belarus have been more directly affected, the Central Asian states less so . . . Central Asia is more dependent on the energy sector, which does not have a strong connection with Russia" (as quoted in Hurst p. 21). The Russian crisis had especially serious effects on Belarus. The value of the Belarusian rubel against the US dollar fell by 80%, which led President Lukashenka of Belarus to issue decrees preventing retail stores from raising prices by more than 2% in any one month; but the decrees created shortages and inflated prices in the illicit "shadow" economy. In September 1998, the transportation of goods out of Belarus was forbidden, because of shortages of basic necessities in the country. The restoration of customs controls after the crisis began, not only in Belarus but elsewhere, again showed the fragility of the Customs Union. Nevertheless, the crisis, which was continuing at the time of writing, may have one positive impact on cooperation within the CIS, as it may foster a trend for producers and consumers alike to turn their attention away from expensive western imports toward goods produced in the CIS.

Conclusion

For all its economic weaknesses, and the distortion of economic decisions by political dogma, the economy of the Soviet Union represented an integrated complex. The role of each republic in the economic process was strictly defined by the planning system, and the economy continued to be largely self-sufficient. By 1989, the share of industrial goods in total imports varied from as low as 0.5% in Kyrgyzstan up to 9.7% in Georgia. Agricultural imports ranged from 1.4% in Kazakhstan to 6% in Armenia. In the same year, more than 95% of output, with the exception of Russia's, was distributed within the Soviet Union itself, while 68.2% of all output leaving Russia itself was distributed to other republics.

As we have seen in this chapter, the severing of long-established links after 1991 had a severe impact on all the CIS countries. To date, attempts to create a common economic space by forming the CIS have failed to produce functioning and mutually beneficial institutions. However, as the effects of the Russian crisis were being felt throughout the region in 1999, there was an increasingly common perception that regional reintegration, whatever the disadvantages, might at least help each country to build up its own economy. In the medium to long term, it may well be a consensus on the national self-interest, in all or most CIS countries, that will best facilitate this difficult process.

Further Reading

Berezovsky, Boris, "SNG from Razval to Cooperation" [The CIS: From Disintegration to Cooperation], in *Nezavisimaya Gazeta*, 1998

Bremmer, Ian, and Ray Taras, editors, *New States, New Politics: Building the Post-Soviet Nation*, Cambridge and New York: Cambridge University Press, 1997

The book is the first truly comprehensive, systematic, and rigorous analysis of nation- and state-building processes in the new states that grew out of the collapse of the Soviet Union. The book replaces an earlier volume by the same editors with a collection of specially commissioned studies by leading specialists.

Bulatov, A., "Zemelnye Otnoshenia v Rynochnoi Ekonomike" [Issues of Agricultural Ownership in a Market Economy], in *Ekonomist*, 1997

Bulatov deals with agricultural reform in the CIS, and assesses some of the main factors preventing the development of private ownership.

Carr, Jonathan, "Inside Russia," in *CIS Today*, Autumn 1998

Carr examines the problems faced both by Russians living and working outside Russia itself, and by people from other CIS countries living and working in Moscow.

Chistyakov, E., and V. Shul'ga, "Integratsionnyi Potentsial SNG i Yego rol' v Razvitii Mirokhozyaistvennykh Svyazei" [The Potential of the CIS for Integration and Its Role in the Development of World Economic Relations], in *Ekonomist*, number 6, 1998

The authors discuss the need for integration within the CIS, while underlining the major obstacles that make this process very difficult.

Eastern Europe and the Commonwealth of Independent States 1999, London: Europa, 1999

This reference book provides a comprehensive description and analysis of 27 post-Communist countries, placing them in their international and historical context. There are now nearly 50 specialist writers contributing to a volume that supplies accurate details, and addresses general background and trends.

EBRD: *Transition Report Update*, London: European Bank for Reconstruction and Development, April 1999

Goscomstat, *Rossia i Strany Sodruzhestva Nezavisimykh Gosudarstv* [Russia and the Countries of the Commonwealth of the Independent States], Moscow: Goscomstat, 1998

Hurst, Sarah, "Down but Not Out," in *CIS Today*, Autumn 1998

The author evaluates the economic impact of the financial crisis of August 1998 on Russia, and its different impact on the CIS.

Inter, number 17, Volgograd, 1999

Kabaev, V., "Sostoianie Nauchnogo Potentsial v Stranakh SNG" [The Current State of the Scientific Potential of the CIS], in *Voprosy Statistiki*, number 1, 1997

Kabaev evaluates the scientific potential of the CIS as a whole, and discusses the problems that, in his view, result from chronic underfunding.

Kaminski, Bartolomiej, editor, *Economic Transition in Russia and the New Independent States of Eurasia*, Armonk, NY: M. E. Sharpe, 1996

This book is the eighth in a projected series of 10 volumes produced by the Russian Littoral project. The series provides a basis for comprehensive scholarly study of the transformation of the ex-Soviet republics into independent states, using systematic analysis of the determinants of their domestic and foreign policies.

Komarov, V., "Uslovia Razvitsia Integratsionnich Protsessov Stran Sodruzhestva," [Conditions of the Development of the Process of Integration in the Commonwealth Countries] in *Ekonomist*, 1997

Komarov addresses some of the issues of cooperation within the CIS, and concludes that none of the member states will be able to rebuild its economy on its own.

Lane, David, *Soviet Society under Perestroika*, London and New York: Routledge, 1992

Lane focuses on the changes that took place under the leadership of Mikhail Gorbachev, providing an introduction to the problems that confronted the reform leadership, and the ways in which they were addressed.

Lebed, Aleksandr, *Za Derzhavu Obidno* [My Country, My Pain], Moscow: Idea, 1995

A former general who is now Governor of Krasnoyarsk region in Russia, Lebed uses this autobiographical book to examine, among many other topics, the question of xenophobia and ethnic conflict in the CIS.

Lukes, Elizabeth, and Tanya Albot, *EBRD Directory of Business Information Sources*, London: Effective Technology, 1996

This reference text provides potential investors with knowledge about the information sources needed to assess and control the risks of investing in the region.

Mikhailov, L., "Sodruzhestvo" [Commonwealth], in *Nezavisimaya Gazeta*, 1998

Shishkov, Y., "Integratsia po Evraziisky" [Eurasian-style Integration], in *Vlast*, number 1, 1997

Ziyadulaev, N., "SNG – Sovremennoe Sostoianie i Perspektivy" [The CIS: The Current Situation and Perspectives], in *Ekonomist*, 1998

The author identifies the major economic problems faced by the CIS, and concludes that lack of investment is among the most urgent issues.

Dr Gennady Polonsky is a Reader in Transitional Economics in the Business School of Buckinghamshire Chilterns University College in England.

Table 3.1   Shares of Selected Countries and Regions in the World's Aggregate GDP, in selected years, 1985–96 (%)

	1985	1990	1993	1995	1996
Soviet Union	7.4	7.6	–	–	–
CIS	–	–	4.1	4.0	2.0
European Community/EU	17.7	20.6	21.0	20.8	22.9
United States	20.7	22.3	23.1	23.6	22.8
Japan	7.5	8.8	9.3	9.7	10.0
China	3.9	5.3	6.9	8.0	10.0

Source: Chistyakov, E., and V. Shul'ga, "Integratsionnyi Potentsial SNG i Yego rol' v Razvitii Mirokhozyaistvennykh Svyazei" [The Potential of the CIS for Integration and Its Role in the Development of World Economic Relations], in *Ekonomist*, number 6, 1998

Table 3.2   GDP in the CIS Countries, 1992–96 (1991 = 100)

	1992	1993	1994	1995	1996
Armenia	58.2	53.1	55.9	59.8	63.3
Azerbaijan	77.4	59.5	47.0	42.2	42.7
Belarus	90.4	83.5	73.0	65.4	67.1
Georgia	55.1	39.0	34.9	35.8	39.8
Kazakhstan	94.7	86.0	75.2	69.0	69.3
Kyrgyzstan	86.1	72.8	58.1	55.0	58.9
Moldova	–	–	69.1	67.8	62.5
Russia	85.5	78.1	68.1	65.4	62.2
Tajikistan	–	83.7	65.9	57.7	48.1
Turkmenistan	–	101.5	84.5	78.0	78.1
Ukraine	90.1	77.3	59.6	52.3	47.1
Uzbekistan	88.9	86.9	82.3	81.6	83.0

Source: Goscomstat, *Rossia i Strany Sodruzhestva Nezavisimykh Gosudarstv*, Moscow: Goscomstat, 1998

Table 3.3   Fixed Capital Investment in the CIS Countries, 1992–96 (1991 = 100)

	1992	*1993*	*1994*	*1995*	*1996*
Armenia	8	6	4	–	–
Azerbaijan	59	36	68	56	117
Belarus	71	60	54	37	35
Georgia	45	17	17	17	18
Kazakhstan	53	32	27	17	11
Kyrgyzstan	75	58	32	58	69
Moldova	74	41	20	17	16
Russia	60	53	40	36	30
Tajikistan	58	58	33	–	–
Turkmenistan	120	174	–	–	–
Ukraine	63	57	44	28	22
Uzbekistan	68	65	50	52	56

Source: Goscomstat, *Rossia i Strany Sodruzhestva Nezavisimykh Gosudarstv*, Moscow: Goscomstat, 1998

Table 3.4   Share of Expenditure on Housing in Fixed Capital Investment in the CIS Countries, 1991–96 (%)

	1991	*1992*	*1993*	*1994*	*1995*	*1996*
Armenia	38	40	39	27	43	19
Azerbaijan	23	36	29	12	22	16
Belarus	21	26	24	25	20	20
Georgia	27	54	68	50	32	29
Kazakhstan	21	20	23	12	6	12
Kyrgyzstan	22	29	32	18	6	4
Moldova	21	34	36	35	30	19
Russia	18	22	23	24	23	20
Tajikistan	21	20	20	–	–	–
Turkmenistan	20	22	31	–	–	–
Ukraine	18	23	28	28	21	19
Uzbekistan	24	30	21	20	12	11

Source: Goscomstat, *Rossia i Strany Sodruzhestva Nezavisimykh Gosudarstv*, Moscow: Goscomstat, 1998

Table 3.5 Agricultural Output in the CIS Countries, 1992 and 1994–96 (1991 = 100)

	Total				Per capita			
	1992	1994	1995	1996	1992	1994	1995	1996
Armenia	87	112	117	119	81	101	106	108
Azerbaijan	75	56	52	54	74	54	50	51
Belarus	91	81	77	79	91	81	77	79
Georgia	87	85	97	102	87	86	98	103
Kazakhstan	101	77	58	53	100	77	58	53
Kyrgyzstan	95	70	68	78	94	69	67	78
Moldova	84	69	71	62	84	69	72	63
Russia	91	76	70	67	91	76	70	67
Tajikistan	100	82	64	53	100	80	61	50
Turkmenistan	91	87	72	71	85	74	60	58
Ukraine	92	78	75	68	91	78	76	70
Uzbekistan	94	87	90	85	91	81	83	78

Source: Goscomstat, *Rossia i Strany Sodruzhestva Nezavisimykh Gosudarstv*, Moscow: Goscomstat, 1998

Table 3.6 Official Rates of Unemployment in the CIS Countries, as of December 31, 1992–96 (% of registered national labor force)[1]

	1992	1993	1994	1995	1996
Armenia	3.4	6.2	5.8	8.2	10.0
Azerbaijan	0.2	0.7	0.8	1.0	1.1
Belarus	0.5	1.4	2.1	2.9	4.0
Georgia	–	–	–	–	1.4
Kazakhstan	0.4	0.6	1.1	2.1	4.2
Kyrgyzstan	0.1	0.2	0.8	3.0	4.5
Moldova	0.7	0.8	1.2	1.4	1.4
Russia	0.8	1.1	2.2	3.2	3.4
Tajikistan	0.4	1.1	1.7	2.0	2.6
Turkmenistan	–	–	–	–	–
Ukraine	0.3	0.3	0.4	0.5	1.5
Uzbekistan	0.1	0.2	0.3	0.3	0.3

1 In every case, the real level of unemployment was probably up to 10 times higher than indicated.

Source: Goscomstat, *Rossia i Strany Sodruzhestva Nezavisimykh Gosudarstv*, Moscow: Goscomstat, 1998

Reforms
and
Prospects

Chapter Four

Russia

Demid Golikov

The Failure of *Perestroika*, 1985–91

Understanding the Russian transition is impossible without first looking at the performance of the Soviet Union in the years leading up to its collapse, for Russia was by far the largest, most populous, and most productive among the Soviet Union's constituent Republics (see also Chapter 1). Following his appointment as General Secretary of the Communist Party of the Soviet Union in February 1985, Mikhail Gorbachev and his allies in the regime launched a program of "reconstruction" (*perestroika*). This called for gradual democratization of the political system, and for reforms of the economy to encourage individual initiative and responsibility. It was the disastrous failure of these reforms that set the scene for the beginning of the present transition.

In 1986, the Soviet government put forward an "acceleration plan" drawn up by leading experts in accordance with the established principles of Communist political economy. The aim was to achieve higher output and consumption by stimulating productivity in intermediate production and machinery. However, the additional investments were wasted and productivity fell still further, since the large state-owned enterprises were prevented from formulating their own investment strategies and had no incentives to invest in promoting economic growth. Next, over the course of 1987–89 the government took its first, faltering steps toward economic liberalization. The State Planning Commission (Gosplan) devolved some of the responsibility for financial management and business strategy to enterprises, and its role was formally restricted to "indicative" planning rather than detailed command over resources. The government also permitted the ownership of capital goods by small-scale private cooperatives, which were given a limited degree of freedom to negotiate employment contracts. The government thus effectively lost control over the profits that had been the main source of its revenues. If it had initiated an official program of privatization at that point, it could have brought about an economically efficient allocation of resources and adjusted the public finances. Instead, it imposed an overoptimistic incomes policy and continued to provide funds for industry.

As a result, national resources were rapidly reallocated from the state into a new private sector – although it was not exactly a private sector in the sense familiar in the West. Since the credit market was still very weak, the small but growing group of genuine private entrepreneurs had only two opportunities open to them. They could either invest their own savings, or they could rent working space, capital, and inputs from state-owned factories, stores or offices. The latter, having been granted the right to manage their own assets, were happy to take part in these arrangements, especially as they were free to set their own prices for privately produced goods and services, while those for products from the public sector remained subject to bureaucratic control. Thus, private economic activity rapidly raised the level of capital utilization and productivity. However, since it was allowed to develop without any institutional or legal controls, a large part of the state's property was soon being managed as if it was fully owned by enterprise managers and/or officials from the ministries that were legally responsible for regulating them.

Meanwhile, the shrinking balance of payments, caused mainly by deterioration in the terms of trade in the oil market, made another contribution to the developing economic crisis. The current account fell from a peak surplus of US$6.7 billion in 1987 to a deficit of US$10.7 billion in 1990, while foreign debt rose to US$54 billion in 1989. As tentative liberalization was transformed into unofficial "privatization" and the current account worsened, the government sought to cover its budget deficit, which rose steadily from 16% of GDP in 1989 to 31% in 1991, by increasing its external borrowing and printing more money. In 1991, the growth of the money supply was four to six times higher than in 1986–89. From 1990 onwards, the economy experienced a permanent shortage of commodities in the state sector, where prices were mostly fixed, alongside inflation in the legitimate commercial sector and in the "informal", quasi-criminal markets, where prices were rising by 10–20% every month by 1991. In an attempt to manage the situation, the government provided all Soviet citizens with consumer vouchers (*talons*), which were supposed to allow them to buy limited amounts of such essentials as sugar, cigarettes, beef (two pounds a month for each person), and soap (two bars a month), at fixed prices. However, by 1991 most Russians could not find even these basic goods on sale in the state-owned stores. Increasing numbers had to spend their days either lining up to receive foreign humanitarian aid, or scrambling to buy, for example, a few kilograms of sugar, only to find that it had usually been moistened by the retailers to give it extra weight. Increasing numbers of individuals tried to avoid the inflation tax and the inefficiency of the financial system by replacing the use of rubles with barter, foreign currency or commodities such as alcohol. By the end of 1991, the Soviet economy was approaching hyperinflation and stagnation.

In August 1991, those elements within the Communist Party that had been suspicious of the movement toward reform, including many of the highest-ranking officers in the Army and the KGB (the security service), launched a coup against Gorbachev while he was away from Moscow. Their avowed aim was to introduce a "special regime" that could restore order. They lasted just four days before collapsing in the face of the strong and effective resistance led by Boris Yeltsin, the President of the Russian Federation (a resistance that, ironically, also included many KGB and Army officers). Their defeat led directly to the dissolution of the Soviet Union, which took place in December 1991, while Yeltsin moved into the Kremlin, the traditional seat of Russian government where the establishment of the Soviet Union had been proclaimed 69 years before.

Gaidar and Liberalization, 1991–92

It was now up to the government of the Russian Federation to prevent an economic crash and hyperinflation, but it was not at all clear how the complex process of transition could be implemented. Russia required reform of its political institutions, far-reaching privatization of most of its enterprises, the restructuring of its industries to take account of market forces, the development of a modernized banking and financial system, and the adjustment of social policy in line with the new conditions. In the event, a sense of urgency pushed the government to begin with the full liberalization of prices and exchange, putting monetary policy at the center of its reforms.

From the very beginning, Yeltsin made a choice in favor of the liberal economists, including Yegor Gaidar, who replaced Ivan Silayev as Prime Minister of Russia in June 1992, and Anatoly Chubais, who called for active restructuring and rapid conversion to free markets. Fierce controversies erupted over almost every issue, ranging from the reorganization of the government and the federal system through the details of economic policy; even the national anthem and heraldic symbols were not adopted without considerable debate. However, at the core of these discussions was the question of which of the various interest groups and newly emerging political factions would gain political power, and therefore enjoy the opportunity to survive and flourish in the new economy. It soon became obvious that liberal reforms, aimed at the radical restructuring of the economy in order to create efficient competitive markets, would work against the interests of all the strongest groups, notably the oil and natural gas exporters, the military, and the agricultural sector, which together had formed the base of the Soviet economy. In other words, after more than 70 years of Communist rule there was no effective political support for liberal ideas. Yeltsin therefore had to turn to the general public. If he could rely on their support, liberal reforms would be successful; otherwise, the economy would develop toward either complete chaos or a market favoring the few who already had power and influence.

The new policies proposed by Yeltsin and the economists he favored did indeed come up against strong resistance from those industries that had become accustomed to being protected by the state, as well as from many of the local authorities in the regions and republics that make up the Russian Federation (see Appendix 4). They in turn received the support of the Communist and nationalist groups that formed the majority in the Congress of People's Deputies, the legislature elected in March 1990. Since then, public opinion had moved on and was generally much more in favor of the reforms than the Communists and their allies were. However, because the reforms were carried out when labor mobility was still very low, more than half the adult population were likely to lose their jobs, just at a time when their savings (if they had any) were being devalued by the inflation that followed the liberalization of prices. Workers and managers, whatever their theoretical views about the contest between markets and central planning, found that their interests coincided and colluded in resisting dismissals. The workers were promised future earnings and benefits, while the managers used their unproductive and excessive workforces as valuable political assets for exerting pressure on the authorities.

On January 2, 1992, the government abandoned controls on the prices of almost every commodity, although liberalization of the prices of oil and oil products was delayed until September that year. Temporary limits were placed on increases in the prices of a small range of consumer goods and services, goods supplied by monopolies, and energy. This partial liberalization of prices represented the first significant compromise between Gaidar and the other reformers, on the one hand, and the industrial lobby, acting together with the opposition in the Federal Assembly, on the other. This concession to gradualism led to inefficient adjustment of relative prices, but nevertheless the beginning was successful. Hyperinflation had been effectively ruled out and economic activity did not collapse. Indeed, a certain degree of dynamism was perceptible in the months that followed.

However, the next compromise between the reformers and their opponents put an end to "shock therapy" in Russia. During the summer of 1992, the restrictive monetary policy was completely discarded, as Viktor Gerashchenko, the new head of the Bank of Russia (the central bank), extended huge flows of credits, amounting to more than 40% of GDP, at interest rates below the rate of inflation. There were three groups of recipients. First, Gerashchenko sought to compensate for what he saw as the adverse effects of liberalization, particularly the liquidity shortage facing uncompetitive enterprises, with loans to major industries in the state sector. These included the huge industries run by the military, which employed up to half of the total labor force (see also Chapter 11), as well as agriculture, and the oil and natural gas industries. Second, he arranged loans through commercial banks for the Russian Arctic and other regions that had long contributed less to domestic output than they received in net transfers from the federal budget. The Congress of People's Deputies compelled the government to continue paying these transfers to the regions, in addition to the loans. Third, the Bank effectively subsidized trade with the other former Soviet republics, which had declared political and economic independence but still used Russian rubles. The resulting upsurge in the money supply was followed by an upsurge in inflation in the fall of 1992, and the monthly inflation rate continued at between 20% and 30% up to the end of 1993, while real interest rates remained deeply negative. By October 1992, the government had practically stopped the flows of credit out of the Bank of Russia. Nevertheless, both Gaidar and then, after he was dismissed in November 1992, the new Finance Minister, Boris Fyodorov, found themselves having to move against the Bank in their attempts to cut the budget deficit. Gerashchenko was to persist in defending inflation, as an unavoidable side effect of liberalization, until a financial crisis in October 1994 compelled him to resign.

In November 1992, Yeltsin's opponents in the Congress of People's Deputies sought to amend the Constitution in order to reduce the powers of the presidency. Yeltsin appeased them and averted the amendment by dismissing Gaidar, who had come to symbolize the shock therapy approach. In fact, Gaidar remained close to Yeltsin as an adviser and served as First Deputy Prime Minister from September 1993 to June 1994. Nevertheless, the initial phase of liberalization had come to a decisive end, and most Russian liberals, including Gaidar and his circle, lost their confidence in Yeltsin sooner or later.

Chernomyrdin and Compromise, 1992–98

Gaidar's successor as Prime Minister was Viktor Chernomyrdin, the former director of the natural gas monopoly Gazprom. Somewhat unexpectedly, given his background in such a powerful state-owned enterprise, Chernomyrdin did not reverse the liberalization of prices, nor did he promote the activist industrial policy demanded by the majority in the Congress of People's Deputies, which would have meant bringing back elements of central planning. Instead Chernomyrdin's government was an unstable coalition, bringing together people with very different backgrounds and opinions, who appeared, disappeared, and sometimes reappeared as the confrontation between Yeltsin and his opponents went on. It quickly became impossible to ascertain what the government's policy was at any given moment. Any one of the numerous Deputy Prime Ministers would not hesitate to sign a document in order to neutralize a decision taken by one of the other Deputy Prime Ministers, or even to announce a "final" decision while the problem that it was said to solve was still being discussed elsewhere in the government. Meanwhile, the money supply, inflation, exchange rates, and other macroeconomic variables carried on being highly volatile.

Monetary expansion continued up to April 1993, when the government began to implement a persistent reduction in the money supply. The tightening of economic policy led the country into another political crisis, in September, when the Congress of People's Deputies voted to impeach Yeltsin. His response was to exercise his constitutional right to dissolve the Congress by decree and to send tanks to surround its meeting place, the White House, in order to force its members to disperse. In December 1993, a new Constitution was approved by referendum, and elections resulted in significant gains for Communist and nationalist groups in the lower house of the new Federal Assembly, the State Duma. Together, they outnumbered Yeltsin's supporters; and they were determined to use their votes to ensure that reform would proceed slowly, if at all.

By the time the State Duma assembled, it was generally understood that most of the credits extended by the Bank of Russia during 1992–93 had been misused. Any credit received at a negative real interest rate – that is, at an interest rate below inflation – was immediately forwarded into more profitable "shadow" investments, or into consumption by enterprise managers, and then sent abroad. It is not surprising that a positive correlation can be traced between the amounts of credit supplied and lost in this way, and the increasing arrears in wages and transaction payments. It was the monetary expansion that prevented the development of competitive markets, preserved the old state industries by redistributing the national income in their favor, and suppressed the emerging small businesses, as well as the nascent middle class associated with them. Restructuring slowed down almost to a complete stop, although the decline in GDP between 1992 and 1996 was less than the decline in industrial output.

At the same time, the preservation of the state industries left the government with limited funds for social welfare, health, education, culture, the legal system, the police, and the military. It tried to reduce its expenditure by delaying the payment of wages to public sector workers and of pensions to the retired. This naturally generated increasing hostility to reform among the population at large, who experienced significant reductions in their real incomes compared to what they had earned in the Soviet period just a few years before. In particular, the shrinking budget for the legal system, the police, and the military created huge problems, as social order deteriorated and illegal economic activities flourished. Corruption and illicit markets had already appeared during the years of *perestroika*, but economic liberalization gave opportunities to those operating in the "shadow economy", as well as to everybody else, to fix their property rights. Criminal organizations eventually took the place of the weakening legal institutions and transformed themselves into private security agencies providing a broad range of services, from supervising the execution of contracts to preventing the entry of new actors into already existing markets.

These developments helped to make the Russian economy very different from the stable and growing economies of the West that provided the model for the reforms. Inadequate regulation and control were responsible for the huge losses that many ordinary Russians suffered as the reforms were implemented. They had to carry the burden of inflation, which is estimated to have been equivalent to 30% of GDP in 1992 and 20% of GDP in 1993. Further, since the financial system was entirely unregulated, they also lost huge amounts of money through investments in fraudulent companies in 1993–94, as well as through the devaluation of privatization vouchers (see below).

Foreign Trade and Investment

One of the most important goals of Gaidar's program had been the liberalization of foreign trade and crossborder capital flows, but its implementation was hampered by the dominant business groups, which deployed nationalistic rhetoric against foreign investors, and in defense of state quotas and licenses. Russia retained the Soviet system for granting "special rights" to certain enterprises for the exclusive export of oil, natural gas, and metals, and it still comprised mainly distributors or wholesale trading companies. This meant that only a small proportion of the revenues from such exports reached the producers of these commodities, who were experiencing an accelerating depreciation of their capital stock. By 1994–95, when the special rights were withdrawn, the enterprises and ministries that had benefited from them had undergone mergers and reorganizations that left them large enough to protect their markets even without state support. It is therefore not surprising to find that virtually all the very wealthy business people in Russia today made at least some of their money from exporting raw materials.

Privatization

Another important policy inherited by Chernomyrdin's government from Gaidar's was the privatization program, which had been devised and implemented by Anatoly Chubais from 1992 onwards. It was successful, if only in the sense that many large enterprises were taken out of government control; but most of them are now in the hands of the "private" sector that began to develop under Gorbachev (as described above). Accordingly, the performance of most of these enterprises has barely improved since privatization. Many of the factories and farms still look to the state for funding, even though responsibility for their financial performance was formally renounced by the state as part of Gorbachev's reforms. Again as in 1987–89, in many of these enterprises the directors are more interested in enriching themselves than in increasing productivity or market share. Unlike in most of the countries of central and eastern Europe, where privatization and the introduction of market capitalism went hand in hand, in Russia (and other post-Soviet economies) privatization has been little more than a formal procedure for fixing property rights, whether there is a market or not. In general, heavy industry in

Russia is still biased toward rent-seeking behavior: the search for subsidies, cheap loans, foreign exchange deals, and other bureaucratic favors, as well as asset-stripping. Meanwhile, increases in market capitalization have been prevented by high inflation, slow progress on institutional reform – especially in relation to the administration of bankruptcies – and continuing state support for inefficient enterprises, even after privatization, which prevents restructuring and protects them from external competitors. Hence, the stock market has played no significant role in the economy.

It was only in 1995 that the Russian government started to privatize the leading state concerns and monopolies. (The high level of monopolization in the Russian economy is part of the legacy from the Soviet period, when it was believed that the efficient allocation of resources and effective coordination in a centrally planned economy required a high level of concentration of productive assets.) Once again, the process was almost entirely controlled by the main interest groups and the new tycoons, who colluded with the industrial ministries, and some members of Chernomyrdin's government, in submitting their bids to the State Property Committee, and purchased the shares in these concerns at very low prices. However, pressure from other interest groups, supported by the opposition parties in the State Duma, ensured that what they regarded as key national assets remained in the hands of the state. Following their own economic interests, both the new business groups and the unsuccessful remnants of Soviet industry sought to protect their market positions. At one of the most important stages of reform, involving fundamental institutional transformation and restructuring of key firms and sectors, the liberals had to fight against an unholy alliance of new and old. The major players in the economy entered upon a kind of competition for monopoly positions, leading to the crowding out of the inefficient older industries as economic and political power became ever more concentrated in the hands of a very small number of people and organizations.

The effects of privatization were somewhat different in the case of small firms. In regions where their transfer to the private sector proceeded rapidly and smoothly, more goods and services were supplied, and their quality improved. By 1992–93, the difference between the two largest cities, Moscow and St Petersburg, was becoming clear. St Petersburg had seen the most intensive privatization of small businesses anywhere in the country and was becoming visibly more prosperous than Moscow as a result. Perhaps the greatest achievement of the privatization campaign is that it has encouraged the development of small businesses, contributing to improvements in the supply of many goods and services to the extent possible in the troubled Russian economy.

The Financial System

There were only three institutions called banks in the Soviet Union, and all three functioned as branches of the central bank in circulating money, making investment decisions, and undertaking foreign exchange transactions (see also Chapter 12). Under Gorbachev's limited reforms, four state banks had been established, in addition to the central bank, to serve different sectors of the economy. After 1988, when basic regulations for commercial banking were enacted, the industry experienced very rapid growth. By 1994–96, there were almost as many banks as in western economies, but almost all of them were very small, even compared to their counterparts in developing countries. Many small banks were established by major firms and industrial groups in order to provide a minimum range of essential transaction services for their owners. The growth of the banking industry was therefore only superficially impressive, and owed much to the laxity of the regulations, as well as to the relatively free access to loans from the Bank of Russia at negative real interest rates (as discussed above).

While the Bank of Russia was supplying such huge flows of liquidity, at the lowest available interest rates, the opportunity costs of loans from the private sector rose significantly. Individuals seeking banking services were crowded out from the loan market, and left with a choice between investing their money in foreign cash or holding the deposits at a negative real interest rate. As a result, before 1995 up to 70–80% of the total liabilities of the Russian commercial banks were attracted at negative real interest rates, a proportion roughly three times greater than for commercial banks in the United States. As in other economies coming out of a period of high inflation, the tightening of monetary policy and financial stabilization inevitably led to a liquidity crisis.

With the monthly inflation rate falling below 10% by the beginning of 1994, the liabilities of the banking industry decreased, but the government helped the banks to avoid a crash by reducing the discount rate, manipulating the reserves, and offering selective support. It offered no help to the thousands of people who had invested huge amounts of money in pyramid schemes. Adjusting to the tightening monetary policy, banks had to decrease their margins and make their real interest rates positive. Extended credits and accepted deposits, measured in real terms, started to grow, following the relatively rapid fall in the previous year. Loans extended to individuals were, and still are, all but nonexistent, while loans extended to industry have been estimated to amount to only around 10% of GDP, a much lower level than in the developed economies.

Having lost cheap credit and subsidies from the government, the state-owned and semiprivatized firms that represented around two thirds of the economy found a simple way to compensate: they stopped paying taxes. The private sector was already accustomed to having as little contact with tax inspectors as possible. The result was that from November 1993 to August 1994 the arrears of the economy to the various government budgets – federal, republican, and provincial – had tripled in real terms, reaching 24% of monthly GDP, or around 25% of the consolidated budget deficit. At the same time, the industrial lobby, ranging from small and failing factories to the prosperous oil giants, collaborated with the local authorities in the provinces to persuade the Federal Assembly to suspend the bankruptcy law, and thus help them to avoid tax in another way. The collusion between the state-owned enterprises and the local authorities – which was never made explicit or official, but was widespread nonetheless – became

another instrument of pressure on the federal government. The enterprises supplied oil, natural gas, electricity, or transportation to the local authorities without insisting on being paid on time, or indeed ever. As a result, the local authorities enjoyed the use of free resources while postponing reforms that might damage the interests of their friendly suppliers. The state-owned enterprises compensated for their losses by avoiding tax payments to the federal government, which was no longer capable of forcing them to pay.

Burdened by the liquidity shortage and the deterioration in the federal finances, the Russian economy finally reached "Black Tuesday," October 11, 1994, when the exchange rate of the ruble against the US dollar fell by 27.5% during a single trading session on the Moscow Exchange. There have been several different interpretations of that event, ranging from sophisticated analyses of the fundamentals in the money market to a simple technical explanation: that the Bank of Russia, either in error or through collusion, failed to intervene when the major commercial banks started to play their speculative games. The latter interpretation makes a great deal of sense, for the shock allowed the authorities to improve the balance sheet a little by making a swap with their US dollar assets. The exchange rate was restored within two days, but the shock had profound consequences. Consumer price inflation surged upwards, while monthly real interest rates fell as low as 3–6% below zero. They remained negative over the following four or five months, even though the banks responded by increasing their nominal rates, the interbank loan market immediately ceased, and the public received another indication of the high risk attached to holding deposits in rubles.

The Default, 1998

One of the numerous Russian paradoxes is that the decline in the inflation rate has not been associated with improvements in the state budget and public finances. The government surrendered to interest group pressure and tried to keep its expenditures high, but failed to collect enough revenue. As has already been mentioned, the easiest way to cover extra spending is to print more money. This is exactly what the Russian authorities did until late 1993, when a system of internal borrowing was launched, in the form of a market in government bonds issued by the Ministry of Finance. Most of these were three-month and six-month discount bills, known as GKOs, but there were also federal coupon papers, known as OFZs. Trading remained insignificant at first, but by June 1994 the borrowing rate had been raised above the rate of return on US dollar assets, allowing a tripling of the rate of growth in debt in real terms. The issuance of government bonds grew steadily, from around 3% of GDP in the summer of 1994 to around 7% in the first half of 1995, and then reached 20% by the spring of 1996.

The strategy was to keep the desired net revenue by adjusting the rate of return. The desired revenue was implicitly determined, with some variations, according to the principle "the more, the better." In effect, it was another pyramid scheme. The effective real return on the bonds became the highest available rate in the economy: depending on the rate of inflation, it was held to an average of 2–4% a month in 1995 and has been fluctuating around 4–6% a month since 1996, sometimes reaching 8%. Around half of the total revenue from government bonds was used to pay the interest on the bonds, further crowding out private investment. However, it helped to reduce inflation and it also helped the banks to survive, as low-interest loans from the central bank in 1992–93 have been replaced by investments in the high-interest bonds. As a result, the banking crisis that had been expected to follow the ending of high inflation was postponed.

Nevertheless, deterioration in the public finances, accompanied by excessive borrowing, would eventually lead to an excessive accumulation of debt and thus to a failure by the government and, probably, the banking industry to continue servicing the debt. The debt redemption schedule for the second half of 1998 and the first half of 1999 appeared to be very tough. It required that the payoffs on bonds should reach around US$3–5 billion, with an additional US$1–3 billion in servicing

the external debt every month, at a time when monthly GDP was estimated at around US$35 billion. The situation was becoming worse because of the deterioration in the balance of trade, which fell from around US$8–12 billion to almost zero. In 1997–98, imports rose more than in any previous year, while world prices for oil and natural gas, Russia's main exports, collapsed. The oil and natural gas industries, faced with a persistent lack of investment, responded predictably by pushing the level of their tax arrears even higher, thus making an additional contribution to the budget deficit.

The financial crisis that started in East Asia in the fall of 1997 seemed likely to cause even more damage and it appeared that Russia's low international investment ratings (B1 from Moody's, and B+ from Standard and Poor's, as of June 1998) might be revised downwards. Meanwhile, the relentless accumulation of unpaid wages and constantly postponed pensions fueled mass unrest. By 1998, very few Russians remained willing to speak in favor of Yeltsin or his policies to opinion pollsters or reporters, and the only political force benefiting from the troubles was the Communist opposition. The Russian economy was approaching deep turmoil.

On March 23, 1998, Yeltsin dismissed Chernomyrdin's government and appointed Sergei Kiriyenko, a 36-year-old banker, as acting Prime Minister. Kiriyenko, who had been an ally of the reformist Boris Nemtsov and was supported by Anatoly Chubais, was unknown to most Russian officials. Partly for that very reason, he seemed more likely than any of the better-known liberals to receive the vote of confidence from the Duma that was necessary for him to continue as Prime Minister. Kiriyenko's government included well-known economists experienced in the reform process, as well as prominent liberal politicians. It took on the economy with a full package of short-term emergency measures, aimed at ending the crisis in the financial markets, and a long-term policy program oriented toward financial stabilization, further economic liberalization, and growth. Again, as in early 1992, it was a policy that threatened the economic interests of all the largest financial and industrial groups – and, just as in

1992, it became evident that such a policy could not be successful without their support.

On July 16, 1998, Kiriyenko's government and the Bank of Russia issued a joint Memorandum on Policies for Economic and Financial Stabilization. They admitted that, despite the adjustment policies implemented by the new government, market confidence had not been restored and capital flows remained volatile. In particular, they declared that the emergency underscored the need to improve revenue collection, including the establishment of units monitoring and controlling payments of current tax liabilities by large taxpayers. In other words, the government acknowledged at last that it had to force them to pay the taxes that they had been allowed to avoid for years. The memorandum also set out a plan for the Ministry of Finance to reduce the level of interest payments in 1998–99 and offset the country's exposure to shifts in market sentiments, by offering holders of GKOs the opportunity to exchange them for US dollar-denominated Eurobonds with long maturities at market rates. It was supposed that bonds denominated in US dollars would generate more confidence than bonds denominated in rubles. This strategy was risky, since the conversion of the debt into foreign currency assets could be interpreted as a signal of declining confidence in the ruble and, if devaluation could not be avoided, the Eurobonds would become the heaviest burden on the budget. This is exactly what happened a few weeks later.

By the beginning of August 1998, it was clear that the government had failed to find support from the Duma, as well as from business leaders. The Duma rejected some of the measures proposed in the memorandum, and all the party leaders spoke out against the government and Yeltsin. This political fiasco became the signal for panic, followed by the collapse of the stock market and a sharp liquidity shortage in the banking system. The real turmoil started in the second week of August. On August 17, the government was compelled to devalue the ruble and impose a 90-day moratorium on a portion of its debt.

Back in March 1998, it had appeared that Kiriyenko had a good chance to turn the tide

of public opinion back to support for liberal reforms. As it turned out, however, the Communists and the business community, each for their own different reasons, joined in an open and successful campaign against the liberals in general and the young, inexperienced Kiriyenko in particular. Indeed, the main domestic impetus for the crisis was the low credibility of Kiriyenko's government: hardly any Russian voter could believe that it could defeat the combination of political demagogues and powerful tycoons that opposed it. The influence of this diverse combination was almost certainly the largest single factor in the financial collapse of August 17. With the help of the Communists, the tycoons had succeeded against the liberals yet again.

The Primakov Interlude

Yeltsin's reaction to the collapse was to blame Kiriyenko, dismiss him and his government, and appoint Viktor Chernomyrdin as acting Prime Minister, in the hope that the tycoons would be appeased by the return of a politician who shared their background and outlook. In the event, the State Duma rejected Chernomyrdin, not once but twice, while the exchange rate went on falling, prices rose by around 40%, and there was a massive shift in consumption toward the cheapest available food and other essentials. As a result, business activity immediately declined, especially in import-related industries and small private firms.

Instead of Chernomyrdin, it was Yevgeni Primakov who was appointed Prime Minister by Yeltsin and approved by the Duma in September 1998. His first task was to bring peace to the political arena, but the economic crisis needed attention too. At the end of December, Primakov revealed his "nine principles" of economic policy. These included using interest rates and international reserves in monetary policy, rather than targeting the money supply; creating "a special development bank in which the state will have a controlling interest"; ensuring the "competitive placement of state investments and provision of state guarantees"; and implementing "an active industrial policy designed to support exports and create large corporations." It was obvious that Primakov, acting in Yeltsin's name, had decided to make placating the majority in the Duma his first priority. This at least conferred some kind of democratic legitimacy on his policies and enabled him to draw individuals from across the political spectrum into his government. However, by the same token it was difficult to see how such a broad-based, ideologically incoherent government, headed by a dedicated advocate of compromise, would be able to implement these proposals – or any others – in an economy that was still dominated by an all too distinctive business community.

It mattered little in the end what Primakov may have hoped to achieve. In May 1999, in the midst of renewed political turmoil, chiefly centered on NATO's conflict with Yugoslavia and the Duma's latest attempt to impeach Yeltsin, the President suddenly announced that Primakov was to blame for "procrastination" over the economy, and dismissed the Prime Minister and all the members of his government. Sergei Stepashin, well known as a Yeltsin loyalist, took Primakov's place.

Conclusion

The Russian business community has not stayed exactly the same throughout the years since the collapse of the Soviet Union. The inherited division among competing interest groups, based on industries, has begun to be transformed into a division based on capital holdings. A few financial groups, consolidated and managed by the major tycoons, control the tradable resources and the leading productive assets in the economy, while a large number of smaller, often regionally based industrial-financial groups, including former state-owned firms, have control over markets in final goods. Some of these dominant groups – notably several of those that have invested in the Moscow region, where around 85% of all Russian capital is concentrated – now look to Yuri Luzhkov, the powerful Mayor of Moscow, as the politician they would like to see winning the presidency when Yeltsin steps down. Other business groups are likely to support Aleksandr Lebed, who is neither a Communist nor a liberal and may be capable of gathering

enough votes from the public without promising changes that would affect major business interests. This division is, however, largely conditional on the economic competition among different financial groups: more or less significant bodies of support may move to other politicians. It remains unlikely, however, that any major business group will openly support Primakov if he chooses to avenge his dismissal from government by running for the presidency.

Looking beyond the short term, the question arises whether Russia will be able to move onto a sustained trend toward stability and economic growth in the 21st century. Its social and economic problems require fundamental, systemic solutions. The failure of Communism, swiftly followed by the failure of *perestroika* under Gorbachev, ensured widespread public support for Yeltsin's program of democratization, but did not attract sufficient support for economic liberalization. Indeed, many Russians still believe that "western economics" cannot be successfully applied in their country, since its cultural and social traditions are – in their view – radically different from those in the rest of the world. It does not follow, of course, that the economic and political upheavals of 1998–99 will lead to a renaissance of the Communist system. Nevertheless, the influence of Communist politicians seems certain to increase, as they exert pressure on the government in favor of reflation, protectionism, and extensive state control, both of the financial system and of the real economy. In promoting these policies, they will claim to speak for the interests of the common people, sometimes in alliance with the nationalists and sometimes in competition with them; yet their support already comes mainly from members of the older generation and their influence will probably wane as that generation passes on.

In the meantime, the influence of Communism can still be felt in other ways, for the Russian turmoil of the 1990s was intrinsically predetermined by the social and economic performance of the Soviet Union. Despite Gorbachev's intentions, *perestroika*, which he envisaged as a way of balancing economic transformation and political reform with institutional stability and a Communist monopoly of power, served only to accelerate the meltdown of the system he devoted most of his life to. The Soviet legacy, combined with the institutional changes and redistribution of economic power during the years of *perestroika*, led directly to the failure of the liberal reforms attempted by Gaidar's government in 1992 and Kiriyenko's government in 1998, and at least discussed by Primakov's government too.

As we begin the 21st century, and see the dawning of a new Europe and other profound geopolitical changes, it would be unreasonable to expect Russia, burdened with this legacy, to turn rapidly or easily toward liberal values and market behavior. Unfortunately, this implies that the Russian economy will have to undergo a much slower, more gradual, and probably more painful process of transformation. It also implies that its living standards will fall further and further behind those of the developed economies; and that Russia will lose its leading positions in culture, education, and technology.

Further Reading

Aslund, Anders, *How Russia Became a Market Economy*, Washington, DC: Brookings Institution, 1995

A readable and comprehensive account of the transition from Communism by a distinguished scholar

Dmitriev, M. E., et al., *Rossiskiye Banki Nakanune Finansovoi Stabilizatsii* [Russian Banks on the Eve of Financial Stabilization], Moscow: Izdatelstvo Norma, 1996

This comprehensive study of banking in Russia includes data on the consolidated balance sheets of banks, and comparisons with their US counterparts.

Gaidar, Yegor, and Karl Otto Pöhl, *Russian Reform / International Money*, Cambridge, MA: MIT Press, 1995

Texts by a leading Russian reformist and a prominent German economist, presenting the problems of economic transition in Russia in the context of the global financial system

Illarionov, A., editor, *Russian Economic Reform: Lost Year*, Moscow: Institute for Economic Analysis, 1994

The authors analyze the situation in Russia up to 1993, emphasizing the huge budget deficit, the weakness of monetary policy, and the government's support of inefficient industries as the main reasons for the continuing economic decline of the country.

Illarionov, A., "Priroda Rossiskoi Inflyatsii" [The Origins of Russian Inflation], in *Voprosi Ekonomiki*, number 1, 1995

The author argues that inflation in Russia is caused by monetary expansion, as in other countries, and not by structural, supply-side or other factors.

Lane, D. S., and C. Ross, *The Transition from Communism to Capitalism: Ruling Elites from Gorbachev to Yeltsin*, London: Macmillan, and New York: St Martin's Press, 1998

Raymond, W. J., and V. Belyakov, editors, *Constitution of the Russian Federation, With Commentaries and Interpretation by American and Russian Scholars*, Lawrenceville, VA: Brunswick, 1994

In addition to a translation of the Constitution, which came into effect in December 1993, and scholarly commentaries on its contents and implications, this volume contains statistics, maps, charts, and selected historical information.

Rosefielde, S., editor, *Efficiency and Russia's Economic Recovery Potential to the Year 2000 and Beyond*, Aldershot and Brookfield, VT: Ashgate, 1998

A thorough analysis of the prospects for the Russian economy, which challenges the optimistic consensus on the impact of the reforms carried out so far

Russian Economic Trends, Moscow: RECEP and Whurr Publishers, quarterly since 1992

This valuable English-language publication contains comprehensive statistical data, with comments and special reports on various issues of economic policy in Russia.

Schleifer, Andrei, and Daniel Treisman, *The Economics and Politics of Transition to an Open Market Economy: Russia*, Paris: OECD, 1998

The authors focus on the problems of restructuring in the Russian economy, the design of the privatization program and effect of macroeconomic policy on economic adjustment.

Sobchak, Anatoly, *For a New Russia: The Mayor of St. Petersburg's Own Story of the Struggle for Justice and Democracy*, New York: Free Press, 1991

Anatoly Sobchak is a prominent Russian politician who was a deputy in the Supreme Soviet under the Communist system, but was later elected on a liberal democratic program as Mayor of Leningrad. The city returned to its original name, St Petersburg, during his term in office. His book gives an insight into the design of Gorbachev's policies, the roles played by key politicians in the democratization of Russia, and the political turmoil that followed the economic collapse of the Soviet Union.

White, Stephen, Alex Pravda, and Zvi Gitelman, editors, *Developments in Russian Politics 4*, London: Macmillan, and Durham, NC: Duke University Press, 1997

This collection analyzes politics and government in Russia (and other successor states), including the presidency, parties and the political system, foreign policy, and legislation.

Yavlinsky, G., and S. Braguinsky, "The Inefficiency of Laissez-faire in Russia: Hysteresis Effects and the Need for Policy-led Transformation," in *Journal of Comparative Economics*, Volume 26, number 1, 1994

Zaostrovtsev, A., *Anti-monopoly Policy and Rent-Seeking in Russia*, Stockholm: Stockholm Institute of Transitional Economies, 1998

The author argues that the rent-seeking motive strongly influences decision-making in the government, as well as the behavior of both state and private enterprises.

Dr Demid Golikov is a Researcher at the School of Economics in St Petersburg, Russia. He has written several papers on Russian economic policy.

Chapter Five

Belarus

Luba Demidkina

As a republic of the Soviet Union up to 1991, Belarus had a remarkably high level of social and economic development, and a reputation for political stability. This combination of factors prompted expectations of a quick and relatively painless transformation after the Soviet Union collapsed. However, these prospects had already faded by that time, largely because of the explosion at the nuclear power station in Chernobyl' in Ukraine in 1986. According to the UN, the Chernobyl' catastrophe was the world's worst ever environmental disaster, releasing radiation 300 times greater than that of the bomb dropped on Hiroshima in 1945. Belarus suffered particularly badly, since 70% of the radioactivity emitted fell on its population. In addition, Belarus had a number of other distinctive features hidden behind the official Soviet statistics. These will be examined in this chapter.

Political Developments

Over the years since the collapse of the Soviet Union, the political system in Belarus has been characterized in turn by the dissolution of the old Communist system, the emergence of aspects of democracy, and, ultimately, the establishment of a dictatorial regime. Certain historical factors preconditioned this peculiar process of political transformation.

Towards Independence

One of the specific features of the country's political development became evident on the eve of the collapse of the Soviet Union: Belarus did not experience the dramatic political turmoil that started to shake the existing regime in Russia, Ukraine, and other republics in the late 1980s. Indeed, it was slow to react to the political changes taking place. Several reasons can be suggested for this.

First, Belarus had some of the most impressive socioeconomic indicators in the late Soviet period. Allowance must be made, of course, for the difficulties involved in relying on Soviet statistics, but comparisons with other Soviet republics are fairly clear nonetheless. By 1991, GDP per capita in Belarus was the highest in the Soviet Union, at US$5,729, compared with the next highest, which were US$5,689 in Latvia, and US$5,396 in Russia (see Turevich 1992a). This relative economic prosperity was accompanied by well-developed systems of education, health care and other social benefits, and might well have contributed to the relative lack of political disturbances.

Second, Belarus was notable for the absence of the type of ethnic conflict that accelerated political developments in Ukraine and the Baltic states. This was partly connected with the homogeneity of the population. In 1989, 77.9% of the population were Belarusian, 13.2% were Russian, and there were also small numbers of Poles, Ukrainians, Jews, and other ethnic groups (see Turevich 1992b). In addition, however, the absence of ethnic conflict can be traced to the fact that Belarusian culture, and especially the language, had never been imposed upon the ethnic minorities. In fact, in 1989 around 80% of ethnic Belarusians spoke Russian. The neglect of national culture was caused by the deliberate policy of suppression and Russification implemented by the Soviet Union, especially in education. In 1980, for example, only 35% of all school students in Belarus were taught in Belarusian, the rest being taught in Russian; and by 1989 even this proportion had dropped, to just 20.8% (see Ryder).

This leads us to the third reason for the delay in the process of change in Belarus. The ideal of national independence, which facilitated political change in neighboring republics, had little popular support in Belarus, since not many Belarusians perceived themselves as distinct, especially from Russians. For example, in the referendum on the future of the Soviet Union conducted in March 1991, more than 80% of those voting in Belarus favored preservation of some sort of union, one of the highest levels of support anywhere (see Men'kouski).

Finally, and more dubiously, some political scientists have suggested that there is a passivity inherent to the Belarusian mentality that has developed over the course of the country's history. Jan Zaprudnik, for example, has claimed that political apathy is more extensive in Belarus than anywhere else in the transition economies, because Belarusians habitually prefer to wait and see what will happen (see Zaprudnik).

Whatever the relative weight of these factors favoring political stability, there were also, of course, counterforces that facilitated political shifts. One was the growth of the national patriotic movement in Belarus, largely facilitated by the first major opposition movement, the Belarusian Popular Front, also known as Renaissance (*Adradzhenne*), which was created in 1988. The Popular Front put a great deal of emphasis on reviving the national identity, and therefore advocated political and economic separation from Russia, and a reorientation toward the West. The leaders of this movement were among the first to bring into the open the mass killings of Belarusians during the Soviet period, by uncovering the bodies of several thousand people killed in Kurapaty, a suburb of the capital city, Minsk.

Another force that brought some turmoil into the political quietude of Belarus was Chernobyl'. The ruling elite, both in the Soviet Union as a whole and in Belarus in particular, concealed the scale and the consequences of the disaster. In 1990, for example Mikhail

Gorbachev, then President of the Soviet Union, refused to visit Minsk to discuss the problem, and this refusal had negative repercussions in the republic. In any case, his subsequent visit brought little assistance to those who needed it (see Ryder).

The Chernobyl' factor, the rising national patriotic sentiment, and the political activity of opposition movements led to a series of strikes and demonstrations in the early 1990s, which undermined the reputation of Belarus as one of the most stable among the Soviet republics. This threatened the power of the Communist Party of Belarus, which was thus forced to make a series of concessions. For example, the Chernobyl' problem received greater publicity, and in January 1990 the Supreme Soviet of Belarus approved a law to make Belarusian the state language. Yet none of this was enough to bring about radical political change: the Communists remained at the helm.

The last Supreme Soviet, elected in March 1990, was overwhelmingly dominated by Communists, who accounted for 84% of its membership. Some seats had been won by representatives of the opposition groups that had formed the Belarusian Democratic Bloc, while the Popular Front had not officially been permitted to campaign in the elections (see Ryder). Nevertheless, in September 1990 the Supreme Soviet adopted a declaration of sovereignty; on July 27, 1991, it declared the independence of Belarus from the Soviet Union; and on August 25, 1991, following the defeat of the attempted coup in Moscow, it completed the formal enactment of independence.

The Early Stages of Transition

In September 1991, the Chairman of the Supreme Soviet, Mikalai Dzemyantei, was dismissed, mainly because he had supported the coup attempt in Moscow. He was replaced by Stanislau Shushkevich, a centrist politician who adopted an active reformist position, while acknowledging the importance of national self-determination and the consequences of the Chernobyl' disaster. He did not remain in charge for long, however. Disagreements soon emerged between Shushkevich and many deputies in the Supreme Soviet, in particular over the drafting of the new Constitution. Shushkevich took a view that turned out to be opposed to that of the majority of deputies, since he favored parliamentarism while the new Constitution, eventually adopted in March 1993, gave Belarus a system centered on a strong presidency, for which elections would be held every five years. There was also to be a new bicameral Parliament, comprising a Council of the Republic and a Chamber of Representatives, as well as a Constitutional Court.

Another bone of contention between Shushkevich and the majority in the Supreme Soviet was the question of signing a Treaty on Collective Security along with the other successor states of the Soviet Union. Shushkevich and the Popular Front opposed signing such a treaty, on the grounds that it contradicted the ideal of making Belarus a neutral country that had been asserted in the declaration of sovereignty. There were also anxieties about a renewal of Russian domination under the terms of the Treaty. It was eventually signed in January 1994. These and other disagreements resulted in the replacement of Shushkevich, also in January 1994, by a transitional figure, Myacheslau Gryb, whose main task was to prepare for elections.

The Regime of Alyaksandr Lukashenka

In the presidential election in July 1994, Alyaksandr Lukashenka received the largest number of votes. The charges of corruption that he leveled against certain political leaders became one of the major issues during the campaign, and brought him considerable popular support. In addition, while having no clear economic program, Lukashenka advocated closer ties with Russia, a deceleration of privatization, and the reimposition of greater state control over the economy.

From the early stages of his period in office, Lukashenka had repeated confrontations with Parliament. One of the first vivid examples came in April 1995, when police attacked and beat several deputies who were on hunger strike, protesting against the President, and evicted others from the Parliament building.

Elections took place in December 1995, and the leading parties in the new legislature were the Communist Party, the Agrarian Party, and the United Civic Party, although independent candidates also took large numbers of seats. Confrontations with the President continued. Lukashenka has also had strained relations with the Constitutional Court: by 1996, around 30 presidential decrees and directives had been judged to be unconstitutional (see Bagdankevich p.129).

Lukashenka twice resolved his conflicts with Parliament by using referendums. The first was held in May 1995, and addressed four issues, with majorities favoring Lukashenka's preferred options:

- giving Russian equal status with Belarusian as an official language;
- moving toward closer integration with Russia;
- abandoning the state insignia and flag adopted at independence, in favor of modified versions of those used in the republic during the Soviet period; and
- amending the Constitution in order to increase the powers of the President.

The second referendum, held in November 1996, also contained four questions proposed by the President. These concerned the following issues, again as resolved in Lukashenka's favor:

- extending the President's term of office and granting him powers of appointment over a wide range of offices;
- altering the significance of Independence Day, celebrated on July 27 since 1991, by moving it to July 3, the date on which Belarus was liberated from occupation by Nazi Germany;
- restricting private ownership of land; and
- maintaining the death penalty.

However, on this occasion there were also three questions proposed by the Chamber of Representatives. These were clearly opposed to the President's position, as they sought to reduce his powers, to empower the Chamber to elect heads of local governments, and to fund state institutions from the budget, as opposed to the non-budgetary fund controlled by the President. None of these proposals was supported by a majority voting in the referendum.

On several occasions, deputies in the Chamber of Representatives tried to impeach President Lukashenka, but these attempts did not come anywhere near success, because the Chamber itself was sharply divided between his supporters and his opponents. In May 1997, when the pro-Lukashenka group found themselves in the majority, Lukashenka appointed its members to a new legislature, the "National Assembly," which has been totally subservient to him, and unilaterally abolished Parliament. Meanwhile, the members of the Constitutional Court have been dismissed, and replaced by Lukashenka's protégés. At present, therefore, the main political parties and movements in Belarus can be roughly but tellingly divided into anti-Lukashenka and pro-Lukashenka groups. From September 1998, the ruling Communist Party, the Liberal Democratic Party, and the Slavic Assembly of "White Russia" (*Belaya Rus*) set about forming a "Popular Patriotic Union" in support of the President. The remaining opposition forces operate on a semilegal basis, and their members are exposed to threats, intimidation, fines, and jail sentences. The two largest opposition groups, the Popular Front and the United Civic Party, operate outside the National Assembly, and are largely restricted to holding illegal public demonstrations and publishing underground newspapers. Nongovernmental organizations, both domestic and foreign, have also come under severe attack. Since Lukashenka could not control three of the largest organizations – the Belarusian Soros Foundation, the National Center for Strategic Initiatives East-West, and the Belarusian Charitable Foundation for the Children of Chernobyl' – he decided to tax them heavily instead.

Lukashenka has flouted any notion of freedom of expression by bringing the entire system of printing and distribution under his control. The few opposition newspapers (mentioned above) are printed in neighboring Lithuania. There are no independent radio or television stations in Belarus, and there is no open access to the Internet or to western periodicals. The armed forces and the police, directly controlled by the President, are used to suppress demonstrators and political activists. The exact number of soldiers is not known but is believed to exceed 100,000 (see Marples). There are around 120,000 police officers, and it is estimated that the concentration of police per head of the population is among the highest in Europe, being, for example, 4.5 times higher than in neighboring Poland (according to *Narodnaya Volya*, February 19, 1999).

The present political regime in Belarus is clearly a dictatorship. The tragedy of the Belarusian people is that the majority, having been taught for decades to listen to authority, not the law, appears to support the regime. Recent polls suggest that Lukashenka remains by far the most popular politician in the country, with the support of around 45% of the electorate (see Marples).

The Economy

The present economic situation is characterized by a deep crisis that owes a great deal to the Soviet legacy, as well as to the activities of President Lukashenka's regime over the past few years. The positive economic developments of the early 1990s, which accompanied the trend toward democracy in the political sphere, have been reversed by the establishment of an ineffective command economy in the late 1990s, complementing the emerging dictatorship.

Plans for Reform

After the collapse of the Soviet Union, several measures were implemented in Belarus with the aim of creating a legal and organizational structure for a reformed economic system by overhauling, for example, forms of property, the banking system, the customs code, entrepreneurship, and state enterprises. In addition, markets in financial instruments, land, labor, and real estate were gradually brought into existence. However, to a large extent these early endeavors were negated by subsequent presidential decisions. For example, one of the major achievements of the early phase of institutional reform was the creation of financial markets and the two-level banking system. By 1998, in contrast, financial services were almost entirely under state control, and were on the brink of collapse. It was in that year that the Currency Exchange was nationalized, and the National Bank of Belarus was put under the direct supervision of the government.

The reform of economic institutions had been a major feature of the various policy programs debated and adopted over the years since independence was declared. The first of these programs was adopted in 1990 by the Belarusian Supreme Soviet. It was largely based on a radical proposal, known as "500 Days," which had been developed that year by the Russian economists Grigori Yavlinsky and Stanislav Shatalin. This was at a time when a less liberal program of transformation, advocated by Mikhail Gorbachev, was being pursued by the Soviet government. In 1994 a second, different program of strict economic measures was adopted, reflecting the strong influence of the neoliberal outlook associated with the IMF in its emphasis on liberalization and stabilization. President Lukashenka then put forward yet another program of transformation, which was somewhat ambiguous, since the options it referred to covered a broad spectrum, including "market socialism," a "multistructural economy," and state control. Finally, in 1995 a fourth program was prepared by the government as a response to the economic crisis. It addressed the period up to 2000, and envisaged stabilization, and the creation of conditions for economic growth, followed by the achievement of growth. This program was severely criticized by opposition parties, which regarded it as shallow and ambiguous. Perhaps it is needless to add that none of these four programs has been implemented.

Macroeconomic Policies

The limited progress made on liberalization during the early 1990s was effectively set aside by the subsequent policies of the President. In 1996, the registration of new enterprises came to a halt, and existing enterprises were required to submit new applications for registration with local governments. As a result, a large number of private enterprises either collapsed or moved into the "shadow" economy. Meanwhile, many enterprises still operate in the Soviet style, working from production plans issued to them by the authorities. In January 1998, a presidential decree gave the state the power to control decision-making in all enterprises through a right of veto over proposals for reorganization, liquidation, alterations in the statutory fund, and managerial changes. In 1997, 65% of prices in Belarus were controlled by the state (see Bagdankevich). To take another example, privatization became erratic after 1991, largely because it was impeded by ideological opposition, first from the parliamentary leadership up to 1995 and then from President Lukashenka and many members of Parliament. Only 12% of property in Belarus is in the hands of the private sector, which employs only 10% of the labor force (see Bagdankevich).

Similarly, measures aimed at bringing about stabilization have suffered from inconsistency and a lack of professionalism. Monetary policy has been determined by political considerations: in 1998, for example, the National Bank was forced to issue credits with interest rates five to six times lower than the rate of inflation. Between 1996 and 1998, enormous expenditures on agriculture, the military, and the upkeep of the presidential administration stimulated inflation, which was officially declared to have reached 80% by 1997 (see Table 5.1). Some economists, however, believe that the actual rate is higher, but is concealed because of heavy state control over prices. State control over exchange rates helped to create a gap of around 300% between the official rate and the unofficial rate by the end of 1998, prompting the devaluation of the Belarusian currency, the rubel, by 200% in 1997 (see Bagdankevich).

Fiscal policy is also highly irregular by the standards normally applied in most countries. Expenditure on social and Chernobyl' programs, on financial support for the economy, and on capital investment has been reduced over the past few years, but defense spending has risen. In 1996, for example, it increased by 5.4%, yet the amount spent on technical support of the armed forces constituted only

4.6% of total defense-related expenditure. A large amount of public funds has also been allocated to the upkeep of the state bureaucracy, and in 1997 the proportion of government expenditure devoted to the civil service almost tripled (see Bagdankevich). In addition to the official state budget there is also a special extrabudgetary presidential fund, although information about its size, and the details of its accounts, are official secrets.

The amount of revenues collected has been below target in recent years. This shortfall is officially attributed to the lack of external financing and the poor performance of privatization programs, but it is mostly due to the failure to collect taxes. In 1996, for example, the collection of taxes on profits and incomes was 37.6% below target, and similar figures applied in relation to customs and excise duties, property taxes, value-added tax and other levies. The 1998 budget made changes in the size and structure of taxes, in order to reduce the overall tax burden, but there was no serious attempt to link these changes to policies on structural reform, industry, or investment. Priority was given to manufacturing and agriculture, leaving the services sector underdeveloped, and the suspension of privatization meant that the state monopolies would not have to face the challenge of competitive private enterprises.

The low level of domestic investment in Belarus reflects the decline in savings. As for foreign investment, in 1997 the total inflow was only US$40 million, and foreign investment per capita was around one tenth of the level in the Baltic states and Poland (see Zlotnikau).

The Problem of Statistics

Before turning to an examination of the main sectors of the economy, we should emphasize that there is one major obstacle to be overcome: both representatives of the Belarusian opposition and well-informed foreign observers have concluded that government statistics are now routinely falsified (see Bagdankevich, Marples, Turevich 1998, Zlotnikau). Thus, according to the official estimates, GDP increased by 10.4% in 1997 and by 8% in 1998 – the highest rates in Europe – while the gross output of manufacturing industry rose by 3.2% (see Table 5.1, and also Karpenka 1999). Given the present state of the economy, as outlined below, these figures are simply impossible to believe. For example, independent estimates suggest that GDP actually decreased, by 1.9%, in 1997. Accordingly, in what follows data supplied by foreign observers and by domestic opposition groups are used wherever possible. However, all figures must be treated with caution, and the motives of all those who supply them should be taken into consideration.

Energy and Raw Materials

The inconsistencies and errors in economic policy have resulted in deterioration in the performance of the main sectors of the economy. However, they would have suffered, in any case, from a relative scarcity of raw materials and energy supplies, which has compelled Belarus to import most of the basic commodities it needs. The country's deposits of potassium salts are the second largest in Europe, and Belarus used to produce around one half of the total output of the Soviet Union. Other deposits include brown coal, combustible shale, limestone, dolomite, marl, and phosphate, as well as ferrous and nonferrous metals; and there are small deposits of high-quality petroleum and natural gas. Peat also used to be a major natural resource for Belarus, but since the explosion at Chernobyl' contaminated it there has been a drastic decline in its use as a fuel. None of these resources can cover more than a fraction of domestic demand.

During the Soviet period the major supplier of oil and natural gas was Russia, which accounted for 90% of all imports of these commodities into Belarus. These imports in turn formed the basis for the country's exports of refined petroleum products. The refining industry was developed in Belarus in order to take advantage of its convenient geographical position, which allowed the construction of two pipelines taking supplies from Russia to the West, and of two refineries, at Mazyr and Navapolacak. With the collapse of the Soviet Union, however, the supply of energy and raw materials dramatically deteriorated. In 1991, the two refineries, which had been working below full capacity, were transferred to Russian ownership. Deliveries were sharply reduced, while prices rose. In 1993, Belarus paid US$21.70 for each ton of Russian oil and US$35.70 for every 1,000 cubic meters of gas; by 1995 it was being charged US$80 and US$53 respectively. Prices of raw materials have also risen, by between 30% and 50%, creating a critical situation in manufacturing. From time to time, Russia has threatened to stop deliveries of fuel and other raw materials because Belarus has failed to pay its debt, which amounted to between US$300 million and US$350 million by 1997. Belarus has tried to bargain with Russia and to pay its debt by bartering Belarusian goods for materials, but the Russians have consistently preferred cash. Indeed, they increased the proportion of energy supplies that must be paid for in cash from 30% at the start of 1998 to 50% by July, and then to 100% by December (see Turevich 1998).

The Belarusian government has taken some steps to improve the supply of energy and raw materials. One approach has been to raise the issue in bilateral negotiations with Russia, as Belarus has sought concessions in return for closer economic and political integration between the two countries. Another, more controversial decision has been to reduce the dependence of Belarus on external sources of energy by starting the construction of nuclear power plants, despite the experience of Chernobyl'.

Manufacturing

Manufacturing is the largest sector in the Belarusian economy, accounting for almost 70% of GDP (see Bagdankevich). The most important industries are machinery, electronics, transportation equipment, chemicals, food-processing, and a range of light industries.

The collapse of the Soviet Union had a dramatic impact on Belarusian industries. According to official statistics, more than 20% of industrial enterprises went bankrupt; unofficial estimates, however, suggest that the figure was closer to 70%. Some economists have even referred to the situation in Belarus as an

example of deindustrialization, since the depreciation of capital assets in industry is believed to be approaching 80% (see Bagdankevich).

There are at least three important reasons for the continuing crisis in manufacturing. First, there has been extensive disruption of the interrepublican trade links that underpinned the Soviet economy. They were vital to the many Belarusian industries that depend on imported raw materials and semimanufactured goods. Second, the export prospects of most Belarusian goods have sharply deteriorated, partly because the decline in spending on research and development has reduced their competitiveness, but partly also because of the loss of traditional markets in Russia and other CIS countries. Third, the Soviet period has left Belarus burdened with a heavy commitment to military production. In 1992, an estimated 120 large enterprises in Belarus were dependent on orders from the military (see Galubovich). Some conversion to production for civilian uses was undertaken, but it had little impact because of the lack of investment to sustain the policy. In 1996, Belarus negotiated a barter exchange of Iranian crude oil for Belarusian manufactured goods, including military equipment, and in 1997 the government signed an agreement with Turkey on cooperation in defense industries and technology. However, many enterprises that used to supply the military are now faced with the decline or even disappearance of their customers, and must survive on government subsidies alone.

In November 1997, the government announced an industrial program that appeared to address the need for structural reform of manufacturing up to the year 2015. The program is based largely on a Keynesian approach to the crisis, leaving the state as the main actor in industrial development, and contains numerous broad statements about the desirability of restructuring, innovation, increasing competition, and developing new markets. It has been criticized by liberal economists, such as those advising the United Civic Party.

Agriculture

Agriculture accounts for around 24% of GDP in Belarus. Since much of the land is poor and the climate is severely continental, animal husbandry and hardy crops predominate. Livestock farming, including pigs, cattle, sheep, and goats, accounts for more than half the total value of agricultural output, while mink, Arctic foxes and silver foxes are farmed for their fur. Belarus used to produce 27% of the Soviet Union's output of flax and 15% of its output of potatoes: its major crops today include both of these, as well as buckwheat, rye, and sugar beet. Other crops, grown in much smaller amounts, include barley, animal fodder, oats, millet, hay, and tobacco (see Ryder).

It now appears that agriculture is undergoing an unprecedented decline. According to estimates by the opposition, state-owned farms are capable of meeting only 50% of the domestic demand for milk, 40% of the demand for meat, and 50% of the demand for grain. The production of vegetables is probably satisfactory, partly because of activity in the private sector, and accounts for perhaps 90% of agricultural production (see National Executive Committee). The sector's problems have been attributed to a variety of factors. First, it is generally agreed that the Chernobyl' disaster caused the radioactive poisoning of around 25% of the country's best farmland and forest, especially in the leading agricultural regions of Homiel and Mahilou. Second, the collective farm system continues to be inefficient, and it has been estimated that up to 97% of collective farms are bankrupt (see Bagdankevich). Third, as the economy has declined financial support for agriculture has deteriorated as a proportion of state spending, even though it has risen in real terms, and there are now increasingly severe shortages of fertilizer, fuel, spare parts, and transportation.

Against this background, the government has resorted to barter, as with oil and gas. In 1992, for example, Belarus imported 2.5 million tons of grain from Kazakhstan in exchange for refrigerators, freezers, and other manufactured goods. In addition, the government has enormously increased the absolute amounts of subsidized credit available to farmers, while deferring the repayment of debt. In 1997, the state subsidized 80% of expenditure on fertilizer, as well as 50% of farmers' spending on fuel and electricity (see Maksymiuk). However, these measures cannot compensate for the failure to launch radical agricultural reform. In the early 1990s, the authorities tried to target inefficiency in agriculture by privatizing farms, but the dominant elite has generally opposed the dissolution of the collective farm system. By the end of 1995, private farms accounted for only around 1% of all agricultural land in Belarus, although 12% of farm employment was in the private sector (see Ryder).

Social Issues

The economic and political changes that have followed the collapse of the Soviet Union have resulted in a significant worsening of social conditions in many of the successor states. However, there is one special factor that has put Belarus in an incomparably more difficult position: the Chernobyl' disaster. Having received 70% of the radiation released by the explosion, the people of Belarus face unprecedented health problems. Some scientists have concluded that Belarusians are threatened with extinction because their gene pool is so severely contaminated (see Roche), and it has been estimated that only 3% of Belarusian children in Belarus can be regarded as enjoying good health (see National Executive Committee). In the early 1990s, the Belarusian government undertook a range of measures aimed at addressing the consequences of the Chernobyl' disaster. Around 20% of the state budget was allocated to implementing them, while the publicity generated abroad attracted some foreign assistance (see Galubovich). However, there has been a decrease in central government expenditures on these measures: the 1998 budget allocated only 9% of total spending to them. Today, around 1.6 million people still live in zones of heavy radioactive fallout, and the government recently announced that it plans to start recultivating land in these zones (see Marples).

Successive governments have also sought to address other social problems associated with the deterioration of the economy. A Social Protection Fund, covering family allowances, pensions, and sickness and disability benefits, and an Employment Fund, which directs employment schemes, supports retraining, and provides unemployment benefits, were both established in 1993. President Lukashenka has claimed that his government has made the provision of social programs a priority, even at the expense of more rapid economic reform, but it appears that the facts do not support this claim. In 1996, for example, overall expenditure on social support and cultural programs was around 75.6% of the amounts planned, while the proportions in specific areas were 89.9% in education and training, 79.7% in cultural programs, 79.3% in social support, and 64.3% in health care (see Turevich 1998).

According to official estimates, only 4% of the labor force were unemployed in 1997 (see Table 5.1); opposition sources put the number of unemployed at around 30% (see Bagdankevich). Even those who have jobs are not necessarily in any better position. The average monthly salary and pension both lie in a range between US$10 and US$30, which is below the minimum amount that can be considered a living wage, and three to eight times lower than in neighboring countries. Thus, more than 80% of the population can be said to be living in real poverty (see Table 5.2). On many collective farms, the monthly salary is less than US$5.00, and even this is not paid regularly. Not surprisingly, almost all of the income that workers do receive is spent on food (see National Executive Committee).

Not only is the population impoverished, but its numbers are declining. The birth rate has been falling for several years, while the death rate has been rising, and infant mortality is believed to be almost twice as high as the average in the United States (see Table 5.2). These demographic trends, combined with rising levels of emigration, have led to a net fall in the population amounting to between 30,000 and 40,000 in every year since 1995 (see Karpenka 1998).

Security Policy

The first step toward establishing statehood and an independent foreign policy was taken in 1991, when independence was declared. The Declaration of Independence itself asserted the rights of the people of Belarus to

self-determination, independence in foreign relations, rejection of nuclear weapons, and neutrality. Belarus started to pursue its own foreign policy after the failure of the Moscow coup in August 1991, and in December the government signed the agreement that established the CIS, initially with only Russia and Ukraine as partners. Belarus then became a member of the CSCE (now the OSCE) in 1992. In 1993, it ratified the first Strategic Arms Reduction Treaty (START 1), and thus committed itself to destroying all the strategic nuclear warheads on its territory, or transferring them to Russia. It also signed the Nuclear Nonproliferation Treaty and the Treaty on reducing conventional forces in Europe (the CFE Treaty) in 1993. However, since Lukashenka came to power the foreign security doctrine of Belarus has changed significantly. The CFE Treaty has been suspended, Belarus has engaged in military cooperation with Turkey and in sales of weapons to Iran (as mentioned above), and in 1997 the country stood at ninth place in the list of the 10 leading arms-exporting countries in the world (see Anis'ka).

Military cooperation between Belarus and other member states of the CIS, especially Russia, should be considered as a separate issue. A highly integrated military complex was built during the Soviet period. Around 120 enterprises in Belarus depended on military orders from Moscow, and Belarus had the highest number of military staff per head of population in any country in Europe. By 1991, the figure was 1:43 in Belarus, while in Russia it was 1:643, and in Ukraine it was 1:98. There were 23 rocket bases and 24 military airfields in Belarus, which also inherited a range of tactical nuclear weapons and 81 intercontinental ballistic missiles (see Zaprudnik).

Close military contacts between Belarus and Russia continued, despite the commitment to neutrality. One of the first violations of that neutrality occurred in 1994, when President Lukashenka, supported by most of the Communist deputies in the Supreme Soviet, signed the CIS Treaty on Collective Security. Russia has been building two military bases in Belarus: one of them forms part of Russia's system of space defense, while the other feeds radio signals to Russian ships and submarines in the Atlantic and the Mediterranean. In 1994, Belarus and Russia signed a package of agreements on the Russian military units stationed in Belarus; in December 1997 they signed another agreement establishing a joint board of officials from their defense ministries; and in December 1998 they signed a Declaration of Intent that provides for the creation of supranational bodies to handle economic and defense policies. Thus, the present security policy of Belarus is very far from fulfilling the declared goal of making the country neutral and non-nuclear.

Regional Economic Cooperation

After Belarus achieved independence, various proposals were put forward for a regional economic strategy. The Belarusian Popular Front, which was then the largest opposition party, proposed that the country should leave the CIS, and create a Baltic/Black Sea Commonwealth, which would also include Estonia, Latvia, Lithuania, Ukraine, and Moldova, as a counterbalance to Russian domination. However, the government of the day, still dominated by Communists, advocated the preservation of the old Soviet geopolitical area, or, if that was not possible, the maintenance of close economic and political ties with Russia. This approach has been adopted by President Lukashenka, who has often stressed the priority of Russia in foreign policy, and has signed several agreements on closer economic integration within the framework of the CIS.

Close cooperation with Russia and other CIS countries is all but inevitable for Belarus. Its trade with Russia and the other member states accounted for more than 60% of all its foreign trade in September 1998. After Russia, Ukraine was Belarus's next largest trading partner, accounting for 7% of its foreign trade. In particular, as has been discussed above, Belarus is heavily dependent on imports of energy supplies and raw materials, mainly from Russia. As for its exports, in 1991 around 90% of the total was sent to Russia and other Soviet republics, and it has been very difficult to change this pattern, given the vulnerability of

Belarusian goods in the face of foreign competition (see Zaprudnik). The Russian position on economic integration with Belarus can be largely explained by security considerations: Belarus remains a sensitive western border area for Russia, against the background of the recent enlargement of NATO and the neutrality of Ukraine.

Nevertheless, it is not at all clear how far the various CIS agreements on economic matters coincide with the national interest of Belarus, and how far they really serve to enhance President Lukashenka's chances of remaining in power. It is certainly true that Lukashenka has taken the initiative in decisions on furthering integration with Russia, and has ignored the opinions of the elected legislature as well as the advice of economists. On the other hand, while the agreements do not require comprehensive reforms, or address long-term economic consequences or alternative priorities, they have had some immediate effects on Belarus. In 1993, Russia reduced the prices it charged for natural gas after Belarus agreed to accept a greater degree of economic cooperation. In 1994, in partial fulfillment of the non-monetary aspects of the monetary union that brought Belarus back into the ruble zone, Russia simplified the export procedures for oil and natural gas. In 1996, Belarus signed an agreement on satisfying mutual claims as between itself and Russia, and then used the bargaining chips that it gained to bring forward the withdrawal of nuclear weapons and Russian troops from its territory. A debt to Russia that totaled US$1.3 billion, or 6.5% of Belarusian GDP, was converted into long-term credits (see Zlotnikau), and Belarus paid for Russian oil and natural gas by means of barter, which accounted for 50% of its trade with Russia in 1997 (although barter was abandoned in 1998, as mentioned above). The customs union with Russia brought two main benefits for Belarus. The high tariffs imposed on goods from outside the union made some Belarusian products competitive in Russia, and exports of cars and televisions to Russia increased in 1997 (see Zlotnikau). The union also allowed Belarus to exploit its transit position to tax goods being taken into and out of Russia across its territory.

These outcomes of regional economic cooperation have tended to enhance the popularity of the President, but it is clear that the economic gains will not last long. Russia finds it increasingly difficult to sell bartered Belarusian goods; Russian oil and natural gas companies have threatened to stop supplying Belarus if they do not receive cash; and Russian troops will not be stationed in Belarus forever. Further, the customs union with Russia has not resolved the country's trade problems. It is still finding it very hard to sell its products to third countries, and in 1998 its foreign trade deficit was around US$1.5 billion (see Karpenka 1999).

Belarus and the Wider World

Aside from the CIS, Belarus is a member of more than 60 international organizations. It joined the IMF and the World Bank in 1992, but loan payments from the IMF were suspended in 1998 after the government departed from the reform program on which loans were conditioned. Belarus has had observer status at the World Trade Organization since January 1995, but its prospects of achieving full membership in the near future are somewhat limited, given its political and economic problems. Unfortunately, these are just two among many indications of the increasing isolation of Belarus from the wider world.

Consider, for example, its relations with Europe and North America. In 1994, around 51% of its exports were directed to western countries, but in 1998 this had dropped to just 30% (see National Executive Committee). In 1998, the most important trading partners outside the CIS were Germany (around 6% of Belarusian trade) and Poland (3%), followed by Austria, the United States, the United Kingdom, Turkey, and China (see Ministry of Statistics). Luiz Marena, the head of an EU delegation that visited Belarus in 1997, stated that there was no basis for negotiations between the EU and Belarus. No further economic agreements between the EU and Belarus are to be signed in the near future, and the ratification of the partnership and cooperation agreement signed in 1995 has

been postponed. A similar situation applies to relations with the United States. In 1997, the US State Department announced that official contact with Belarus would be reduced to a minimum, and that all its aid programs, except those that support free media and democratic institutions, would be suspended.

Confrontation with the West culminated in June 1998 in Lukashenka's decision to expel diplomats representing the EU and its members, the United States, and six other western countries, which all responded by expelling Belarusian diplomats. The ambassadors of the EU countries (but not the US ambassador) returned to the country in January 1999. However, any hope of improving relations was negated just two months later, as NATO launched air strikes on Yugoslavia and Lukashenka declared his wholehearted support for the Yugoslav regime.

Conclusion

Belarus is faced with grave problems in its economy, its society, its political system, and its foreign relations. The first step toward recovery from its crisis must be the removal of the present regime, which would permit the restoration of at least a degree of democracy, and also end the corruption and incompetence of the present ruling elite. The withdrawal of state controls over the economy and the widening of the country's geopolitical horizons also appear to be indispensable if Belarus is ever to make significant progress. Finally, Belarus is also faced with a threat to its very existence: it needs international attention and support, because it cannot hope to overcome the consequences of the Chernobyl' disaster on its own.

Further Reading

Anis'ka, Syargei, "Provokatsiya kak vid Konkurentsii" [Provocation as a Type of Competition], in *Belaruskaya Delavaya Gazeta*, February 24, 1999

Bagdankevich, S., *Kak Zhili? Kak Zhivem? Kak Budem Zhit? 1994–1997* [How Did We Live? How Do We Live? How Shall We Live? 1994–97], St Petersburg: VIRD, 1998

A valuable analysis of the Belarusian economy, in Russian, by a prominent neoliberal politician who uses some unusually reliable statistical indicators

Belarusian Review, The, The Belarusian-American Association, Inc., quarterly publication

In addition to the items by Marples and Turevich cited below, this journal (e-mail: BelReview@aol.com) contains useful and reliable statistical data difficult to obtain inside Belarus itself, as well as other analytical articles covering economic, political, social, cultural, and historical issues.

Bremmer, Ian, and Ray Taras, editors, *New States, New Politics: Building the Post-Soviet Nations,* Cambridge and New York: Cambridge University Press, 1997

A collection of 20 papers on politics in the region since 1991, including an analysis of Belarus by Jan Zaprudnik (cited separately below)

Galubovich, M. I., et al., *Ekanamikhnaya Historiya Belarusi* [Economic History of Belarus], Minsk: Ekspaperspektiva, 1995

A comprehensive economic study, in Belarusian, covering development from the earliest settlements in Belarus up to the 1990s

Karpenka, Genadsiy, "Otkrytoye Pis'mo Presidentu Respubliki Belarus Lukashenko A. G." [Open Letter to A. G. Lukashenka, President of the Republic of Belarus], in *Narodnaya Volya,* December 3, 1998

This article, and the one following, are among many informative pieces by Karpenka on the economy and politics of Belarus. A former Deputy Chairman of the country's Chamber of Representatives, and a prominent figure in the opposition to President Lukashenka, he died in April 1999, aged only 49.

Karpenka, Genadsiy, "Belaruskaya Ekonomika: Stepen'razvala, Putsi Vyhoda" [The Belarusian Economy: A Degree of Collapse, Ways of Recovery], in *Naviny,* February 10, 1999

Maksymiuk, Jan, "Redeveloping Developed Socialism in Belarus," available on the Internet at www.ruf.rice.edu/~sergei/belarus/economy/economy.html, 1998

Marples, David, "Belarus: An Analysis of the Lukashenka Regime," Part I, "The Economy," in *Belarusian Review,* Summer 1997

An objective and wide-ranging view of the Belarusian economy from the outside

Men'kouski, V. I., "Abvyashchen'ne nexalezhnastsi Respubliki Belarus" [Declarations of Independence of the Republic of Belarus], in Abetsedarskaya, A., et al., *Historiya Belarusi* [History of Belarus], Minsk: Ekspaperspektiva, 1998

A useful introductory text, in Belarusian, for those interested in these documents

Ministry of Statistics and Analysis, *Statistical Yearbook of the Republic of Belarus,* Minsk: Ministry of Statistics and Analysis, 1998; *Vneshnyaya Torgovlya Respubliki Belarus* [Foreign Trade of the Republic of Belarus], Minsk: Informstat, 1999

Official statistical information, whether in English or in Belarusian, must be treated with caution, for the reasons given in the chapter.

National Executive Committee, "Zayavleniye Natsional'nogo Ispolnitsel'nogo Komitseta Respubliki Belarus: O Situatsii v Ekonomike i Prognoze ego Razvitsiya na Blixhayshiy Period" [Note of the National Executive Committee of the Republic of Belarus on the Economic Situation, and Prospects for Development in the Coming Period], in *Narodnaya Volya,* November 23, 1998

Polevikov, Sergei, *Sergei Polevikov's Belarus,* Internet site at www.ruf.rice.edu/~sergei/belarus

Roche, Adi, *Children of Chernobyl,* London: HarperCollins, 1996

A very moving book, rich in detail, describing the dramatic impact of the Chernobyl' disaster on Belarus

Ryder, Andrew, "Belarus," in *Eastern Europe and the CIS,* London: Europa, 1997

A useful overview of political, economic and social development in Belarus

Turevich, Art (1992a), "Belarus in 1992," in *Belarusian Review,* Winter 1992

A comprehensive analysis of the country's political, economic and social development during 1992

Turevich, Art (1992b), "Belarus Economy," in *Belarusian Review,* Spring 1992

Valuable statistical data, alongside a thoughtful analytical review of the economy

Turevich, Art (1998), "Belarus 'Economic Miracle' Unraveling," in *Belarusian Review*, Spring 1998

Useful statistical material of a type that is almost impossible to obtain inside Belarus

Zaprudnik, Jan, "Belarus: From Statehood to Empire?" in Bremmer and Taras, cited above

An excellent analysis of Belarusian statehood, using interesting historical materials

Zlotnikau, Lavon, "Economic Growth in Belarus: Fact or Fiction?" available on the Internet at www.ruf.rice.edu/~sergei/belarus/economy/economy.html, 1998

Luba Demidkina is a citizen of Belarus residing in the EU.

Table 5.1 Demographic and Economic Indicators for Belarus, 1990–97

	1990	1991	1992	1993	1994	1995	1996	1997
Resident population (thousands)	10,212	10,233	10,298	10,319	10,297	10,264	10,236	10,204
under working age	2,501	2,493	2,489	2,468	2,425	2,371	2,311	2,246
of working age	5,680	5,677	5,703	5,720	5,722	5,731	5,749	5,782
above working age	2,031	2,063	2,106	2,131	2,150	2,162	2,176	2,176
Registered unemployed (thousands)	–	2.3	24.0	66.3	101.2	131.0	182.5	126.2
Change in GDP (%)	–	–1.2	–9.6	–7.6	–12.6	–10.1	0.8	0.4
Receipts of the state budget (% of GDP)	35.7	29.9	32.3	36.7	36.4	29.6	27.5	32.2
Expenditures of the state budget (% of GDP)	33.3	28.2	34.2	42.3	39.9	42.3	29.5	34.4
Consumer price inflation (%)	–	247.5	1,659.1	2,096.5	2,059.9	344.0	139.3	163.1

Sources: Bagdankevich, S., *Kak Zhili? Kak Zhivem? Kak Budem Zhit? 1994–1997* [How Did We Live? How Do We Live? How Shall We Live? 1994–1997], St Petersburg: VIRD, 1998; *Ekamamichesliye Tendentsii v Belarusi: Dekabr 1996* [Economic Trends in Belarus: December 1996], Minsk: TACIS, 1996; Ministry of Statistics and Analysis, *Statistical Yearbook of the Republic of Belarus*, Minsk: Ministry of Statistics and Analysis, 1998; Turevich, Art, "Belarus 'Economic Miracle' Unraveling", in *Belarusian Review*, Spring 1998

Table 5.2   Social Indicators for Belarus, 1990–95

	1990	*1991*	*1992*	*1993*	*1994*	*1995*
Life expectancy (years)	71.1	70.7	70.3	69.2	68.9	68.6
Male	66.3	65.5	64.9	63.8	63.5	62.9
Female	75.6	75.5	75.4	74.4	74.3	74.3
Birth rate (per 1,000 people)	13.9	12.9	12.4	11.3	10.7	9.8
Death rate (per 1,000 people)	10.7	11.2	11.3	12.4	12.6	13.0
Infant mortality						
(per 1,000 live births)	11.9	12.1	12.3	12.5	13.2	13.3
Consumers' spending on food						
(% of total consumers' spending)	28.0	30.0	34.0	40.0	44.0	59.0
Mean annual income (BR thousands)	2.4	4.6	39.6	589.6	1,242.5	7,408.9
Minimum consumption budget						
(BR thousands)	1.5	2.9	24.9	371.4	1,155.5	6,964.4
Minimum consumption budget						
(% of average annual income)	62.8	63.9	62.7	65.3	92.8	94.0
People with incomes at or below						
the minimum consumption budget						
(thousands)	510.0	1,400.1	1,448.4	2,551.0	5,485.3	8,265.8
(% of total population)	5.0	13.1	14.0	24.6	53.0	80.4

Source: *Ekamamichesliye Tendentsii v Belarusi: Dekabr 1996* [Economic Trends in Belarus: December 1996], Minsk: TACIS, 1996

Chapter Six

Ukraine

Paul Kubicek

The emergence of an independent Ukrainian state sealed the fate of the USSR and changed the landscape of Europe. Zbigniew Brzezinski has declared the creation of Ukraine "one of the three most important geopolitical developments of the century" (see Ryabchuk 1994a). Initially, there was great enthusiasm for Ukraine at home and abroad, as more than 90% of those voting in a referendum on December 1, 1991, approved of independence and the Deutsche Bank, for example, forecast a rosy future for the new state's economy (see Motyl). However, the celebrations have given way to a lingering post-Soviet hangover, as Ukrainian leaders have discovered it is far easier to declare independence than to build functioning economic and political institutions, maintain the trust of the citizenry, solve ethnic and regional problems, or mend fences with Russia. While there have been some positive achievements, notably the preservation of Ukrainian independence despite all the trials, severe problems remain, as the economy languishes, corruption mounts, and the public has become disillusioned and frustrated. Ukraine enters the 21st century on rather shaky ground. Rather than trace the developments leading to Ukraine's independence, which has been ably done elsewhere (see Solchanyk 1992; Motyl; Wilson; and Kuzio and Wilson), this chapter will focus on developments in the post-Soviet period, which has been marked by a sense of continuous crisis and profound disappointment.

"Ukrainianization" of the Economy

Any discussion of post-Soviet Ukraine must begin with the economy, which has been described by many as the site of Ukraine's greatest crisis, a crisis that contributes to its political and security problems. In general, reform has been piecemeal at best, although the economic free fall of 1992–94 has ended and support has been provided by the West. Anecdotally, it is worth noting that the verb "to Ukrainianize" (*ukrainizirovat'*) has assumed a pejorative meaning in Russian, "to bring to ruin".

The greatest problems that Ukraine has faced have been runaway inflation, a precipitous drop in production, and declining living standards for most Ukrainians (see Table 6.1). Clearly, there is little but bad news to report about economic developments. Hyperinflation was the most noticeable problem in the years immediately following the collapse of the Soviet Union. The causes of this inflation were numerous: laws of supply and demand acting in an economy with chronic shortages, speculation, increased costs of imported fuel, and some price liberalization. The primary culprit, however, was less economic than political: the giant subsidies and loans granted by the government to prop up insolvent state enterprises, and the unrestrained printing of money. This phenomenon was especially noticeable in 1992–93, when Leonid Kuchma, a former plant director himself, was Prime Minister. Critics charged his government with preserving the Soviet principles of *nomenklatura* (see Glossary). Taras Stets'kiv, an adviser, resigned, arguing that the government's policies were controlled by "corrupt banking bureaucrats and the influential directorate," which had "strangled" the economy, and that the government itself represented only the "industrial oligarchy and the state sector of the economy" (see Stets'kiv). By 1996, however, inflation had been brought down to double digits under the leadership of President Kuchma, thanks in large part to relative budget austerity, and to foreign pressure and support. This gave the government some breathing space in August 1996 to carry out the introduction of the hrivna, the Ukrainian currency, which had been delayed because the government feared hyperinflation would complicate it and make it more costly. The hope has been that once inflation was under control, a general economic recovery could begin.

The data do not support this notion. True, the drop in GDP and production is less than before, but through 1997 (and presumably 1998, as Russia fell into deeper crisis) production was still declining. Again, the costs for the drop in production are many: loss of ties to markets and suppliers in other Soviet republics; lack of fuel; an end to the production of entirely unwanted products; an oppressive tax system that forces movement into the underground economy (estimated to be 20–50% of the economy); breakdown of discipline and order; antiquated technology; and ineffective macroeconomic policies. One study in 1993 concluded that the overall coefficient of production efficiency in Ukraine was an abysmal 0.14 (the maximum being 1) and that the country was producing only 2.2% of its potential (see *Holos Ukrainy*). As production dropped and the tax base shriveled up or moved underground, tax rates soared ever higher, and economic activity moved away from production into various forms of speculation. Later, relative budget austerity also contributed to the decline in production, by limiting the funds available for enterprises. While few firms have officially gone bankrupt and closed their doors, many are near-dormant and workers are at best periodically paid. By 1997, the good news was that the economy had come near to bottoming out; the bad news was that it would still take many years for production to return to the levels reached in the Soviet period.

Abysmal economic performance has meant a sharp drop in living standards and a high level of overall dissatisfaction. Wages have clearly failed to keep up with inflation. One analysis concluded that between December 1991 and August 1993 wages rose by only 37% as much as inflation (see Lukinov), and it is clear that from 1993 to 1998 real wages did not substantially increase. In 1994, even government data showed that over 80% of the population received less than the subsistence level defined by the government (see *Slavia Press Digest*). As budgets were trimmed, workers were not even paid their paltry wages on time. Wage arrears in Ukraine by the end of 1998 totaled over US$2.5 billion, but protest remained muted because workers had lost faith in both the government and the unions to solve their problems (see Kubicek 1999).

Obviously, such developments lead to public frustration and disappointment. Surveys conducted by the Democratic Initiatives Center reveal that Ukrainians overwhelming rate both the overall economic situation in the country as very poor and their own standard of living as poor, and as lower than before the collapse of the Soviet Union. They also have little confidence in the future. Data from Central and Eastern Eurobarometer surveys for 1992–96 (see Table 6.2) show very low levels of satisfaction and hope, although there has been some improvement since 1994. Still, these figures provide little reason for optimism, and low levels of satisfaction feed into the problems of low trust in state institutions (discussed below) and skepticism about economic reform. For example, in a 1995 survey conducted by the Kyiv Institute of Sociology, only 31.4% of respondents thought that people like themselves would benefit from the introduction of private property, and only 12% of respondents claimed to support capitalism (see Kubicek 1997). While improving economic conditions is consistently listed as the top priority among Ukrainians, it is also notable that there were almost twice as many respondents to a 1997 survey who thought the economy should return to the state it was in before *perestroika* (see Glossary) than respondents who thought that transition to the market should occur – 38% versus 20% (see *Politichny Portret Ukrainy*).

To make matters worse, while Ukrainians have definitely experienced a "shock," there has been very little "therapy." The Ukrainian elite in the period immediately following independence did not use its window of opportunity to launch ambitious and far-reaching reforms. Instead, the basic features of the Soviet command economy were preserved: state ownership of land and industrial enterprises, state planning and direction, distorted price structures, and lack of competition. While some smaller enterprises were rented out or privatized in 1992–94, corruption was endemic, as bribes were needed to obtain property rights, directors used their positions to engage in "spontaneous privatization," and mafia structures demanded protection money from private entrepreneurs. Many Ukrainian observers noted that the various laws and programs on privatization were spinning their wheels as the basic foundations of the command economy were not dismantled, and private business had to compete on an uneven playing field against the state sector (see Shevchenko, Cherniak, and Drobiazko). Those who endorsed market-oriented reforms found themselves essentially shut out of the policy-making process. In the words of Yurii Nechaev, co-director of the Center for Market Reforms, "it's no use offering rubies to pigs when they're content to play in the mud" (in an interview with the author, 1994).

There was a moment of hope for reformers in 1994, after Leonid Kuchma assumed the presidency. Bucking expectations that he would again serve the interests of the old guard, he declared that Ukraine had no choice but to move ahead with radical economic reforms. He managed to push through a privatization program, issue privatization vouchers, trim the budget deficit, free prices, and win aid and support from the West. However, in order to win domestic support for these measures, he had to appease the centrist factions in the legislature, then called the Verkhovna Rada, or Supreme Council, who were mainly either state directors, or ex-directors transformed into owners of large enterprises. The results included more perks and subsidies to the *nomenklatura*, and widespread allegations of corruption. "Clan" politics became the norm, and

patron-client relations, not market principles, were dominant. As in Russia, "*nomenklatura* privatization" was widespread, and the transfers of ownership did not help to jump-start the economy. Government privatization targets were habitually unfulfilled. For example, in late 1995 the government reported that it had received only US$11 million of the US$526 million it had expected in privatization receipts, and the 1997 program netted only US$350 million of the almost US$1 billion expected (see OMRI and *Kyiv Post*, February 6, 1998).

By 1998, the initial hopes in Kuchma had been dashed. The government could do little more than hope to secure new international loans to pay off its mounting foreign and domestic debt. It could only make ends meet by not paying workers, and by early 1998 layoffs of government workers were being discussed. Corruption had grown and the "oligarchization" of politics was evident. A repeat of the Russian debacle of the summer of 1998 was very possible, and the government was considering printing money to prevent total financial collapse. Meanwhile, the international community has lost confidence in the Ukrainian reform project. One western diplomat called the leadership "opportunistic scum" (according to a report in *The Economist* in 1998), and George Soros, who had previously backed many programs in Ukraine, said he had "given up on Ukraine," which, in his view, "lacks political will and any kind of leadership" (as quoted in the *Washington Post*).

Comparative economic data confirm Ukraine's status as a reform laggard. For example, in the *World Bank Development Report* of 1996, which focused on transition economies, Ukraine's score for liberalization (on a scale from 1 to 10) was 5.7, compared to 8.9 for Poland and 6.9 for Russia, while the share of private sector output was only 37% of GDP, compared with 58% for Poland and 59% for Russia (see World Bank). These figures put Ukraine behind Russia, and all the countries of central and eastern Europe, in progress on market reforms. By the end of 1997, Ukraine brought up the rear of the league table of transition economies compiled by the European Bank for Reconstruction and Development, even behind basket cases such as Albania or Bulgaria (see *The Economist*).

The consensus view now is that foreign investment is the best way Ukraine can extricate itself from its predicament. President Kuchma even declared in early 1998 that the planned privatization of several large enterprises should be delayed until "real investors come." The problem is that Ukraine has attracted only a paltry amount of foreign investment. By 1996, the total was US$1.1 billion, compared with US$10 billion for Poland and even US$2 billion for Romania. Fears of corruption and unclear regulations have alarmed governments and transnational companies. As the US Secretary of State Madeleine Albright has stated: "We very much have kind of a chicken and egg problem, in that they [Ukraine] are in serious economic problems because they're not able to attract investment, and one of the reasons they're not is that they haven't been able to undertake all their economic reforms" (as quoted in *Kyiv Post*, March 6, 1998). Getting out of this vicious circle looks no easier now than it did in 1992. The economic problems in Ukraine are far from over.

Political Developments Since 1991

As in the economic arena, independence did not bring rapid or far-reaching changes in the political sphere. On the same day Ukrainians voted for independence, 62% of those taking part in the election for the presidency voted for Leonid Kravchuk, rejecting candidates associated with the "national democratic" Popular Movement for Restructuring (Rukh). Kravchuk had been in favor of independence, but had only been recently converted to the nationalist cause. Previously, he had been head of the Ideology Department of the Ukrainian Communist Party, and had served as Chairman of the republic's Supreme Soviet (the former legislature).

Kravchuk's election was paradigmatic of how prominent elements from the Communist Party preserved their positions in independent Ukraine. This new elite, commonly labeled the "party of power" (*partiia vlady*), comprised

pragmatically oriented members of the old *nomenklatura* who were characterized by "economic and political conservatism, a penchant for authoritarianism and command-administrative methods, and clan connections" (according to Ryabchuk 1994b). Taras Kuzio has suggested that post-Soviet Ukraine was run by a cadre of 1,500 or so people, almost all of whom came from the *apparat* (see Glossary) of the Communist Party (see Kuzio). While this group made an effort to shed its skin and wrap itself in the Ukrainian flag, its commitment to the democratic process was questionable. Reformers in government were dismissed or resigned in frustration, and Viacheslav Chornovil, the leader of Rukh, lamented that "we have surrendered our ideals of democracy to hands that have always been indifferent or hostile to them" (see Chornovil). Others referred to the situation as a "debauched democracy" (see Miasnykov) or feared a counterrevolution, led by these former Communists, that would "attack ideas of democracy and civil society" (see Prykhod'ko and Bujvol).

While the country remained at peace, Kravchuk's term of office (1991–94) was not marked by political stability. The country had three Prime Ministers, there was no new Constitution to guide action or resolve disputes over competing branches of power, signature campaigns tried to force the dissolution of the legislature, and many laws were never implemented. Ukrainians spoke of a crisis of authority as the President and the Communist-dominated legislature sparred over power, and local elites often acted as they saw fit, without regard to any law or authority at the center. In June 1993, the deteriorating economic situation helped fuel miners' strikes, which were resolved only after new legislative and presidential elections were promised.

In March 1994, Ukrainians went to the polls to choose a new legislature, the Supreme Council (as mentioned above), replacing the Supreme Soviet, elected in 1990 and dominated by anti-reform Communists, which was blamed for many of the country's ills. National democratic parties such as Rukh, and pro-reform groups, such as the Inter-regional Reform Bloc, hoped to take advantage of public frustration with the status quo. However, the elections were conducted under a flawed majoritarian electoral law that allowed labor collectives and groups of voters, as well as parties, to nominate candidates, and required a turnout of at least 50% to validate the election in each constituency. As a result, parties were relatively unimportant: only 11% of the 5,835 declared candidates were from political parties. Because many voters were apathetic, turnout in some districts did not meet the 50% threshold, and, despite repeat elections, 34 seats out of 450 remained unfilled.

The results were not encouraging to most pro-reform candidates. The non-Communist opposition was divided among dozens of parties and movements, and was vulnerable to the criticisms of those who associated the market, nationalism, and reform with socio-economic disaster. Candidates from the Communist, Socialist, and Agrarian Parties fared well, winning 27.8% of the seats in the initial elections, but over half of all the candidates elected were "independents." Most of these were state directors or managers of collective farms, and were not very amenable to political or economic liberalization.

Once the new legislature had convened, fractions were formed which allowed one to determine its members' affiliations more clearly (see Table 6.3). The Communists, Socialists and Agrarians formed the largest single bloc, but it did not have a majority, while the national democratic groups did not have substantial voting power. However, the center, comprised mainly of deputies without any party affiliation, has been supportive of some reform measures and has not pushed for integration with Russia, although it has been claimed that many deputies in this group have been beneficiaries of a massive amount of corruption.

In the summer of 1994, Ukrainians again went to the polls to elect a President. Seven candidates ran, but the battle came down to a contest between two Leonids, Kravchuk and Kuchma, both of whom were rooted in the "party of power." Kravchuk portrayed himself as a defender of the Ukrainian state, but his campaign was rather vacuous, and the Kyiv newspaper *Nezavisimost'* even offered readers US$150 if they could prove that Kravchuk had a serious electoral program (see Kuzio). Kuchma, a former Prime Minister and director of a missile factory, was backed by the industrial lobby, and emphasized improving relations with Russia. His own economic program was also nebulous, as he alternated between favoring reform and calling for "business as usual." Kuchma was ultimately elected with 52% of the vote, and was the overwhelming choice in the more industrial and Russified regions of eastern and southern Ukraine.

As mentioned above, Kuchma has pushed through some economic reform programs. He has also tilted Ukraine further away from Russia and toward the West, and successfully used the threat of a referendum to persuade the legislature to pass the new Constitution, in June 1996, thus resolving a longstanding dispute. The Constitution grants a great deal of power to the presidency, establishes rules for local government, makes Ukrainian the sole official language, and declares Ukraine a unitary state, with Crimea as an autonomous republic within it (see Wolczuk).

In general, however, there has been no significant change in the political life of the country under Kuchma. While one does not hear the term "party of power" as much as before, one does hear about the influence of regional clans, especially those from Donets'k and Dnipropetrovs'k, over the government. Politicians from the old *nomenklatura* still dominate. National democratic groups have little power on their own and, as under Kravchuk, are compelled to back the President in battles with the legislature, which has been renamed the Narodna Rada, or People's Council, under the new Constitution. Kuchma, like Kravchuk, has tried to centralize executive power, and has dismissed two Prime Ministers, Evhen Marchuk and Pavlo Lazarenko, when they demonstrated some independence and became critical of him. As was the case with Kravchuk, he has also turned a blind eye to corruption. Lazarenko, a crony of Kuchma's from Dnipropetrovs'k who became Prime Minister in 1996, was reputed to be the richest man in Ukraine, thanks to manipulation of energy export licenses (before his arrest in Switzerland on money-laundering charges in December 1998).

It is therefore not surprising that trust in political institutions, parties, and politicians is abysmally low in Ukraine. Data gathered by the Democratic Initiatives Center in Kyiv in 1994–97 (see Table 6.4) indicate that around 70% of respondents do not trust Rukh or the nationalists, 65% do not trust the legislature, roughly half do not trust the President, and, with the exception of Kuchma in 1995 and 1996, politicians are generally less trusted than astrologers. It is also striking that the Communist Party consistently receives a higher score on questions of trust than Rukh does.

This assessment was shown to be broadly reliable in the most recent elections for the People's Council, conducted on March 29, 1998. This time, half the 450 seats were filled by the winners in 225 electoral districts, and half were filled from national party lists. To win seats by list, a party had to get at least 4% of the total number of votes cast nationally, but there was no requirement of a minimum turnout. As one could predict, this system, similar to the one used in Russia, encouraged the further development of parties, although a large number of wealthy businesspeople or farm directors ran as independents in the single-member districts.

The results produced little change in the overall composition of the People's Council (see Table 6.5). Once again, the Communists and their allies did much better than the national democratic groups, but the decisive votes belong to the centrists, again dominated by elements from the erstwhile "party of power." Hromada is led by Lazarenko; the United Social Democrats are led by Kravchuk and Marchuk; the Popular Democratic Party was created by Kuchma and is nominally led by the present Prime Minister, Valery Pustovoytenko; and even the Greens are, ironically, largely backed by leading figures in the energy industries, who hope to capitalize on the positive image associated with that party label.

Political life in Ukraine is now centered on the presidential election scheduled for October 1999. Kuchma will run again, and his primary challengers appear likely to be Lazarenko and Oleksandr Moroz, a former Chairman of the legislature, who is a leading critic of Kuchma and head of the Socialist Party. Lazarenko's arrest (see above) has complicated the picture and made forecasts more difficult. If, as seems likely, the main threat to Kuchma comes from Moroz and his supporters, Rukh and other national democratic parties may not even nominate a candidate, and may instead throw their support behind the President as the guardian of Ukrainian statehood, as they did in 1994. Given the weaknesses of his opponents, Kuchma is likely to be reelected, but the safest bet is that, regardless of who wins, dramatic changes are not in order.

The Regional Factor in Ukraine

Any analysis of contemporary Ukraine must include discussion of the regional divisions in the country. Ukrainians are wont to say that there is not just one Ukraine, but two, three, or maybe four or five. Regions can be identified based upon historical experience, language, ethnic composition, religion, foreign connections, and economic structure. The most common approach is to divide the country in half, roughly along the Dniepr river, between a western region, ethnically Ukrainian and oriented toward the West, and an eastern region, industrialized and Russified, or Sovietized. A more nuanced treatment of region, however, would look at five separate regions (see Table 6.6 and Figure 6.1).

The eastern region is the most heavily industrialized and urbanized area of the country. Next to Crimea, it also has the highest percentage of ethnic Russians, particularly in the provinces (*oblasts*) of Donets'k and Luhans'k, and Russian is the primary language spoken in large cities. This region was integrated into the Russian empire centuries ago, and has extensive crossborder links with Russia; its people tend to see maintaining ties with Russia, and protecting the rights of Russians and Russian-speakers, as priorities. A notable, residual "Soviet" identity has been found by some who have studied this region, a phenomenon that may confound Ukrainian state-building efforts (see Pirie; Miller et al.). These *oblasts* also have a number of large, smokestack industries and mining operations, which account for the fact that the region's output per capita is higher than average, but which are not likely to be profitable without maintenance of state subsidies. The region has been hit harder than average by the drop in industrial production, and for this reason eastern Ukrainians are typically more cautious on movements toward the market, and favor preserving much of the Soviet support system.

The western region has a completely different history, ethnic composition, and economic structure. Most of this region was incorporated into the Soviet Union only in 1939, meaning it escaped the worst of the Stalinist repression. Previously, it had been part of the Austro-Hungarian Empire up to 1918, and then had been divided among Poland, Romania, Hungary, and Czechoslovakia. Many of its residents harbor memories of life before Soviet rule, and affiliate with the Uniate (Greek Catholic) Church; some of them fought against Soviet occupation into the early 1950s. Anti-Russian feelings run deep here, and few Russians live in the region. Ukrainian nationalist feelings are very strong, especially in the three *oblasts* of Galicia – L'viv, Ivano-Frankivs'k, and Ternopil' – and many of the leading figures in the nationalist movement come from here. Economically, agriculture and light industry predominate, and the region sees the West as the most likely and promising economic partner.

The people of the large central region are mostly Ukrainian-speaking, although Russian is the more frequently heard language in the capital city, Kyiv. The center largely lacks traditions of Ukrainian nationalism, due in large part to the famine and repression during the Stalinist era, which crushed any incipient formation of national identity. Since independence, it has followed a relatively moderate political course, receptive to some of the calls for national rebirth from western Ukraine, but also responsive to the reaction emanating from the East. Its economy is mixed between industry (largely in Kyiv) and agriculture, and it has generally fared better than the eastern region since 1990.

The ethnic composition and economic structure of the southern region fall somewhere between those of the central and eastern regions. There is a sizable Russian minority, again particularly in the cities. There was for a time a movement, based in Odessa, that sought a separate identity for this region, as "Novorossiya" (New Russia), but it failed to attract public support. Ukrainian national consciousness has been low in this region, and because of its port cities it has a more cosmopolitan atmosphere than other regions. It is also more urbanized than average, and contains some large enterprises, like those in the eastern region, although the overall presence of industry is at a lower level. Issues of economic autonomy have been high on the agenda of the region's elite, although in general it is the most politically quiescent region in the country.

Crimea deserves a category all to itself (see Dawson). Unlike all the other regions of Ukraine, it has an ethnic Russian majority. Given the fact that it was transferred from Russian to Ukrainian jurisdiction as recently as 1954, on a whim of Khrushchev's, it is hardly surprising that the residents of this peninsula continue to identify strongly with Russia (or the Soviet Union). Broken ties with Russia have hurt the economy, which included a sizable tourism industry catering to visitors from Russia. A separatist movement developed, Russian politicians claimed Crimea as a part of Russia, and local politicians pushed hard for more autonomy and/or union with Russia. A Crimean Constitution that proclaimed the region's sovereignty was promulgated in 1992 and again in 1994. The issue of Crimea's status, and the dispute with Russia over the Soviet Black Sea Fleet stationed in Sevastopol, were both resolved in March 1995, when the Ukrainian government suspended the Crimean Constitution, abolished the Crimean presidency, and forced the region to cancel a vote on a proposed "Slavic Union" (see also below). A new Constitution for the peninsula was approved in the fall of 1995.

Given these disparities and the fact that Ukraine is effectively a new state, building a unified, civic identity among the various peoples and regions is a major task for Ukrainian elites. Both Kravchuk and Kuchma have eschewed any effort to impose an exclusively "Ukrainian" vision on the state, but ethnic and regional questions constitute major cleavages in Ukrainian political life, and have flared into major political disputes. Examples include debates over the state language; whether the population should be defined as the "Ukrainian people" or the "people of Ukraine"; education policy; relations with Russia and the CIS; referendums for economic autonomy in Donets'k and Luhans'k; the question of a unitary or federal structure for the state; the rights of local councils; and, most clearly, the status of Crimea. Many of these issues were resolved when the Constitution was adopted, and the general direction of policy has been toward central control and Ukrainianization, with Crimea's autonomous status being an anomaly.

While the most significant disputes appear to be receding into the past, far less progress has been made on constructing a cohesive national identity. In general, the pattern is that those living in the western region, the heartland of Ukrainian nationalism, associate much more strongly with the state than those in the East, particularly ethnic Russians. For example, surveys conducted by researchers from the University of Iowa in 1997 found that 50% of Russians in eastern Ukraine thought of themselves as "Soviet" a "great deal of the time," and only 23% felt pride in seeing the Ukrainian flag. The corresponding figures for ethnic Ukrainians in western Ukraine are 4% and 71%, but it is notable that their findings show less loyalty and attachment to Ukraine, among *all* residents of the country, compared with data from 1995 (see Miller et al.). They conclude that ethnic/national schisms are still pervasive, complicating efforts at state-building and reform.

The clearest evidence of regional schisms comes from voting patterns. Voters in the western region tend to back nationalist or national democratic candidates; voters in the East, the South, and Crimea tend to favor the Communists or other parties that promise rights for Russian-speakers and closer ties with Russia; voters in the central region waver between these two positions. This pattern has held in all national elections (see Table 6.7). In December 1991, the highest degree of support for independence was in western Ukraine, although it should be stressed that majorities in all the regions, including Crimea, voted for independence. At the same time, the

ex-Communist Kravchuk, promising stability and with only a moderately nationalist platform, won the presidential election in all the regions except western Ukraine, where Chornovil was the primary choice. By 1994, however, Kravchuk himself had become a symbol of Ukrainian statehood, and he won in all but one of the *oblasts* to the west of the Dniepr river, while Kuchma, clearly the candidate of the Russophone voters, won in the eastern and southern regions. The polarization was particularly acute in Galicia, where Kravchuk won more than 90% of the votes cast, and in Donets'k, Luhans'k, and Crimea, where Kuchma won more than 85%.

In the legislative elections in both 1994 and 1998, Communist, Socialist, and Agrarian candidates dominated in the eastern and southern regions, while nationalist candidates from parties such as Rukh, the Republican Party, or Reforms and Order picked up almost all of their support in the western *oblasts* and in the city of Kyiv. The changes in the electoral law make complete comparisons difficult, but the breakdown of voting and elected deputies by region is striking.

To the extent that party cleavages reflect regional/ethnic cleavages in Ukraine, one would expect processes of national integration to be difficult. It is true, as some researchers have noted, that all Ukrainians can agree that the economy is poor and that politicians are not to be trusted (see Hesli et al.), but significant differences remain on foreign policy, language and cultural rights for minorities, and economic reform policies. Trying to find a "happy medium" that will satisfy voters from all the different regions – or at least not substantially alienate them – continues to be a major challenge. Failure to ameliorate regional differences will contribute to fears of political instability, intensify partisan political rivalries, and work against the norms and procedures of democratic compromise.

A Shifting Balance Between Russia and the West

As if all its domestic troubles were not enough, Ukraine has also faced immense challenges in foreign policy. It is caught, figuratively and literally, between East and West, and Ukrainian elites have tried to craft a foreign policy to balance a variety of interests. The priorities have been relations with Russia and with the West, preserving Ukrainian security, and promoting beneficial economic ties.

Relations with Russia are complex and represent one of the most important issues for Ukrainian leaders. On the one hand, Russia is perceived as the primary threat to Ukraine's security. Ukrainian leaders do not want to fall again into Moscow's orbit, or allow Russia to interfere in Ukrainian domestic issues, notably over the status of Crimea. On the other hand, Russia is Ukraine's largest trading partner, it relies on Russia for its energy needs, and there are a host of ties between industries and individuals on both sides of the border. Thus, relations with Russia need to be amicable, but Kyiv does not want to rely too heavily or exclusively on Moscow.

Many problems remain, however (see Motyl; D'Anieri; and Sherr). Ukrainians and Russians have disputed Ukraine's inheritance of nuclear weapons and the Black Sea Fleet from the Soviet Union; the status of Crimea and ethnic Russians in Ukraine; Ukraine's mounting energy debts to Russia; and the powers of the CIS. Overlaying all of these is the fact that some Russians are not willing to recognize Ukraine as an independent state, since they see Ukraine as having a special place in Russian history, culture, and identity. While the nature of the centuries of interaction between the two nations is a matter of some dispute – was it imperialist or mutually beneficial? – there is no doubt that many Russians view Ukraine and Ukrainians as an essential part of themselves. For example, Nikolai Travkin of the Russian Democratic Party has opined that "history requires that Russia's relations with Ukraine be qualitatively different from its relations with other foreign countries" (see Travkin). Other prominent Russians, including Aleksandr Solzhenitsyn and Vladimir Zhirinovsky, have been even more explicit, claiming that Ukraine should become part of a greater Slavic state with Russia. This sentiment finds wide support among Russians and even among a large number of Ukrainians. For example, surveys conducted in 1994 found that 78% of Russian

respondents thought Ukraine should become part of Russia, and that 36% of those in Ukraine (majorities in Crimea, Donets'k, and Luhans'k) were in favor of some sort of union with Russia (see Laba).

In the first years of Ukraine's independence, Russian politicians acted in a menacing manner toward Ukraine. Many claimed Crimea as a part of Russia and pushed for dual citizenship for ethnic Russians in Ukraine. Russia also helped make Ukraine an international pariah because it refused to surrender its nuclear weapons, and refused to sign a treaty that would unequivocally recognize Ukraine's borders. Gas cutoffs were common, as Russia demanded either political concessions or payment of an enormous energy debt, which amounted to US$4 billion by 1995. One Russian official even advised western countries not to upgrade their facilities in Kyiv, since they would once again become mere consulates. Despite the pressures and the economic hardship, however, Kyiv did not budge on key issues such as Crimea or the nuclear weapons. Sovereignty was safeguarded at all costs (see D'Anieri).

By 1994, some thought that the Russian policy of pressure on Ukraine would pay off. Leonid Kuchma, promising to defend the interests of the largely pro-Russian industrial lobby and build "Fewer Walls, More Bridges" with Russia, was elected President. Many thought that Kuchma would pursue integration with Russia and bow to many of its demands in Crimea. Yet these expectations were not realized. Kuchma proved to be an adroit bargainer, and continued to defend Ukrainian sovereignty against Russian assaults. While he did agree to dismantle the country's nuclear weapons and sign the Nuclear Nonproliferation Treaty of 1968, these decisions were clearly implemented more with Washington than Moscow in mind. In return, he won security guarantees, went on a highly publicized trip to Washington, and gained western aid for his economic reform program. By 1997, the IMF had supplied Ukraine with around US$3.5 billion in aid, and Ukraine received more US foreign aid than any other country except Israel and Egypt. Ukraine also became the first country to enter a Partnership for Peace with NATO. By 1996, Ukraine was clearly leaning toward, and receiving solid support from, the West, and in 1997 Kuchma even proposed an "11+1" arrangement for the CIS, dropping Ukraine's status in its Economic Union from associate to observer (see Appendix 4). Some even see Ukraine heading a new bloc, together with Georgia, Azerbaijan, and Moldova, to counter Russian influence within the CIS.

Rather than upping the ante with Kyiv, Moscow began to back down. When Kuchma reasserted control over Crimea in early 1995 by dismissing the region's President and its legislature, Moscow maintained that this was an internal affair of Ukraine. Linkage between Ukrainian debt and the status of Crimea was dropped, and the debt was successfully rescheduled in 1995. By late summer 1996, preparations were being made for both a treaty on borders and the division of the Black Sea Fleet. In May 1997, after another delay, President Yeltsin made his long awaited and often postponed trip to Kyiv, signing agreements on both issues, and also agreed on provisions on Ukrainian debt and the removal of various trade barriers with Ukraine. While both sides stand to benefit, one detailed report suggested that the agreements are highly favorable to Ukraine, in some ways better than those the Russians had backed away from eight months earlier (see Sherr).

Clearly, Kuchma's pro-western policy had paid dividends. Not only was he receiving badly needed economic assistance, but he had also gained a stronger hand in relations with Russia. He used this to his advantage in February 1995, connecting the rescheduling of Ukraine's debt with the IMF's disbursement of funds for Russia and therefore receiving Russian concessions. In 1996, as Kuchma teetered toward backing the expansion of NATO and upgrading Ukraine's relations with that organization to a "special partnership," Russia found itself outmaneuvered. With the West firmly backing Ukraine – the US Senate even applauded Ukraine for preventing the emergence of an organization to promote the reintegration of post-Soviet states – Moscow was forced to treat Kyiv as an equal.

Of all the areas discussed in this chapter, foreign policy has been the one in which Ukraine has enjoyed the most success. In 1991–94, it was weak and diplomatically isolated, an easy target for Russian pressure. It managed, however, not to back down, and after 1994, when it could feel more secure, due to its better relations with the West, it was able to assert itself. While it officially professes neutrality, and signed a 10-year economic cooperation treaty with Russia at the end of 1997, there is little doubt that it has become an important partner of the West. In July 1997, Ukraine even signed a special charter with NATO, receiving security guarantees from the alliance. More western assistance is being negotiated, including a US$2.3 billion loan from the IMF in 1998, although a host of economic concerns still worry western lenders and investors. Nonetheless, Ukraine's security and survival as an independent state now seems fully assured.

Prospects for Development

While the worst of the post-Soviet crisis may be behind Ukraine, it is hard to be sanguine about prospects for future development. True, there have been some significant accomplishments in recent years: the adoption of the new Constitution and a series of democratically conducted elections; the resolution of the thorny questions of Crimea, the Black Sea Fleet, and the state language; the introduction of the new currency; international treaties with all neighboring states that recognize Ukraine's borders; and the provision of western economic assistance and security guarantees. Compared with 1992, Ukrainian statehood is more secure than ever before. The predictions that Ukraine would collapse as an independent state (see Rumer) now seem misplaced.

Nonetheless, most Ukrainians would agree that there is little hope for solutions to the country's severe problems. The economy continues to languish, corruption flourishes, and the enthusiasm of the first years after independence has given way to frustration and alienation. Regional divisions are still marked, as diametrically opposed visions of the country's future are held by those in the East and the South, on the one hand, and those in the West, on the other. Elections produce no real changes, as politicians continue to muddle through the crisis. A key point is that independence was not accompanied by a turnover in the elite, or by the adoption of a radical program for economic reform. Faith in all politicians has been lost, and calls for more rapid economic reform fail to attract voters. How Ukraine will get out of this hole – into which Russia has also fallen – is a very difficult question to answer.

The safest prediction is that what will happen at time t+1 is the same as that which held at time t. This would seem to hold well in the Ukrainian case, given the fact that no corrective has been found or is readily available for many of the country's basic problems. If one were to predict change, it would be most likely in a backward direction, meaning the election of an unreformed Communist or ex-Communist President (perhaps Moroz), together with a People's Council dominated by his supporters. Conceivably, such a combination could try to reanimate a state-dominated economy and seek close ties with Russia that would undermine Ukrainian sovereignty. However, this seems unlikely, as the Communists and their allies have been unable to attract a majority of voters, business interests have been created that would oppose the reimposition of Communism, and moving closer to Russia is far less attractive after the collapse of the Russian economy in 1998. However, change leading to more reforms seems even more unlikely, given the inability of the national democrats to expand their base of support, the negative connotation of the market for many voters, and the rise of industrial oligarchs who profit handsomely at present but would fare poorly under genuine market conditions (see Kubicek 1999). These oligarchs have dominated Ukrainian politics since independence, and there are no rivals from above or below to their continued reign.

Thus, while Ukrainians can take solace in the fact the state has not collapsed, the underlying economic issues have not been handled well, and it will take years for the country to get back to the levels of production and income achieved when it was part of the Soviet Union. Democratic institutions are in place, but corruption is rampant, and public confidence in political figures and institutions is low. Regional divisions remain important, and festering problems play into the hands of the Communist opposition. There is no sign of movement from below, or of the presence of credible elites that might give one confidence that the basic problems in the country can be resolved. The opening phrase of the national anthem, "Ukraine is not dead yet," perhaps best sums up the country's status as it enters the 21st century.

Further Reading

Cherniak, Vladimir, "Privatizatsiia ili Kollektivizat-siia?" [Privatization or Collectivization?], in *Nezavisimost'*, May 6, 1994

Chornovil, Viacheslav, "Pro Sorsialno-polychni stan v Ukraini i Zavdannia Rukhy" [The Sociopolitical Situation in Ukraine, and the Tasks of Rukh], in *Vysoky Zamok* (L'viv), December 8, 1992

An important text by the founder and leader of Rukh, who died in a road accident in March 1999 after a long career as a prominent Ukrainian nationalist

D'Anieri, Paul, *Economic Interdependence in Ukrainian-Russian Relations*, New York: State University of New York Press, 1998

An in-depth study focusing on the economic ties between these states and their political effects, particularly on Ukrainian sovereignty

Dawson, Jane, "Ethnicity, Ideology and Geopolitics in Crimea," in *Communist and Post-Communist Studies*, Volume 30, number 4, December 1997

An examination of the major issues affecting Crimea and its often difficult relations with Kyiv

Dolishnii, Mariian, "Regional Aspects of Ukraine's Economic Development," in I. S. Koropeckyj, editor, *The Ukrainian Economy*, Cambridge, MA: Harvard University Press, 1992

A good source on economic patterns in Ukraine in the late Soviet period

Drobiazko, Anatolii, "Banky i Promyshlennost': Bity Nebitogo Vezet?" [Banks and Industry: Leading to the Non-existent?], *UNIAN-Biznes*, July 5, 1994

The Economist: "A Truly Dreadful Prospect," March 28, 1998

Harris, Chauncy, "The New Russian Minorities: A Statistical Overview," in *Post-Soviet* Geography, Volume 34, number 1, 1993

A comprehensive look at Russian minorities in a variety of post-Soviet states, and the problems their presence causes for domestic and international politics

Hesli, Vicki, William Reisinger, and Arthur Miller, "Political Party Development in Divided Societies: the Case of Ukraine," in *Electoral Studies*, Volume 17, number 2, June 1998

This article presents research based upon survey evidence examining political cleavages in Ukraine. Primary attention is given to regional divisions and international orientation of voters.

Holos Ukrainy, February 4, 1994

Kubicek, Paul, "Post-Soviet Ukraine: In Search of a Constituency for Reform," in *Journal of Communist Studies and Transition Politics*, Volume 13, number 3, September 1997

A look at the barriers to adoption of reform in Ukraine, utilizing public opinion surveys and assessment of interest group activity

Kubicek, Paul, *The State, Interest Associations, and Corporatism in Post-Soviet Ukraine*, Ann Arbor: University of Michigan Press, 1999

A study of economic interest associations in Ukraine, and their effect on political and economic reform. It finds that a "state corporatist" system still exists in Ukraine, and that links between old guard politicians and interest groups inhibit economic liberalization.

Kuzio, Taras, *Ukraine: State and Nation Building*, London and New York: Routledge, 1998

A comprehensive look at some of the most important issues facing Ukraine: building a national identity, language politics, regionalism, and creation of new myths and symbols

Kuzio, Taras, and Andrew Wilson, *Ukraine: Perestroika to Independence*, New York: St Martin's Press, and London: Macmillan, 1998

The authors trace the changes in Ukraine from 1985 to 1991, particularly how sovereignty and independence gained support among political elites and the population as a whole.

Kyiv Post, various issues

A good English-language source for events in Ukraine

Laba, Roman, "The Russian-Ukrainian Conflict: State, Nation, and Identity," in *European Security*, Volume 4, number 3, Autumn 1995

A historical review of Russian-Ukrainian relations, with a discussion of how the two sides currently view each other

Lukinov, I., "Inflatsiyna Polityka, yiyi Ruynivni Naslidky i Shliakhy ikh Podolannia" [Inflation Policy, its Ruinous Results, and Ways to Overcome it], in *Ekonomika Ukrainy*, January 1994

Miasnykov, Oleh, "Autorytaryzm. Shche ne Rezhym, Ale vzhe i ne Symptomy" [Authoritarianism: Still Not a Regime, But Also Not a Symptom], in *Viche* (Kyiv), March 1994

Miller, Arthur, Thomas Klobucar, William Reisinger, and Vicki Hesli, "Social Identities in Russia, Ukraine, and Lithuania", in *Post-Soviet Affairs*, Volume 14, number 3, July-September 1998

Research from surveys examining identities in three states. They find a strong class-based identity, although in Ukraine a national/ethnic identity is also important.

Motyl, Alexander, *Dilemmas of Independence: Ukraine after Totalitarianism*, New York: Council on Foreign Relations, 1993

Motyl reviews the push for independence in Ukraine, as well as the fundamental issues facing Ukraine in the initial post-Soviet period.

Nezavisimost': "Khaos: v Gosudarstve, v Parlamente" [Chaos: In the State, and in Parliament], July 29, 1994

Open Media Research Institute (OMRI), *OMRI Economic Digest*, November 23, 1995

Pirie, Paul, "National Identity and Politics in Southern and Eastern Ukraine," in *Europe-Asia* Studies, Volume 48, number 7, November 1996

A review of survey evidence and voting behavior in these regions in Ukraine that tries to account for their continued "Soviet" orientation

Politichny Portret Ukrainy: "Ukrains'ke Suspil'stvo 1994–1997" [Ukrainian Society, 1994–97], number 20, 1998

Prykhod'ko, Gregorii, and Boris Bujvol, "Revoliutsiia pislia Revoliutsiia v Ukraini" [The Revolution after the Revolution in Ukraine] in *Ratusha* (L'viv), November 12, 1992

Rumer, Eugene, "Eurasian Letter: Will Ukraine Return to Russia?" in *Foreign Policy*, number 96, Fall 1994

A pessimistic assessment of developments and prospects for Ukraine

Ryabchuk, Mykola (1994a), "Between Civil Society and the New Etatism: Democracy and State-Building in Ukraine," in Michael Kennedy, editor, *Envisioning Eastern Europe: Postcommunist Cultural Studies*, Ann Arbor: University of Michigan Press, 1994

An excellent and critical review of the uses of nationalism in post-Soviet Ukraine by the political elites and the national democratic opposition

Ryabchuk, Mykola (1994b), "Chy Isnuye v Ukraini 'Partiia Vlady'?" [Is There a 'Party of Power' in Ukraine?], in *UNIAN-Polityka*, May 10–16, 1994

Sherr, James, "Russia-Ukraine *Rapprochement?*: The Black Sea Fleet Accords," in *Survival*, Volume 39, number 1, Autumn 1997

Sherr reviews Russian-Ukrainian relations, assesses the 1997 treaty, and argues that Ukraine largely got the better of the deal.

Shevchenko, Yaroslavna, "Reformy i Zakonodavcha Baza" [Reforms and the Legislative Foundation], in *Polityka i chas*, December 1993

Slavia Press Digest: "Poll Reflects Drastic Mood," March 15, 1994

Solchanyk, Roman, editor, *Ukraine: From Chernobyl to Sovereignty*, London: Macmillan, and New York: St. Martin's Press, 1992

A collection of articles and documents tracking the independence movement in Ukraine

Solchanyk, Roman, "The Post-Soviet Transition in Ukraine: Prospects for Stability," in Taras Kuzio, editor, *Contemporary Ukraine: Dynamics of Post-Soviet Transformation*, Armonk, NY: M. E. Sharpe, 1998

Solchanyk reviews developments in Ukraine since 1992, focusing in particular on political parties

and movements, regional tensions, and relations with Russia.

Stets'kiv, Taras, "Try Tsviakhy v Domovynu Ukrains'koyi Nezalezhnosti" [Three Nails to Assist Ukrainian Independence], in *Post-Postup*, August 25, 1993

Travkin, Nikolai, "Russia, Ukraine, and Eastern Europe," in Stephen Sestanovich, editor, *Rethinking Russia's National Interests*, Washington, DC: Center for Strategic and International Studies, 1994

An assessment by a Russian official about how the new independent Ukrainian state should fit into Russian strategic and economic thinking

Washington Post: "Soros Announces Cuts at Foundation," November 13, 1998

Wilson, Andrew, *Ukrainian Nationalism in the 1990s: A Minority Faith*, Cambridge and New York: Cambridge University Press, 1996

This is a comprehensive and somewhat critical assessment of the Ukrainian nationalist movement in the contemporary period. Wilson finds that nationalist discourse in Ukraine is far from dominant, and is restricted primarily to the western region of the country.

Wolczuk, Kataryna, "The Politics of Constitution Making in Ukraine," in Kuzio as cited under Solchanyk above

This chapter traces the complex and often acrimonious debates over the Ukrainian Constitution, finally adopted in 1996.

World Bank, *From Plan to Market: World Development Report 1996*, Oxford and New York: Oxford University Press, 1996

A thorough review of many of the economic issues facing post-Communist states. An important resource.

Dr Paul Kubicek is Kenneth Boulding Postdoctoral Fellow in the Institute of Behavioral Sciences at the University of Colorado.

Table 6.1   Economic Performance of Ukraine, 1992–97 (% except as shown)

	1992	1993	1994	1995	1996	1997
GDP	−12.5	−7.2	−24.3	−12.0	−10.0	−3.2
Industrial output	−9.0	−7.4	−28.0	−11.5	−5.1	−1.8
Agricultural output	−11.0	−16.5	−16.0	−4.0	−9.0	−7.2
Inflation	1,210	4,735	842	375	39	10
Foreign debt (US$ millions)	n.a.	396	3,624	4,828	9,170	10,243

Sources: European Bank for Reconstruction and Development, World Bank, Ukrainian Ministry of Finance

---

Table 6.2   Public Dissatisfaction in Ukraine, 1992–96 (% of respondents)

	1992	1993	1994	1995	1996
Reporting satisfaction with overall direction of country	28.5	12.0	14.3	15.4	17.4
Reporting satisfaction with democracy	18.2	14.8	15.4	14.9	17.9
Reporting improvement in household finances	16.1	4.4	5.6	8.6	8.6
Expressing hope in the future	22.7	11.1	12.5	15.8	18.7

Source: Central and Eastern Eurobarometer Surveys

Table 6.3   Fractions in the People's Council of Ukraine, as of February 1997 (numbers of seats)

Communists and their Allies (36%)	149
Communists	86
Socialists	25
Agrarians of Ukraine	38
Center (41%)	171
Constitutional Center	56
Unity	37
Inter-regional Group	28
Social-Market Choice	25
Independents	25
National Democrats (14%)	56
Reforms	29
Rukh	27

Source: Solchanyk, Roman, "The Post-Soviet Transition in Ukraine: Prospects for Stability," in Taras Kuzio, editor, *Contemporary Ukraine: Dynamics of Post-Soviet Transformation*, Armonk, NY: M. E. Sharpe, 1998, p. 26

Table 6.4 Public Trust in Parties, State Institutions, and Astrologers in Ukraine, 1994–97 (index from 1, lowest, to 5, highest)

	Rukh	Nationalists	Communists	President	Legislature	Astrologers
1994	1.97	1.84	2.27	2.33	2.29	2.50
1995	1.82	1.72	2.12	2.86	2.13	2.48
1996	1.88	1.81	2.14	2.55	2.09	2.43
1997	1.88	1.81	2.14	2.28	2.03	2.30

Source: *Politichny Portret Ukrainy*, "Ukrains´ke Suspil´stvo 1994–1997," number 20, 1998, pp. 9–11

Table 6.5 Results of Elections for the People's Council of Ukraine, March 1998

	Votes (% of Total)	Party List Seats	Single-member Seats	Total Seats
Communists and their Allies	37.3	127	39	166
Communist Party	24.7	84	32	116
Socialist-Agrarian Alliance	8.6	29	6	35
Progressive Socialist Party	4.0	14	1	15
Center	31.2	66	44	110
Popular Democratic Party	5.0	17	11	28
Hromada	4.7	16	10	26
Greens	5.4	19	0	19
United Social Democrats	0	14	4	18
Agrarian Party	3.7	0	9	9
Others	8.4	0	10	10
National Democrats	16.5	32	32	64
Rukh	9.4	32	13	45
Reforms and Order	3.1	0	3	3
Forward Ukraine	1.7	0	7	7
Others	2.3	0	6	6
Extreme Right	3.4	0	5	5
Independents and Others	n.a.	0	91	91
Totals	88.4	225	209	434

Source: Official returns, as reported by the International Foundation for Electoral Systems

Table 6.6   Regional Differences in Ukraine, 1989 and 1996 (%)

	Proportion of total national population, 1996	Urban population, 1996	Ethnic Russians, 1989	Proportion of total agricultural output, 1989	Proportion of total industrial output, 1989
West	22.1	49.8	5	22.0	16.5
L'viv	5.4	60.9	7	3.9	5.1
Ternopil'	2.3	43.7	2	3.3	1.5
Ivano-Frankivs'k	2.9	43.3	4	2.1	2.2
Center	26.7	64.4	10	34.1	23.9
East	35.7	82.7	34	26.4	48.2
Donets'k	10.1	90.3	44	4.9	13.7
Luhans'k	5.4	86.4	45	3.3	7.4
South	10.1	65.2	24	12.8	8.3
Crimea	5.1	70.5	67	4.7	3.1
Totals		67.8	22		

Sources: Dolishnii, Mariian, "Regional Aspects of Ukraine's Economic Development," in I. S. Koropeckyj, editor, *The Ukrainian Economy*, Cambridge, MA: Harvard University Press, 1992; Harris, Chauncy, "The New Russian Minorities: A Statistical Overview," in *Post-Soviet Geography*, Volume 34, number 1, 1993; UN, *Human Development Report 1997*

Table 6.7   Regional Voting Patterns in Ukraine: Votes Cast in Favor of Selected Options and Presidential Candidates, 1991–98 (%)

	Independence, 1991	Kravchuk, 1991	Kravchuk, 1994	Communists and Allies, 1998	National Democrats, 1998
West	97	37	73	15.5	31.4
L'viv	98	12	94	6.4	48.4
Ternopil'	98	17	95	5.4	35.0
Ivano-Frankivs'k	99	14	95	5.4	34.8
Center	95	69	51	43.0	14.6
East	88	71	25	44.4	6.7
Donets'k	84	72	21	41.3	6.3
Luhans'k	84	76	12	55.5	4.0
South	87	71	37	43.4	10.3
Crimea	54	54	10	45.7	7.8
National	90	62	45	37.2	15.6

Sources: Wilson, Andrew, *Ukrainian Nationalism in the 1990s: A Minority Faith*, Cambridge and New York: Cambridge University Press, 1997; F-4 Political Research Center, Kyiv; official returns, as reported by the International Foundation for Electoral Systems

Figure 6.1   Ukraine and its Regions

Chapter Seven

The Five States of Central Asia

Michael Kaser

The five republics of Central Asia are bounded to the East and Southeast by mountains, which have remained unsettled, as have the deserts occupying the center and the West of the group. However, their rolling or flat terrains are open in all other directions, and have always invited immigration and nomadism. Indeed, of all the territories brought under Russian rule by force of arms, none had inherited a civilization as ancient as that of Central Asia. In Turkmenistan settled agriculture can be traced back to the fifth millennium BCE, and irrigation in the basins of the classical rivers Oxus (Amu Darya) and Jaxartes (Syr Darya) in succeeding millennia furnished the rich surpluses for a cultured society when Slavs were barely covering their subsistence. Integrated into a great Islamic network after the Arab invasions of the seventh century CE, the region's empires fostered science and architecture. The fame of Bokhara and Samarkand, both in modern Uzbekistan, is founded as much on the early mathematicians and astronomers of these cities as on their magnificent buildings.

Dependence on Russia, Isolation from the World

By the middle of the 19th century, however, when Central Asia was targeted for expansion by the Russian and British empires, its culture had stagnated and its governments had fragmented. Rival penetrations, from British India in the South and from Russian Siberia in the North could have added around 4 million people, as many as then populated Siberia or the newly conquered Russian Caucasus, to

either of the two empires (Parker p. 308). Russia's acquisitions in the "Great Game" immortalized by Rudyard Kipling were halted by the buffer zones of Afghanistan, Persia (now Iran), and Tibet (see Hopkirk). Each empire thereby fenced the other out in order to protect their captive supplies – cotton was a high priority for both – and their markets of millions of consumers. If the buffer had extended to the Emirates of Bokhara and Khiva, and the Khanate of Kokand, or even if free trade had been the economic policy of the Russian imperial government, Turkestan (as most of Central Asia was then generally known) might have gained rail connections to northern India through Persia and Afghanistan, and enjoyed commercial options outside underdeveloped Russia.

Despite the Great Power status that imperial Russia achieved at the Congress of Vienna in 1815, which was derived essentially from its territorial extent, it was a poor country – its GDP per capita was in 1913 about the same as Japan's (see Maddison) – and Central Asia was its dependency. World politics could have evolved quite differently if there had been easy communication between Central Asia, the Persian Gulf, and the Indian subcontinent. The Russian Emperor Paul I had dispatched, but soon recalled, a Cossack force to conquer India in 1800–01, and in 1917, a mere three weeks after the Bolsheviks' October Revolution in Petrograd (as St Petersburg had become), the new government, the Soviet of People's Commissars, appealed for revolt among "all Muslim Toilers of Russia and the East," specifying Indians as well as the nearer Turkic and Iranian peoples (Carr p. 232). Putatively more likely than the export of the Russian Revolution was the reverse historical option. Reinforced by British imperial arms, Russian colonial officers who supported the anti-Bolshevik "Whites," the autonomous native rulers, and the nationalist *basmachi* (guerilla fighters) might successfully have resisted subordination to the Commissars. The Bolshevik seizure of Tashkent (now in Uzbekistan) in November 1917 was indeed temporarily dislodged, and the counterrevolutionaries were said to have signed an agreement with the UK government, through its Military Mission in Meshed, for British protection over Turkestan for 55 years (Ellis p. 139).

Instead, Central Asia remained isolated within what became (in 1922) the Soviet Union. Maritime trade, the cheapest mode of international transport, became accessible to the region only after the collapse of the Soviet Union, when the Turkmen and Iranian railways were linked at Sarakhs in 1996. Not a single rail track, and only the poorest of roads, crossed a politically determined barrier that was rendered hermetic by the repressive regime of Stalin and, during part of the Cold War, by a western defensive wall formed by the Central Treaty Organization (CENTO), the equivalent of NATO along the Soviet Union's southern flank from 1955 to 1979.

The actual course of history kept Central Asia under the rule of Moscow. The Soviet government delimited the borders of the five countries in 1924. Turkmenistan and Uzbekistan became Union Republics in that year, while the other three were autonomous republics – Tajikistan within Uzbekistan, Kazakhstan and Kyrgyzstan within Russia – until they too became Union Republics, Tajikistan in 1929 and the latter two in 1936. For most purposes, however, these republics had little power, until the Communist Party leadership of Mikhail Gorbachev weakened the federal state's control over both citizens and the lower constituents of the government system. Unlike in most other Union Republics, no strong nationalist movements had emerged in parallel to *perestroika*, for politicians of the eponymous nationalities had reached tacit power-sharing accords with the All-Union authorities. Nominally still pursuant to Stalin's

dictum, "national in form, socialist in content," Soviet governments had long relied on "national cadres" for the governance of both Union Republics and, within most of them, Autonomous Republics. (After 1936 there was only one Autonomous Republic within Central Asia, Karakalpakstan, which had been detached from Kazakhstan in 1932 to form part of Uzbekistan). The participation of Communists from the ethnic groups of Central Asia in leading Party and state positions roughly correlated with the sizes of those groups in relation to resident (many long-resident) Slavs. The 1989 census, the last so far conducted throughout Central Asia, counted 72% Turkmen and 10% Russians in Turkmenistan, 71% Uzbeks and 8% Russians in Uzbekistan, 62% Tajiks and 8% Russians in Tajikistan, 52% Kyrgyz and 22% Russians in Kyrgyzstan, but 40% Kazakhs and 38% Russians in Kazakhstan. This last pair of figures reflects the events of the 1930s, when denomadization and collectivization caused the death, by killing and famine, of 1.75 million Kazakhs, and the permanent emigration of another 650,000, rendering Kazakhs a minority in their own land (Akiner p. 45).

Political Developments

On the eve of independence, four of the republics in Central Asia had members of their eponymous nationalities as First Party Secretaries. All four of these individuals seamlessly became Presidents of the new states.

In Soviet Kazakhstan, Russians and Kazakhs had usually alternated as Party leader, but when, in December 1986, Gorbachev replaced Dinmukhamed Kunayev, a Kazakh, with Gennady Kunayev, an ethnic Russian, the capital city, Almaty (Alma Ata in Russian), experienced its first nationalist riot. In June 1989, the Party leadership was passed to Nursultan Nazarbayev, who had been Chairman of the Kazakh Council of Ministers since 1984. In April 1990, Nazarbayev was appointed by the Supreme Soviet (legislature) of the republic to the new post of President. He was elected as sole candidate in a national poll in December 1991, apparently on 98.8% of the vote, and gained re-election for a further seven years in a contested election in January 1999, apparently with 82% of the vote. International observers from the OSCE said that the latter election "fell far short of the standards to which Kazakhstan is committed as an OSCE participating state."

Saparmurat Niyazov, the leader of Turkmenistan, has been in power the longest of the four. He became First Secretary of the Communist Party of Turkmenistan in 1984, before *perestroika* began, and was elected unopposed, apparently gaining 98.3% of the votes cast, in October 1990. He was re-elected on 99.5% of the votes in June 1992, and had his term extended by referendum in January 1994 on 99.9% of the votes; it was confirmed in July 1998 that a presidential election would be held in 2002. If President Niyazov, who was designated Turkmenbashi, Leader of the Turkmen, in October 1993, runs again – although heart problems could intervene – the indications are that his hold on the country would continue.

Islam Karimov had been Party First Secretary of Uzbekistan only since 1989 when, in March 1990, the Supreme Soviet of the country appointed him to the new executive presidency. A popular election in December 1991 confirmed him in that office, apparently on 86% of the votes, and his term was extended to 2000 by referendum in March 1995, on 99.9% of the votes.

In Tajikistan, Kakhar Makkhamov had been Communist Party leader since 1985, and gained the support of the Supreme Soviet of the republic to become President in November 1990. His failure to condemn the abortive coup in Moscow of August 1991 forced his resignation. He was briefly succeeded by Rakhmon Nabiyev for the first months of civil war, in which Islamist and democratic parties confronted the former Communists, but Imamali Rakhmonov was sworn in as head of state by a wholly Communist government in November 1992. Two years later, in November 1994, Rakhmonov won 58% of the votes in those districts of the country that remained under the control of government forces, mainly around the capital, Dushanbe, and in the region of Külob. The civil war, which was regional more than political in its divisiveness, formally ended in June 1997, and the power previously held mainly by Külobis was shared with the leader of the Islamic Renaissance Party, Sayed Abdullo Nuri, who became Chairman of a new National Reconciliation Council in July 1997.

The exception to the pattern of Communist leaders staying in power was in Kyrgyzstan, which from May 1993 has been officially known as the Kyrgyz Republic, to avoid the ethnic implication of the "-stan" suffix. In June 1990, more than 500 people were killed in riots between ethnic Kyrgyz and ethnic Uzbeks, in a land dispute for which Absamat Masalev, the Party leader, was blamed. In the following October, the Supreme Soviet gave the new post of executive President not to Masaliyev, but to the Chairman of the Kyrgyz Academy of Sciences, Askar Akayev. Having won 95% of the votes cast in an election in October 1991, he had his term extended in January 1994, apparently by 96% of the votes cast in a referendum, and was re-elected in December 1995 by 72% of those voting. In July 1998 he was authorized by the Constitutional Court to stand for a third term, in an election due in 2000.

Detachment from Russia

The continuation from the Soviet period of near-unanimous voting for entrenched leaders did not mean prolonging the old dependence on Moscow, except in Tajikistan. There, the civil war compelled the Communist succession to rely heavily on Russia, where Tajikistan and the other former Union Republics are often distinguished from other foreign countries by being termed "the near abroad." Russian troops, along with contingents from the armies of other states in Central Asia, stayed to guard the frontier against the Taliban in Afghanistan, and its ruble remained the currency of Tajikistan until 1995. President Rakhmonov declared in July 1993 that "without Russia, neither Tajikistan nor the Tajik people would exist" (Webber p. 26).

Elsewhere, liberation from the tutelage of Russia was required in order to offset the scant concern for independence that national leaders had manifested as the Soviet Union approached dissolution in the second half of 1991. Kazakhstan was in fact the last Union

Republic to declare its independence, on December 16, 1991, and the first non-Slav republic to adhere to the accord on a new grouping, the CIS, reached by Belarus, Ukraine and Russia on December 8 (see Chapter 2). The five republics of Central Asia all joined the CIS officially on December 13, 1991. Kyrgyzstan and Uzbekistan had been the first to state that they regarded themselves as independent, on August 31, and had been followed by Tajikistan, on September 9, and Turkmenistan, on October 27.

Although each of the new states made the majority language its official medium, Russian was retained in Kazakhstan as the language of interethnic communication, under the Constitution of January 1993, and both there and in Kyrgyzstan the national language continued to be written in Cyrillic letters. The two other Turkic tongues, Turkmen and Uzbek, reverted to the Roman script that all had adopted, in emulation of Kemal Atatürk's policy in Turkey, between 1928 and 1940. The Tajik decision to convert its written language, which is related to Farsi, to the script used in Iran has not yet been implemented.

All five states were admitted to membership of the UN on March 5, 1992, and simultaneously declared a "partnership" among themselves. Since then, four have become involved in group relationships, while Turkmenistan has declared itself "neutral," and was recognized as such by the UN General Assembly in December 1995. Bilateral security treaties now link the four other states with Russia, and a common peacekeeping force for Central Asia, agreed in May 1996, has been placed at the disposal of the UN, and may only be used under UN auspices (Jonson pp. 39–40). Uzbekistan, however, left the CIS Collective Security Treaty in January 1999. Although CIS members declared an Economic Union in March 1993, they have been reluctant to devolve any substantive operations to it. Indeed, President Akayev of Kyrgyzstan has called the CIS "a unique phenomenon inconsistent with the conventional norms of international cooperation" (Kumar p. 38). Belarus, Kazakhstan, and Russia formed a tighter Customs Union in January 1995, and were joined by Kyrgyzstan in March 1996. A

Community of Integrated States was established in March 1996 by Belarus, Kazakhstan, Kyrgyzstan, and Russia, and declared open not only to other CIS states but to others. So far, only Tajikistan has taken up the offer, in 1998. Even this "Quadrilateral" has not managed to harmonize its trade regulations, import duties or quantitative trade restrictions. At its meeting in October 1997, Valery Serov, a Deputy Prime Minister of Russia, declared that "the main question is how to breathe life into the quadripartite agreements of the Customs Union" (Jonson p. 57). Further problems arose when Kyrgyzstan was admitted to the World Trade Organization, the first CIS state to gain admittance, in October 1998; Kazakhstan looks likely to gain membership during 1999. Russia is also negotiating entry. In January 1994, Kazakhstan, Kyrgyzstan, and Uzbekistan established a more limited Central Asian Economic Union; it was expanded to include Tajikistan in March 1998.

Disarticulation from Russia was not offset by adherence to other political blocs, although the new states were ready to join bodies with religious, cultural or economic bases. Examples of each of these are, respectively, the Organization of the Islamic Conference, the UNESCO Silk Road Program, and the EU-sponsored Transport Corridor Europe-Central Asia (TRACECA). All five have joined NATO's program of Partnerships for Peace.

Paths to Nation-building

The variant legacies of past Russian colonialism and Soviet all-Union planning underlie the differences in the relationships between these five countries and Russia since independence. Each of the five has also had its own individual experience in creating a state where previously there had been a single "Soviet" citizenship for nearly 70 years.

Before the 1917 revolutions, Slavs from elsewhere in the Russian empire had long migrated into Central Asia, to take part in administration, military operations, mining, or industrial and agricultural development. Migration continued for the same purposes under Soviet rule, and the internal passports introduced by Stalin, which identified their holders by one of the 130 or so Soviet nationalities, permitted settlement anywhere within Soviet borders (with some exceptions, such as residence in certain urban areas). However, very many others were transported there involuntarily, or under the system of labor direction. Already in the 1930s, political prisoners were sent to the remote mining areas of Kazakhstan, and more were shipped to all parts of Central Asia until the amnesties of 1956. The heaviest influx, however, was of entire national groups suspected or accused of disloyalty: Koreans from the Soviet Far East; Germans from the Volga region; Tatars from Crimea; Kalmyks, Chechens, and Ingush from the Northern Caucasus; and Meskhetians from Georgia. After Stalin's death in 1953, they were gradually permitted to return to their home regions, but in many cases their former land and houses had been seized by others, and there was nowhere for them to go. Georgia, for example, refused to accept the Meskhetians, Ukraine made many difficulties for Tatars, Ossetians had taken Ingush land, and Russians had settled the historic homeland of the Volga Germans.

Following Stalin as Soviet leader, Nikita Khrushchev sought to remedy the food shortage induced by forced collectivization by establishing state farms, with youthful Slav volunteers, on the semiarid steppes, under the "Virgin Lands" campaign. From 1954 until the campaign was abandoned in 1956, 35 million hectares were put under cultivation, but many settlers left when much of the land, subject to wind erosion when plowed, became a dust bowl. Those who remained added substantially to the Russian population of northern and central Kazakhstan.

It was perhaps inevitable that members of the eponymous nationalities would take the leading positions in central and local government after independence, and that immigrants – whatever the length or manner of their establishment – would feel insecure. Violence against them was very rare – about 100 people died in an Uzbek riot against Meskhetians in June 1989 – but, as the 1989 census (quoted above) showed, residents not of the titular nationality were in the range of 60% of those enumerated in Kazakhstan and 28%

of those in Tajikistan. A degree of homogenization ensued. Between 1989 and 1995, 1.45 million Russians left the five republics, and 245,000 Germans emigrated from ex-Soviet countries, mostly these same republics. The civil war in Tajikistan and traditional mutual suspicion between Uzbeks and Tajiks also led to the repatriation of many Uzbeks. Indeed, by 1995 that immigration and the tapering down of Russian emigration swung the migration balance of Uzbekistan from negative to positive.

Nevertheless, more was needed for sound nation-building than changes in ethnic proportions, although what was specifically required depended on the recent history of each country. Besides perpetrating the mass deaths of Kazakhs in the denomadization of the 1930s, the Soviet authorities had minimized Kazakh culture. The two experiences reinforced each other, for Kazakh culture had been tied to nomadism, and the cities of the 19th century and the first half of the 20th century were Russian creations. In Uzbekistan, on the other hand, Soviet policy had been to accentuate an Uzbek self-identity in the countryside, where the peasants had formerly been known as Sarts, not as Uzbeks, to compensate for urban cultures that were Russian in Tashkent, and Tajik in Bokhara and Samarkand. In the four republics of predominantly Turkic stock, a single powerful leader undertook the task of nation-building, but the state of Iranian stock, Tajikistan, remains weak and cruelly divided.

Regional Differentiation within the Five States

Whatever the power radiating from the capital city in each of the five states, it is counterbalanced by regional or clan loyalties. The differentiation has often been traced to "tribes" or "clans," but the affinity may better be described as by lineage, because, while some groups are defined by genealogy, others are related by place of origin. Lineage is politically significant everywhere, but especially in Tajikistan and Turkmenistan. President Karimov has launched a powerful attack on it in Uzbekistan; private sector managers find it constraining in Kazakhstan; and large Slav minorities, as well as the penetration of Russian market forces, have offset its impact in Kazakhstan and Kyrgyzstan. In Kazakhstan, Kyrgyzstan, and Turkmenistan, where the terrain is relatively uniform, it may broadly be described as "clannish," while in Uzbekistan and Tajikistan oases, river basins, and mountain-hemmed valleys have dictated groupings that are specifically regional but enhanced by lineage affinities.

In Kazakhstan, there are three lineage divisions, referred to by the term *zhuz*, which means "part" or "portion" but is commonly translated as "Horde," in reference to their common origins in Genghis Khan's Golden Horde. The Big or Senior Horde occupies the South and West, with Almaty, the former capital, as its chief city; the Middle Horde occupies a North-South belt in the middle of the country, centered on the city known as Aqmola until it was inaugurated as the new national capital, under the name Astana, in June 1998; and the Little or Junior Horde occupies the Northwest and West. There is a further sub-lineage group that distinguishes those who claim descent from Genghis Khan himself, but this has no economic or territorial significance. As throughout the former Soviet Union, bribery and corruption permeate the quasiliberalized economy, and they are reinforced by affinity linkages, but Kazakh heads of businesses have expressed frustration at having to take account of clan rivalries for appointments within enterprises, and in allocating contracts and orders.

Kyrgyzstan is divided into two regions. The North contains the national capital, Bishkek, most of the industry and hydroelectric power, the sugar beet area, and the sole major tourist zone, Lake Ysyk-Köl. It is also President Akayev's home region. The South occupies part of the Fergana (or Farghona) Valley and a mountainous region shared with three enclaves of Uzbekistan. It was the home of Absamat Masaliev, the Kyrgyz Communist Party leader whom Akayev displaced in 1990.

The quadripartite division of Uzbekistan has particularly exercised President Karimov. He is especially sensitive to minority issues, not only because of the large number of Tajiks in his territory, but also because he took office as leader of the Uzbek Communist Party in June 1989, at the time of the riots against Meskhetians (mentioned above). There were further disturbances, arising from protests against the economic shock of price rises and cuts in social benefits in January 1992, early in his first term as President of independent Uzbekistan. Over the next four years, he replaced all but one of the 13 regional leaders (*hokim*) with persons whom he judged loyal to him. In a book published in 1997, he devoted chapters to "Religious Extremism and Fundamentalism" and to "Regionalism and Clans." The background to the first involves the underground Islamic Renaissance Party and the growing strength of fundamentalism in the Fergana Valley. In the second, he contrasted the "powerful repressive machinery" and the "thick veil of silence" that had obscured "conflicts caused by the rival interests of opposing clans" during the Soviet period with the present overtness of "separatist trends in the regions [that] pose a real threat to the integrity of the state" (Karimov pp. 59–66). The Fergana Valley is potentially the most dissident of the five regions, for Namangan is the focus of Islamic fundamentalism, and the division of the Valley among three republics has created numerous external and internal minorities.

In Turkmenistan, President Niyazov has such complete control that no regional political divergence is allowed. As "Leader of the Turkmen," he has among his advisers representatives of the main geographical regions and tribal groups, although in all there are around 30 tribes and more than 1,000 clans. The Tekke occupy central Turkmenistan, with the capital, Ashgabat (Ashkhabad in Russian), as their main city, and they are the community of President Niyazov himself. Their region has become the site of much infrastructure investment, including luxury hotels, great monuments, and a large mosque at Geok Tepe, commemorating the historic last battle with the Russian army in 1881, in which 14,500 Tekke were killed. The Yomud occupy the Caspian Sea littoral and are potentially the richest, due to their oil deposits and their location on the lines of transit between Kazakhstan, Iran, and Azerbaijan, by rail, sea, and pipeline. The

Saryk, who occupy the East, were economically the most favored in the Soviet period, when the Karakum Canal opened the region to intensive cotton-growing. The East also has commercial promise in a vast gas deposit, to be exploited for sale in Pakistan and possibly in India, and in a proposed new rail link with Iran. By contrast, the Ersary are the poorest group, occupying the mountainous zone towards the frontier with Afghanistan. Their Dashhowuz region is isolated from the rest of the country by desert, and has been badly affected by the drying of the Aral Sea and the salination of former cotton areas.

In Tajikistan since 1992, civil war, the irruptions of warlords, and roving criminal gangs have destroyed what little economic unity the country once had. The central zone, which is directly administered by the national government, and includes the capital city, Dushanbe, and the region of Gharm, has had widely differing experiences from those of the country's three other regions. Dushanbe was founded by Russian settlers, and it remained a strongly Russian city until their mass exodus in 1992–93; there was an industrial base and substantial generation of hydroelectricity brought a large aluminum smelter. Gharm has a very entrepreneurial population but few resources apart from agriculture: it was the main supplier of grain and vegetables, especially potatoes, to the rest of the country. The Gharmis took advantage of agrarian reform in 1996 to set up small private farms. The elite of the Leninobod region (Leninabad in Russian) – still so called, although the regional capital has reverted to the name Khujand – virtually monopolized the leading political offices in the Soviet period: every First Party Secretary since World War II was born in Khujand or nearby. Most Soviet industrialization was concentrated in the region, partly because of ease of transportation from and into Uzbekistan, and then to the rest of the Soviet Union. Külob, in contrast, had little to export other than cotton, and its capital, Qürghon Teppa, was the center of fierce fighting between the established population, many of them Uzbeks, and the Gharmis brought into the valley of the Vakhsh, a tributary of the Amu Darya, to cultivate cotton in the 1960s. War

devastation now ranks it as the poorest region of the country. Finally, the Autonomous Region of Badakhshoni Kuni is mostly high barren mountain, but has unexploited minerals and hydroelectricity. It was frequently cut off from the rest of Tajikistan because the single road to its capital, Khorugh, hugs the frontier with Afghanistan, and was often closed by fighting. The Aga Khan Foundation supports Ismaili coreligionists in agricultural development, and there is a certain revival of Zoroastrianism.

The Economies of Central Asia

Resources

Throughout the history of Central Asia, economic life reflected the mode of food production – arable farming based on adequate rain and snow, and a minimum of frost-free days, in the North; oasis, irrigated, and high-insolation agriculture in the South, where cotton has long been the principal crop; and arable cultivation, mixed with stockbreeding nomadism, and transhumance between them in the highland East. This three-way division still constitutes the basic regional differentiation of the five countries as a group, but each is overlaid by the differential impact of industrialization, widely initiated by the evacuation of plant from regions threatened by the Nazi invasion of 1941, and pursued during the Cold War also as being remote from potential attack.

Industrialization has centered on extraction of Central Asia's varied mineral resources (see also Chapter 10). The state with the broadest array of minerals is Kazakhstan, ranging from fossil fuels through base metals to rare and precious ores. Merely to list the metals indicates the country's long-term potential: barite, beryllium, bismuth, chromite, copper, gold, iron, lead, manganese, silver, tantalum, titanium, uranium, wolfram, and zinc. Their extraction and processing declined after independence, because demand fell in the rest of the former Soviet Union, and in the post-Communist countries of central and east Europe. However, following privatization, strategic investors from abroad have engaged in extensive restructuring and new investment, notably for chrome in Aqtöbe (Aktyubinsk in Russian), iron, steel, and coke in Qaraghandy (Karaganda), and copper in Zhezqazghan (Zhezkagan). The US oil corporation Chevron was invited into a joint venture to exploit the new Tengiz deposit even before the Soviet Union was dissolved. Joined later by other western corporations, and one Russian firm, they will export substantial quantities when a pipeline is built by the Caspian Pipeline Consortium to the Russian Black Sea oil port of Novorossisk. A group of western corporations, the leading Russian firm Gazprom, and the Kazakh utility are jointly exploiting the large Karachaganak gas deposits, output from which feeds into the Russian pipeline network supplying former Soviet states, as well as eastern, western and southern Europe.

Kyrgyzstan, too, has an impressive range of minerals – including antimony, arsenic, gypsum, lead, mercury, and uranium – but its biggest export earner is gold. The Kumtor deposit is estimated to be the world's eighth largest (comprising 516 tons, of which 290 tones are to be extracted between 1996 and 2015). Operations are in the hands of a joint venture by the Kyrgyz government and Cameco of Canada.

Uzbekistan, similarly, gains significant income from joint ventures in goldmining. At Zarafshan the foreign partner is the Newmont Mining Company of the United States, which entered the partnership even before the breakup of the Soviet Union; at Amantaytau the partner is the UK corporation Lonrho; and at Angren, which has the country's largest reserves (160 tons), Mitsui of Japan and Newmont are both participants. Other minerals in Uzbekistan are copper, fluorspar, lead, molybdenum, uranium, wolfram, and zinc.

Turkmenistan must rely for future foreign earnings on its oil and natural gas, but all exports go into the Russian pipeline system, apart from a little of each sold to neighboring Iran. An ambitious scheme to lay pipelines for natural gas, and later for oil, through Afghanistan, to supply Pakistan and India, has been elaborated by the US corporation Unocal, to the point of training Afghan workers, but its realization awaits agreement on long-term security. Oil pipelines under the

Caspian Sea to Baku in Azerbaijan, or through Iran for the Persian Gulf, are under consideration by the governments concerned. The US government has warned Turkmenistan and other Caspian states against greater cooperation with Iran, but has accepted the proposed transit of Turkmen gas through Iran for sale to Turkish – and possibly Balkan – consumers. Turkmenistan also has deposits of bromine, iodine, strontium, and sulfur.

Recent hostilities and persistent insecurity still limit the mining and processing of Tajik natural resources, which include bismuth, boron, columbium, copper, gold, lead, mercury, molybdenum, silver, tantalum, wolfram, and zinc. Soviet planning placed a large aluminum works at Tursunzade, to valorize the hydroelectricity generated in the Vakhsh Valley and elsewhere, but it had to rely on imported bauxite and – like one of the two operational gold mines (Devaz, jointly run with a UK firm) – it was shut down for long periods during the civil war. Another gold mine, at Zeravshan in the peaceful Leninobod region, is operated in a joint venture with Nelson Gold of Canada, and furnishes some export earnings.

Two states in Central Asia have interests in the oil and natural gas deposits under the Caspian Sea. Those offshore from Kazakhstan are the southernmost extension of the Volga-Urals sedimentary basin in Russia, while those offshore from Turkmenistan form part of a basin of which the western limits are under Grozny, in the breakaway Russian republic of Chechnya, and Baku. An undersea area between the two basins is unlikely to yield hydrocarbons. The rights of the five littoral states have become a source of political contention, and a solution proposed by Russia and Kazakhstan in March 1998 awaits multilateral agreement.

Another unsolved problem is the control and allocation of water, an essential component of farming and urban life in the arid regions. In April 1992, the five governments established an Interstate Coordinating Commission on Water Management, but the fundamental conflict between upstream states generating hydroelectricity and those downstream dependent on irrigation awaits settlement (Rumer pp. 268–9). Excessive use of water for ornamental fountains and gardens in Ashgabat has created water shortages for Turkmen farmers.

The Shocks of Economic Change

Each of the five states of Central Asia was affected on independence by a series of economic shocks, compensation for which took time. To begin with, they inherited economies more open to foreign trade than corresponding market economies at similar incomes per capita. In 1988, the sum of imports and exports as a share of GNP was 34% in Kazakhstan, 39% each in Turkmenistan and Uzbekistan, 42% in Tajikistan, and 45% in Kyrgyzstan, while according to the World Bank the average for "low income" countries is 35%. They were thus vulnerable to shocks transmitted through trade, in their cases from the collapse in supplies and demand in the post-Communist countries with which they predominantly traded. The shock arrived at a period when the Soviet economic mechanism was being dismantled, and mechanisms to support and regulate the private sector were not yet in place. In particular, the centralized financial system of the former Soviet Union had substantially supplemented republican revenues. Requirements for expenditure were more constant, and the newly independent ministries of finance were immediately confronted with large budget deficits.

Because the Russian ruble continued to circulate throughout Central Asia until 1993, and in Tajikistan until 1995, the five states had to follow Russia's lead, and removed controls on nearly all retail and wholesale prices within one month of Russia's removal of them on January 2, 1992. Demand that had been long pent up pushed prices into a rapid inflation, which could be little checked by the evocation of more supplies, for trade relations with other ex-Soviet states were disrupted, and there was insufficient domestic capacity. As prices rose and budget deficits widened, the recently established central banks created ruble credits to facilitate government payments, and to respond to the calls for liquidity by new commercial banks, which at the time were still state-owned. Inflation in 1992, the first full year of independence, reached 1,504% in Kazakhstan, and 855% in Kyrgyzstan – each

influenced by their predominant economic orientation toward Russia, where inflation was 1,529% – but it was still high in Tajikistan, at 822%, and in Turkmenistan, at 770%. In Uzbekistan, however, remaining price controls and an ingenious scheme of entitlements to basic household necessities kept inflation down to 415%. The governments of Turkmenistan and Uzbekistan also set limits to the response of market forces by adopting suspicious attitudes to petty traders and slowing the pace of privatization (Pomfret p. 98).

Stabilization with New Currencies

It was Russian inflation that bore the brunt of the creation of ruble credits by central banks in the CIS. The IMF tried in vain to help the CIS countries make a single currency operate effectively until 1993, when it made a loan under its first Systemic Transformation Facility to Russia conditional on the restriction of the monetary issue to the point at which the exchange rate of the ruble to the US dollar would appreciate. This set in place an "exchange rate anchor" for macroeconomic stability, but a consequence was that the issue of rubles by banks elsewhere in the CIS would have to be determined in Moscow. Only Tajikistan, where the beleaguered government was wholly dependent on Russian support, accepted that condition, and retained the Russian currency until May 1995, when it issued its own ruble; the four others took steps to set up independent currencies. The Kyrgyz som appeared in May 1993, and the Kazakh tenge, the Turkmen manat, and the Uzbek sum in November. The advice and support of the IMF were decisive in diminishing the rate of inflation in Kyrgyzstan and – via the Russian ruble – Tajikistan: during 1994 their rates were respectively 278% and 350%, while Russia's was 309%. The states which delayed or declined linkage with the IMF experienced hyperinflation in 1994, at levels worse than in any other year after independence year: 1,550% in Uzbekistan, 1,880% in Kazakhstan, and as much as 2,714% in Turkmenistan.

Policies for monetary stabilization and market liberalization, inspired by the IMF, subsequently moderated inflation in Kazakhstan and Kyrgyzstan in 1997, to 17% and 26% respectively. Each government was confident enough to make its currency convertible (both on current account, the latter also on capital account). Each was assured further support for both budgets and the external account by the IMF, and Kazakhstan enjoyed substantial foreign direct investment, mostly into its hydrocarbon industries, amounting to US$2.9 billion in 1997 alone. Uzbekistan forfeited IMF support in October 1996, when poor cotton and grain harvests, presaging, respectively, lower exports and higher imports, led it to impose exchange controls, which are due to be lifted in 2000. It showed inflation at 73% in 1997. Turkmenistan, where President Niyazov has steered clear of commitments to the IMF, had inflation of 84% in 1997, and in Tajikistan, where a fragile peace had emerged only in the course of the year, inflation was at 85%.

Output under the Continuing Influence of Russia

The year 1996 was a turning point in relations between the five states and Russia, for it was then that the sum of their imports and exports with CIS partners fell below half. The decline in exchanges with these other countries, notably with Russia, but also with the states in central and eastern Europe that had once been members of Comecon, was a prime cause of the collapse of industrial production. This contributed, especially in Kazakhstan and Kyrgyzstan, to reducing GNP to well below late Soviet levels (see Tables 7.1 and 7.2).

However, employment was much less affected, and in 1997 it was generally close to or above the levels recorded in 1989. The contrast arises partly because agricultural output held up better, and because decollectivization did not result in any significant shift of the rural population, although private small-holdings have become the norm in Tajikistan and Uzbekistan. In 1997 and 1998, aggregate output in all five countries was still well below that of 1989.

The welfare derived from lower outputs may, however, be better overall than in the "shortage economy" of Soviet times, because the goods and services supplied, whether domestically and imported, conform to market-expressed demand. The Soviet ethos of "production at all costs" also occasioned considerable environmental damage, exemplified in Central Asia by the drying up of the Aral Sea, the closure of the noxious antimony mines in Kyrgyzstan, and the fluorosis induced downwind in Uzbekistan by lack of filtration at the Tursunzade aluminum plant in Tajikistan.

The gap between the richest and the poorest in the countries of Central Asia has significantly widened following the privatization of state enterprises, and the emergence of much unregulated financial and trade activity. Opportunities for corruption, and the production and trade of narcotics, have put illicit gains in the hands of a few. The social safety net is lower and more porous than in Soviet times, and poverty is becoming a serious problem. In Kyrgyzstan, for example, a sample survey conducted in 1993 indicated that 53% of the population were in "severe poverty," based on their money incomes and benefits (Falkingham et al. p.86).

The Russian financial crisis of August 1998 had effects on the Central Asian economies that are taking time to work through. The sharp devaluation of the ruble against the US dollar, from R6.00 at the start of the year to R22.00 by the end, was much greater than in the case of the other main currencies of the region. Devaluation ranged from the strong Kazakh tenge (from KT78.00 to KT84.00) to the weak Uzbek sum (from UzS200 to UzS465 at the unofficial rate). Goods from Central Asia were rendered less competitive than domestic supplies in Russian markets, but Russian goods became cheaper in Central Asia. The renewed decline in Russian economic activity, signaled by a fall in GDP of 5% and a resurgence of inflation to 84%, has put pressure on governments and businesses to turn increasingly to outside partners for exports. However, Kazakhstan and Turkmenistan, which rely on oil and gas for future earnings, are having to contemplate the continuation of low prices for their sales, and a slackening of the inflow of foreign investment. Turkmenistan and Uzbekistan, which have cotton as their principal export (it accounted for 36% of Uzbek exports in 1996 and 1997), have experienced declining crops and lower world prices. To these countries in their first years of independence, after emerging from captivity within the centrally planned Soviet Union, the world economy has not been kind.

Further Reading

Akiner, Shirin, *The Formation of Kazakh Identity: From Tribe to Nation-State*, London: Royal Institute of International Affairs, 1995

This summary history of the Kazakh people and language includes an analysis of the post-Soviet balance between "Westernizer" and Moslem conformities, in which the nomadic tradition is evoked against tendencies to Islamic fundamentalism.

Carr, E. H., *The Bolshevik Revolution 1917–1923*, Volume 3, London: Macmillan, 1953

Carr's 14 volumes, under the collective title *A History of Soviet Russia*, cover political and economic history between 1917 and 1929.

Davies, Robert W., *The Industrialization of Soviet Russia*, in progress, with four volumes published so far, London: Macmillan, and Cambridge, MA: Harvard University Press, various dates

Davies takes up the economic history of the Soviet Union where Carr stopped, in 1929.

Ellis, C. H., "Operations in Transcaspia 1918–1919 and the 26 Commissars' Case," in *St Antony's Papers*, number 6, London: Chatto and Windus, 1959

The definitive study, by a participating officer, of British military intervention in Russian Turkestan at the time of the Bolshevik Revolution

Falkingham, Jane, Jeni Klugman, Sheila Marnie, and John Micklewright, editors, *Household Welfare in Central Asia*, London: Macmillan, and New York: St Martin's Press, 1997

Fifteen contributors report on social surveys that reveal the extent of poverty, inadequate nutrition and labor market conditions, mainly in Kazakhstan and Uzbekistan.

Hopkirk, Peter, *The Great Game: On Secret Service in High Asia*, London: John Murray, 1990; Oxford and New York: Oxford University Press, 1991 and 1997

As well as being a highly readable account of 19th-century forays and conquests by the British and the Russians in Central Asia, the book lists nearly 300 publications on the topic.

Jonson, Lena, *Russia and Central Asia: A New Web of Relations*, London: Royal Institute of International Affairs, 1998

Lena Jonson considers the realignment of political and economic relations that followed the breakup of the Soviet Union, and demonstrates the weakening of cultural and economic ties between Central Asia and Russia, as well as the unreceptiveness of governments to Russian proposals for political and military alliances.

Karimov, Islam, *Uzbekistan on the Threshold of the 21st Century*, London: Curzon, 1997

This is a translation into English of the President's wide-ranging program for combating religious and ethnic extremism, regional rivalries, and ecological damage, and establishing a national identity, a supportive social policy, and economic growth in his country.

Kumar, Narendra, *President Akaev of Kyrghyzstan: A Political Biography*, New Delhi: Har-Anand Publications, 1998

The authorized biography of the Kyrgyz President, by an Indian journalist, this book covers his personal career, his scientific research in optics and related engineering, and his expectations for the 21st century.

Maddison, Angus, *Economic Growth in Japan and the USSR*, London: Allen and Unwin, and New York: Norton, 1969

A detailed compilation and comparison of the national products of the two countries between 1913 and 1965; subsequent work has somewhat modified the relativities shown.

Manas, translated by Walter May, two volumes, Moscow and Bishkek: Kirgiz National Commission for UNESCO, 1995

This is an excessively colloquial translation (omitting the erotic passages) of the national epic of the Turkic Central Asian nomads, handed down and supplemented over a millennium by Kyrgyz bards, but not put in written form until the 1850s.

Parker, William H., *An Historical Geography of Russia*, London: University of London Press, and Chicago, IL: Aldine Publishing, 1968

Central Asia is considered only after its incorporation into the Russian empire, but the description of all parts of the former Soviet Union includes the economy and demography of the region up to the early 1960s. The extensive bibliography concentrates on the Slav-settled areas.

Pomfret, Richard, *Asian Economies in Transition: Reforming Centrally Planned Economies*, Cheltenham and Brookfield, VT: Edward Elgar, 1996

A collection of studies on all the Asian transition economies, including one on the five states of Central Asia and another on their replacement of the ruble with national currencies

Rumer, Boris, and Stanislav Zhukov, editors, *Central Asia: The Challenges of Independence*, Armonk, NY: M. E. Sharpe, 1998

Eleven papers, six by the editors themselves, devoted largely to the economies of Central Asia, especially of the two largest, Kazakhstan and Uzbekistan, with reference to domestic performance, international trade, foreign investment, and agrarian reform

UN Economic Commission for Europe, *Economic Survey of Europe in 1996–1997*, New York and Geneva: United Nations, 1997

Chapter 4, "The Central Asian Economies 1991–1996," is a sequel to the Commission's first economic analysis of the region (in *Economic Bulletin for Europe*, Volume 9, number 3, November 1957), which still bears reexamination for its light on Soviet regional economic policy. The chapter considers the problems of marketizing the previously centrally planned and subsidized economies, their evolution since independence, and their prospects for the future.

Webber, Mark, *CIS Integration Trends: Russia and the Former Soviet South*, London: Royal Institute of International Affairs, 1997

Webber examines the early political and strategic disintegration of the CIS, up to 1994, and the subsequent process of stabilization and reintegration. Each of the countries in Central Asia and Transcaucasia is treated, and measures of military, economic and political cooperation are reviewed.

Periodicals

A number of international organizations publish current analyses and statistics on a regular basis.

The NIS/TACIS service of the European Commission (the executive body of the EU) publishes quarterly *Economic Trends* for Kazakhstan and Uzbekistan, compiled by national teams collaborating with research institutions in an EU state. The IMF publishes a *Staff Country Report* after mission visits; titles are listed, as they are published, in the fortnightly *IMF Survey*, which also summarizes agreements reached with member states, and furnishes economic context and forecasts. The UN Economic Commission for Europe (in Geneva) publishes three times a year an *Economic Survey of Europe*, containing analyses of developments in all its member states, together with extensive statistical provision; it also publishes *Trends in Europe and North America*, a statistical abstract of economic and social data for 55 states in more readily comparable form for transition economies than the larger *United Nations Statistical Yearbook*. Last, but far from least, the European Bank for Reconstruction and Development (in London) produces an annual *Transition Report*, also with authoritative analyses and its own statistics and forecasts. This appears in October/November, and in advance of its annual general meeting in April there are both a general *Update* and, for each of its countries of operation, an annual *Country Profile*. These profiles are directed to businesses.

Businesses also form the main target audience for the quarterly *Country Reports* and annual *Country Profiles* of the Economist Intelligence Unit, and for monthlies such as *New Markets Monthly* and *Russia Express: Reporting the Republics of the Former Soviet Union* (Monmouth, Gwent). Shorter notes on a range of developments in each country are published in *ABREES* and *Central Asia Newsfile*. All these private sector publications are British, and are issued in London, except as shown.

Michael Kaser is Emeritus Fellow of St Antony's College and Reader Emeritus in Economics in the University of Oxford, and Honorary Professor at the Institute for German Studies in the University of Birmingham in England. Among his many books and articles on the former Soviet Union and the CIS countries are *Soviet Economics* (London: Weidenfeld and Nicolson, 1970), *Privatization in the CIS* (London: Royal Institute of International Affairs, 1995), and *The Economies of Kazakhstan and Uzbekistan* (London: Royal Institute of International Affairs, 1997). He was a coeditor of *The Cambridge Encyclopedia of Russia and the Former Soviet Union* (Cambridge and New York: Cambridge University Press, 1994).

Table 7.1   Real GNP in the Five States of Central Asia, 1990–97 (1989 = 100)

	1990	1991	1992	1993	1994	1995	1996	1997
Kazakhstan	99.0	88.1	83.4	75.8	66.2	60.8	61.1	62.3
Kyrgyzstan	104.8	96.5	83.1	70.3	56.2	53.1	56.9	62.5
Tajikistan	100.2	91.7	63.3	53.0	41.7	35.6	30.4	30.9
Turkmenistan	101.8	97.0	82.5	83.7	69.7	64.4	64.4	54.8
Uzbekistan	99.2	98.7	87.7	85.7	81.2	80.5	81.9	86.1

Source: UN Economic Commission for Europe

Table 7.2   Real Gross Industrial Output in the Five States of Central Asia, 1990–97 (1989 = 100)

	1990	1991	1992	1993	1994	1995	1996	1997
Kazakhstan	99.2	98.3	84.7	72.2	51.9	47.7	47.8	49.7
Kyrgyzstan	99.4	99.1	72.9	54.5	39.2	32.2	35.1	52.8
Tajikistan	101.2	97.6	73.9	68.1	50.8	43.9	33.4	32.6
Turkmenistan	103.2	108.2	92.0	95.7	72.1	67.5	79.5	55.7
Uzbekistan	101.8	103.3	96.4	99.9	101.5	101.6	107.7	114.7

Source: UN Economic Commission for Europe

Chapter Eight

The Three Caucasian States

Michael Kaser

For two of the Caucasian states, Armenia and Georgia, national identities had been formed as early as the fourth century by conversion to Christianity. Their religious affiliation soon had to be defended against pressure from their southern, Islamic neighbors. It was retained, through national language, social forms, and culture, throughout the centuries, and after they were conquered by imperial Russia around the start of the 19th century.

Azerbaijan, in contrast, was historically torn between the Ottoman and Persian empires, until it was divided in 1828 between Persia and Russia, at the line of the river known to the ancient Greeks as the Araxes but as the Araz in Azeri, and as the Aras in Armenian, where it forms part of the frontier with Turkey. The autonomy which the local rulers, the khans, had previously enjoyed had, however, established a strong sense of Azeri nationality on both sides of the frontier. In 1946, the western powers, through the newly created UN, frustrated attempts by the Soviet government to annex Iranian Azerbaijan, where the Tudeh Party canalized democratic and Azeri nationalist opposition to the Shah into a favorable attitude to the Soviet Union.

Under Russian rule, Azerbaijan broadened its ethnic mix at the end of the 19th century. The Nobel brothers from Sweden made Baku, its capital, the world's largest supplier of oil, through a pipeline to the Georgian Black Sea port of Batumi, and Slavs and Armenians immigrated to service the economic boom. Azeris had scant share in that prosperity: in the enterprises owned by the Nobels, for example, Christians outnumbered Moslems (Garskova and Akhanchi p. 182). Ethnic antipathies surfaced during the unrest that followed the Revolution in Russia in 1905, when Azeris rioted against Armenians.

In the wake of the Revolutions of 1917, the three nations declared their independence. Transiently united in a Democratic Federal Republic of Transcaucasia, they each created their own states in May 1918. They were briefly protected by British troops sent to guard supply lines to Persia and India against the Bolsheviks, who had withdrawn Russia from the war against Germany and Turkey. Left to themselves, Azerbaijan fell to Russian revolutionary forces in April 1920, Armenia in the following November, and Georgia in February 1921. The three states were formed into a Transcaucasian Soviet Federative Socialist Republic which became a founder member of the Soviet Union in 1922, but each reverted to a separate status as a Union Republic under the Soviet Constitution of 1936. Further admixtures of population took place, for similar economic reasons, as the three states were industrialized under the Soviet Five-year Plans.

A Turbulent Rebirth of Historical States

By the time of the Soviet census of 1989 (the last to date), the states had been little affected by Russian immigration, but contained shares of each other's peoples. The population of Armenia was 93% Armenian, 3% Azeri, and less than 2% Russian, alongside Ukrainians, Greeks, and Assyrians. Azerbaijan comprised 83% Azeris, 6% Armenians, and 6% Russians, alongside Georgians, Kurds, Jews, and Turks. Georgia, meanwhile, enumerated 70% Georgians, 8% Armenians, and 6% Russians, with smaller numbers of Ossetians, Abkhazians, Greeks, Ukrainians, Jews, and Kurds.

By 1989, ethnic tolerance, once enforced in the name of "socialist internationalism," was already weakening in parallel with the dissolution of the Communist Party's monopoly on power and of the repressive machinery of the centralized Soviet state. Religious and nationalist antipathies between Armenia and Azerbaijan had been exacerbated at the very start of Soviet rule. In 1921, Josef Stalin, then People's Commissar for Nationalities, allocated Nagorno-Karabakh, a region largely populated by Armenians, to become an enclave wholly within Azerbaijan, albeit with "autonomous" status. He also allocated Nakhichevan, an Azeri-populated district of Armenia, to be made into an enclave of Azerbaijan, physically separated from the rest of that country by eastern Armenia. In February 1988, Karabakh (known to Armenians as Karabagh or Artsakh) provided the first explosion of ethnic violence when Soviet political control was relaxed by the *perestroika* (restructuring) of Mikhail Gorbachev (1985–91). Anti-Armenian riots, in which there were 32 deaths, occurred in one city in Azerbaijan, Sumgait (Sumqayit in Azeri), in February 1988. They arose from protests against the decision of the Karabakh legislature to press for the region to be transferred to Armenia. The Soviet government of Azerbaijan responded by disbanding the Karabakh authorities, but after the Armenian Supreme Soviet had approved the transfer – even though the All-Union Supreme Soviet had denounced it – the Armenian government afforded informal military and supply support for the Karabakh rebels. The Karabakh militia not only gained control of their region and expelled the Azeri population, but gained the Lachin corridor, linking the enclave to Armenia proper. After prolonged international mediation during intermittent hostilities, all parties agreed a ceasefire in July 1994. The frontiers between the two countries remain closed, and the Nakhichevan enclave has land communication with its metropolis only via Iran.

Georgia was the first Union Republic to declare its independence from the Soviet Union, in April 1991, followed by Armenia in September and Azerbaijan in October. In each country, the relatively free elections after independence was declared were decisive in displaying support for strongly nationalist candidates. Zviad Gamsakhurdia was elected President of Georgia in May 1991, with 86% of the votes cast; Levon Ter-Petrosian was elected President of Armenia in October 1991, winning 87% of the votes; and Abulfaz Elchibey was elected President of Azerbaijan in June 1992, obtaining 55% of the votes. Hostilities in all three states nevertheless offered poor conditions for strengthening democracy.

In Georgia, Gamsakhurdia was scarcely established constitutionally as President when he was accused of seeking a dictatorship. In January 1992, he was compelled to flee when Tbilisi, the capital of Georgia, was captured by two paramilitary forces, the National Guard under Tengiz Kitovani and the Mkhedrioni Knights (or Horsemen) under Dzhaba Ioseliani (Aves p. 177). During the ensuing civil war, Gamsakhurdia was killed, reportedly by his own hand, in November 1993. Kitovani and Ioseliani, together with a former Prime Minister, Tengiz Sigua, vainly tried to reconcile the rebel factions, to regain control of breakaway provinces, and to staunch crime, drug trafficking, and banditry.

Georgia includes five regions in which separatist movements have appeared since the collapse of the Soviet system. Three are ethnically divergent. Two of these, Abkhazia and South Ossetia, have declared themselves independent, and have elected their own presidents, but they have failed to obtain any international recognition. A new Georgian Prime Minister, Vazha Lortkipanidze, who came to office in August 1998, has declared his priority to be a settlement with them as autonomous entities. The UN has an Observer Mission in the country (UNOMIG), while Russia and the OSCE have been assisting in mediation. A third region, Mengrelia, the former core of support for Gamsakhurdia, has been reintegrated. The other two regions, Adzharia and Javakhetia, are religiously divergent: their ethnically Georgian populations were converted to Islam under Turkish rule. They are both now virtually autonomous under the protection of Russian garrisons (see Kurbanov, and also Akıncı). The majority of Georgian Moslems live in Adzharia, in loose but peaceful communion with Tbilisi, under its President Aslan Abashidze, grandson of the chairman of the legislature of semi-independent Adzharia in 1918–21. The Moslems in Javakhetia, known as Meskhetians, are Sunni (most of the Moslems in the Caucasus follow the Shi'a tradition). In 1944, when they numbered around 100,000, they were deported by Stalin, mostly to Uzbekistan. When around 70,000 of these Sunni Moslems fled violence against them in Uzbekistan, in June 1989, 46,000 of them took refuge in Azerbaijan, the only Moslem country apart from Iran with a Shi'ite majority. Meanwhile, their original homeland in Georgia had been taken by Armenians, who now number 55% of the region's population, alongside Georgians (30%) and Russians (5%). The clashes between Meskhetians and Uzbeks have made the government of Uzbekistan anxious to return the forced settlers to their pre-1944 homes, but this is opposed by the Armenians now on their land. Any deterioration in relations between Georgia and Armenia could provoke irredentism in Javakhetia – a danger of more than local significance, because the routes of a new railway and of a proposed oil pipeline to Turkey lie through its central valley.

Against such fissiparity must be set a profound sense of identity among the eponymous nationalities of the three Caucasian states. The liberalization of the practice of religion has enhanced the public demonstration of the respective expressions of Orthodox Christianity, under the Catholicos-Patriarch of All Georgia, Iliya II; of Monophysite Christianity, under the Catholicos of All Armenians, Supreme Patriarch Garegin II; and of Islam, under the Moslem Board of Transcaucasia, chaired by Sheikh Allashukur Pashezade. The latter is a Shi'ite, but there is a Sunni Deputy Chairman. The Caucasian conflicts have been perceived as religious wars only by a minority, and contrary to the declarations of various religious leaders.

Separate alphabets have always distinguished the Armenian and Georgian languages from Russian, which uses the Cyrillic alphabet. Azeri was written in the Arabic alphabet until 1930, but Cyrillic was adopted for Azeri at the same time as it was introduced for writing the other Turkic languages in the Soviet Union (mainly in Central Asia). At independence, a return to the Arabic alphabet was mooted, but the decision went in favor of the Roman alphabet instead, in a form close to, but not identical with, that in use in Turkey.

Political Developments

In March 1992, Eduard Shevardnadze became Chairman of the State Council that had been established to govern Georgia when President Gamsakhurdia went into exile (see above). Shevardnadze had been the leader of the Georgian Communist Party between 1971 and 1985, and had returned to the country after serving as Foreign Minister of the Soviet Union up to August 1991. He ruthlessly suppressed both criminals and nationalists, restored law and order in the non-separatist areas, and brought about both international acceptance of his government and the ending of hyperinflation. He was elected President in October 1992, winning 96% in those areas where voting was feasible, and was re-elected in November 1995 with 75% of the votes cast. Attempts on his life in August 1995 and February 1998 were, however, indications of immanent disorder, as was the displacement of nearly 500,000 people who are seeking to return to their homes.

The war over Nagorno-Karabakh drove 185,000 Azeris out of Armenia and 299,000 Armenians out of Azerbaijan, and *de facto* transferred the Karabakh region and the Lachin corridor to Armenian rule. These military reverses eroded the authority of President Elchibey of Azerbaijan, who fled to his native region, the Autonomous Republic of Nakhichevan, as Heydar Aliyev took power, in June 1993. Aliyev had been Communist Party leader in Azerbaijan from 1969 to 1982, when he went to Moscow as First Deputy Prime Minister of the Soviet Union. He lost that post early in Gorbachev's *perestroika*, having been accused of corruption, and returned to Nakhichevan, which was his native region too. After consolidating power in that enclave, and resigning from the Communist Party, he became Chairman of its regional assembly (Mejlis) in September 1991. The success of his coup was confirmed by his election as President in October 1993, with 98.8% of the votes cast, although the opposition parties boycotted the voting. Aliyev was re-elected with 76% of the votes cast in October 1998, in the face of another opposition boycott.

In Armenia, President Ter-Petrosian lost popular support amid accusations that he condoned abuses of human rights, and, although he was re-elected with 52% of the votes cast in an imperfect election in September 1996, he was compelled to resign in February 1998. He was replaced the following month by Robert Kocharian, who consolidated a 39% first-round vote in February with a 59% in the second round in March. Within 10 days of his victory, the new President met President Aliyev in Moscow to relaunch negotiations on Nagorno-Karabakh. They met again at a summit in Baku in September 1998 to initiate the EU-led Transport Corridor Europe-Central Asia (TRACECA), but Aliyev added a protocol that Azerbaijan was not thereby to be bound to any involvement with Armenia.

In early 1999, when this was written, none of the three Presidents of the Caucasian states had the authoritarian status that some of their counterparts had imposed elsewhere in the CIS. Their power was limited not so much by public and parliamentary opposition – which is under some constraint – but by the weakness of central authority. The writ of the longest in office, Shevardnadze, runs in only a limited part of Georgia, and where it does it is often defied, as a kidnapping of UN officials by armed supporters of former President Gamsakhurdia exhibited in February 1998. Aliyev, whose term has been almost as long, has confronted opposition rallies with police violence and arrests, as occurred in the run-up to the October 1998 election. Kocharian came direct from the presidency of Karabakh to his present office, and hence has the power to meld the province and the main territory, and,

perhaps, to carry both with him in a settlement with Azerbaijan. In all three countries, normal economic life is still inhibited by widespread disrespect for law and order, as unsettled conflicts, both within the Caucasus and to its North – in North Ossetia, Ingushetia, Chechnya, and Dagestan – have put guns into the hands of criminals as well as oppositionists.

Fluctuating Relations with Russia and the CIS

The disturbed condition of the North Caucasus is one of the problems in the relations between the three states and Russia, and all three have had to seek to distance themselves from it. Three stages can be distinguished in the independence period, common to all three states (Aves pp. 175–6). Initially, as each was establishing its separation from the Soviet Union, Russia was perceived not only as inhibiting a clean break, but, at a time of emerging separatism, as fomenting ethnic conflict to weaken them. A second stage can be identified as two of the three governments came to appreciate a mutuality of interest with Russia – Georgia for aid to constitute its armed forces and Armenia to establish alliances to protect its interests. In June 1992, the Russo-Georgian Dagomys Agreement bartered ex-Soviet equipment for the Georgian army against a cession of effective sovereignty over South Ossetia, exacted by Russia amid concern that the secessionists there would try to link up with its own republic of North Ossetia. In May 1992, the Turkish government's threats against Armenia for fomenting skirmishes in the Azeri enclave of Nakhichevan drove Armenia into a close strategic relationship with Russia, which supported the consolidation of the new Armenian army and its incorporation of the irregulars who had taken over Karabakh. Azerbaijan was the loser as these ties were established and the frontier with Russia was closed. In a third stage, both Georgian and Armenian dependence on Russia increased, with Russian army bases on the territory of each – as well as in separatist Abkhazia, with which Russia sought to mediate agreement with Georgia. Azerbaijan put further space between itself and Russia in September 1994, as President Aliyev's government signed the "deal of the century" with a consortium of international corporations. This was a concession, agreed with Elchibey's government but renegotiated by Aliyev's, to exploit oil under the Caspian Sea, generating expectations of wealth that would transform the country into the regional power. The Russian government, however, forced the consortium to admit a Russian oil company and to divide the evacuation of "early oil" between pipelines through to a Russian Black Sea port and through a rehabilitated pipeline to a Georgian Black Sea port. The pipeline through Russia was the first to be ready – taking offshore crude to Novorossisk in November 1997 – but that through Georgia was to become available only in the course of 1999. Its terminus was to be located in Supsa, rather than in Batumi, the port favored by the Nobels and their successors (see above), which is the capital of autonomous and unreliable Adzharia. Conflicts of national economic interests are focused on the Caspian Sea dispute and the routing of the pipelines from those basins (see below, and also Chapter 10).

Oil transportation is an important motivation behind the creation of an interstate consultative alliance by Georgia, Ukraine, Azerbaijan, and Moldova, nicknamed GUAM. Established by three of these states in late 1996, the partnership added Moldova in October 1997 and held its first regular political consultation the following month. Its prime economic motivation is the assurance of the supply of Azeri oil by pipeline through Georgia and thence by tanker between Black Sea ports to provide for Ukrainian and Moldovan requirements. Onward pipeline shipment of oil to markets in central and eastern Europe is also envisaged, avoiding passage through Russia. Politically, GUAM is declared not to be directed against the interests of "any country," and it may acquire new members, but a certain defensiveness is to be discerned towards Russia and Armenia, which have strong mutual links. The governments of the two Caucasian members of GUAM have expressed dissatisfaction with Russia's failure to mediate satisfactorily over Abkhazia and Karabakh. Azerbaijan distanced itself further from Russia

and the rest of the CIS in January 1999, when it followed Uzbekistan's lead and pulled out of the CIS Collective Security Treaty. This implied that Azerbaijan would have to negotiate bilaterally with each of the other CIS participants on defense matters.

The Economies of the Caucasus

The Pursuit of Latitudinal Relationships

The western powers perceived their interests to lie in weakening the relationships between the three new states and Russia, without encouraging Iran to occupy any power vacuum, and in fostering their ties with Turkey, a NATO member. Since a similar policy broadly prevailed with respect to the five new states of Central Asia, where the dangers of Islamic fundamentalism could also be seen in relation to Afghanistan, the geographic axis of the relationships that the West desired was along a line of latitude rather than, as within the Soviet Union, along lines of longitude. The export of the potential wealth to be derived from Caspian hydrocarbons, and the burgeoning trade that should accompany the opening of market economies, also led in the same latitudinal direction. The present trend is thus to resume historical flows across the Black and Caspian Seas, and with Iran and Turkey, in place of the three states' almost exclusive political and economic orientation toward the North. Just as the symbol of the past was the "Georgian Military Highway" from Russia, completed in 1817 as the Russian empire took over the Caucasus (1801–31), so the present trend involves a symbolic return to the ancient Silk Road, which ran between Europe and China in classical and medieval times. Under both emperors and Soviets – briefly interrupted by independence in 1918–22 – the conduits of political authority, and of capital and commerce, had originated in Moscow. Oil from Baku, gold from Armenia, and subtropical produce from Georgia typified the export goods of the Caucasus that, under the centrally planned economy, were almost exclusively consumed within the Soviet Union. Azerbaijan was the sole Soviet producer of certain equipment for the oil industry, and Russia's output of refined petroleum suffered when hostilities after independence cut off supplies.

In establishing an economic dimension to independence, the three states differed on membership of the CIS. Armenia was in the second wave of members, just days after its foundation, Georgia was the last member to join, and Azerbaijan quit it between October 1992 and September 1993. Since independence, trade outside the CIS has increased at the expense of that with the CIS, in all three states. This is clear from comparisons between their exchanges with the rest of the Soviet Union in 1988 and their exports to the rest of the CIS in 1997, omitting unregistered trade and trade with the Baltic states (ECE number 1 p. 171; ECE number 3 p. 96). Armenian exports to the rest of the CIS dropped from 98% of its total exports to 43%, and imports from 82% to 34%. Azerbaijani exports dropped from 94% to 41%, and imports from 75% to 42%. Finally, Georgian exports dropped from 93% to 58%, and imports from 80% to 36%. In 1997, Iran outranked Russia as Azerbaijan's principal partner for both exports and imports; it came second after Russia for both trade flows in Armenia. Turkey ranked second after Russia as the destination of exports from Georgia; it was about equal with Azerbaijan, and also second after Russia, as the source of imports. It was in this context that the western powers sought to promote – and Russia to oppose – economic relations along a line formed by the Balkans, the Black Sea, the Caucasus, and the Caspian Sea through the TRACECA Program. This received the approval of all three governments at a summit meeting in Baku in September 1998.

Foreign companies were beginning to enter the three new domestic economies even before the breakup of the Soviet Union, and were particularly attracted to Azerbaijan's oil wealth as soon as the country gained its independence. Since privatization, they have been joined by domestically based businesspeople, and a prime requirement on the governments is to make their commercial criteria and environment transparent and predictable. Cumulative foreign direct investment between 1989 and 1998 has been estimated by the European Bank for Reconstruction and Development at US$265 million in Armenia, US$3.23 billion in Azerbaijan, and US$512 million in Georgia (EBRD p. 81).

Resources

From the first commercial extraction in 1872 until Stalin's Five-year Plans, starting in 1929, Baku's oil dominated the economy of Azerbaijan. As energy demand multiplied and the existing onshore reserves were exhausted, a "Second Baku" was opened up among the Volga-Urals deposits, and Azerbaijan's production entered a decline, from which an upturn began only in 1998 with offshore oil exploited by international corporations. The potential of offshore reserves had long been recognized, and had been exploited by relatively primitive methods since 1964. In addition, thermal electricity using oil and natural gas, together with alunite deposits, furnished a basis for an aluminum industry at Sumgait, created after World War II as part of a complex of steel-making, heavy engineering, and chemicals production. Cobalt, copper, lead, molybdenum, and zinc are also extracted.

Georgia was important to the Soviet industrial base for its manganese at Chiaturi, which, together with iron ore from Azerbaijan, was the pretext for establishing a steel industry at Rustavi. Georgian coal was, however, unsuitable for coking, and imports of metallurgical coke from Russia and Ukraine have been interrupted by lack of transport through secessionist Abkhazia, which also has a grip on the domestic coalmines. Other mining and quarrying includes arsenic, barite, perlite, quartz, and talc.

Alexander the Great conquered Armenia in order to secure a supply of gold, but it was not until 1961, late in the Soviet period, that Armenia opened up a gold deposit that had been neglected since the Roman occupation (Kaser p. 582). Copper and molybdenum deposits have also been commercially exploited, and the availability of gemstones is the basis of an important jewelry industry. Bauxite from Guinea was imported through Batumi to supply aluminum production in Azerbaijan and Georgia.

In both Georgia and Armenia, the hydro-electric potential of the mountainous regions has been harnessed, mostly since World War II, in major cascades such as Lake Sevan in Armenia and the Inguri river in Georgia. Azerbaijan, however, suffers from an extreme shortage of water, even though its coastal cities, villages, and arable area are in danger of inundation as the level of the Caspian Sea rises.

Caspian Environmental and Political Problems

In 1999, the Sumgait and Rustavi complexes were confronted, on the 50th anniversary of their foundation, by serious environmental problems. The disappearance of their markets and the strangulation of their supplies of raw material had created rust belts where steel had once ruled. In Sumgait particularly, the erection of plants producing aluminum, caustic soda, and synthetic rubber with little filtration or safe disposal of waste had contaminated the air, the water, and the soil. Stricter provisions are being observed by the international corporations operating in the Caspian Sea, but fears are being expressed that pollution by petroleum leakage cannot fail to increase. At an International Conference on the Problems of the Caspian, held in Baku in 1992, the concentration of oil and phenols in the coastal waters of northern Azerbaijan was reported to be four to six times the permitted maximum (Feshbach p. 58).

A treaty on navigation on the Caspian, signed by Russia and Persia in February 1921, and another treaty signed by the Soviet Union and Iran in March 1940 on bilateral equality of treatment in Caspian ports, both implied that the Sea was for the common use of the two states (Roberts p. 50). The independence of Azerbaijan, Kazakhstan, and Turkmenistan added three further state participants in the exploitation of the Caspian bed, all of whom eventually came to a preference for separately demarcated "economic zones," while Russia and Iran held to the principle of common exploitation. Russia came round to the concept of demarcation in July 1998, when President Yeltsin of Russia and President Nazarbayev of Kazakhstan agreed on mutual delimitation

of the northern Caspian, and announced their preparation of a draft agreement on the entire Sea, which would be presented to the other three riparian states. The five states are nevertheless already collaborating in a Transboundary Diagnostic Analysis and Strategic Action Program for the Caspian Ecosystem, within the Caspian Environment Program, which is a joint operation of the UN Development Program, the UN Environment Program, the World Bank and the EU's TACIS program, and has its headquarters in Baku.

Establishing Separate National Economies

The shifts in political and economic relationships described above took place in parallel with political restructuring and the creation of independent economies. In common with all post-Soviet states, those in the Caucasus experienced a "management shock" and an "economic shock," as new administrative and management entities were fashioned as a result of decentralization of power and deregulation of prices. The separation of their economies from what had been a single Soviet economy meant a loss of the financial transfers from Moscow that had helped to balance republican budgets. The confrontational nature of the relations among them, and with their neighbors, required, among other changes, the early creation of frontier and customs points, as well as legislation to favor nationals, for example through the preclusion of double nationality.

The transformation of each country's branch of the former State Bank (Gosbank) into a national central bank came equally early in the transition. There were already embryonic commercial banking networks, for two-tier banking had previously been established by the grant of autonomy to state-owned commercial banks by Gosbank. Over time, two of the three governments disposed of shares in such banks: by 1998 the Armenian government owned only the State Savings Bank, and in Georgia the government sold off all its banks in 1995. In Azerbaijan, however, the government has held on to four banks, which in 1997 accounted for 80% of all bank assets. In a survey conducted by a team from the IMF,

Armenia and Georgia were ranked as having made "substantial progress" on central bank reform, but Azerbaijan was found to have made only "moderate progress." Only Georgia was assessed as making "substantial progress" on restructuring commercial banking, Armenia and Azerbaijan's progress being only "moderate" (IMF p. 4). The rapid establishment of new economic institutions, especially in conditions of civil unrest and national military mobilization, offered all too many opportunities for corruption and crime, and it will be some time before normal conditions prevail.

The Worst of the Post-Soviet Recessions

Georgia suffered the worst recession of any CIS member – its GNP in 1994 was a mere 23% of the level in 1989 – but Azerbaijan's reached a nadir of 37% of that level in 1995, and Armenia's fell to 44% in 1993 (see Table 8.1). Even by 1998, the three economies combined generated only two fifths of their output of 1989. However, by 1998, thanks to rising oil production, Azerbaijan's GNP had reached 42% of the level of 1989, and Armenia was at 40%: Georgia, however was down at 35%. They had also passed through the worst experiences of inflation in the CIS. The consumer price indices in all three states were at their most explosive in 1994 – rising (year on year) by 22,470% in Georgia, 4,964% in Armenia, and 1,664% in Azerbaijan – but price stability had been achieved by 1998 (see also below). Despite the array of blockades and interrupted transport routes, foreign trade did not fall proportionately with output, and in 1997 the ratio of trade to GDP was at least double that in 1988 (ECE number 1 p. 172).

The breakup of the national planning system of the Soviet Union, and of the guaranteed relationships with other state enterprises in Comecon, were prime factors behind the catastrophic industrial recessions after independence (see Table 8.2). Georgia recorded the worst fall in any CIS state: in 1997, it generated just 18% of its industrial production in 1989. Armenia's industrial output showed a collapse to 40% in 1993, and by 1997 it registered only 43% of its industrial output in 1989.

Because its oil output declined, as well as its manufacturing, Azerbaijan's aggregate industrial output has shown a steady decline, and in 1997 it was 42% of the level of 1989, for substantial flows of Caspian oil began only in the later months of that year.

Privatization

The privatization of agriculture was crucial in countries with high shares of national output generated in that sector – 30% in Armenia, 28% in Georgia, and 20% in Azerbaijan as of 1997. Armenia had decollectivized even before the Soviet Union fell apart, under legislation enacted in January 1991. The collective and state farms were handed over to their members and workers, but the new owners were not permitted to sell their land in the first three years of ownership. Georgia gave leasehold title to those on state and collective farms, and did not allow sales of land until March 1996. Transfer to freehold has been slow in the zones controlled by the Georgian government, but is already the predominant form of tenure in the secessionist regions of Abkhazia and South Ossetia. In Azerbaijan, collective and state farmers took the law into their own hands, and effectively privatized their shares of the farmland, a situation which legislation enacted in August 1996 began to formalize. Both there and in Georgia, governments faced with atomized agricultural sectors persisted with one instrument of control introduced in the Soviet period – selective compulsory procurement from farmers – but these controls were lifted in 1993–94.

In other sectors of the three economies, most small enterprises were quickly denationalized, but medium-sized and large firms stayed in state ownership until privatization programs started in 1994–96. By 1997, the private sector was generating around 55% of GNP in Armenia and Georgia, but only 40% in Azerbaijan.

Overcoming Macroeconomic Imbalances

The war in Nagorno-Karabakh, and the inability to collect taxes in a disturbed economy, pushed the Armenian government's budget deficit to 54% of GDP in 1993, but it had been cut to 6% by 1998. Azerbaijan, too, had a deficit peaking in that war year, 1993, but at 13% of GDP; and this was reduced to 4% by 1998. Georgia's fiscal deficit reached 14% of GDP in 1993, also its worst year, due to civil hostilities, but this had been cut to 3% by 1998. Because such huge early deficits had to be monetized, in the absence of facilities to borrow, inflation turned to hyperinflation, which was at its worst in the year following the peak fiscal deficits (see above). Hyperinflation had been fueled by arbitrary increments in fixed prices in 1991 – a tripling in Armenia and a doubling in Georgia – and by the bungling of a partial demonetization of high-value banknotes. Next, the liberalization of prices in January 1992 had set off a vicious spiral, as supply fell instead of rising. The new currencies introduced in 1993 were initially weak, and hyperinflation continued through 1994. Since 1995, however, the currencies have strengthened, and by 1998 Azerbaijan's inflation rate averaged less than 1%, Georgia's was 4%, and Armenia's was 11%.

The overcoming of inflation in constrained conditions has been remarkable, and reflects the reduction in military expenditures, as ceasefires held, as well as the revival of economic activities which could generate tax revenue. Credit is also due to the IMF, which in April 1993 introduced a new credit program for transition economies, the Systemic Transformation Facility. Each state has an Enhanced Structural Adjustment Facility covering three years to 1999: Armenia's credit is for US$154 million, Azerbaijan's for US$131 million, and Georgia's for US$233 million. The conditions for these credits involved the limitation of central bank financing of budget deficits, the reduction of subsidies for production, the full liberalization of prices, and further privatization.

External Imbalances

None of the three economies has achieved balance on external accounts. Their traditional exports of farm produce were much reduced by disruptions to transportation and to farm supplies, by the abolition of Soviet agricultural procurement programs, and by the growth of consumption on farms when land went into private ownership. By 1997, food products and farm produce provided 33% of Georgian exports, but were offset by 21% of imports, excluding tobacco products, which alone were 12% of imports. They accounted for 12% of exports from Armenia, which had a food deficit – 24% of its imports were of food in 1997 – but they accounted for only 7% of exports from Azerbaijan, where 19% of imports were of food.

The sale of Armenia's Yerevan Cognac Distillery to the French firm Pernod Ricard, in 1998, promised a revival of the country's best-known export item. Georgian tea plantations were being replanted and improved, some by a German firm, Martin Bauer. Azerbaijan's cotton crop was stabilized at around 300,000 metric tons and its tobacco crop at 20,000 metric tons, each representing around half the harvests achieved in the Soviet period. Both crops are now mainly for export. A serious decline for Azerbaijan's exports was that of caviar, due to pollution and poaching in the Caspian Sea.

All three countries inherited engineering plants from the Soviet period, and machinery and equipment continue to command a modest place in exports. In 1997 they made up 22% of Armenia's exports, 5% of Azerbaijan's, and a mere 1% of Georgia's, against their imports in the same product group: 21% of Azerbaijan's imports, despite a decline in equipment for the oil industry, 12% of Armenia's, and 5% of Georgia's.

Being energy-deficient, Armenia and Georgia suffered a substantial loss on their terms of trade when their suppliers elsewhere in the CIS began to charge world-market prices from 1993 onward. At that time, Azerbaijan's oil output was declining, reaching its nadir in 1994, and its exports, which also bottomed out in 1994, hence made little quantitative gain from the price changes. Georgia's dependence on imports of natural gas from Russia and Turkmenistan, and of oil from Azerbaijan, was reduced because of its inability to pay for the supplies: by 1995, imports stood at around 25% of the level in 1990. By the end of 1997, the state had incurred external arrears of over US$400 million in its purchases, and in consequence supplies were being doled only against cash. Armenia's agreement with Turkmenistan for natural gas ended on January 1, 1996, when transactions reverted to a cash basis, and both Armenia and Georgia have endured power cuts, as natural gas is used in generating electricity. Armenia has recommissioned one of the two units of the nuclear power plant at Medzamor, which had supplied the capital, Yerevan, but which had been closed after the earthquake of December 1988 (see also Chapter 10). With the shipment of "early oil" from the new Caspian wells, in November 1997, the prospects for Azerbaijan's earnings are bright, but in early 1999 the route for a Main Export Pipeline was still under discussion.

The outcome of these trends in exports and imports, and of the evolution of trade in invisibles (services), was that in 1998 Armenia ran a deficit on its current external account equal to 29% of its GDP, while Azerbaijan's was 33% of its GDP; Georgia, on the other hand, had reduced its deficit to 8% of GDP, from 23% in 1994. In all three states, the real appreciation of their new currencies against the US dollar must have reduced the competitiveness of export products and encouraged imports.

Trade and Payments Commitments

The EU and Canada have accorded "most favored nation" (MFN) status to all three states, and treated them as within the Generalized System of Preferences, since 1992; the United States accorded them MFN status in 1993. Armenia applied for membership of the World Trade Organization (WTO) as early as 1993, and Georgia submitted its membership application in July 1996: they could both expect membership in 1999. Azerbaijan did not apply until July 1997, and by early 1999 it had not submitted its initiating memorandum to the WTO. All three states have concluded partnership and cooperation agreements with the EU, but, pending ratification, the EU has interim agreements with them.

Armenia accepted Article VIII of the IMF, on current account convertibility, with effect from 1997. Azerbaijan practices *de facto* current account convertibility, which the government expects to formalize as an Article VIII commitment in 1999. Georgia allows full convertibility on current account. Secessionist unrest and porous frontiers have favored money-laundering and capital flight. Inward remittances constitute small incomes for Georgia and Azerbaijan, but are larger for Armenia because of its large diaspora abroad, which also provides entrepreneurship, expertise, and capital for small and medium-sized businesses. Banks reporting to the Bank for International Settlements showed that, as of June 1998, entities in all three Caucasian states had aggregate assets in excess of liabilities. Central bank reserves measured against average monthly current account expenditures were lowest in Georgia and highest in Azerbaijan.

The New Currencies

At the end of 1992, the benefit of the Russian issuance of rubles to the other CIS states, which were then still using them, was equivalent to a drain of 11.7% of Russia's GDP, but to an increase of 52% in the GDP of Georgia, 49% in Armenia, and 26% in Azerbaijan. The IMF insisted that the Russian government had to restrict its money issue, which could only be achieved by taking control of issue in the other states using the ruble. In July 1993, the Russian central bank withdrew existing paper money, and declared that it would issue the new units only on condition that it was given that control. All three Caucasian states opted instead for separate currencies.

Azerbaijan had already issued its manat, in August 1992, initially as a parallel currency to the ruble. Since it became a freestanding national currency, the manat has exhibited appreciation in real terms – discounting for domestic and US inflation – due principally to the inward transfer of foreign currencies from the oil consortiums.

Georgia, too, had come to monetary independence before the ruble zone collapsed, having introduced its coupon in April 1993. However, the coupon depreciated rapidly during the subsequent hyperinflation, from 8,000 to the US dollar to 1 million between August 1993 and August 1994. After the UN mediated a temporary settlement between

Abkhazian separatists and the Georgian government, and Georgia joined the CIS, the IMF negotiated a stabilization program, and the lari was introduced in September 1995; one lari was exchanged for 1 million coupons.

The Armenian government introduced the dram in November 1993. It declined from AD77 to the US dollar to AD400 in November 1995, but subsequently, like the manat, it appreciated in real terms. Again like the manat, the lari has undergone a very considerable appreciation against the ruble since the Russian financial crisis of August 1998.

Further Reading

Akıncı, Uurğ, "Javakhetia: The Bottleneck of [the] Baku-Ceyhan Pipeline," in *Silk Road: A Journal of West Asian Studies*, Volume 1, number 2, December 1997

Starting with a brief history of the region, the author, the US Bureau Chief for the *Turkish Daily News*, places its ethnic problems in the context of other issues confronting Georgia.

Aves, Jonathan, "The Caucasus States: The Regional Security Complex," in Roy Allison and Christoph Bluth, editors, *Security Dilemmas in Russia and Eurasia*, London: Royal Institute of International Affairs, 1998

This is one of a number of chapters by specialists studying national, regional, and global aspects of security in the post-Soviet states, as well as multilateral security problems.

EBRD: *Transition Report 1998*, London: European Bank for Reconstruction and Development, 1998

This edition of an annual survey of economic transition in central and eastern Europe, and in the CIS, has special reference to financial services.

ECE number 1: Economic Commission for Europe, *Economic Survey of Europe*, number 1, New York and Geneva: UN, 1998

Chapter 4, "The Three Caucasian Economies 1991–1997," is an analytical account the difficulties brought by independence and macroeconomic instability, the policies and institutional changes initiated, and the problems of efficiently using natural resources.

ECE number 3: Economic Commission for Europe, *Economic Survey of Europe*, number 3, New York and Geneva: UN, 1998

Chapter 3, "Foreign Trade of Transition Economies," is the ECE Secretariat's regular annual review of trade developments in the transition states. It is accompanied by a separate chapter reviewing trade in the established market economies of the continent.

Feshbach, Murray, *Ecological Disaster: Cleaning Up the Hidden Legacy of the Soviet Regime*, New York: Twentieth Century Fund, 1995

Feshbach examines the evidence of widespread pollution and environmental damage consequent upon Soviet industrialization, and studies the consequences of inadequate measures after the Chernobyl' nuclear catastrophe in 1986, as well as the effects of the preparation and testing of nuclear, chemical, and biological weapons.

Garskova, Irina, and Parvin Akhanchi, "Discrimination in the Labour Market in the Baku Oil Industry," in Abel Aganbegyan, Oleg Bogomolov, and Michael Kaser, editors, *Economics in a Changing World*, Volume 1, *System Transformation: Eastern and Western Assessments*, London: Macmillan, and New York: St Martin's Press, 1994

A study of the records of companies operating in Azerbaijan shows discrimination in wages and hiring of workers by ethnic origin.

IMF, *Central Bank Reform in the Baltics, Russia, and the Other Countries of the Former Soviet Union*, Washington, DC: IMF, December 1997

The restructuring of central banks and commercial banks is examined for 15 countries, in a comparative context.

Kaser, Michael, "The Soviet Gold-mining Industry," in Robert G. Jensen, Theodore Shabad, and Arthur W. Wright, editors, *Soviet Natural Resources in the World Economy*, Chicago: University of Chicago Press, 1983

This is one of 31 chapters reviewing the state of western knowledge (at the time of publication) about the production, transportation, and trading of natural resources in the former Soviet Union. Despite the official secrecy then prevailing, the estimates of western scholars were generally accurate.

Kurbanov, R. and E., "Religion and Politics in the Caucasus," in Michael Bourdeaux, editor, *The Politics of Religion in Russia and the New States of Eurasia*, Armonk, NY: M. E. Sharpe, 1995

This chapter forms part of a comprehensive survey, edited by the Founder Director of the Keston Institute, Oxford, of the gains and difficulties of organized religion in the former Soviet Union.

Roberts, John, *Caspian Pipelines*, London: Royal Institute of International Affairs, 1996

A study of the economic and political viability of the exploitation of oil and natural gas deposits around and under the Caspian Sea, and of proposed export pipelines

Periodicals

A number of international organizations publish current analyses and statistics on a regular basis. The NIS/TACIS service of the European Commission (the executive body of the EU) publishes quarterly *Economic Trends*, compiled by national teams collaborating with research institutions in an EU state. The IMF publishes a *Staff Country Report* after mission visits; titles are listed, as they are published, in the fortnightly *IMF Survey*, which also summarizes agreements reached with member states, and furnishes economic context and forecasts. The UN Economic Commission for Europe (in Geneva) publishes three times a year an *Economic Survey of Europe*, containing analyses of developments in all its member states, together with extensive statistical provision; it also publishes *Trends in Europe and North America*, a statistical abstract of economic and social data for 55 states in more readily comparable form for transition economies than the larger

United Nations Statistical Yearbook. Last, but far from least, the European Bank for Reconstruction and Development (in London) produces an annual *Transition Report*, also with authoritative analyses and its own statistics and forecasts. This appears in October/November, and in advance of its annual general meeting in April there are both a general *Update* and, for each of its countries of operation, an annual *Country Profile*. These profiles are directed to businesses.

Businesses also form the main target audience for the quarterly *Country Reports* and annual *Country Profiles* of the Economist Intelligence Unit (London), and for monthlies such as *New Markets Monthly* and *Russia Express: Reporting the Republics of the Former Soviet Union* (Monmouth, Gwent). Shorter notes on a range of developments in each country are published in *ABREES* (London).

Michael Kaser is Emeritus Fellow of St Antony's College and Reader Emeritus in Economics in the University of Oxford, and Honorary Professor at the Institute for German Studies in the University of Birmingham in England. Among his many books and articles on the former Soviet Union and the CIS countries are *Soviet Economics* (London: Weidenfeld and Nicolson, 1970), *Privatization in the CIS* (London: Royal Institute of International Affairs, 1995), and *The Economies of Kazakhstan and Uzbekistan* (London: Royal Institute of International Affairs, 1997). He was a coeditor of *The Cambridge Encyclopedia of Russia and the Former Soviet Union* (Cambridge and New York: Cambridge University Press, 1994).

Table 8.1   Real GNP in the Three Caucasian States, 1990–97 (1989 = 100)

	1990	1991	1992	1993	1994	1995	1996	1997
Armenia	94.5	83.4	48.6	44.3	46.7	49.9	52.8	54.4
Azerbaijan	88.3	87.7	67.9	52.2	41.9	37.0	37.4	39.6
Georgia	84.9	67.0	36.9	26.1	23.4	24.0	26.6	29.6

Source: UN Economic Commission for Europe

Table 8.2   Real Gross Industrial Output in the Three Caucasian States, 1990–97 (1989 = 100)

	1990	1991	1992	1993	1994	1995	1996	1997
Armenia	92.5	85.4	44.2	39.7	41.8	42.4	43.0	43.4
Azerbaijan	93.7	98.2	74.9	69.7	53.9	44.6	41.6	41.7
Georgia	94.3	73.0	39.6	29.0	17.5	15.8	17.0	18.4

Source: UN Economic Commission for Europe

Chapter Nine

Moldova

Ronald J. Hill

In contrast to the other European countries that have emerged from the former Soviet Union – Russia, Ukraine, Armenia, Azerbaijan, and Georgia – Belarus and Moldova stand out as countries for which ideas of nationhood and statehood were developed and imposed only in the 20th century, by the Soviet Union itself. In the case of Moldova, its post-Soviet history has been marked by a search for a clear identity, and by a struggle to assert itself and even to survive culturally, politically and economically.

The Moldavian Soviet Socialist Republic was the second smallest of the Soviet Union's constituent republics, after Armenia. It largely comprised the province of Bessarabia, bordered by the rivers Prut to the West and Dniester (or Dnestr) to the East, and by the Black Sea and the Danube to the South, which was incorporated into the Russian empire in the 19th century. Between the two World Wars, it was administered as part of Romania, reverting fully to Soviet control in 1944. Finally, after World War II, its territory was modified with the addition of Transnistria, a strip of land that was formerly part of Ukraine but had a mainly Russian population. As a result, it was sandwiched between Romania to the West and Ukraine to the East, North, and South.

During the Soviet period, representatives of non-native groups – principally Russians and Ukrainians – moved into the republic, while some of the local population moved elsewhere. Nevertheless, despite occasional significant difficulties, including anti-Jewish pogroms in the first decade of the 20th century, interethnic relations have been relatively harmonious.

Even so, issues relating to the ethnic and cultural composition of the population were significant in identifying the republic's status. It was a movement for reunification with Romania that pushed Moldavia to seek separation from the Soviet Union in the late 1980s, and inhibited it from full membership of the CIS at the outset. The same push by Romanian nationalists, in harmony with a long-expressed irredentist aspiration on the part of Romania, also led to a split with Transnistria, which has come to be one of the major political and economic problems for the new state. The management of the ethnic dimension of the population has become one of the most delicate issues in the creation of Moldovan nationhood and statehood, with implications for development and for the very survival of the country.

Territory and Population

Moldova's area of 33,700 square kilometers makes it one of the smallest countries in Europe. It has a population of around 4.3 million, of whom 53.4% live in rural areas, reflecting the predominantly agrarian basis of the economy (see below).

Moldova's population has steadily expanded since World War II, thanks to both immigration and a high birth rate. The pace of urbanization has been relatively high. The population of the capital city, Chişinău (Kishinev in Russian), expanded from 216,000 in 1959 to 356,000 in 1970 and reached more than 750,000 by the end of the 1990s. Chişinău also acquired the attributes of a capital city, including universities and an Academy of

Sciences, a television and radio center, government buildings, hospitals, hotels, museums, theaters and concert halls, and the country's only major airport, which acquired international status with the collapse of the Soviet Union. Meanwhile, other cities, such as Tiraspol and Bălţi (Beltsy), gained the characteristics of regional centers, with administrative, educational, cultural, and trading establishments, as well as industrial enterprises that steadily attracted population from the rural hinterland.

A striking feature of the population is its ethnic diversity, reflecting the country's historic location on the frontier between the Russian empire and the Balkans. Around 65% of the total population are culturally Romanian – their culture is sometimes referred to as "Moldo-Romanian" – and in the Soviet period the Moldavians were identified as a distinct ethnic group. Ukrainians form the next largest group, at 14.2%, followed by Russians, who account for 13%. Another significant group comprises the Turkic-speaking, Christian Gagauz (4% of the total), of whom around 153,000 live within the borders of Moldova. (A further 36,000 live across the southern border in Ukraine and small numbers remain in Bulgaria, from where the Gagauz migrated in the second half of the 18th century.) There are also long-established minorities of Bulgarians, Roma, Jews, Germans, Belarusians, Tatars, Poles, and Greeks. The Jewish population of Chişinău was the object of a vicious pogrom in 1903 and many of the remaining Jews left for Israel in the 1970s.

While interethnic relations have generally been good in Moldova, language has become a source of tension that could again become significant in the future. In the late 1980s, the issue of language was a central factor in the anti-Soviet demonstrations that hit the country during the era of *glasnost*. Several generations of Russification included the use of the Cyrillic script for Moldavian, which was declared a distinct language as an element in Moscow's policy of separating Soviet Moldavia from Romania. This led to a demand for the restoration of the Roman alphabet and the adoption of Romanian as the national language. Both demands were conceded by the Communist government on August 31, 1989, but the move was resented by the Gagauz and other minorities. Indeed, it directly contributed to the declaration of an autonomous republic in the South in August 1990 – later formally constituted as Gagauz-Yeri – and to the declaration of independence in the region based on Tiraspol, in the form of the Dnestr Moldavian Republic (see below). Issues of language and culture arose again with the Bulgarian community in the South, which opposed new administrative arrangements that it felt would be disadvantageous.

Independence

Even before the collapse of the Soviet Union at the end of 1991, Moldova had moved some way towards an independent existence, fueled by a desire on the part of one section of the population to unite with Romania, particularly following the overthrow of the Ceauşescu regime in December 1989. For example, the republic's Supreme Soviet declared Moldovan sovereignty in June 1990 and the referendum on a "renewed union," held by Gorbachev on March 17, 1991, was boycotted by Moldavia (along with some other Soviet republics). On May 23, 1991, following a separate local referendum, the country renamed itself the Republic of Moldova, and the Supreme Soviet became the Parliament (Parlamentul). Following the replacement of the Soviet Union by the CIS, Moldova declined to become an integral member of the new organization until 1993. As a constitutionally declared neutral country, it remains outside the military cooperation of the CIS and it even sold some MiG fighters to the United States in 1997.

In 1989, with demonstrations in favor of recognition of Romanian as the official state language and the adoption of the Roman alphabet, nationalists in the Popular Front movement in Moldova pushed for outright union with Romania. This movement alarmed the non-Romanian speakers, who together accounted for over one third of the population. These included the largely Russian-speaking population of Transnistria and the Gagauz population in the South, both of which demanded autonomy (and would hold unofficial referendums on the issue in September 1991). The Soviet political elite in the capital, notably Mircea Snegur, tacked with the prevailing wind. Following the elections of March 1990, which, as in other Soviet republics, broke the Communist Party's political monopoly, Moldova steadily acquired greater independence from the center, and, after the attempted coup of August 1991 against Gorbachev, it declared its independence on August 27.

Romania was the first country to recognize the new state. In fact, nationalist rhetoric in Moldova was matched by irredentist rhetoric on the other side of the Prut, where the România Mare party and other political movements pushed for unification. Interethnic confrontation became a serious problem for the first time in modern Moldovan history, with Russian and Ukrainian intellectuals being sacked from positions they had held for decades. This fueled the fears of minorities, and led to defensive actions among the Gagauz and in Transnistria, no doubt with encouragement from politicians in Russia. Transnistria came to rely on the protection of the Russian 14th Army. Independence, therefore, was accompanied by a sense of uncertainty as ethnic mobilization steadily gripped the country. For a relatively brief period at the turn of the 1980s and 1990s, life was made extremely uncomfortable for the more than 1 million people whose native language was not Moldovan.

However, competitive maneuvering within the political elite diverted attention to other issues. Snegur overwhelmingly secured his own election as President in December 1991, and a relative moderate, Andrei Sangheli, became Prime Minister in a government that promoted an effective program of reform and a more measured approach to interethnic relations. When parliamentary elections were called for February 1994, economic reform, the separatist crisis, and the country's international orientation dominated a campaign that resulted in a defeat for the pro-Romanian parties. This was largely due to the mobilization by the reform Communists and other moderate parties of a strong public opinion in favor of interethnic harmony and collaboration in the cause of reform.

Nevertheless, a poll conducted in the summer of 1992 had revealed significant differences among members of different ethnic groups in their attitudes to the country's orientation, whether toward Romania, toward Russia and the CIS, or in favor of national independence. Russians and Ukrainians were particularly wary of both pro-Romanian moves and national independence. On issues of everyday economics and politics, however, there was remarkable unity, and personal animosity against members of other ethnic communities was not high. Perhaps even more surprising was the strong attachment to the notion of independent Moldovan statehood, which was also reflected in the results of the referendum on unification with Romania, held on March 6, 1994 (at a time when reconstituting the Soviet Union was no longer possible). On a turnout of 75% of eligible voters, 95% voted for independent statehood and against unification with Romania. Interestingly, an opinion poll conducted in Romania in May 1992 had indicated that less than one fifth of Romanians wanted early unification with Moldova anyway.

As an independent state, Moldova has expanded its international links. It joined the UN in March 1992, and was offered membership of the World Bank and the IMF less than two months later. Treaties and agreements with Romania, Ukraine, and Russia were signed, ambassadors were exchanged with a number of countries in the region and further afield, and, partly in response to the imposition of a high tariff regime on its exports, Moldova became a full member of the CIS in the autumn of 1993 (ratified by its Parliament in April 1994). In March 1994, President Snegur signed NATO's Partnership for Peace agreement, and before the end of the year he also signed trade agreements with European countries and a partnership arrangement with the EU. In a further indication of a shifting orientation, in February 1996 Moldova followed Romania and Bulgaria in obtaining membership of the Agence de la Francophonie, principally an organization that unites former French colonies with metropolitan France, even though none of the three is either French-speaking or former French territory.

Political Developments

Moldova was a state that had never existed in history, with borders not of its choosing and one of these (and an important piece of territory) in dispute, and with a population and a political elite that had no experience of functioning in a democratic fashion, and very little experience of performing the functions of modern government. There was a pool of talent and scholarship on which to draw for advice, but the administrative elite had no training for running an independent state, managing a currency or dealing with the rest of the world – or for doing all of this in conditions of extremely severe economic dislocation, exacerbated by internal conflict. In addition, given the complex ethnic composition of the population, and the patently confused question of relations with Romania, Russia, and Ukraine, the task of creating a distinct Moldovan identity and allegiance naturally featured near the top of the political agenda. The search for a distinctive "national idea" continues. Further, the political culture of the Communist system had not trained politicians to seek compromise, which may be regarded as part of the essence of democracy. If the performance of the political and administrative elite has been less than was hoped for or expected, that is hardly to be wondered at.

The Soviet Constitution of 1977, however much amended, was not a suitable vehicle for establishing the political and economic arrangements for a society that aimed at creating a completely new system of a different type. Accordingly, a new Constitution was adopted in July 1994, following the referendum referred to above. It is still too early to say whether it is capable of securing stable and competent government, and some signs suggest that it may be inadequate.

The Constitution was designed, in part, to prevent an excessive concentration of power in the hands of the President, by creating a particular form of separation of powers in a "semipresidential" system, rather than the "presidential republic" that Snegur wished for. In any case, Snegur failed in his attempt to secure another term in office, being defeated by Petru Lucinschi, another former

Communist who had become Speaker of the Parliament, in the presidential election of December 1, 1996. Lucinschi's victory owed much to his program of moderately paced reform, ethnic harmony, and a moderate orientation toward Russia.

The President's most crucial role is to choose the Prime Minister-designate, who is then obliged to select members of a government whose composition broadly reflects the strength of the parties in the Parliament. In consultation with the President, the Prime Minister-designate devises a program for its term of office. The list of ministers and the program are then presented to the Parliament for approval. Clearly, a principal function of the Parliament lies in approving the government and its program, and a formal ruling requires a minimum of 52 of its 101 members.

Parliamentary deputies are elected through a system of proportional representation based entirely on party lists, the whole country being regarded as a single constituency. Thirteen parties and blocs competed in the first election under this system, held in February 1994 (as mentioned above). The result was a victory for the Democratic Agrarian Party, which won 56 seats on 43.18% of the votes cast, while only three other parties gained representation.

Fresh elections in the spring of 1998, with a new President in office, involved 15 parties and electoral blocs, alongside 67 independent candidates. In the new Parliament, the Communist Party forms the largest party bloc, with 40 seats. Its nearest rival, then called the Democratic Convention of Moldova but since renamed the Alliance for Democracy and Reforms, won 26 seats. Its largest component group is the Party of Revival and Accord, led by ex-President Snegur, but it also includes the Christian Democratic Popular Front. The centrist Bloc for a Democratic and Prosperous Moldova, which supports President Lucinschi, won 24 seats. Finally, the center-right Party of Democratic Forces came in with 11 seats.

President Lucinschi selected the outgoing Prime Minister, Ion Ciubuk, who had been an agricultural administrator in the Communist period, to form a new administration, which would be expected to find the Communist deputies in opposition to it. However, in the economic and political turbulence that flowed from the Russian economic crisis of late 1998, this administration failed to survive even a year in office. On February 1, 1999, Ciubuk tendered his resignation, on the grounds that he was unable to consolidate the government because of the political diversity among its members, although critics focused on his own incompetence. The government fell, leading over the following weeks to a virtual constitutional crisis.

A new center-right government was appointed in March 1999, following a very close vote in Parliament. Led by Prime Minister Ion Sturza (born 1960), it comprises representatives of all three of the non-Communist groupings mentioned above. In a press release, it identified progress toward eventual membership of the EU as its principal foreign policy goal. With that in mind, it aims to establish the country's image as a favorable location for investment. Domestically, it intends to press ahead with structural reforms, establish stricter financial discipline, and reform the administration. In addition, and not surprisingly, it expressed its intention to halt social decline and secure the welfare of vulnerable sections of society.

In the meantime, the existing arrangement for forming governments clearly allows a great deal of scope for conflict. The President is elected on the basis of a program; political parties, in presenting their lists of candidates for election, also present their own programs; and the government, under a Prime Minister selected by the President, also has its own program. Several different political agendas may therefore be in competition with one another, particularly at the start of a parliamentary term. President Lucinschi, like his predecessor, has concluded that a presidential republic was required, to give the President the authority to act decisively when the parliamentary arithmetic results in potential instability. A referendum on the issue was held in May 1999, but the turnout of voters fell below the 60% level required to validate its result.

Further, the selection of representatives exclusively on the basis of party lists effectively divorces the deputies from the electorate, since no given member of the Parliament can be said

to represent the interests of a particular group of electors. In these circumstances, public control over their representatives is minimal and power accrues to party leaderships. It may be difficult for the public to sustain interest in political matters over which they have no influence, and disillusionment may well set in as politicians play their games with little or no concern for the public. This is clearly not likely to contribute to the building of a participant political culture that could sustain democratic values, practices, and institutions. Nor is there much democracy at the local level.

In present circumstances, however, many citizens may well feel that the niceties of democratic constitution-making are of less significance than overcoming the economic crisis, which has left the rural population, in particular, far worse off than it was in the Soviet period, with practically no sign of improvement, as the small national economy is buffeted by international developments.

The Problem of Transnistria

In 1990, when a pro-Romanian movement appeared to be politically dominant in Moldavian politics, the leading politicians in Transnistria, centered on the city of Tiraspol, declared the establishment of the Dnestr Moldavian Republic ("Pridnestrovskaya Moldavskaya Respublika" in their preferred language, Russian). This mini-republic remains an economic and political liability to Moldova as a whole. While Gagauz-Yeri in the South, which had a similar aim of resisting Romanianization, successfully negotiated the establishment of autonomous status in March 1992, the authorities in Tiraspol have steadfastly refused to reach an agreement, despite pledges written into the Constitution of the Republic of Moldova. Instead, the Republic has devised its own constitution, with official versions in Moldavian (Romanian written in Cyrillic script), Russian, and Ukrainian, and its own currency, the Dnestr ruble, featuring a portrait of the Russian general Count Aleksandr Suvorov (1730–1800), who founded Tiraspol in 1792. The Dnestr Republic also retains many features from the Soviet period, including the red flag with a green horizontal stripe – unlike that of the Republic of Moldova, which is essentially the Romanian tricolor with the superimposition of a stylized eagle – and there are still statues of Lenin in front of the Tiraspol city council building and the headquarters of the republic's government. The currency has suffered tremendous inflation, and living standards have been propped up by grossly undercharging for energy and other resources. Of the US$439 million owed by Moldova to Gazprom by 1999, US$364 million had been incurred by Transnistria. In addition, a Russian garrison remains in Tiraspol, in contravention of the Constitution of the Republic of Moldova, which is formally recognized by Moscow. This Russian force played a critical role in supporting the breakaway territory in the summer of 1992.

The justification for the rebellion hinged initially on Moldova's attitude towards Romania. The Tiraspol government's position is that the formation of the Dnestr Republic is "historically based, juridically legal, and morally justified by the consequence of the development of historical processes." The territory was never part of the Romanian state, and around 48% of its population today are Ukrainian or Russian; the Moldavian population of the region accounts for around 40%. Its economic, political and trade orientation has always been toward Ukraine and Russia rather than to Romania. Its government has declared that "Moldova can give [us] nothing . . . apart from international recognition." However, given its minute size and strategic vulnerability, it seems inconceivable that the Dnestr Republic could survive indefinitely, except by being propped up by political support and economic subsidies, in whatever form, from Russia or Ukraine.

The mere fact that there is a secessionist territory deters foreign investment in Moldova, which has not reached the levels needed to effect the transition to a modern, trade-oriented economy. The stability of the country still appears in doubt following the brief but intense military conflict in Transnistria in the summer of 1992. There was particularly bitter fighting in July that year in Bendery, the second city in the Dnestr Republic but also its only significant population center, on the right bank

of the Dniester. This resulted in up to 500 deaths and involved the intervention of Russian forces under General Aleksandr Lebed. Clear evidence that Russia regards the breakaway territory as important for its own security and other interests raises further doubts about the integrity of the Republic of Moldova. Repeated attempts to resolve the matter, with the assistance of Russia, Ukraine, and the OSCE, have failed, even though, in June 1996, Moldova offered Transnistria both a special status (comparable with that accorded to Gagauz-Yeri in the South) and a constitutional guarantee of its right to consider its position if the question of unifying Moldova with Romania should ever arise again.

Quite apart from deterring inward investment, the unresolved issue of the Dnestr Republic has a deleterious effect in other ways. Transnistria's section of the international border with Ukraine is effectively open, permitting a liberal inflow of goods on which duty is not charged, and which may include drugs and other contraband, as well as an inflow of criminal elements from Russia, Ukraine, and perhaps points further East. Despite its openness, this border is also holding back the revival of Moldova's exports to Ukraine and Russia, particularly following the destruction of bridges across the Dniester. The major oil and natural gas pipelines into Moldova also pass through the territory of Transnistria, adding further to the vulnerability of the rest of Moldova. The Tiraspol authorities, by contrast, regard trade with what they still call "Bessarabia" as "foreign trade," and are as likely to impose import duties on goods from Chişinău and Bălţi as on goods from Germany. As a result, supermarkets in Tiraspol may contain products from western Europe, including foodstuffs, but nothing from elsewhere in Moldova. This substantially reduces the scale of the Moldovan domestic market.

Finally, the *de facto* secession of Transnistria deprives the Moldovan government of access to the revenues of industrial enterprises in that region, where around 40% of the whole country's manufacturing plant was located in the Soviet period. This includes a power station, a steelworks, a cement works, and a number of engineering, clothing, and food-processing establishments. The manufacturing base of Moldova is thus to a considerable extent beyond the reach of the government in Chişinău. Like most of the economy, these enterprises are in need of modernization, a task that would be much easier, and would be to everyone's benefit, if it could be achieved by the foreign direct investment that is inhibited by the political impasse. Negotiations between the Moldovan and Transnistrian governments still take place from time to time, generally with the involvement of the OSCE, as well as the governments of Russia and Ukraine, but there has been little sign of conciliation, let alone successful compromise.

The Economy

In 1997, around 43% of the net material product of Moldova (excluding Transnistria) was based on agriculture, which employed more than 35% of the labor force. In the same year, agriculture and the food-processing industries together accounted for around 75% of the country's exports (again excluding Transnistria). Moldova's main crops have traditionally been grapes, of which a large proportion are made into wines and cognac; tobacco, particularly in the arid southern region; maize, sunflower, sugar beet, and potatoes; as well as apples, walnuts, and other products of horticulture. Dairy and meat production, particularly pork, are also significant.

During the Soviet period, the Moldavian republic was the site of experimental production and management methods in agriculture. However, following the breakup of the large state and collective farms, much of the productive capacity of agriculture lies idle for want of capital for investment in machinery and fertilizers. Success in producing tomato and apple juice is limited by a relative glut on the market, which renders the cultivation and harvesting of these fruits scarcely worthwhile. The traditional wine-making industry, likewise, cannot compete effectively on the collapsed Russian market, and it is reported that Moldovan wine is being relabeled and marketed as the produce of Bulgaria, a country that has penetrated western European markets with cheap table wine. Agriculture has also been singularly unsuccessful in attracting investment from foreign partners. Finding markets to replace those lost in Russia and Ukraine is extremely difficult, given the country's limited access to western Europe. As a result of all these factors, the volume of agricultural production in 1998 stood at 85% of its level as of 1997.

Manufacturing is to be found mainly in Transnistria. Light industry, including the assembly of tractors and washing machines, food-processing, footwear, textiles, and clothing industries were developed, as well as energy production and some heavy engineering in the region based on the city of Tiraspol. However, the almost total lack of domestic energy and mineral resources made the republic heavily dependent on other parts of the Soviet Union for supplies of the requirements for economic development, and for a market for its produce. Production goes on within the confines of the Dnestr Moldavian Republic – for example, footwear from the region is believed to be on sale in western Europe, but with labeling other than Moldovan – but, as has been discussed above, with little or no benefit to the rest of Moldova.

With no outlet to the sea, Moldova depends heavily on supply routes that have become far less reliable than in the Soviet era. Trade with the East, including Russia, the main supplier of energy and other raw materials, and formerly the major market for Moldova's economic output, has to pass through Ukraine, a country also in economic distress and of uncertain political stability (see Chapter 6). Routes to western and central Europe also depend on passage through Ukraine to the North or across a small number of river crossings to Romania to the West. (In the period of Communist rule, there were just one road crossing and one rail crossing over the Prut.) The creation of a coherent national economy, capable of trading with the rest of the world, is one of the major tasks facing the new state.

The Moldovan state is relatively weak, with few of the mechanisms needed for administering an effective tax regime, and little of the experience necessary for effective policy making and the exercise of state authority. It is not surprising in these circumstances that the level of illegal or semilegal economic activity is very high. Estimates of the scale of such activity range from a minimum of 20% up to 50%, although a figure of 70% is occasionally claimed.

Economic Changes, 1991–98

Economic decline, leading to virtual collapse, was a prime cause of the fall of the Communist system, in Moldova as much as anywhere else; and the travails of *perestroika* only exacerbated the situation. Moldova suffered the disruption of economic links with other parts of the Soviet Union when that country collapsed in 1991. Heavily dependent on Russia and Ukraine for its energy imports, it was affected particularly seriously when Russia demanded payment in hard currency for oil and natural gas. Moldova lacked the ability to develop products for sale in western markets, and was unable to sell into the distressed traditional economies of Russia and Ukraine.

In effect, the 1990s have been the first period in the history of Moldova that it has not been entirely within a Russian-dominated economic area. Until independence was achieved, Moldova was effectively isolated from the world economy. It did not have its own currency, and all its trade was conducted through the All-Union Ministry of Foreign Trade in Moscow. In 1989, 95% of its "exports" were to other Soviet republics. The bulk of these goods would not have matched world standards. Accordingly, the reorientation of the economy toward exporting to the West, however desirable and necessary, requires massive investment and effort at all levels, from product design and production to packaging and marketing.

Following the dismemberment of the Soviet Union, the performance of the Moldovan economy declined precipitously, and with the imposition of trade barriers by other former Soviet states the position further deteriorated. As we have seen, only 5% of the republic's "exports" had gone outside the Soviet Union in 1989. The new impediments to trade compounded the serious position, and the economic failure of the major markets for Moldova's products placed the republic in an exceptionally difficult position. Imports rose steadily from the time of independence, and without matching sales the trade balance deteriorated sharply. Between 1989 and 1997, GDP fell by around 60%, leading to an average monthly income of a mere US$33, among the lowest in Europe.

The country's heavy dependence on trade, notably on imports of energy, but also of most other inputs into industrial production, left it especially vulnerable to the disturbances in the economies of Russia and Ukraine; the breakup of the Soviet airline Aeroflot, and of the rail and road transport systems of the former Soviet Union, made a difficult situation even more acute. Russia's insistence on payment for energy in hard currency from 1992, together with accompanying price rises, raised the share of energy in the total value of Moldova's imports from 16% in 1991 to 43% in 1992, contributing to a decrease in GDP of 21% in 1992 alone. Moldova also shared the experience, common to many of the transition economies, of initial hyperinflation following the liberalization of prices: annual inflation reached 1,200% in 1992.

A better performance in 1993 was followed by a decline of 30% in 1994. The loss of markets in the East was compensated for, although not very quickly, by the opening of links to the West, including four new bridges across the Prut and the influx of western investment. The new Moldovan currency, the leu (not to be confused with the Romanian leu), was introduced in November 1993, and has generally been maintained at relatively stable exchange rates against western currencies. An article published in *The Economist* of London in 1995 has been much quoted by Moldovan government sources, since it praised Moldova as an excellent example of management of the transition to a market economy. In particular, inflation was brought under control, with the annual rate falling to 105% in 1994, 30% in 1995, and then down to a manageable 3% in subsequent years.

Nevertheless, the economy has continued to display all the signs of distress common to the region. The official unemployment rate, at less than 3% in 1998 (see also Table 3.6), was outweighed several times by the numbers of workers engaged in part-time employment, officially "on leave" or affected by seasonal fluctuations in agricultural work. By the end of 1998, the average income per capita was in the region of US$30 a month and the shadow economy accounted for up to 50% of GDP – some unofficial estimates placed it even higher. By 1997, GDP had fallen to only 35% of the level reached in 1989, the steepest decline in the region, and it has subsequently fallen further.

The Effects of the Russian Crisis, 1998–99

Hopes for stabilization, engendered by growth of 1.3% in 1997, were dashed following the turbulence caused by the collapse of the Russian ruble in the second half of 1998, which was disastrous for Moldova. Prices rose rapidly, and the value of the leu against the US dollar fell steadily, from less than ML5.00 before the crisis to ML9.50 in mid-March 1999, despite costly attempts by the national bank to sustain its value: foreign reserves fell by more than US$200 million during 1998. Inflation surged to 10 per cent for 1998. During the period from January to October 1998, the country's trade imbalance reached US$348.1 million, and exports declined by 2.1 and 1.7 times in September and October 1998 compared with the same months in 1997. On November 1, 1998, the total external debt reached US$1.3 billion and the accumulated arrears on the government's debt servicing rose to US$68.4 million.

Inadequate infrastructure in key sectors such as agricultural processing, and the unresolved issue of the breakaway eastern region, add to the international turbulence to present bleak prospects for the economy. By the spring of 1999, Gazprom, the main Russian supplier of natural gas to Moldova, had halved the quantity supplied and threatened to cut it off completely unless repayments of debts totaling US$439 million were repaid in cash, not in Moldovan state bonds. In addition, the state budget has been in disarray. Its deficit rose to around ML950 million (approaching US$100 million) by the end of 1998, and the state's payments of pensions and wages were in arrears. The collapse of Ion Ciubuk's government (see above) led the IMF to delay payment of a loan that had been agreed in early 1999.

Prospects

The immediate prospects appear bleak indeed. Lacking a clear identity to assist its foreign marketing strategy, and unable to produce other than fairly basic agricultural commodities for sale for hard currency, Moldova has found that its economic viability is under constant threat. The perpetuation of the division between Transnistria and the rest of the country hampers attempts to present an image of a stable and responsible democracy; so too, perhaps, does lingering suspicion that the country may, after all, eventually unite with Romania. Perceptions of political instability are not mitigated by the inability of the political parties to function on the basis of responsibility and compromise. Any attempt to project a distinct image of a reliable and confident trading partner or a site for secure inward investment is thus rendered problematic. Without a clear "image," based on developing a distinct sense of nationhood through a broadly accepted "national idea," marketing is blocked by ignorance. The outside world knows very little about Moldova (and the existence of a province called Moldavia inside Romania only causes further confusion); in addition, any image that Moldova does have is tarnished by the continuing dispute with Transnistria.

Nevertheless, academics and research institutes have been looking into the possible future development of the country. An underlying assumption is that the dispute with Transnistria will eventually be resolved by some sort of compromise, although it would require action on the part of Russia. Repeated interventions by Russian politicians are seen as affronts by the leadership of Moldova, although they are generally restricted to speeches and articles, and are therefore less immediately irritating than the continued presence of Russian troops on Moldovan territory. In principle, continuing and developing economic ties with Russia offer a possible way forward. However, apart from the political difficulties, there is now no common border between the two countries. The unproven stability and security of Ukraine as a transit corridor for Moldova's trade with Russia, and Russia's own economic and political woes, make that prospect unattractive. Closer association or even union with Ukraine would be geographically more logical, but that alternative is nowhere discussed. Even the Dnestr Republic's leadership in Tiraspol considers union with Russia an option, but, curiously, not union with Ukraine.

Incorporation into Romania also remains a theoretical possibility. Contacts with that country have been expanding, facilitated by the construction of new bridges across the Prut. Incorporation is certainly a long-term aspiration of many Romanian politicians, but the Moldovan referendum of March 1994 showed a widespread preference for full independence over the alternative of becoming a border province of Romania, associated with what is already a relatively backward part of that country. Another consideration, of course, is that any such development in the future would undoubtedly result in the permanent loss of Transnistria; and Gagauz-Yeri might also opt out.

Membership of the EU, for both Romania and Moldova, should not be ruled out, although it may not be achieved for 20 years or more. There is a developing perception that the future of Moldova lies in the EU, as was explicitly stated by the new government formed in March 1999. The country's economic condition will clearly not permit early membership. In any case, as a small, open economy with heavy dependence on trade, Moldova would wish and, perhaps, need to maintain strong links with its eastern neighbors, in addition to expanding links with central and western Europe, and with the South. Turkey, for example, is becoming a significant trading partner. In the meantime, Moldova stands to gain from the eastward expansion of the EU, particularly if some of the infrastructure developments that are contemplated, including North-South and East-West highways, come to pass. Analysts also point out that, despite being a largely agricultural region, like some other potential new EU members, Moldova would represent a minute fraction of EU production,

far less than any of the potential new members before it in the queue. Moldova's threat to the EU would be tiny, while the benefit to Moldova would be colossal.

The establishment of EU membership as a goal of Moldovan policy, even as a long-term aspiration, should serve to focus public and elite attention on the tasks of modernization and democratization, without which closer links to the West cannot be attained. However, if this becomes an established part of Moldovan thinking before a resolution of the Transnistrian dispute has been achieved, it may serve to entrench still further the eastward-oriented and backward-looking leadership of the Dnestr Republic. If Ukraine were to join the EU, however, along with Romania, it would be very difficult for the whole of Moldova not to be drawn along.

For the immediate future, Moldova's most urgent needs are for constitutional reforms, including a settlement of the status of Transnistria, along with other ethnic claims that continue to arise; a streamlining of government; and, above all, the accumulation of experience by the whole population, but especially by the political and administrative elites. Such developments, indeed, are vital for winning the active support of a population whose standard of living has declined catastrophically in the course of the 1990s. The problematic question of the nation's identity may resolve itself if conditions can be achieved to attract both domestic and international support.

Further Reading

Crowther, William, "The Politics of Democratization in Post-Communist Moldova," in Karen Dawisha and Bruce Parrott, editors, *Democratic Changes and Authoritarian Reactions in Russia, Ukraine, Belarus, and Moldova*, Cambridge and New York: Cambridge University Press, 1997

Dyer, Donald L., editor, *Studies in Moldovan: The History, Culture, Language and Contemporary Politics of the People of Moldova*, Boulder, CO: East European Monographs, 1996

This is the most reliable and wide-ranging among the small number of worthwhile studies of Moldova available in English.

Hamm, Michael F., editor, *Moldova: The Forgotten Republic*, a special issue of *Nationality Papers*, Volume 26, number 1, March 1998

In addition to the article by Charles King cited below, the contributions by Jeff Chinn and Steven D. Roper, Pål Kolstø and Andrei Malgin, and William Crowther are of particular relevance to an understanding of contemporary Moldova.

King, Charles, "Ethnicity and Institutional Reform: The Dynamics of 'Indigenization' in the Moldovan ASSR," in *Nationalities Papers*, Volume 26, number 1, March 1998

King, Charles, *The Moldovans: Negotiable Nationalism on a European Frontier*, Stanford, CA: Hoover Institution Press, 1999

This is the most comprehensive study of modern Moldova and its identity by a single author available in English.

Skvortsova, Alla, "The Russians in Moldova: Political Orientations," in Ray Taras, editor, *National Identities and Ethnic Minorities in Eastern Europe*, London: Macmillan, and New York: St Martin's Press, 1998

UN Development Program, *National Human Development Report*, Chişinău: UN Development Program Moldova, annual publication

This regular report on the work done by the Program in Moldova, including Transnistria, provides useful information.

Van Meurs, Wim P., *The Bessarabian Question in Communist Historiography: Nationalist and Communist Politics and History-Writing*, New York: East European Monographs, 1994

Websites

Readers interested in following current events in Moldova are advised to consult Internet sources such as http://news.ournet.md. The official Government of Moldova website is at http://www.moldova.md. The annual surveys of the Center for Strategic Studies and Reforms are to be found at http://www.un.md/cisr. Radio Free Europe/Radio Liberty provides daily reports on developments in central and eastern Europe, Russia, the Caucasus, and Central Asia at www.rferl.org/newsline.

Ronald J. Hill is Professor of Comparative Government in the Department of Political Science at the University of Dublin (Trinity College), Ireland. His publications include *Soviet Political Elites: The Case of Tiraspol* (Oxford: Martin Robertson, 1977), *The Soviet Union: Politics, Economics and Society* (second edition, London and New York: Pinter, 1989), and, as editor, *Beyond Stalinism: Communist Political Evolution* (London: Frank Cass, 1992). Professor Hill would like to acknowledge the use in this chapter of materials produced by the Center for Strategic Studies and Reform in Chişinău and to express his gratitude to its Director, Dr Anatol Gudîm, for permission to make use of the work of the Center, particularly its *Strategy for Development* and the work of Octavian Şofransky.

Economic
and
Social Issues

Chapter Ten

Energy and Raw Materials

Olga Kuznetsova

The energy and raw materials industries of the CIS countries have been going through momentous changes ever since the demise of the Soviet Union. Attempts to optimize the production of energy and raw materials within the Soviet Union as a whole had resulted in its various republics specializing in the production of particular resources. Now that these republics have become independent states, each one faces the challenge of transforming the profile of its energy and raw materials industries, in order to utilize its own resources to the full. Some countries have found themselves reassuringly rich in many of the most important resources, such as oil, natural gas or uranium, and they enjoy the full attention of the major international companies, which are anxious to find their way to the treasures hidden under their territories. Other newly independent states must come to terms with the new reality of being poor in natural resources, and must pay the full price of buying energy and raw materials in world markets.

Russia

Russia is very rich in a vast variety of natural reserves. Its deposits of natural gas, coal, and oil are among the largest in the world; the Ural Mountains contain almost every mineral available on the planet; in Siberia and the Russian Far East, there are oil, natural gas, coal, timber, rare and precious metals, and diamonds. The country's energy potential is also very high. Within the CIS as a whole, Russia holds around 75% of confirmed coal resources; nearly 90% of known oil and natural gas reserves; around 60% of ferrous ores and

raw materials for aluminum production; 90% of the region's tin and nickel; around 33% of its lead and mercury; more than 50% of its copper, zinc, and natural salt; 40% of its molybdenum and wolfram (or tungsten); around 67% of its potassium, phosphorus, and apatites; 80% of its hydro resources; and 90% of its timber.

Most of these resources are located in climatically unfavorable areas, remote from ports, and are difficult to develop. Nevertheless, Russia's enormous wealth in natural resources has attracted the interest of potential investors from all over the world. The oil and natural gas industries have been particularly successful in securing inflows of funds from abroad. At the same time, the further growth of foreign participation is hindered by the widespread perception that Russia carries a high political risk, as well as by relatively poor infrastructure, limited pipeline access, and high levels of nominal taxation on most kinds of natural resources.

Oil, Natural Gas, and Coal

Russia's proven oil reserves amount to 50 billion barrels. They are predominantly concentrated in Western Siberia, where the principal fields are at Samotlor, Romashkino, Mamontov, Fedorov, Lyantor, Arlan, Krasnolenin, Vatyegan, and Sutormin. The region as a whole supplies around two thirds of Russian oil, while its four largest fields account for more than half of the national output. The Volga-Ural region produces the second largest amount of oil. The explored resources of Russia's Arctic territories are smaller but they also attract many western investors. Most of Russia's new oilrigs, however, are in the Tyumen *oblast* (region) and near the island of Sakhalin (also an *oblast* within the Russian federal system) in the Russian Far East.

Total reserves of natural gas have been estimated to amount to around 1.75 trillion cubic feet. The major producing fields are Urengoy, Yamburg, Orenburg, Medvezhje, Severo-Urengoy, and Vyngapurov. The first three account for roughly 80% of the country's output of natural gas.

Russia's coal reserves have been estimated to amount to 220 billion short tons. The major coal-producing basins are in Chelyabinsk, Kansko-Achinsk, Kuznetsk, Lena, the Moscow *oblast*, Pechora, Raychikhinsk, Taymyr, Zyryanka, and the southern part of the Sakha republic (also known by its Russian name, Yakutia).

Non-nuclear Electricity

Around 69% of Russia's capacity for generating electricity is in the form of fossil-fired thermal plants. Natural gas alone provides 65% of the fuel required by these plants, and this share is expected to grow. Another 20% is hydroelectric, and 10% is nuclear (discussed below). Power generation has been falling at a dramatic rate as a result of the economic crisis that has continued ever since the collapse of the Soviet Union. In 1997, the amount of electricity generated was 23% below the peak reached in 1990.

Russia produces around 834 terawatt hours of electricity each year. Output is dominated by the joint stock company Unified Electric Systems (UES), which owns more than 50 of the largest thermal and hydroelectric plants, as well as the country's unified power grid, and oversees the 72 regional electricity companies. As one would expect, the government regards UES as a natural monopoly, and it operates under the control of the Ministry of Fuel and Energy, which is responsible for all energy supplies except nuclear power.

At present, total generation capacity is 205 gigawatts, down from 213 gigawatts in 1990. The industry is in need of funds to support the upgrading of equipment upgrades, and the

rationalization of inefficient and obsolete capacity. In the early 1980s, 6 gigawatts of new capacity were built each year, but only 1 gigawatt has been added in each of the past few years; in addition, by 2003 half of the non-nuclear power plants in the country will have exceeded their rated service lives. Government officials have estimated that the country will need from US$3 billion to US$5 billion a year in the period 1998–2000, and from US$6 billion to US$11 billion a year in the period 2001–05, if it is to carry out its plans to replace and expand capacity in full.

Hydroelectricity, which remains under state control, accounts for 43 gigawatts of Russian generating capacity. More than 70% of this total is accounted for by 11 gigantic plants, each with a capacity of more than 1 gigawatt, the largest being Sayano-Shushenskaya (6.4 gigawatts), Krasnoyarskaya (6.0 gigawatts), and Bratskaya in Irkutsk *oblast* (4.5 gigawatts). However, less than 20% of Russia's annual hydroelectric potential of around 852 terawatt hours is being used at present.

Russia is one of 20 countries in the world that employ geothermal power. So far, its exploitation of this renewable resource has been concentrated in the Kamchatka *oblast*, which has a total of nine geothermal fields, with an estimated aggregate capacity of 380 to 550 megawatts. There is a single 11-megawatt geothermal plant, built in 1966, at Pauzhetskaya, but a 7-megawatt addition is being planned, and is due to be completed by 2010, while another plant, with a capacity of 80 megawatts, is already under construction at Mutnovsk, also in Kamchatka *oblast*. A 30-megawatt geothermal plant is being built on Iturup, one of the Kurile Islands ceded to the Soviet Union by Japan in 1945.

Russia imports electricity from Central Asia, but it exports around the same amount to Finland, as well as to other CIS countries. Russian electricity exports could increase if a planned power line is built from Irkutsk *oblast* to China. The line could take three to four years to build, and could export up to 18 terawatt hours each year. The expected revenues could then be used to support the enhancement of the country's potential for hydroelectricity. The Russian government anticipates that the construction of these plants could lead to a surplus of 65 terawatt hours a year in Eastern Siberia by 2010; this surplus could be exported to Asian countries. Other planned international transmission projects include the Baltic Ring, and the United Power Supply System of the Black Sea and Caspian Sea countries (on the Caspian see also below). As a member of the Black Sea Economic Cooperation (BSEC) group, Russia has joined in setting up a Black Sea and Balkan regional economic center to help coordinate energy strategies, such as finding the best locations for pipelines through the region.

Nuclear Power

The nuclear power industry is treated separately from other forms of electricity generation. It is administered by the Ministry of Atomic Energy (Minatom), and is operated by the consortium Rosenergoatom, which runs the nine civilian nuclear power plants. In all, Russia has 29 nuclear reactors producing electricity, with a total capacity of around 21 gigawatts. The authorities claim that these reactors are safer than those anywhere else in the world except Germany and Japan, as demonstrated by the statistics on accidents in 1997. Nonetheless, safety continues to be a source of concern, especially with regard to the 16 relatively old light-water-cooled, graphite-moderated reactors, which were built to the same design as the plant at Chernobyl' in Ukraine.

Minatom has plans to add 8 gigawatts of nuclear generating capacity by 2010. A new reactor at Kalinin is set to become operational during 1999, and two others are to be built, at Kursk and Rostov, at an average cost of US$1.5 billion each. However, the economic crisis is likely to put these plans in jeopardy.

In addition, a new generation of mobile nuclear reactors, to be used for generating electricity and for desalinating water, has been designed by a Minatom design bureau in Nizhnii Novgorod, in collaboration with the Kurchatov Atomic Energy Institute in Moscow. The design was based on the reactors used in nuclear-powered icebreakers. The advantages that they offer, notably for use in the Arctic

region, are that they will not require refueling for up to four years at a time, and will operate for up to 40 years in all. Their use will therefore need to be interrupted only once every 13 years, so that they can be returned to Murmansk for maintenance. The electricity produced by these mobile plants is five times cheaper than electricity from other available sources, and they will pay for themselves after only 10 years of use.

Timber

More than 70% of the 789 million hectares of stocked forest land in Russia are covered with coniferous trees, while deciduous forests account for around 157 million hectares, or around 20%, of the stocked forest land, as well as for around 20% of growing stock. The balance consists of species, mainly located in eastern Russia, that do not contribute a significant share of the aggregated inventory.

Western Russia (European Russia and Western Siberia) provides two thirds of the short-term and medium-term fiber supply of the country, more than half of which is supported by deciduous forests. One third of the medium-term to long-term fiber is located in western Russia, nearly 60% of which is supported by deciduous forests. In contrast, Eastern Russia, which accounts for the remaining one third of short-term to medium-term fiber, is dominated by coniferous forests, which support around 75% of its total.

Gold

The richest gold deposits in Russia are located in the Amur, Kamchatka, and Magadan *oblasts*, and in the Sakha republic. Among the most highly developed gold fields are the Centralno-Aldanskoye, the Verkhne-Indigirskoye, the Allakhunskoye, and the Kularskoye.

Resources in Northern Russia

Northern Russia is uniquely well-provided with minerals. More than 700 different minerals are available, 100 of which were first discovered in this region. Among the most important are phosphate (35% of the entire stock obtainable in the CIS), nonferrous metals (30%), rare metals (80%), kyanite (93%), feldspar and pegmatite (37%), and iron ores. The estimated stock of titanium is around 50 million tons.

Although the region's reserves of oil and natural gas are extensive, their development requires considerable investment. The large East Barents and West Kara oil reserves are located in the Barents and Kara Seas. Research has indicated that prospective oilfields could yield up to 40 million tons over the first 10 to 15 years of the 21st century. Natural gas resources in that part of the Barents Sea that does not freeze have been estimated at more than 35 billion cubic feet.

The world's largest gas condensate field, Shtokmanovskoye, is located on the Barents Sea shelf, around 370 miles off the coast of the Kola Peninsula. Its estimated production potential is 106 billion cubic feet. Other large gas fields, still undeveloped, are Ledovoye, Ludlovsk, Severokildinsk, Murmansk, Pomorsk, Severogulyayevsk, Rusanovsk, and Leningrad.

Resources in Other Regions

The mineral resources of southern Russia include oil, natural gas, iron, manganese, mercury, apatites, phosphorites, coal, and copper.

The Volga-Urals region has the world's largest and richest deposits of iron ore, as well as copper, zinc, titanium, bauxite, gold, silver, precious and semiprecious stones, nickel, ilmenite, marble, high-quality dimension stone, and, in the republics of Bashkortostan, Tatarstan, and Udmurtia, reserves of oil and natural gas. In addition, there are deposits of bituminous shale, peat, and gypsum.

Siberia possesses a wealth of natural resources in addition to the natural gas, oil, hydroelectric sources, and timber already mentioned. These include manganese, copper, mercury, rare-earth metals, ferrous and non-ferrous metals, brown and hard coal, gold, platinum, high-quality marbles, precious and semiprecious stones, potassium, table salt, mica, talc, titanium, and niobium.

The Sakha republic is best-known for its diamonds, which are extracted from both veins and placers (superficial gravel or similar deposits containing particles of gold). It is also one of Russia's leading producers of gold and tin, and has sizable reserves of coal, copper, iron, antimony, oil, natural gas, and timber.

The Russian Far East possesses enormous natural resources of oil and natural gas, in the Sakhalin and Kamchatka *oblasts*; gold, in the Amur, Kamchatka, and Magadan *oblasts*; and iron ore, including one of the richest deposits, with 37.1% iron content, in Gagarinsk. It also has silver, brown and bituminous coal, titanium, apatite, zeolite, tufa, kaolin, phosphatide, chalcedony, limestone, dolomite, timber, and other construction materials.

Chukotka, which became a separate *oblast* in 1992, is rich in tin and mercury ores, gold, coal, natural gas, and building materials. Chukotka has Russia's second-largest deposits of gold, in the Bilibinsky, Smidtovsky, and Chaunsky districts, as well as its second-largest deposits of wolfram. Tin is mined in the Chaunsky and Iultinsky districts, and coal is mined in Anadyr. Chukotka is a region in which small nuclear power plants, installed on barges, are spreading fast.

Primor'ye *kray* (sometimes referred to as the Maritime region) is a supplier of spar, boron, and zinc. Its coal deposits are approaching exhaustion, while its timber resources remain rich. Primor'ye has four power plants, but they are inefficient. They consume coal from the region's mines, and fuel oil delivered from Siberia.

Around 87% of the area of Sakhalin is covered with forests. The average amount of timber available is estimated to be around 23 billion cubic feet. The main species are spruce (35.8%), fir (28.8%), and larch (22.7%). The most valuable timber comes from the central parts of the island. The forests are rich in fur-bearing animals, and the sea around the island is rich in fish, other sea animals, and other resources. The total quota of fish allotted to the island is 1.4 million tons a year, while the total quota of sea invertebrates is 345,000 tons a year. Sakhalin has proven offshore oil reserves of around 1.5 billion barrels; its onshore oil reserves are almost exhausted, but its natural gas reserves are substantial. Medium-quality coal deposits can support production for many years to come, but manufacturing costs are high.

The Kurile Islands have substantial reserves of titanium and sulfur, and gold has also been found there.

Belarus

Belarus is poor in energy supplies, as well as in other natural resources. Thermal plants generate a share of domestic electricity, but Belarus imports more than 90% of its primary energy, mainly from Russia.

There are only marginal deposits of oil and natural gas. Domestic production of oil and natural gas satisfies less than 15% and 3% of domestic needs, respectively. Belarus hosts two important pipelines transporting oil out of Russia: the northern branch of the Druzhba oil pipeline goes through Belarus to an oil terminal at Ventspils, in Latvia; the Northern Lights gas pipeline goes through Belarus to Poland. The country has inherited from the Soviet Union sizable but vastly underused refining capacities, both for oil and for natural gas, built around these pipelines.

Peat has been used for fuel in the past, but is now avoided because of contamination following the explosion of the nuclear power plant at Chernobyl' in Ukraine in 1986. Although recent geological exploration indicates that Belarus may have significant reserves of brown coal, huge investments would be required to start its commercial extraction.

Ukraine

Ukraine serves as a major transit corridor for oil and natural gas coming from Russia and Central Asia to Europe. Oil is transported through the Druzhba pipeline, and more than 90% of Russia's exports of natural gas also pass through Ukraine, via another pipeline. Ukraine, which is a member of the BSEC group, is seeking to develop its role as a transit route for natural gas and oil through its Black Sea port of Odessa.

Oil, Natural Gas, and Coal

At the start of 1998, the US Energy Information Administration estimated that proven oil reserves in Ukraine amounted to around 395 million barrels. Domestic production is not sufficient to meet domestic demand, of which nearly 80% must be met by imports. The major oil fields are at Stynawske, Dolina, and Bugruvativske, and in the Black Sea.

Proven reserves of natural gas in Ukraine amount to around 39.6 trillion cubic feet, but the country relies heavily on supplies from Russia and Central Asia. The government of Ukraine has shown a strong interest in the industrial extraction of coal-bed methane, which has a potential for supplementing natural gas.

Ukraine also has massive deposits of coal in the Donets'k Basin, which is also known as the Greater Donbas.

Electricity

Ukraine's power plants were deeply integrated into the electricity industry of the former Soviet Union, but restructuring began after independence was achieved. The government has proclaimed an ambitious goal of committing US$1 billion each year to the modernization of up to 25% of nominal generating capacity by 2001, but the implementation of this project has been delayed by a shortage of funds.

Ukraine operates five nuclear plants, employing 14 reactors, at Khmel'nyts'kiy, Zaporizhya, Yuzhno-Ukrainka, Rivne, and Chernobyl'. Chernobyl' receives more attention than the others because of the explosion in 1986. In December 1995, the Group of Seven leading industrialized countries, and the International Atomic Energy Agency, signed a Memorandum of Understanding with Ukraine on a comprehensive program to support the closure of the Chernobyl' plant by 2000, and to revitalize the Ukrainian electricity industry. Discussions of the future profile of Ukraine's energy industry have also been overshadowed by concern about the construction of two more nuclear reactors, which has been frozen since independence. Completing these reactors would be the cheapest way to meet anticipated demand, but ecologically minded experts claim that the available generation capacity should be sufficient, and propose instead that Ukraine should concentrate on rehabilitating its existing thermal and hydroelectric power plants.

Kazakhstan

Kazakhstan is very well-endowed with natural mineral and energy resources, ranking second after Russia among the CIS countries. More than 1,000 types of valuable ores are available for excavation at almost 3,000 sites. Kazakhstan is the world's leading producer of barite, lead and wolfram; it ranks second in production of chromite ore, silver and zinc; it ranks third in output of manganese; and it is also among the 10 leading producers of copper, iron ore, and gold. Its deposits of lead, zinc, manganese, and copper all have a very high metal content. Kazakhstan's Ministry of Geology has estimated that the value of its confirmed mineral reserves exceeds US$1 trillion. Not surprisingly, mining attracts particular interest from foreign investors.

Kazakhstan holds 16 billion tons of iron ore, around 8% of the world's reserves, of which nearly half can be mined. Manganese deposits total around 600 million tons, around 17% of the total for the CIS. However, chromium is economically more valuable to Kazakhstan than manganese, as Kazakhstan holds 95% of the total chromium reserves of the CIS, or around 30% of the world's deposits, and is the sole producer of chromium in the northern hemisphere. Kazakhstan holds almost 25% of the world's deposits of uranium, amounting to more than 1 million tons of ore.

Oil, Natural Gas, and Coal

The International Energy Agency (an organ of the OECD) has put Kazakhstan's onshore reserves of oil at 2.7% of global reserves, or around 10% of Saudi Arabia's recoverable reserves. There are 130 confirmed oil fields in the country, of which one half are producing. Around 94% of the country's residual commercial oil reserves are located in its western regions (*oblys*) of Atyraú, Aqtöbe (formerly known as Aktyubinsk), and Mangghystaú, in Uralsk, and in the Caspian depression. The Tengiz oilfield is the largest: it contains 6–9 billion barrels of proven oil reserves. The development of offshore deposits in the Caspian Sea (discussed below) will constitute the next major step in the growth of the oil industry.

Kazakhstan ships the bulk of its oil exports to the West through the Russian port of Novorossisk, which has direct pipeline connections to main oilfields. The transportation system is seen as a bottleneck for Kazakhstan's efforts to increase its oil revenues. Six export pipeline projects, focused on European and Asian markets, are now under consideration. The pipeline planned to link the Tengiz field with Novorossisk may become operational in 2001.

Commercial reserves of natural gas have been estimated at around 68 trillion cubic feet, with residual reserves at around 65 trillion cubic feet. The Karachaganak field, the largest of 75 fields available, contains nearly 73% of all the residual reserves in the country. This field is an extension of Russia's Orenburg field.

There are major coal deposits at two locations. Those in Qaraghandy (Karaganda in Russian) contain mostly high-quality coking coal; those in Ekibastuz contain mainly brown (sub-bituminous) coal, which is used in power plants.

Electricity

Kazakhstan ranks third among the CIS countries in energy output. Its electricity industry has faced numerous problems following the dissolution of the Soviet Union. In the Soviet period, the transmission and distribution systems of Kazakhstan were designed as two separate regional networks: one, in the North of the country, is still linked to the Russian network, while the other, in the South, is part of the power and irrigation network for Central Asia. Although Kazakhstan generates enough electricity to meet most of its domestic demand, the separation of the networks has resulted in its becoming both an exporter of around 1.7 million kilowatt hours a year, and an importer of around 8.6 million kilowatt hours a year, in accordance with regional needs.

Kazakhstan has 54 thermoelectric power plants, mainly run on coal, although as of 1997 oil accounted for 2% of its primary energy supplies, and natural gas accounted for 8%. There are also five hydroelectric plants (generating another 8% of the country's primary energy), and one nuclear plant (generating 2% of the total). There are many obsolete facilities, causing losses during transmission and distribution of nearly 15% of the electricity produced. Generating equipment is generally 20 years old, or even older, and relatively inefficient; levels of pollution are high because 80% of electricity (as of 1997) is generated by coal-fired plants burning dirty high-ash coal. The situation may improve if cleaner sources of power, such as hydroelectricity, are put to greater use, especially as only 10% of the country's huge hydroelectric potential is used at present. Multinational companies from the United States and elsewhere have bought shareholdings in key Kazakh power facilities, and around 85% of the generation system is in the hands of the private sector.

Gold

There are 146 known gold deposits in Kazakhstan, but almost half of the reserves are concentrated in just eight of them. The three largest deposits are at Vasilkovskoe, Bakyrchik, and Akbakai. Vasilkovskoe is one of the largest goldfields in the world: it holds 150–200 million tons of ore, with a gold content of 2.8 grams a ton, giving it an estimated value of US$3 billion. The potential for goldmining is very strong because of the size of the reserves, the high gold content in the ore, and production costs that are low by world standards.

Kyrgyzstan

Kyrgyzstan has abundant hydroelectric resources, important coal reserves, and minor deposits of oil and natural gas. It exports electricity and imports coal, natural gas, and petroleum products.

Oil, Natural Gas, and Coal

At present Kyrgyzstan produces only very small quantities of oil, around 800,000 tons each year, and virtually all its natural gas is imported. However, most of its territory has not yet been explored for hydrocarbons, and it is believed that there are undiscovered reserves, especially in the Fergana (or Farghona) Valley,

which Kyrgyzstan shares with Tajikistan and Uzbekistan.

Coal reserves are estimated to amount to as much as 3 billion tons, of which only 8% are technically recoverable. Around 10% of these recoverable reserves are in areas close to existing mining operations, making it relatively cheap to develop them. Small private mines produce 12% of the coal. One major problem is that the bulk of the recoverable reserves are located in the southern part of the country, while the bulk of the demand is in the North. Transportation is difficult and expensive, making it more cost-efficient for northern Kyrgyzstan to import coal from Kazakhstan. In addition, Kyrgyzstan produces relatively coarse coal, and fine coal dust, which are not easy to market. Attempts to manufacture coal briquettes, which would make the coal more salable, have been unsuccessful so far. The coalmining industry needs further exploration and research into economically recoverable reserves.

Electricity

The total installed capacity in Kyrgyzstan is 3,545 megawatts. Around 80% of the country's electricity is produced in hydroelectric plants; the other 20% is contributed by thermal plants at Bishkek and Osh. Kyrgyzstan's electricity system is part of the integrated power and irrigation system for Central Asia. Its annual output of electricity exceeds its total domestic consumption. Kyrgyzstan exploits only around 10% of its hydroelectric potential, which is estimated to be 26,000 megawatts, but if two proposed dams are completed at Kambarata, total installed capacity would increase by 2,260 megawatts.

Energy is a very important part of the national economy. Electricity is a major export product, and has a high potential for attracting foreign investors. However, the government has not yet announced a coherent policy for the further development of the industry.

Tajikistan

Tajikistan has a vast variety of mineral and organic resources. These include one of the world's largest deposits of uranium, while a large deposit of antimony has been discovered in the Khovland district. Tajikistan is also relatively rich in silver, as well as in gold (see below). Its deposits of silver ore have been estimated at 60,000 tons; the largest deposit, which alone contains around 38,000 tons, is in Bolshoi Kanemansur. Many of the country's mineral deposits are suitable for relatively inexpensive open-pit mining, but they are found in mountainous regions, where extreme weather conditions prevail, and transportation is difficult.

Oil, Natural Gas, and Coal

Tajikistan has proven reserves of 300 million barrels of oil, and 1 trillion cubic feet of natural gas, but production of both is marginal, satisfying just 6% of domestic demand. Tajikistan must therefore purchase almost all oil and petroleum products from other CIS countries, while for natural gas it relies heavily on imports from Uzbekistan and Turkmenistan in particular. Several potentially important coal deposits have been identified, but none has yet been exploited.

Electricity

Tajikistan had a generation capacity of 3.8 gigawatts, and an output of 14 billion kilowatt hours, in 1997. Hydroelectricity accounts for 76% of total energy output, and the country's hydroelectric capacity is second only to Russia's among CIS countries. Nevertheless, this resource is underused, and the Pamir Mountains offer ample reserves that have yet to be exploited.

The largest single source of electricity in the country is the Nurek hydroelectric plant, one of the largest in Central Asia. Construction of another immense power plant, the Rogun dam, started in the Soviet period, with the intention of supplying electricity to all of Soviet Central Asia. Once it has been completed, its output will eventually be equal to total national output at present. The government is anxious to identify foreign financing to finish the construction of the Rogun complex, in order to turn electricity into a major export product.

Gold

There are more than 30 known gold fields, of which only a few have been prospected. Annual output of gold is less than 3 tons. The main producer is the Zeravshan Gold Company, a Tajik-British joint venture; two other gold mines are also joint ventures. The largest mine, at Devaz, has proven reserves of around 25 tons and produces less than 0.5 tons each year.

Turkmenistan

Turkmenistan possesses the world's third-largest deposit of sulfur, in the Karakum Desert, and huge reserves of other raw materials, including sodium sulfate, sodium chloride, kaolin, native salt, and ozocerite. There are also deposits of bentonite clays, mineral paints, stones, and gypsum. Turkmenistan is also rich in natural building materials, such as clays, which are used to make hard ceramic for processing into bricks and drainage pipes. However, many resources are underused. Of 149 mineral fields, only 50 have been developed, and only one third of the available sulfur fields are under commercial excavation. The government is trying to develop eight major geological areas, with foreign participation: these include the promising shelf of the South Caspian depression, the Middle Caspian offshore, the Pre-Kopetdag depression, western Kopet-Dag, Misiryanskaya, and the right bank of the Amu Darya (the Amu River).

Oil and Natural Gas

Turkmenistan borders the Caspian Sea, a very promising area for oil and natural gas exploration (see below). At present, however, oil resources are relatively undeveloped. Proven oil reserves in Turkmenistan amount to 546 million barrels, while potential reserves may be as much as 6 billion barrels. Most oil comes from the Chelken district; the major oilfields are Kotur Teppe and Nebit-Dag. Oil production has been steadily increasing since 1995, but one of the main obstacles hindering further development is the lack of export routes. Although new pipelines are under consideration, they will not be operational in the near future, so oil companies have been looking for other routes and participating in oil swaps. In addition, the dispute between Turkmenistan and Azerbaijan over the offshore field known as Serdar in Turkmenistan but as Kyapaz in Azerbaijan continues to prevent its· development.

Turkmenistan is believed to contain the world's fourth-largest reserves of natural gas (after Russia, the United States, and Iran): the total was estimated during the Soviet period at somewhere between 353 trillion cubic feet and 494 trillion cubic feet. The largest fields are in the Amu Darya basin, one half of the country's reserves being located in the immense Dauletabad-Donmez field. There are large reserves of natural gas in the Murgab basin – particularly the giant Yashlar deposit, which contains an estimated 27 trillion cubic feet – and in the Kopet-Dag trough. Turkmenistan is capable of producing more than 28 trillion cubic feet of natural gas each year, most of which is available for export. As with oil, access to export routes is a serious obstacle to the development of the industry. Turkmenistan must rely almost entirely on the Russian pipeline network to get its natural gas to foreign customers.

Electricity

Turkmenistan has a generation capacity of 4 gigawatts. Output is around 9.4 billion kilowatt hours a year, but only around two thirds of generated energy is consumed domestically. At present, the excess is exported to Kazakhstan, although there are plans to provide electricity to Iran, Turkey, and Pakistan via Afghanistan.

Mining

Mining is concentrated in the *welayat* (region) of Balkan. The bentonite clays of the Oglanlinsky deposit, located on the northern slopes of the Bolshoy Balkhan ridge, are considered to be among the most important rock ores in Turkmenistan, and their quality has no match elsewhere in the CIS. They serve many users in metallurgy, pottery, food processing, and wine production.

The basalt ores of the Turkmenbashi peninsula are employed in producing reclamation construction mineral fibers, heat and sound insulation, and fibrous concrete.

The Ahal *welayat* is the main supplier of building materials in the country. This region has 32 fields with proven reserves of dolomites, kaolins, and other raw materials that are used in the production of cement, glass, bricks, china, and other building materials.

About 40 million tons of alunite ore are deposited in the Zulfagar rocky field and the Zaklin field.

The Lebap *welayat* has 34 mineral fields with proven reserves of natural sulfur, celestine, natural salt, potassium, carbon, marble onyx, and various raw materials used for making building materials, but only 13 fields are commercially used. The Govurdak and Garlyuk rocky field is the main source of natural sulfur.

Uzbekistan

Uzbekistan possesses deposits of coal, gold, nonferrous metals, and mineral fertilizers, but its principal natural resources are oil and natural gas. It is estimated that 63% of the country sits on hydrocarbon deposits. The Fergana basin, located under the Fergana Valley, is thought to have the highest potential. It is estimated to contain 4 billion barrels of oil, as well as several trillion cubic feet of natural gas.

A landlocked country with a shortage of export pipelines, Uzbekistan is actively seeking to increase its export capability. It uses foreign technical assistance to evaluate the feasibility of using a part of its pipeline network to tie into a proposed pipeline that will serve the whole of Central Asia, linking its oilfields to a new deepwater port on the Arabian Sea coast of Pakistan. In addition, Uzbekistan is trying to link up to the proposed 1,800-mile pipeline from Kazakhstan to China.

Oil, Natural Gas, and Coal

The production of oil and natural gas is managed by Uzbekneftegas, a state-owned corporation. The major oilfields are at Mingbulok and Kokdumalok. Oil production has substantially increased since Uzbekistan became independent, and Uzbekneftegas has forecast that oil output will reach 10 million tons by 2000, and 12 million tons by 2010. However, specialists outside the country are skeptical that such growth is feasible. There are significant oil reserves, but the oil is high in sulfur content. Uzbekneftegas has identified 32 new oil and natural gas fields to be developed, an additional 18 for rehabilitation, and nine more blocks for exploration.

Uzbekistan ranks among the world's 10 largest producers of natural gas, and has increased output substantially since it became independent. The extraction of natural gas is concentrated mostly in the southeastern part of the country; the major fields are at Gazli, Shurtan, Kokdumalok, and Kandym. Uzbekistan is taking short-term measures to increase production by upgrading facilities at existing fields, and is seeking to raise the capital required for longer-term development through joint ventures with foreign investors. As part of its program to become self-sufficient in energy, Uzbekistan is encouraging domestic users to convert to natural gas. It also exports natural gas to southern Kazakhstan, Kyrgyzstan, Tajikistan, and Ukraine.

Uzbekistan's coal reserves are concentrated primarily in the Angren, Baisun, and Shargun deposits. Production at Angren, mostly of brown coal (lignite), accounts for more than 80% of total production. The modernization of production facilities is expected to increase output by more than 300,000 tons a year. The Angren mine already has modern coal gasification technology installed underground, to produce natural gas for the Angren power plant. Additional investment at the Shargun deposit is expected to double or triple its production of high-quality coal, from levels of around 200,000 tons a year, while the completion of a new mine at Baisun could quintuple its output of 100,000 tons a year. Other investments planned include the recovery of kaolin and other byproducts, and the development of further coal gasification projects.

Electricity

Uzbekistan's major power plants are in the valley of the Syr Darya (Syr River), and at Tashkent, Angren, and Nawoiy. The two largest gas-fired plants, in the Syr Darya and at Nawoiy, account together for around one third of all the generating capacity in the country. Electricity is generated mainly by thermal plants powered with natural gas, and smaller proportions come from coal-fired and hydroelectric facilities. Uzbekistan has installed generating capacity of 11.8 gigawatts.

The Energy Ministry has plans to increase capacity by 4 gigawatts, through the rehabilitation of existing plants and the construction of new facilities. Projects include the renovation of the Syr Darya complex, using funds from the European Bank for Reconstruction and Development; the construction of a thermal plant near Termez; the renovation of the coal-fired plants at Angren and Tashkent; and the construction of a 400-megawatt hydroelectric plant near Pskent.

Metals

The center of Uzbekistan's mining industry is the *wiloyat* (region) of Nawoiy, where most of the country's deposits of gold, and of other minerals, are located. The deposits of gold are the fourth-largest in the world, and around 70 tons of gold are produced each year, making Uzbekistan the world's seventh-largest producer, even though only 25% of proven fields are in use. In 1992, the government entered into a joint venture with the Newmont Mining Company of the United States to produce an estimated 5 million ounces of gold from the Muruntau mine over the next 16 years.

Other important mineral reserves include uranium, copper, zinc, wolfram, silver, molybdenum, and lead. Uzbekistan is one of the world's major uranium producers, and copper production is also on a very large scale. The Almalyk mining and metallurgical works near Tashkent processes most of Uzbekistan's copper and zinc.

Armenia

Armenia's mineral deposits are relatively small. They consist of copper, coal, molybdenum, zinc, aluminum, and gold. Its proven reserves of oil and natural gas are negligible.

Armenia occupies the position of a transit center for Transcaucasia, particularly for oil exports from Azerbaijan and Kazakhstan to Turkey and western markets. Even though it does not have a coast on the Black Sea, Armenia is also a member of the BSEC.

Oil, Natural Gas, and Coal

Oil products are imported from Russia and Iran. In an effort to become more self-sufficient in energy, Armenia has begun a oil and gas exploration program, worth US$15 million, which has been contracted to a foreign firm. Four areas with potential for oil and gas extraction were identified.

Armenia has received all its natural gas from Turkmenistan, via Russia, since Azerbaijan and Turkey imposed a blockade on the country in the early 1990s. The supplies from Turkmenistan have become unreliable, however, because of ethnic and civil unrest in the Caucasus, pipeline accidents, and non-payment of debts. Seeking an alternative, Armenia has started talks with Iran on building a 90-mile pipeline, which would cost around US$120 million, to supply Iranian natural gas. Existing pipelines consist of 994 miles of high-pressure transmission lines and 6,835 miles of low-pressure transmission lines, reaching around 500,000 consumers. Of this network only around 1,240 miles are in operation.

Experimental coalmining is conducted in Ijevan. The coal is used in limited production of coal and peat briquettes. There are four regions of coal and bituminous shale deposits, in Ijevan, Shamout, Jarur, and Jermanis, estimated to total 118 million tons, but the government has no intention of developing coal-based generation of electricity.

Non-nuclear Electricity

Up to 70% of Armenia's electricity is produced in hydroelectric plants, several of which are on the Razdan river. While the country has installed capacity that exceeds its present demand, many of the facilities are obsolete, and in need of rehabilitation and modernization. The major plants are in Yerevan,

Hrazdan, and Sevan-Hrazdan; the energy distribution system is controlled by the Ministry of Energy. In 1996, Armenia put through a substantial reform of its electricity industry by separating the utilities into companies engaged in generation, transmission, and distribution.

Armenia has three fully operational geothermal power plants, in Yerevan, Hrazdan, and Vanadzor, which have exceeded their projected operating lifespans. Armenia is an active volcanic region, and experts have identified six territories with geothermal potential. Wind energy is at the experimental stage, while the exploitation of solar energy also has good prospects, since Armenia enjoys 2,500–2,700 hours of direct sunlight each year.

The Armenian transmission network was built as a part of the Transcaucasian power pool, which has fallen apart following ethnic conflicts and power shortages. Interconnections still link Armenia with Georgia and Azerbaijan, as well as with Nagorno-Karabakh and Nakhichevan, but none is operational at present. In 1997 the Armenian electricity grid was connected to the Iranian grid.

Nuclear Power

Both units at the Medzamor nuclear power plant that serves the capital city, Yerevan, were closed in 1989, several months after the earthquake of December 1988, because of fears about their safety. However, the government took the controversial decision to reactivate them, in response to the country's desperate shortage of electricity. Unit 2 was reopened in November 1995, increasing Armenia's electricity generation by 40%, and enabling electricity to be supplied without interruption for the first time in years. The government plans to reactivate Unit 1 after performing extensive renovation, and in the long term it hopes to build a new plant on the site, as the retirement of Unit 2 is scheduled for 2004.

Azerbaijan

Azerbaijan, one of the world's oldest oil-producing regions, is still enormously rich in oil, as well as in natural gas. There are also notable deposits containing aluminum. Azerbaijan is another CIS country that has joined the BSEC group, although it does not have a coast on the Black Sea.

Oil and Natural Gas

In the Soviet period oil production gradually moved to Siberia and other regions, but since it became independent Azerbaijan has focused on restoring production. Although there are no official estimates for the country's total reserves, experts in the industry have suggested that the deposits under the Caspian Sea may be as large as those under the North Sea (as discussed in more detail below). Some specialists put the maximum potential as high as 40 billion barrels. Virtually every major oil company in the world has shown some interest in Azeri oil, most of which is located offshore in deepwater fields, such as Gunashli, 60 miles off the Azeri coast, which accounts for more than half of the country's output of oil.

At the moment, most natural gas comes as a byproduct from the offshore oil fields. However, a major offshore field, containing an estimated 900 billion cubic feet of natural gas, was recently discovered not far from the city of Nakhichevan. Natural gas reserves in discovered fields alone come close to 6.5 trillion cubic feet.

Electricity

There are eight thermal plants, accounting for more than 80% of total capacity, and five hydroelectric plants. Two thirds of thermal capacity is powered by *mazut* (residual fuel oil), with natural gas as a secondary fuel. The electricity industry is desperately short of the funds required to upgrade its aging facilities. More than half of the turbo-generators and boilers have been in use for more than 40 years, and because of financial problems the equipment is also poorly maintained. Power cuts are frequent, and there is a lot of wastage of electricity during transmission and distribution. The power grid of Azerbaijan is connected with the neighboring grids of Dagestan (in Russia) and Georgia.

Georgia

Georgia's mineral deposits include arsenic, barite, coal, copper, manganese, perlite, quartz, and talc. The country lacks any significant domestic fuel reserves, and is dependent on neighboring states for its energy supply. The weakness of the electricity industry is seen as a major obstacle to the country's economic growth; the development of hydroelectricity appears to be the most efficient way to enhance Georgia's self-sufficiency in energy.

Georgia may benefit from being positioned on the routes between neighboring energy-rich states and western markets. It is one of several contenders for the main export pipeline carrying 1 million barrels of oil a day for an international consortium extracting oil in the Azeri sector of the Caspian Sea. A feasibility study, costing US$1.4 million, was under way in early 1999. Another possibility is the expansion of the shipment of oil from fields in Kazakhstan across Georgia to its port of Batumi on the Black Sea. In addition, Ukraine has set up a pilot project to transport oil by rail across Georgia to the Ukrainian port of Odessa; and Georgia has joined the BSEC group.

Oil, Natural Gas, and Coal

Around 580 million tons of oil have been discovered in southern and eastern Georgia, but many other parts of the country have never been explored. Despite its limited resources, Georgia is now taking steps to increase domestic oil production, through production-sharing and joint ventures with foreign companies. The Kura basin and the Black Sea region are growing in importance. The government has forecast that around 5 million tons of crude oil will be extracted each year by 2000.

Georgia has limited reserves of natural gas, and they remain largely untapped. No natural gas is extracted for commercial use, yet in 1993, for example, natural gas, nearly all of which was imported, accounted for 44% of fuel consumption. Imports from Turkmenistan arrive via the North Caucasus-Transcaucasian pipeline through Russia.

Coal reserves have been estimated at 700 million tons. The two largest deposits, both in the breakaway republic of Abkhazia, have been estimated to contain 250 million tons and 80 million tons, respectively. Coal is mined in Abkhazia and near Kutaisi.

Electricity

The electricity system of Georgia is going through hard times. Its effective generation capacity has fallen to a meager 1,575 megawatts, following the closure of many thermal plants because of fuel shortages, and equipment is generally very old and poorly maintained. Almost 30% of electricity is lost during transmission and distribution.

The bulk of electricity is produced from hydro resources, but further development is hindered by lack of investment. Only 10% of Georgia's estimated 100 billion kilowatt hours of hydro resources are in use, as only eight of its 72 power plants are hydroelectric. Georgia also has favorable conditions for the development of wind energy in the areas of Poti and Batumi along the Black Sea, in the center of the country, in the suburbs of the capital, Tbilisi, and at more than 160 other sites. There are also sources of geothermal energy.

Moldova

Moldova is generously supplied with cement components, and gypsum, limestone, sand, and raw materials for bricks and tiles. Deposits of oil and brown coal have been discovered in the South of the country, and their industrial importance is now being assessed.

Energy is mostly imported: domestic inputs account for only 5% of fuel and electricity production. Moldova depends almost entirely on Russia for oil, and nearly half of its electricity comes from Russia and Ukraine. The total capacity of all its power plants is around 3 million kilowatt hours, and the backbone of the national energy system is the thermal power plant in Dniestrovsk, which has a capacity of 2.5 million kilowatt hours. The national grid is already interconnected with Ukraine's, and steps have been taken to connect it with Romania's. Like those two countries, Moldova is a member of the BSEC group, despite having no Black Sea coast.

Despite its limited endowment of reliable hydrocarbon reserves, Moldova plans to collaborate with western companies to produce 100,000 tons of oil a year from the Valenskoye field, which has estimated commercial reserves of 10 million tons, as well as nearly 180 million cubic feet of natural gas from the Viktorovskoye field, which has around 869 billion cubic feet of reserves.

Since independence, domestic and industrial consumption of energy has been rationed as part of a nationwide conservation program aimed at reducing the amounts spent on buying energy abroad. Moldova is also actively investigating alternative energy sources, such as solar, wind, and geothermal power.

The Potential of the Caspian Region

The Caspian Sea, which conceals six separate hydrocarbon basins beneath its surface, appears to hold great promise for up to five CIS countries, and indeed for the world, in the coming century (see also Chapters 7 and 8). Although the exploration of the area is at an early phase, the proven oil reserves for the entire Caspian Sea region already amount to somewhere between 15 billion and 29 billion barrels (see Table 10.1), a level comparable to the proven reserves of the United States (22 billion barrels) or the North Sea (17 billion barrels). As for natural gas (see Table 10.2), at between 236 trillion and 337 trillion cubic feet, confirmed reserves are almost equal to those in North America (300 trillion cubic feet). Since prognosticated reserves of both these hydrocarbons are as large as proven reserves, the region is likely to become one of the most important sources of energy supply in the world in the 21st century. However, the development of the Caspian Sea's potential, and of the region as a whole, has proved to be a messy business. The seabed has become the epicenter of a major international dispute over ownership rights among the five littoral states: Azerbaijan, Iran, Kazakhstan, Russia, and Turkmenistan. Uzbekistan, which does not border the Caspian Sea directly, also wants to be involved in the decision-making process, because it shares several of the region's hydrocarbon basins, as well as some of the proposed routes for exporting oil and natural gas.

Further Reading

Aves, Jonathan, *Post-Soviet Transcaucasia*, London: Royal Institute of International Affairs, 1993

Aves highlights socioeconomic developments in the region in the early 1990s.

Ellman, Michael, and Vladimir Kontorovich, editors, *The Disintegration of the Soviet Economic System*, London and New York: Routledge, 1992

An in-depth analysis of the economic, social and political processes that resulted in the collapse of the Soviet economy and the disintegration of the Soviet Union

Gustafson T., *Crisis Amid Plenty: The Politics of Soviet Energy under Brezhnev and Gorbachev*, Princeton, NJ: Princeton University Press, 1989

A thorough account of the development of the Soviet Union's energy supplies, and the responses of the government, from the 1960s to the 1980s

Jensen, R. G., et al., *Soviet Natural Resources in the World Economy*, Chicago, IL: University of Chicago Press, 1983

Inevitably outdated in many respects, but still a valuable source of information on the natural resources of the Soviet Union in its closing years, described in an international context

Lewis, R. A., *Geographic Perspectives on Soviet Central Asia*, London and New York: Routledge, 1992

A useful source of information on the physical and human geography of the five states in Central Asia as they entered the transition process

Locatelli, C., "The Reorganization of the Russian Hydrocarbons Industry – An Overview," in *Energy Policy*, Volume 23, number 9, 1995

This article presents an outline of the changes that took place in the industry in Gorbachev's Soviet Union and Yeltsin's Russia.

Mercedes Balmaceda, Margarita, "Gas, Oil and the Linkage between Domestic and Foreign Policies: The Case of Ukraine," in *Europe-Asia Studies*, Volume 50, number 2, 1998

This article investigates the connections between energy supply and policy-making in Ukraine in the post-Soviet period.

Nove, Alec, *An Economic History of the USSR 1917–1991*, London and New York: Penguin Books, 1992

This is a new edition of a highly informative analysis of the development of the Soviet economy.

Ogutcu, M., "Eurasian Energy Prospects and Politics – Need for a Long-term Western Strategy," in *Futures*, Volume 27, number 1, 1995

This article explains how future developments in the Caspian region may affect the security of western energy supplies.

Rodgers A., editor, *The Soviet Far East: Geographic Perspectives on Development*, London and New York: Routledge, 1990

An interesting text that focuses on the potential of the Soviet (now Russian) Far East for further development

Rosenberg, Christoph, and Tapio Saavalinen, "Dealing with Azerbaijan's Oil Boom," in *Finance and Development*, Volume 35, number 3, Washington, DC: IMF, 1998

This article highlights the problems faced by Azerbaijan's oil industry as it approaches the 21st century.

Shaw, Denis J. B., editor, *The Post-Soviet Republics: A Systematic Geography*, Harlow: Longman, and New York: John Wiley, 1995

A comprehensive handbook on the CIS countries, with useful references

US Commercial Service, *Guide for American Business: Energy Markets of Europe, Russia, and the NIS*, Washington, DC: US Department of Commerce, 1998.

US Embassy in Azerbaijan, *Industry Subsector Analysis: Power Generation*, Baku: April 1997

Watson, J., "Foreign Investment in Russia: The Case of the Oil Industry," in *Europe-Asia Studies*, Volume 48, number 3, 1995

This article investigates the challenges facing foreign investors in the Russian oil industry.

Wood, A., and R. A. French, *The Development of Siberia: People and Resources*, London: Macmillan, and New York: St Martin's Press, 1989

A geographic study that still offers a great deal of valuable information and insight into this crucial region of Russia

Dr Olga Kuznetsova is a Research Fellow in the International Business Unit at Manchester Metropolitan University in England.

Table 10.1   Oil Reserves in the Caspian Region, 1997 (billions of barrels)

	Proven	Probable	Total
Kazakhstan	10–16	85	95–101
Turkmenistan	1.4–1.5	32	34
Azerbaijan	3.6–11	27	31–38
Iran[1]	0	12	12
Russia[1]	0.2	5	5
Uzbekistan	0.2–0.3	1	1
Total	15.4–29	163	178–191

1 Only those fields that are adjacent to the Caspian Sea are included here.

Source: US Energy Information Administration

Table 10.2   Gas Reserves in the Caspian Region, 1997 (trillions of cubic feet)

	Proven	Probable	Total
Kazakhstan	53–83	88	141–171
Turkmenistan	98–155	159	257–314
Azerbaijan	11	35	46
Iran[1]	0	11	11
Russia[1]	n. a.	n. a.	n. a.
Uzbekistan	74–88	35	109–123
Total	236–337	328	564–665

1 Only those fields that are adjacent to the Caspian Sea are included here.

Source: US Energy Information Administration

Chapter Eleven

Change and Continuity in Manufacturing

Marianne Afanassieva

In order to analyze developments in the manufacturing sector in the CIS countries, it is essential to look at the structural legacy of Soviet industry. To a large extent, the successor states of the Soviet Union have inherited their industrial structures from the single national economic complex that developed during the Soviet times. The Soviet economy had been developed as a closely linked system of enterprises and associations of enterprises scattered across an enormous territory, with supply chains crossing the borders of the former Soviet republics. There was an overemphasis on manufacturing and defense production, while the production of consumer goods and the development of service industries were relatively neglected.

Two other main factors have contributed to the formation of the present industrial structures. First, following the dissolution of the Soviet Union in 1991, and the consequent shocks to the system as the transition away from a command economy accelerated, most countries in the CIS sought to lessen or abandon the inherited overemphasis on manufacturing. In many cases, however, this has been replaced by a new kind of excessive reliance, either on an overdeveloped export-oriented raw materials sector or on new services, especially in the area of finance. Second, there have been attempts to reestablish some of the ruptured economic links among industrial enterprises, through the creation of transnational financial-industrial groups and holding companies. Some co-operation has also been occurring among the

countries that have inherited the bulk of the former military-industrial complex of the Soviet Union.

The Legacy of the Soviet System

The Soviet economy was a highly centralized system, into which the economies of the former republics were tightly integrated. As has been mentioned, the legacy of the structural imbalances of the Soviet economy was reflected in the dominance of heavy industry, with a special emphasis on the defense complex and heavy machinery. The priority given to the development of these industries, known in Soviet parlance as the "first group of production," had been at the expense of the "second group," which comprised the industries producing consumer goods and food.

Engineering was by far the largest manufacturing industry in the Soviet period: by the 1980s, it accounted for almost 30% of total gross output and employed 16 million people, or around 43% of the industrial labor force (see Cooper 1994). The foundations of a modern machine-building industry had been laid in the 1930s, with the establishment of many large new enterprises for the manufacture of machine tools, motor vehicles, tractors, aircraft, and heavy machinery. These enterprises included a number located East of the Ural Mountains, which together formed a strong production base that offered a secure location for military production during World War II. After the war, Soviet engineering's areas of particular strength continued to include the production of aircraft and heavy industrial machinery, in addition to equipment for generating and transmitting electricity. The production of machine tools in particular became one of the largest and most overextended manufacturing industries in the Soviet economy. The relatively low level of development of information technology created increasingly serious problems for the Soviet Union as it sought to match western achievements in microelectronics and computing.

Production for military use represented around one third of total Soviet engineering output. It was supervised by a specialized Military-Industrial Commission, along with nine ministries, each of which was in charge of a branch of industry comprising different types of production facilities. The military-industrial complex included both scientific and production complexes, which were capable of developing and manufacturing prototypes of machinery following the full production cycle from the initial idea to mass production. Since 1989, when President Mikhail Gorbachev first announced reductions in military expenditure, state orders and funding for defense production have steadily declined throughout the CIS. While some enterprises have expanded and diversified their range of exports, giving rise to new concerns about weapons proliferation, many enterprises in this group have been undergoing a painful conversion from military to civilian production.

The defense capabilities of the various CIS countries, and the difficulties they face in promoting conversion to civilian production, largely depend on the extent to which each of them inherited parts of the Soviet military-industrial complex. Although the Soviet planners encouraged a high degree of cooperation among the Union republics on production for military purposes, there was a massive concentration of resources in the European republics. Thus, of almost 55,000 defense enterprises, design bureaus, and research institutes involved in Soviet defense production in the 1980s, Russia had 73%, Ukraine 14%, Belarus 3.3%, and Moldova 1%, with the remaining units being spread among Kazakhstan (1% of the total number) and the other republics (see

Benediktov and Khrustalev). The most extensive cooperation developed between Russia and Ukraine, the two republics that housed the largest parts of the defense industry, and this has continued into the post-Soviet era.

Russia's inheritance from the Soviet Union included almost all the facilities for the development and production of nuclear weapons. Ukraine was left in possession of a major development and production center for strategic missiles; one of the principal tank design and manufacturing bases; unique facilities for the building of heavy surface naval vessels, ship propulsion units and heavy transport aircraft; the Soviet Union's largest manufacturer of airplane engines; and important centers for radar and optical systems. Belarus had major manufacturers of electronic components, optical and radar systems, and missile transporters. Kazakhstan was less strategically sensitive, but nevertheless housed important producers of infantry weapons and naval armaments. Georgia and Uzbekistan had enterprises building combat and transport aircraft. However, some significant capabilities were lost with the collapse of the Soviet Union (see Cooper 1998).

In addition, the economies of the newly independent states that developed after the collapse of the Soviet Union inherited a number of other main features, albeit to varying degrees (see Schroeder). First, they tended to be significantly more specialized than western market economies. Instead of being allowed to evolve economic activities that could serve the needs of their own populations across a broad range, each of the Union republics that made up the Soviet federation was compelled to adopt a policy of economic specialization. This was typically centered on very large enterprises designed by the Soviet planners to serve the perceived needs of the entire Soviet Union. This tendency to concentrate resources and effort on a few, large-scale activities was reinforced, from the first Five-year Plan (1929–33) onward, by the construction of entire new cities around single industrial plants, which very often became monopoly producers of goods.

Second, the basic components of their economies were seriously distorted or damaged during the Soviet period. Again as a result of decades of central planning, capital stocks, labor forces, and natural resources were all allocated in ways that had little or no relation to local or regional needs and aspirations. The emphasis on rapid and large-scale industrialization imposed a bias toward relatively low levels of technology, which was mainly used to maintain very large production runs. High levels of environmental damage resulted in many parts of the Soviet Union.

Third, all the CIS countries are marked by the legacy of Soviet economic culture. The Soviet institutional framework was based on state ownership of most property, the restriction of financial services to little more than basic accounting, and a corps of officials accustomed to giving commands and intervening in most forms of economic activity. As a result, the newly independent states inherited economic environments in which managers and workers alike were unaccustomed either to economic insecurity or to market competition.

The Challenge of Transition

The manufacturing sector in the CIS countries was hit hard by the breakup of the Soviet Union, which disrupted supply systems, orders and transportation, and was followed by a growth in demand for imported goods. The overspecialized, distorted, and often technologically backward industrial endowments of each country were often such as to ensure that only a few plants were equipped to produce goods that were in demand, and were efficient enough to make their products competitive in the market place.

Regrettably, it is not possible to adopt the obviously desirable approach of compiling and comparing data from all 12 countries in order to trace general trends of development. Information from some of the successor states is seriously inadequate or even inaccurate, while in others divergences in statistical concepts and measurements have reduced comparability between different countries (see Hanson). Even if these problems did not exist, the variations among the states in the extent and patterns of price liberalization since 1991 would have made any compilation of overall numbers unreliable. Thus, the changes

in Russia, which is by far the largest of the 12 economies in any case, must be used to provide at least some indication of the overall changes in structure throughout the CIS.

The post-Soviet Russian economy can be divided into three main sectors: the natural resources sector, comprising fuel production, electrical energy, and ferrous and nonferrous metallurgy; machine-building, including the defense industries discussed above; and agriculture, together with food-processing and a variety of light industries. The natural resources sector is now the backbone of the Russian economy. It is largely export-oriented, and is highly efficient and competitive. It employs only 3 million people, or less than 5% of the labor force, but it accounts for around 15% of GDP, 50% of gross industrial output, and more than 70% of export earnings. Labor productivity in this sector is between five and seven times higher than in the other two sectors, although, somewhat surprisingly, its capital intensiveness is almost the same (see Popov). With some exceptions, the other two sectors are much less efficient and much less competitive. In many cases, Russian industries are being squeezed out by foreign companies, even in the domestic market.

It can be expected that, given such differentials in economic potential, both labor and capital in a market economy should transfer from less efficient activities to more efficient ones. This is what has actually happened in recent years. In the first stages of the transition in Russia, between 1989 and 1994, there was a marked decline in the contribution of manufacturing to GDP, as measured in current prices, while the shares of distribution and other services rose, and the share of agriculture also declined sharply. Within the manufacturing sector, the decline in engineering, and in the textiles and clothing industries, was substantially greater than in other industries. The share of the natural resources sector in overall industrial output rose from 23% in 1990 to 51% in 1996, while the share of machine-building fell from 31% to 16%, and that of light industry from 12% to 2%. The number of people employed in machine-building has shrunk to around half of its level in 1991, and is now around 5 million.

These dramatic changes can be explained partly by the different dynamics in prices. The prices of fuel, energy, and metals have been rising faster than those of the output of machine-building and, especially, agricultural products. At the same time, the volume of output in the natural resources sector has been contracting more slowly than that of the manufacturing and processing industries. The share of the natural resources sector in investment has also been rising, from 5% in 1991 to 46% in 1996, while the share of machine-building dropped from 10% to 5%.

Further – and despite the problems discussed below – there have been some significant structural changes in the types and conditions of production, and in the sizes of enterprises, across the CIS. In broad terms, economic actors can be classified into three groups, according to the extent to which they have been able to move from dependence on the state to autonomy within markets (see Plyshevsky). A more or less complete transition to market conditions has been achieved by those large and medium-sized enterprises that have survived the economic and financial difficulties of the 1990s, as well as by many banks, by relatively cost-effective smaller producers, and, most notoriously, by the "shadow" economy (see below). The transition is proving to be much more difficult, as one might expect, for those enterprises that have low profitability, are making losses, carry a large burden of debts, or are hampered by arrears in payments from other economic actors. Finally, in Russia as elsewhere, the defense industries, scientific research, many types of agriculture, and almost all social services are surviving, where they have not been cut or closed down, only with the continuing support of the various governments.

Obstacles to Further Change

The manufacturing sector in the CIS countries continues to be burdened with a number of problems, not of all of which can be traced directly to the Soviet period. The structure of industrial output in most of the 12 countries is still dominated by extraction rather than processing industries. The effective demand for manufactured products is still very low and direct investment in the manufacturing sector still carries relatively high levels of risk. In addition, ever since the financial crisis struck East Asia in late 1997 there has also been an unfavorable climate for exports on the world's raw materials markets. These issues are of special relevance to Kazakhstan, for example, where manufacturing industry accounts for 20.7% of GDP and 22.2% of employment, and there are limited opportunities for diversifying the products being exported (see TACIS). It must also be emphasized that the industrial sector throughout the region remains inefficient, mainly due to the lack of sufficient productive investment, exacerbated by the lack of international competitiveness, the extensive degree of state ownership, and the lack of marketing skills. Many enterprises operate at very low capacity. In Moldova, for example, average capacity utilization was below 50% as of the third quarter of 1998, while in Uzbekistan it was only around 54% (see TACIS).

As for aggregate GDP growth rates across the whole of the CIS, there was modest growth of around 1.1% in 1997, and expansion continued up to June 1998. However, this was followed by contraction in the second half of the year, equivalent to an annual rate of around -2.6% (see Tables 11.1 and 11.2). This was largely a reflection of the impact of two major shocks on the economies of the CIS over 1998: the collapse in demand for, and the prices of, primary commodities resulting from the continuing crisis in East Asia; and the repercussions of the Russian financial crisis in August that year.

However, rates of growth in GDP and industrial output are by no means uniform across the region: aggregate figures must therefore be handled with care. The combination of internal fragility and the disruption of trade with Russia have not created favorable conditions for GDP growth in Ukraine or in Moldova, following a modest recovery in 1997, and decline could well continue into 1999. As for Belarus, official statistics give a deceptive picture of economic recovery, which is largely due to an expansion of cheap credit, and disregard for increasing internal and external imbalances. The five states of Central Asia are predominantly primary commodity exporters and have thus been seriously affected by the collapse in commodity prices on the world markets. On a more positive note, growth rates in the three Caucasian economies were sustained during the first half of 1998, particularly in Azerbaijan, where the economy benefited from extensive investment in oil production and related industries (see UNECE).

Nevertheless, it is generally still the case, across the CIS, that whatever growth does occur tends to be mostly in the basic extractive industries, with the result that the inherited structure of each economy tends to be preserved rather than overhauled, thus damaging the international competitiveness of these countries. In most CIS countries, growth is still to a large extent dependent on the activities of unrestructured enterprises, and is not supported by newly founded and more flexible economic agents. This means that each economy has a very limited material base, and is dependent on various forms of paternalistic support from the state.

One of the main factors exacerbating this situation is the relatively low level of investment, which in several CIS countries is actually decreasing (see Table 11.3). It has been estimated that as of 1997 investment in most CIS countries was at a similar level to that achieved in the Soviet Union in 1964, or around 29% of the level reached in 1991 (see Chistyakov and Shul'ga). Those states that have significant endowments of natural resources – notably Azerbaijan, Kazakhstan, Turkmenistan, and Uzbekistan – have at least some significant potential to attract investment. However, others, such as Belarus, were required to specialize in manufacturing under the Soviet system and have not been able to raise the quality of their "human capital" much above the inherited Soviet average (see Hanson).

The Current Situation

It is indicative of the current state of the transition process that barter trade has been increasing across all these categories. Indeed, there is an increasing demonetization of trade and economic intermediation, and a large

part of the economy in every CIS country comprises actors who are striving to hide themselves from the attentions of the government and the media. These "shadow" economies have grown to phenomenal proportions, and many of the legal and regulatory functions of the state, above all in Russia, are being undertaken by private, often criminal, organizations (see Ericson). The share of the shadow economy in the GDP of Russia has been estimated at around 25% (see Plyshevsky). Much of the activity associated with the unofficial economies consists of misreported or undeclared economic activities performed by registered enterprises using the same assets that are used to produce output for the formal economies (see EBRD). These enterprises are particularly sensitive to changes in the relative costs of official and unofficial activities, such as changes in business regulations and taxation, changes in the state's capacity, and changes in the level of bribes required to avoid detection by tax authorities or government regulators. These processes clearly have an adverse effect on the prospects for structural change in industry. The decrease in officially registered output is taking place alongside the simultaneous expansion of the shadow economy, which is adjusting to the market much more quickly, notably in the production of consumer goods and the provision of services. However, its operations are diverting funds from being invested in manufacturing industry and other sectors of the economy, preventing any overall improvement in the structure of production overall.

The formal economies of the CIS countries account for around 10% of the world's aggregate industrial potential, and their connections with the rest of the world are on a rising trend. In 1990, internal trade among the various Union republics amounted to 72.1% of the total value of Soviet exports; by 1996, the share of intra-CIS trade within the total exports of CIS countries was only around 27%. The share of products with high value added has undergone a drastic decline, which suggests that the utilization of the region's scientific and technical potential is deteriorating. At present, there is no investment-supported demand for high technology and its products inside the CIS. As a result, production is stagnating and the technological base available in the 12 countries is increasingly obsolescent. Existing advantages are gradually being lost across a wide range of manufacturing activities, notably in aerospace technology, arms production, nuclear physics, energy production, machine-building, and biotechnology (see Chistyakov and Shul'ga).

Against this background of difficult and even worsening conditions, one of the best ways in which CIS countries can hope to revive their economies, and perhaps even to begin expanding again, is to reestablish the cross-border economic links among enterprises and regions. They could then focus on developing domestic production aimed at consumption across the region. In this regard, it will be crucial to allow domestically produced goods to compete freely and fairly throughout the CIS economic space, in order to attain superior levels of quality and cost efficiency.

One specific route to reviving cooperation has been provided through the "agreement on assistance in creation and development of production, commercial, credit and finance, insurance, and mixed transnational associations," which was signed by all 12 CIS governments in April 1994. This agreement explicitly emphasizes the possibility of creating transnational associations in any area of economic activity, in various forms. In particular, the creation of "financial-industrial groups" has been viewed by the CIS governments as a key element in the attempt to restore and maintain cooperative links among partner enterprises located in different successor states. These groups are formed through holding companies or through merging capital into partnerships (see Slepov et al.).

Some financial-industrial groups have already succeeded in reuniting enterprises that had close economic relations during the Soviet period. For example, the Russian-Belarusian group BelRusavto has brought together automobile plants in Belarus and the large Russian Mogilev automobile plant, a plant in Minsk that makes wheels, the Avtodizel joint stock company that makes engines in Yaroslavl, the Tutayev motor plant, and a Yaroslavl plant that makes fuel equipment (see Kozik and Kokhno). Similar structures are being developed within the CIS-wide defense industry. Russia, Belarus, and Ukraine are participating in an interstate joint stock company, Vympel; the International Aviamotors group includes enterprises in Russia and Ukraine; and one interstate joint stock company, Formmash, involves cooperation between Ukraine, Belarus, and Latvia, a non-CIS country that nevertheless shares a Soviet industrial legacy.

The obvious danger inherent in the development of these and other types of cooperation is that manufacturing in the CIS countries could become increasingly oriented toward producing goods for sale only within the CIS economic space itself. This in turn would have the perverse effect of enhancing the region's isolation from the rest of the world, just at a time when economic interactions among states and regions are generally increasing, and even becoming essential to continued growth. As the CIS countries enter the 21st century, they still bear all the marks of the Soviet industrial and cultural legacy that was bequeathed to them in 1991 – and the prospects for far-reaching restructuring are not very bright.

Further Reading

Benediktov, M., and Y. Khrustalev, "Integratsiya Voyennoi Industrii Stran SNG" [Integration of the Defense Industry in the CIS Countries], in *MEiMO*, number 12, 1998

This article compares trends toward integration in the defense industries of the United States and western Europe with trends in the CIS countries.

Chistyakov, E., and V. Shul'ga, "Integratsionnyi Potentsial SNG i Yego rol' v Razvitii Mirokhozyaistvennykh Svyazei" [The Potential of the CIS for Integration and Its Role in the Development of World Economic Relations], in *Ekonomist*, number 6, 1998

The authors analyze the industrial potential of the CIS, comparing it with that of the Soviet Union and focusing on changing relations with the rest of the world economy.

Cooper, Julian, "Engineering", in Archie Brown, Michael Kaser, and Gerald S. Smith, editors, *The Cambridge Encyclopedia of Russia and the Former Soviet Union*, Cambridge and New York: Cambridge University Press, 1994

This short but informative article outlines the main developments in the engineering industry in the Soviet Union and then in Russia.

Cooper, Julian, "The Future of the Russian Defence Industry," in Roy Allison and Christopher Bluth, editors, *Security Dilemmas in Russia and Eurasia*, London: Royal Institute of International Affairs, 1998

Cooper focuses here on the problems and prospects of the defense industry in Russia.

EBRD: European Bank for Reconstruction and Development, *Transition Report 1997*: *Enterprise Performance and Growth*, London: European Bank for Reconstruction and Development, 1997

The main focus of this edition of an authoritative publication is on the restructuring of enterprises in all the transition economies, but there are also analyses of reforms in individual countries.

Ericson, Richard E., "Economics and the Russian Transition," in *Slavic Review*, Volume 57, number 3, Fall 1998

This is an insightful critical review of several recent publications on the transition process in the largest of the CIS countries.

Hanson, Philip, "The Economies of the Former USSR: An Overview," in *Eastern Europe and the Commonwealth of Independent States 1997*, London: Europa, 1996

Hanson provides a useful historical overview of trends in GDP, economic relations, and foreign trade in the successor states to the Soviet Union.

Kozik, L., and P. Kokhno, "Protsessy Ekonomicheskoi Integratsii Gosudarstv SNG" [Processes of Economic Integration in CIS Countries], in *Ekonomist*, number 2, 1998

This article presents an analysis of the problems of integration facing the CIS countries, with special reference to Belarus.

Plyshevsky, B., "Struktura Proizvodstva" [The Structure of Production], in *Ekonomist*, number 12, 1997

The author outlines the structural problems of transition, both in general terms and with special reference to Russia.

Popov, Vladimir, "Vyvoz Syr'a – Eto ne Stydno" [Exporting Raw Materials is not Shameful], in *Ekspert*, number 41, November 2, 1998

A discussion of the changing structure of the Russian economy

Schroeder, Gertrude, "Economic Transformation in the Post-Soviet Republics: An Overview," in Bartolomiej Kaminski, editor, *Economic Transition in Russia and the New Independent States of Eurasia*, Armonk, NY: M. E. Sharpe, 1996

This is a valuable survey of the common features, and divergences, in economic development in the successor states to the Soviet Union.

Slepov, V. A., O. V. Voronenko, and D. B. Kryuchin, "FPG: Sovremennye Tendentsii Razvitiya" [Financial-industrial Groups: Contemporary Development Tendencies], in *Finansy*, number 4, 1998

The authors discuss the general problems of creating financial-industrial groups, using the example of the Korporatsiya Glavsreduralprodukt group, which is engaged in supplying processed foods in the Sverdlovsk region.

TACIS, *Economic Trends*, quarterly publication, Brussels: TACIS

TACIS is a program of the EU concerned with supporting the transition process in the CIS countries and Mongolia. It issues country-specific reports in the various editions of this publication.

UNECE: UN Economic Commission for Europe, *The Economic Survey of Europe*, number 3, Geneva; UN Economic Commission for Europe, 1998

This authoritative publication is packed with information and insights on the transition economies, and on their relations with the other member states of the organization in western Europe and North America. Large parts of this publication are available online (at www.unece.org).

Marianna Afanassieva is a Research Fellow in the Local Economic Development in Transition Economies Unit (LEDTEU) of the School of Languages and European Studies at the University of Wolverhampton in England.

Table 11.1 Changes in Gross Industrial Output in the CIS Countries, 1994–96 (%)

	1994	1995	1996
Armenia	5.3	2.4	1.0
Azerbaijan	−22.7	−17.2	−6.7
Belarus	−17.1	−11.9	3.2
Georgia	−39.7	−9.8	7.7
Kazakhstan	−28.1	−8.2	0.3
Kyrgyzstan	−28.0	−17.8	10.8
Moldova	−27.7	−3.9	−8.5
Russia	−20.9	−3.3	−5.0
Tajikistan	−25.4	−5.1	−19.8
Turkmenistan	−24.7	−6.4	17.9
Ukraine	−27.3	−12.0	−5.1
Uzbekistan	1.6	0.1	6.0
CIS	−21.5	−5.8	−3.4

Source: UN, *World Economic and Social Survey*, New York: UN, 1997

Table 11.2 Changes in GDP and Industrial Output in the CIS Countries, 1996, 1997, and January to June 1998 (%)

	GDP			Industrial Output		
	1996	1997	1998 First Half	1996	1997	1998 First Half
Armenia	5.8	3.1	6.7	1.4	0.9	3.2
Azerbaijan	1.3	5.8	9.1	−6.7	0.3	0.7
Belarus	2.8	10.4	12.5	3.5	18.8	13.5
Georgia	11.0	11.3	8.9	7.7	8.1	0.8
Kazakhstan	0.5	2.0	1.7	0.3	4.0	1.1
Kyrgyzstan	7.1	9.9	5.0	8.8	50.4	23.5
Moldova	−7.8	1.3	−4.7	−6.5	n. a.	2.3
Russia	−3.5	0.8	−0.5	−4.0	1.9	0.1
Tajikistan	−16.7	1.7	2.6	−23.9	−2.5	12.5
Turkmenistan	0.1	−15.0	3.0	17.9	−30	−5
Ukraine	−10.0	−3.2	0.2	−5.1	−1.8	0.7
Uzbekistan	1.7	5.2	4.0	6.0	6.5	5.5
CIS	−3.4	1.1	0.8	−2.8	2.5	1.8

Source: UN Economic Commission for Europe, *The Economic Survey of Europe*, number 3, Geneva: UN Economic Commission for Europe, 1998

Table 11.3 **Changes in Gross Investment in the CIS Countries (except Turkmenistan), 1993–96 (%)**

	1993	1994	1995	1996
Armenia	−24.0	−35.0	n. a.	n. a.
Azerbaijan	−39.0	89.0	−18.0	74.0
Belarus	−15.0	−11.0	−31.0	−10.0
Georgia	−62.0	−0.5	2.0	19.0
Kazakhstan	−39.0	−15.0	−38.0	−35.0
Kyrgyzstan	−31.0	−42.0	82.0	18.0
Moldova	−44.0	−51.0	−17.0	−15.0
Russia	−12.0	−26.0	−10.0	−18.0
Tajikistan	n. a.	−43.0	−25.0	n. a.
Ukraine	−10.0	−23.0	−35.0	−20.0
Uzbekistan	−5.0	−22.0	4.0	7.0
CIS	−10.0	−22.1	−18.9	−15.9

Source: UN, *World Economic and Social Survey*, New York: UN, 1997

Chapter Twelve

Financial Services

Olga Kuznetsova

The structure and performance of the financial services in the CIS countries share many common features, because they all descend from the same origin, the Soviet financial system. This system was very different from those accepted in developed market economies, in that it was firmly based on public property, state monopoly, and central planning. After the collapse of the Soviet Union, the newly independent states set themselves the targets of upgrading and restructuring their financial services, so that they could meet the standards and requirements of a new economic environment. Achievements vary from country to country. The transformation of financial services is only one of many reforms required to complete the transition process successfully, and the pace of change in this area cannot be very different from the speed of reforms in other areas. Hence, although the CIS countries had the same starting point, the current level of financial services in the different states is now a prime indicator of their general commitment to reforms.

From State Control to Liberalization

The Soviet Union had only a handful of banks apart from the State Bank (Gosbank), and all were state-owned. They specialized in particular economic sectors, such as agriculture, manufacturing, construction, or foreign trade, and their principal function was to help with the fulfillment of the state plan. They mostly dealt with state-owned enterprises and collective farms. The needs of the public were served by a savings bank, the Sberegatelnyi Bank or Sberbank, which was spun off from Gosbank in the late 1980s (and which still exists: see below). All the Soviet banks were extremely centralized, with headquarters in Moscow and branches or offices in republics and regions. Throughout the Union, all major procedures, services, and products were identical. The only other organizations providing financial services were the Inspection for State Insurance of the All-Union Ministry of Finance, known as Gosstrakh; and another state agency, Ingosstrakh, which provided insurance coverage for Soviet business activities abroad. Because money played a restricted role in the Soviet economy, many modern financial products and services familiar in the West did not exist. Financial institutions operated primarily in areas of savings and lending, but mostly supervised financial flows and allocated financial resources on behalf of the state. Profit-seeking was never their real mission.

After independence was achieved, the 12 Union Republic branches of Gosbank became independent central banks, on the model of their counterparts in the West, while the local networks of the Soviet banks served as the foundations for national financial systems. It is not surprising, therefore, that in most CIS countries one may still find large specialized banks focusing on particular industries. In some cases, state banks were broken up and privatized, to give birth to many smaller banks. A new wave of banks, finance companies, and other financial institutions created by private capital has swept across the region, but it is probably only in Russia that any of these has become really important.

In all the CIS countries, the development of new financial systems was prejudiced by an overall decline in economic performance and high rates of inflation. As a result, banks accumulated significant amounts of non-performing loans. On the other hand, their deposit bases suffered following the collapse of living standards. Numerous financial scandals, and some high-profile cases of fraud, substantially undermined the credibility of banks and the financial system in general. In these circumstances, it is not surprising that banks and other financial institutions have failed to achieve high standards, or that the quality and range of products and services provided do not grow as fast as they might be expected to. For example, within the CIS banks have joined the Society for Worldwide Interbank Financial Telecommunications (SWIFT), which provides data communication and transaction processing services to banks around the world, only in Ukraine, Kazakhstan, Armenia, and Moldova. In addition, some banks have started to move into increasingly sophisticated banking activities in which they lack expertise. This has made the banking business very risky both for customers and for the providers of services. The imminent threat of a banking crisis has become a fact of life in many of the CIS countries.

In addition, in all the CIS countries both the providers of insurance services and their customers are financially very weak. The majority of insurance companies operating in CIS countries are very small by western standards, and their numbers are changing all the time as a result of mergers, bankruptcies, and new ventures. Around 70% of the entire CIS insurance market is controlled by 200 companies. Clearly, insurance provision will have to pass through a period of thorough reorganization before it can become capable of meeting the requirements of increasingly sophisticated economies. In the meantime, the CIS countries have tried to coordinate their efforts to support the development of the industry through common principles and regulations, aimed at the creation of a "united insurance area," and they have established an Advisory Council on Insurance as an affiliate of the Interstate Economic Council.

Finally, the progress of banking, insurance, and other financial services in the CIS countries is compromised because of poor or inadequate financial legislation, political interference, the criminalization of many economic activities, and the uncertain business climate. Years after the beginning of reforms, only banking and insurance services have seen significant development, while other financial services and products, such as private sector pensions, personal investment plans or mortgages, remain in a rudimentary state. Even the supply of reliable recent data on financial services is inadequate in some CIS countries: hence the relative lack of detail below on securities markets and the insurance industry.

Russia

Although the progress of reforms in Russia has been difficult and erratic, financial services have been developing at a rapid pace, and the country boasts the most advanced financial system anywhere in the CIS. Nevertheless, the scale, reliability, and range of services are still far below the level that has become standard in western economies.

Banking is the most advanced of the financial services in Russia. Market reforms led to a dramatic increase in the number of banks, which peaked at 2,600 in 1997, largely resulting from the commercialization of the regional branches of former state banks as they gained independent status. Later, however, the introduction of more stringent legal requirements and the growth of competition reduced the number of banks to just under 1,700 at the beginning of 1998. The dramatic financial crisis in August 1998 put an end to the existence of dozens of banks, including some of the largest. The consequences of the crisis are certain to play a major long-term role in determining the development of the industry well into the 21st century. Most importantly, the crisis has fatally undermined public confidence in banks and forced the government to tighten its grip on the banking industry.

Banking remains highly concentrated. Before the crisis of 1998, Russia's 200 largest banks held nearly 85% of all banking assets (according to *Finansovye Izvestia*, October 7,

1997). Access to banking services is very unequal in different parts of the country. Of the 30 largest banks, 27 are based in Moscow and three in St Petersburg (Bank of Russia p. 18). Services provided outside these financial centers are generally inadequate and below standard, although most of the leading regional banks offer full services for corporate clients, including payments throughout Russia and through correspondent banks abroad. The standard services offered by both Moscow-based and regional banks are demand accounts, denominated in rubles and in foreign currencies; saving accounts; and certificate of deposit accounts. However, no reliable inter-bank clearing system exists, partly due to the inadequacy of the telecommunications infrastructure and the lack of a fully developed regulatory framework. Credit cards are increasingly being used as means of payment.

Whatever their size or location, Russian banks have never had a reputation for being reliable. In 1997, for example, Viktor Chernomyrdin, then Prime Minister, maintained that more than 50% of domestic banks were sound, although western estimates have never exceeded 2% (see OECD, and Sutela). Two years later, Viktor Gerashchenko, the head of the Bank of Russia announced that, in the wake of the crisis of 1998, only 350 to 400 commercial banks would ultimately remain open. For years there has been talk of closing down at least some of Russia's inept, inefficient and often criminally controlled banks. Many of them are nothing more than licensed money-laundering operations. One result of the crisis has been that banks, whatever their private connections, have also had to seek state support or authorization to stay in business and improve their credibility. This in turn has increased the role and responsibility of the Bank of Russia. It was founded on July 13, 1990, through the transformation of the Russian Republican Office of Gosbank, and was initially called the State Bank of the Russian Federation. Following the dissolution of the Soviet Union in December 1991, the Bank was instructed by the Russian Supreme Soviet to assume full control over the assets, technical facilities, and other resources of Gosbank, and all its institutions, enterprises,

and organizations, on Russian territory. In 1992, following the establishment of a single centralized federal treasury system accountable to the Ministry of Finance, the Bank was no longer required to make cash transactions servicing the federal budget. In April 1995, the Bank terminated direct lending to finance the federal budget deficit, and stopped extending centralized, targeted credits to individual industries and sectors of the economy.

Before August 1998, it was characteristic that commercial banks saw operations in the market for short-term state bonds as their main source of income: returns in that market climbed occasionally to 250%, allowing the banks to pay lucrative rates on deposits. Other activities were neglected. In fact, of R120 trillion (US$21 billion) in banking credits issued in 1996, only 1.2% were medium- and long-term credits to businesses (see Berezanskaya). The default on the government's debts resulted in millions of Russians losing all the savings that they had entrusted to banks, since the only bank in which deposits by the public are guaranteed by the state is Sberbank. It now holds more than 70% of non-corporate deposits in Russia. Private banks have been working hard trying to attract what is thought to be billions of rubles-worth of "under the mattress" savings, but the crisis has made this task even more daunting.

Since the first foreign bank obtained a license to operate in Russia as early as 1992, more than a dozen other western banks have received licenses. The government has established a ceiling of 12% on the share of foreign capital in the total statutory capital of all banks in Russia: before the crisis the actual share was just over 4%.

The Moscow Interbank Currency Exchange trades a larger volume of currencies than any of its rivals in Russia, and also has the largest number of financial institutions as members. Currency exchanges are also active in St Petersburg, Omsk, Yekaterinburg, Novosibirsk, Vladivostok, and a number of other cities. Trading sessions in hard currency contracts also take place on the Moscow Central Stock and Currency Exchange.

Financial services other than banking are scarce, although there are some private pension funds, financial and investment companies, and institutions for brokerage and dealing. The demand for insurance products greatly exceeds the capacity of the insurance industry, which is characterized by a lack of reliable and efficient service-providers, very low financial capacity in the majority of firms, and a tendency to narrow specialization. While there are around 2,000 insurance companies operating in the Russian market, more than 50% of all premium payments are collected by the leading 50 or 60 firms (according to *Trud-7*, December 11, 1998). The underwriting market is represented by only 19 companies.

Belarus

The banking industry was the first in Belarus to attempt to redesign itself in the light of new economic realities soon after the country gained independence. A new two-tier system was created, with the National Bank of Belarus, established in 1991, supervising a number of commercial banks spread around the country. As a whole, however, the financial system is poorly developed, insurance being the only area where non-banking financial services are offered.

Despite the relatively early start in dismantling the Soviet legacy in supervision and operations, very little has been achieved. The slow progress towards adopting modern market principles is a direct consequence of the political orientation of the government, which since 1995 has aimed at the conservation of central planning, public ownership, and state domination in the economy. Financial services have been geared to implementing functions very similar to those fulfilled by the Soviet banks, as instruments of state control.

The four largest banks in the country are Belagroprombank, Belpromstroybank, Sberbank, and Belvnyeshekonombank. These are specialized banks, dealing with the agricultural sector, manufacturing industries, personal savings, and foreign operations, respectively, and all four evolved from former Soviet banks with similar specialized functions. Yet Sberbank is the only wholly state-owned bank: the other three are either limited liability companies or joint stock companies. Together

they account for more than 75% of banking assets. Most of the 34 other commercial banks have been founded either by Belarus enterprises and organizations or by individuals: as of March 1998, however, only 23 of them were operational and only seven met the requirements on minimum capital. No new commercial banks were registered during 1997, while some were struck off the state register (National Bank of Belarus p. 19). Indeed, banks in this category have been prone to bankruptcy, as very low profitability is a distinctive feature of the country's banking industry. To protect these banks the government has pursued a policy of imposing restrictions on non-domestic banks, but, unlike in Russia, there is no ceiling on the share of foreign capital in the national market for banking services. The lack of adequate and effective legislation and the deterioration in the economy have prevented any significant positive developments.

Dependence on trade with Russia kept Belarus within the ruble zone until well after the dissolution of the Soviet Union. The Belarus rubel was introduced in 1992, in response to a shortage of Russian rubles with which to pay fuel and other debts to Russia. It quickly became known colloquially as the *zaychyk* ("hare"), in reference not only to the design on the one-rubel bill, but also to the way its value went down in leaps and bounds. It has since recovered somewhat, and has become, like other new currencies, a symbol of nationhood. Nevertheless, its value remains officially tied to that of the Russian ruble, and the government of Belarus has continued with efforts toward economic and monetary union with Russia.

Belarus has three commodity and stock exchanges. The securities market was created at the end of 1992, and is licensed and supervised by a state inspectorate. Over-the-counter trading dominates the securities market, with Russian corporate shares and bonds the most actively traded items.

Ukraine

As in most of the CIS countries, banking and financial services in Ukraine are underdeveloped by western standards, and many financial products and services are missing from its markets. The national economy is still predominantly cash-based and, despite the efforts of the government and technical assistance by international agencies, the financial system remains weak, unstable, and in need of restructuring. The National Bank of Ukraine closely controls banking operations, chiefly in an attempt to curb the spread of semilegal activities following the growth of the "shadow" economy. The major problems faced by Ukrainian banks are bad loans, lack of sufficient resources, and the high cost of credit.

The Ukrainian banking system includes more than 200 banks, some with foreign participation. Most of these banks were founded by entrepreneurs and firms after independence, but it was a very small group of institutions that took over the assets and operations of the former Soviet banks, and which still stands out. The industry is dominated by nine banks, the three largest being Ukrayina Bank, which serves agriculture and has the largest net assets; Prominvestbank, which specializes in funding construction and capital investment; and Oshchadbank, a savings bank that was formerly a branch of the Soviet Sberbank. Ukrainian banks adopted international accounting standards in 1998; the country also has a well-developed electronic payment system and is linked to SWIFT (defined above).

Ukraine offers foreign banks liberal treatment: they are allowed to carry out all the activities open to domestic banks. In 1998, the National Bank abolished the rule that had required that the authorized capital of foreign-owned banks should not exceed 15% of the statutory capital of all the banks in the country. However, despite this favorable legal regime, foreign banking capital has shown no inclination to rush into establishing its presence in Ukraine.

According to research by the US State Department, the securities market in Kyiv, the capital, is reportedly the fifth largest among the 27 "emerging" post-Communist markets (in the CIS and in central and eastern Europe). Virtually all of the registered secondary market activity is conducted through the nationwide electronic trading system. However, it has been claimed (again based on US State Department research) that the lion's share of trading, around 75%, is not reported to licensed markets.

Kazakhstan

The backbone of the Kazakh banking system is the National Bank of the Republic of Kazakhstan. Among its other duties as a central bank, it controls the supply of the Kazakh tenge, the national currency introduced in November 1993.

Every bank in the country has to register with the National Bank and obtain a license: 76 were licensed as of early 1998. The banking sector is dominated by nine very large banks. Five are fully owned by the government – the Kazakhstan Export-Importbank, the Housing Construction Bank, the Government Budget Bank, the Rehabilitation Bank, and the Turan-Alem Bank – and 35 others are privately owned commercial banks based in the former capital city, Almaty. The two largest commercial banks, whether measured by assets, branch networks or scope of operations, are Kazkommertsbank and the Halyk Savings Bank. The latter, which inherited the assets, infrastructure, and customers of the Kazakh branch of the Soviet Sberbank, now controls more than 40% of personal savings in the country, and is the only bank in the country with a comprehensive branch network. The Halyk Savings Bank, the Turan-Alem Bank, and the Dutch institution ABN AMRO together control more than 60% of all banking assets in Kazakhstan.

As in Russia, there is a limit on the share of foreign capital in the overall assets of the banking industry, which in Kazakhstan is set at 25%. Some leading international banks, including Société Générale and Citibank, were quick to establish their presence, alongside banks from China, Russia, the Netherlands, and Turkey, but the limit has not yet been reached. Twelve foreign banks have full operating licenses, although ABN AMRO is the only foreign bank to run a full-scale branch.

The banking system of Kazakhstan is still at a formative stage, and its parameters, in particular the number of operational banks, change almost on a monthly basis. There has been a steady trend for the number of banks to decline through mergers and acquisitions, but also, more importantly, because of the attempts of the National Bank to impose discipline and promote efficiency, notably by making liquidity and capitalization requirements tougher. The National Bank recently issued rules requiring banks to complete the adoption of international standards on capitalization, the quantity and diversification of assets, management, accounting, and the transmission and protection of information by December 31, 2000. Failure to meet these standards will lead to liquidation or reorganization; and withdrawal of licenses issued to private banks has already become quite common. Despite these attempts, the banking system is beset with such fundamental problems as low levels of capitalization, tight liquidity, and high levels of non-performing loans. Interest rates are prohibitively high. The short duration of credit, the inexperience of loan officers, and uncertainty in applying new banking laws are additional issues. As a result of all these factors, the banking industry underperforms: banks provide only 1–3% of all the financial resources required by the national economy.

Since 1998, banks in Kazakhstan have been allowed to hold pension deposits, which the government hopes will help them to enhance their operational assets. Kazakhstan now has nine pension savings funds, eight of which are private while the ninth is state-run. The pension reform now under way, the most ambitious in the CIS, is expected to provide for two types of pension funds, corporate and personal.

The only stock market in the country is the Kazakhstan Stock Exchange, which was incorporated in 1997. Only holders of licenses issued by the National Securities Commission, a state regulatory agency, are allowed to trade. There are a number of financial companies involved in brokerage and dealing. Trading by banks is restricted to government securities, but they can also act as corporate securities custodians. Treasury bills account for the largest share of turnover; domestic corporate equities and foreign currencies are also traded, but volumes are low.

Nearly 170 registered investment funds have been established. They have succeeded in attracting 67% of the vouchers issued to the population during the government's privatization campaign, which are to be exchanged for shares in several thousand enterprises.

Kyrgyzstan

The banking industry is the most developed branch of the financial services in Kyrgyzstan. The strong and independent central bank, the National Bank of Kyrgyzstan, issues the Kyrgyz som, the national currency introduced in May 1993, and supervises nearly 20 commercial banks. The free flow of financial resources and free trade in foreign currencies have been fully implemented, but there is a relatively limited range of credit instruments available, and legislation and accounting systems are neither completely transparent nor fully aligned with international standards. Consequently, the private sector continues to operate mainly on a cash basis.

The National Bank of Kyrgyzstan, like most of the central banks in the CIS, is actively seeking to modernize and upgrade the financial system. It has created a special agency for debt restructuring and reorganization of banks, as well as an Agricultural Finance Corporation to revive the supply of credit for farms. As of January 1998, all Kyrgyz legal entities other than institutions funded by the state budget are required to operate according to the international standards for accounting and reporting.

The national banking system is still quite weak, however, as non-performing assets represent an estimated 80–90% of total banking assets. The other problem is severe undercapitalization. Only the former Soviet state banks have anything approaching nationwide coverage. Several of the small, new private banks are well-run, but their activities are confined to the capital, Bishkek, and surrounding areas. Real interest rates remain high and long-term credit is not available; most banks make profits mainly from trading in foreign currencies.

Foreign banks can be opened and operate under a written agreement with the Foreign Ministry for three years initially, with subsequent mandatory reapplication for an extension. Very little export finance is available, and most imports are paid for by cash or cash transfer.

The Kyrgyz Stock Exchange, which is a member of the Federation of Euro-Asian Stock Exchanges, began listing and trading the securities of privatized companies in May 1995. The Maksat Commercial Bank won a tender to become the clearing bank for the Exchange, which is regulated by a semiautonomous State Securities Agency.

There are also 15 investment funds, two pension funds, one savings company, and more than 400 other financial institutions. These include around 40 insurance companies, all of which are owned by domestic capital, including one owned by the state. Foreign companies may penetrate the market only by setting up joint ventures or signing agreements of reinsurance with Kyrgyz companies. The spectrum of insurance services is narrow: according to the State Insurance Supervision Board, life and other forms of personal insurance account for 79% of all insurance premiums, property insurance for 18%, and liability insurance for the remaining 3%.

Tajikistan

The National Bank of Tajikistan and the large specialized banks, the legacy of the Soviet banking system, remain in command of the financial system of the country, and banking regulations still draw heavily on Soviet patterns. The same is true of the accounting system used by domestic banks. The banking culture in the country is in its infancy: cash is still the dominant method of payment and the use of checks is marginal. Heavy-handed interference by the state is a prominent feature of the Tajik financial system. Business customers, for example, are not allowed to cash their bank deposits freely, and interest rates, which are negative in real terms, are also subject to controls.

The leading institution in mobilizing the savings of the population is the savings bank, Sberbank, which enjoys a unique status. It is outside the scope of the National Bank's supervisory powers and reports directly to the legislature, the Supreme Assembly. Sberbank recently started to expand its lending activities, in which it did not have previous experience,

with a focus on smaller enterprises, private firms, and individuals. The bank has the most extensive branch network in the country and all deposits in them are guaranteed by the state.

Similarly, deposits in the Khatlon Reconstruction and Development Bank also have a government guarantee. The Khatlon Bank was established by the government with a mission to assist in the development of the Khatlon region. It is expected that it will be closed down when the development project for which it was created comes to an end.

The remainder of the industry comprises a range of "state commercial" banks, privately owned commercial institutions, and cooperative banks. The differences among these categories are related to their capital structure rather than to their functions. Prominent in the first category is the Tajikistan Bank for Foreign Economic Activities, which was once the Tajik division of the Soviet Bank for Foreign Trade (Vneshtorgbank); it is not in fact a state-owned entity, although the state does back up its borrowings. It manages foreign exchange reserves under the authority of the Ministry of Finance. The leading commercial banks are Agroprombank, which serves agriculture, Orienbank, which serves manufacturing and construction, and Tajikbankbusiness, which focuses on trade, local industries, and small enterprises. Together, these three institutions account for more than 96% of bank lending. Since January 1998, the statutory minimum capital requirement for commercial banks has been fixed at US$1 million, which is a very high threshold by national standards, preventing any rapid increase in the number of banks in the country.

The reform of the banking system, which is still in progress, started in 1994 with financial aid from the World Bank, the IMF, and the European Bank for Reconstruction and Development (EBRD), and technical assistance from western corporations. One particular problem that must be addressed is the generally low level of professional experience and training among banking staff, following the mass emigration of Russian personnel in the 1990s. This shortage has created a severe constraint on the growth of banks. For example, Sberbank has been forced to restrict credit operations to just two of its branches, in the capital, Dushanbe, and in Khujand (formerly Leninobod), because there are not enough fully trained employees to maintain credit departments at other branches.

The Tajik ruble was introduced in May 1995, as the fifth and last of the new currencies of Central Asia. It is traded on the Tajik Interbank Currency Exchange, a closed-stock company established by seven commercial banks and the National Bank. Auctions are carefully controlled by the government.

Additionally, there are one state insurance company, the Tajik descendant of the Soviet Gosstrakh, and seven privately owned insurance companies.

Turkmenistan

The banking system of Turkmenistan is underdeveloped by western standards, despite the efforts by some banks in the country to increase the range and quality of their services, and to establish relations with foreign banks. The national currency, the Turkmen manat, was introduced in November 1993. It has been weakened by persistent inflation and the slowness of the reform process.

All banks, whether commercial or stateowned, domestic or foreign, must be registered with the State Central Bank of Turkmenistan. The Central Bank issues two types of license: a general license, which allows conversion of the Turkmen manat into hard currency, and vice versa, at the current exchange rate, and an internal license, which allows the purchase of hard currency at foreign exchange auctions when certain requirements are met. Most commercial banks have been granted only internal licenses.

There are 67 banks in Turkmenistan. Two are fully owned by the state: Sberbank, the national savings bank; and the Turkmenistan Bank for Foreign Economic Activities, which is the primary fiscal agent for the government, securing financing for all governmental commercial transactions and handling all foreign exchange operations. There are 52 agricultural cooperative banks (*daykhanbanks*), supervised by a national Daykhancenterbank, and 13 commercial banks.

A securities market organized and managed by the state started operations in Turkmenistan in 1994. Its slow progress and small volumes present serious obstacles to the growth of trading in stocks and bonds.

Uzbekistan

The Uzbek banking system has been slow to shake off the features inherited from the Soviet period. It is still dominated by the state, and comprises a few specialized "super banks," servicing the needs of particular segments of the economy, such as agriculture or construction. However, the laws and regulations contain nothing to preclude a commercial bank from doing business with all categories of customers. Foreign banks have started to show a cautious interest in Uzbekistan, and some have representative offices in the country, but full-scale operations by foreign banks are not allowed in the domestic market.

The National Bank of Uzbekistan, established in 1992, is the core of the financial system. It has had responsibility for issuing the national currency, the Uzbek sum, since it was introduced in November 1993, and it controls around 60% of all banking assets. The other major state bank is the National Bank for Foreign Economic Activity, which implements almost 95% of all external payments through correspondent accounts with foreign banks. It was established in 1991 to monitor the use of foreign currency resources, promote exports, and stimulate foreign economic activity. It has 17 branches in key areas across the country. The Agricultural-Industrial Bank of Uzbekistan (Uzpakhtabank) and the Industrial Bank of Uzbekistan (Uzpromstroybank) are large state-owned banks dealing almost exclusively with state-owned farms and industrial enterprises, respectively.

Access to hard currency is very limited in Uzbekistan. Every company earning hard currency is obligated to exchange 30% of its revenues at the official rate, under a policy aimed at preventing hard currency transactions outside the banking system. It also helps the government to maintain strict controls over the money supply and to subsidize state purchases of priority imports. Nevertheless, the policy has provoked the establishment of an illicit market in foreign currency.

Armenia

The contribution of financial services to the national economy of Armenia is very modest by any standards. This is a reflection of the low level of development of these services, as well as the relative lack of demand for them among a population whose living standards have collapsed and who have not acquired market habits to any great extent.

The Central Bank of Armenia was not fully established until 1994 and is not yet wholly independent in policy-making. The state also controls the national savings bank, Hnaibank, and owns shares in the three largest commercial banks, Ardshinbank, Haieconombank, and Haiagrobank. All five of these institutions derived from branches of Soviet banks. In addition, there were 31 commercial banks in Armenia as of February 1999, and foreign banks also have representation in the country.

The spectrum of activities of Armenian banks is not wide by western standards. Only a few banks are involved in operations with securities, mainly government Treasury bills. These few banks are mostly active in the primary market and, as a rule, prefer to use their own funds rather than act as intermediaries for clients. The ability of banks to invest and provide credit is limited by their under-capitalization. Only a very small number of banks can provide loans exceeding US$20,000 or its equivalent. Lending operations are predominantly short-term and at very high rates of interest, up to 50–70% annually. Banks usually demand collateral of equal or higher market value, such as real estate, automobiles or gold. The number of private banks has more than halved since 1996, as the Central Bank has started to make capitalization requirements tighter, pushing the most under-capitalized banks into closure or mergers with stronger banks.

In the face of close supervision and increasing competition, the commercial banks are working toward implementing inter-national accounting standards and improving their performance. Banking reform has moved somewhat more slowly in Armenia than in other CIS countries. In late 1991, the special-ized state banks of the Soviet system were converted into joint-stock commercial banks, and some new commercial banks were formed, but, at least formally, the State Bank of Armenia and the Bank for Foreign Economic Activities remained branches of state banks in Moscow. The consequences included lack of control by Armenia over monetary policy until the national currency, the dram, was introduced in November 1993. Significant assistance to the development of the banking industry is being provided through bilateral foreign advice and assistance, and multilateral financing, for example to support the installa-tion of an interbank electronic transfer and data exchange system.

Azerbaijan

Financial services play a secondary role in the economy of Azerbaijan, where cash transac-tions dominate. The banking system is small and the level of public trust in it is not high. It is dominated by the International Bank of Azerbaijan, the healthiest of the four state-owned banks. The other three are technically bankrupt, and are undergoing a restructuring program designed by the World Bank: they are unable to lend money. Meanwhile, the number of privately owned banks varies constantly, and none has established a significant or lasting position in the industry. Most western firms that have dealings in or with Azerbaijan make use of either the International Bank or one of the six foreign-owned banks, although domestic banks are generally used for payments transactions. The World Bank and the EBRD are both active in financing public infrastructure projects, while these and other international institutions provide technical assistance and training to some private banks.

The Baku Interbank Currency Exchange holds interbank auctions of foreign exchange. It has also conducted auctions of Treasury bills for the Ministry of Finance. The national currency, the Azerbaijani manat, was introduced in August 1992. Since 1993, it has been fully convertible, and it can be openly exchanged at foreign exchange shops throughout the capital city, Baku. Companies with foreign capital participation may freely expatriate profits from their business in Azerbaijan.

There is no stock exchange, nor are there any other organized capital markets.

Georgia

Private commercial banks began operations in Georgia in 1989, two years before the Soviet Union collapsed, and their number grew rapidly following the introduction of new banking legislation in 1991–92. Meanwhile, the banks in the public sector ended their relationships with their former parent banks in Moscow during 1991, and the National Bank of Georgia was created as an independent central bank. Nevertheless, Georgia remained in the ruble zone until as recently as September 1995, when it introduced its fully convertible national currency, the lari.

The five largest commercial banks, all of which originated from Soviet state banks, share between them 95% of all national credit resources. The Commercial Banking Law allows the National Bank to intervene against monopolistic practices and to instigate proceedings to liquidate banks that do not comply with prudential banking practice.

Moldova

The banking industry is a major provider of financial services in Moldova. At the center of the system is the National Bank of Moldova, established in June 1991. There are 21 commercial banks, of which five have domestic licenses, allowing them to carry out foreign exchange operations in the home market only, while the other 16 have general licenses, enabling them to perform international foreign exchange operations. The Interbank Foreign Currency Exchange is the main wholesale market for foreign currency in the country. The national currency, the Moldovan leu (which must be distinguished from the Romanian leu), is one of the most stable currencies in the CIS.

The National Bank has taken measures to raise the profile of the national banking system.

International accounting standards were introduced as early as 1995, and banks that do not comply with the regulations may be reorganized or liquidated. There are no restrictions on setting up foreign banks or their branches in the territory of Moldova.

The Moldova Stock Exchange was incorporated in December 1994 and held its first trading session on June 26, 1995. It is a closed joint-stock company regulated under the Law on Securities and Stock Exchanges. Thanks to foreign assistance, the Exchange is equipped with the modern technologies necessary to support its operations, and the shares of more than 500 privatized enterprises and commercial banks are included in its quotation list.

Further Reading

Association of the Ukrainian Banks, *Report*, Kyiv: annual publication

> This regular report, based mainly on official sources of information, provides details of changes in the practice and performance of Ukrainian banks.

Bank of Russia, *Vestnik Banka Rossii* [Bank of Russia Bulletin], number 84, Moscow: Bank of Russia, 1998

> One in a regular series of collections of documents, information, and regulations issued by the central bank of Russia

Belyanova, Elena, "Likelihood of Bank Crisis in Russia," in *The Russian Economic Barometer*, number 2, 1995

> This prescient article evaluates the economic factors that posed a threat to banking in Russia at the time that it was published.

Berezanskaya, L., "Chubais Asks Banks to Invest in Industry," in *St Petersburg Times*, April 28-May 4, 1997

EBRD, "Kazakhstan: Country Profile," London: European Bank for Reconstruction and Development, 1996

> A technical and analytical survey of the details and major trends in the transition in Kazakhstan

Finansy, number 3, 1998

> This issue of a useful Russian-language periodical includes information on trends in the development of the insurance industry in the CIS.

Marber, Peter, "Banking the Bear: Financial Marketization in Russia," in *The Columbia Journal of World Business*, Winter 1994

An investigation of the first signs of increasing access to capital in Russia, following the adoption of western standards

National Bank of Belarus, "Bankovskaya Sistema Belarusi: Tsifri i Facti" [The Banking System of Belarus: Data and Facts], in *Bankovskyi Vestnik* [Banking Bulletin], number 3, March 1998

This article provides some official statistics on the banking industry of Belarus.

OECD, *Economic Surveys – Russian Federation*, Paris: OECD, 1997

In this edition of an occasional publication, the largest section is dedicated to an evaluation of the activities of commercial banks, but the survey also includes some assessments and recommendations in the area of macroeconomic stabilization and structural reforms, as well as informative tables and a statistical annex.

Roe, Alan, Alan Siegelman, and Tim King, *Analyzing Financial Sectors in Transition: With Reference to the Former Soviet Union*, Washington, DC: World Bank, 1998

A comprehensive overview of banking, monetary and fiscal policy, and other aspects of finance in the CIS

Russian and East European Finance and Trade, Volume 30, number 5, 1994

This special issue of a leading journal in the field is devoted to studies of the transformation of banking and other financial services in Russia, Poland, and Hungary.

Sutela, Pekka, "The Role of Banks in Financing Russian Economic Growth," in *Post-Soviet Geography and Economics*, Volume 39, number 2, 1998

Sutela examines the contribution of the banking industry to stimulating economic growth and gives a brief account of the recent progress of the industry.

World Bank, *Tajikistan: The World Bank Country Study*, Washington, DC: World Bank, 1994

This review of the major trends in the transition in Tajikistan was conducted and completed as the country was moving from civil war to an uneasy peace. Nevertheless, it contains much valuable and relevant material.

World Bank, *From Plan to Market: World Development Report 1996*, Oxford and New York: Oxford University Press, 1996

A set of cross-country comparisons, highlighting various aspects of development in the transition economies, not only in the CIS but also in central and eastern Europe

Dr Olga Kuznetsova is a Research Fellow in the International Business Unit at Manchester Metropolitan University in England.

Chapter Thirteen

Social Divisions in CIS Countries

Stuart Griffin

Many of the Soviet Union's successor states have been plagued by serious social instability, which has frequently manifested itself in the form of interethnic violence. However, it is often debatable whether deep-rooted "ethnic tension" is truly the cause of social divisions, or whether it merely provides a suitable conduit for the political ambitions of prominent local figures. Many of the successor states have little or no experience of independent statehood and are handicapped by a weak sense of "nationhood." It is almost inevitable, therefore, that they have found the process of state-building extremely difficult. The general economic malaise among the CIS countries is another major source of social unrest, crime, and conflict.

Russia

With a landmass of around 6.5 million square miles – almost twice the size of the United States – and a population of around 147 million, Russia is by far the largest of the ex-Soviet states. Its fragile political institutions, its problematic federal system, and the difficulties of transition to a market economy have been heavily exploited by organized crime. Political instability has largely been confined to power struggles in the center, but the brutal Chechen war, which raged during the winter of 1994–95 and continued sporadically into 1996, was an ominous reminder of tension between Moscow and some of the autonomous regions.

Russia has struggled to come to terms with the end of the Soviet Union, and the political and social adjustments that this has entailed. According to T. H. Rigby, in Russia "the combination of its ethnonational diversity with the loss of its imperial role imbue the issue of national identity with a particular intensity, exceeded only in the former Yugoslavia" (Rigby in Saikal and Maley pp. 207–8). The resolution of Russia's identity crisis, which it is still struggling with, is a key factor in the future stability not only of Russia itself but of the entire CIS region, especially in the light of continuing tensions over the future of the 25 million ethnic Russians living outside Russia. This became an especially sensitive issue as the Soviet Union broke up. Hard-line elements in Russia advocated an aggressive foreign policy to "protect" them, while radical nationalists in the other successor states exploited fear and distrust of the Russian residents, often ex-Soviet military personnel, to engender "national" unity.

Ethnic Russians constitute nearly 80% of Russia's population, but that leaves around 29 million people who belong to around 130 other ethnic groups (see Appendix 5). Russia is a highly secularized society that generally accepts the great religious diversity among these groups. There are potential sources of division both in nationalist sentiment in European Russia, which often equates being Russian with being Christian, and in the revival of Islamic societies in some areas. In practice, however, religion has so far mattered less than the distribution of power.

Many ethnic minorities are concentrated in outlying autonomous areas, notably in the Caucasus and the Far East, linked to Moscow through a hybrid federalism that mixes national and territorial conceptions (see, for example, Sakwa). Twenty-one "national" republics and 11 "national-territorial" areas (autonomous *okrugs* and autonomous *oblasts*) sit uneasily alongside 57 other territorial units (*krays*, *oblasts*, and the two major cities of Moscow and St Petersburg) that are significant only as convenient administrative districts. The division of powers among these units took on special significance after 1990, when centrifugal tendencies within the Soviet Union led to a spate of unilateral declarations of sovereignty, culminating in Russia's own declaration of independence in August 1991.

Nevertheless, few of the federal units have directly questioned their position within a Russian federation that provides them with some degree of social and economic security. No one ethnic minority represents more than 5% of the total population, and the two largest minority groups – the Tatars (4.5%) and the Ukrainians (2.9%) – are widely dispersed. Thus, the scope for interethnic civil war and widespread irredentism is considerably less than is often implied. An additional factor that the republics have to take into account is the presence in most of them of substantial Russian populations. For example, Tatarstan, which has been among the most vociferous advocates of self-rule, has a population almost equally divided between ethnic Tatars and ethnic Russians. Many regions, notably in Siberia and the Far East, also have grievances concerning their economic exploitation during the Soviet period, and some have voiced concerns over the state of native language training and cultural facilities (see Dawisha and Parrott pp. 67–8). However, so far these grievances have rarely been translated into serious separatist activity, other than in the troubled North Caucasus (see below).

Instead of independence, then, the republics and regions appear to be seeking as much self-rule as possible, by pressing Moscow to grant greater fiscal, judicial, and administrative powers. The Federal Treaty, finally signed, after years of difficult negotiation, on March 31, 1992, recognized the different types of federal units, and accorded them nominally equal rights and obligations. The republics were allowed to adopt some of the trappings of statehood, notably their own constitutions: most have since created their own judiciaries and

many have introduced presidential systems of rule. Only Chechen-Ingushetia and Tatarstan refused to sign the Treaty. The Chechen Republic had declared its independence, both from Russia and Chechen-Ingushetia, the previous November, making negotiations impossible, while Tatarstan was holding out for a bilateral treaty, according it stronger sovereign status, which was agreed on February 15, 1994.

The War in Chechnya

If any region can be seen to symbolize the difficulties of federalism it is the North Caucasus. The Caucasus Mountains are home to ethnically diverse but culturally similar peoples divided among nine republics: Adygei, Chechnya, Dagestan, Ingushetia, Kabardino-Balkaria, Karachai-Circassia, and North Ossetia in Russia; Abkhazia and Adzharia in Georgia (see below). These political divisions, a legacy of the Soviet period, bear little resemblance to the realities of a region where kinship ties and honor codes often mean more than the abstract concept of the state. Further, the republics are somewhat arbitrarily organized, with ethnic groups often separated by state boundaries, most obviously the division between North Ossetia in Russia and South Ossetia in Georgia. Not surprisingly, the region has been the source of much interethnic antagonism, as many North Caucasian peoples have challenged the authority of both Russia and Georgia.

In August 1989, the North Caucasian republics inside Russia formed the Assembly of Mountain Peoples of the Caucasus (AGNK) to represent their common interests. Renamed the Confederation of Mountain Peoples of the Caucasus (KGNK) in November 1991, this had become a very significant and unpredictable organization by 1992. It was capable of raising considerable paramilitary forces, which were used on several occasions to reinforce Abkhazian and South Ossetian forces in Georgia. The high proportion of Chechen units involved in KGNK military activities and their high quality were ominous signs for Russia itself.

Following an effective political coup in Chechnya, which saw Major-General

Dzhokhar Dudayev come to prominence in 1990 and then formalize control over Chechen politics by "winning" a questionable presidential election on October 27, 1991, Chechnya unilaterally declared independence (as mentioned above) in November 1991. President Boris Yeltsin wished to respond strongly by imposing a state of emergency on the region, but this was generally felt to be too vigorous a reaction and so Russia settled on economic sanctions. Over the following three years, Dudayev consolidated his control, building up Chechnya's armed forces and strengthening his own power-base to become a *de facto* dictator. Simultaneously, as economic sanctions bit deeply, the republic became a notorious center for organized crime. Attempts by the Russian intelligence service, the FSK, to overthrow his regime, which was far from universally popular within Chechnya, only consolidated support for Dudayev, perhaps indicating that anti-Russian sentiment was stronger even than the desire for democratic rule.

An undeclared war escalated throughout 1994, until Russia finally launched a full-scale invasion on December 11. The brutal fighting that followed took Moscow by surprise. Russian forces faced tortuous street-fighting against a highly committed enemy through the Chechen capital, Grozny. After the presidential palace was captured, on January 19, 1995, Dudayev's remaining forces retreated into the mountains and continued to harass Russian forces from there. Only after Dudayev's death in battle in April 1996 was a lasting ceasefire brokered, in August the same year. A peace agreement signed in May 1997 requires both parties to resolve their differences permanently by 2001.

The Chechen war raised many questions about the efficacy of Russian federalism, particularly its ethnonational element. Aside from the indiscriminate use of force by Russian troops, which saw civilian casualties run into tens of thousands, the invasion was ordered without due regard for federal procedures and carried out with spectacular ineptitude. The Yeltsin government's credibility suffered badly, as many of the regional elites questioned Moscow's commitment to the new Russian Constitution (see below). The war also height-ened political tension at the heart of the federal government, exacerbating arguments over the potentially explosive issue of national identity.

The Struggle for the Future of Russia

Although Chechnya is the most high-profile manifestation of instability in Russia, it is the political struggle at the heart of central government that holds the key to Russia's destiny. The creation of a viable national identity, often closely interwoven with problems of economic rehabilitation, lies at the heart of successful state-building.

T. H. Rigby has identified four broad groupings in Russian politics: the democrats, who wish to take the quickest path to free markets and democracy; the centrists, who prefer a slower, incremental approach; the Communists, who wish to preserve the Soviet system in some form; and the patriots, who are determined to reassert a unique Russian identity (see Rigby in Saikal and Maley). However, diversity of opinion within these broad groupings has inhibited party formation and further clouded the political landscape. Within the patriotic grouping, for example, we can perhaps distinguish between "patriots," who advocate a more intro-spective form of nationalism built cooperatively from within, and "nationalists," who generally espouse a more aggressive, imperialist form of nationalism (see Sakwa). While the democrats and, to a lesser extent, the centrists argue that Russia must come to terms with the demise of the Soviet Union, hard-line Communists and nationalists continue to push for the reassertion of Russian dominance in the CIS region. The establishment of coherent long-term policies has thus been impeded by fundamental disagreements over the very nature of Russian society.

These disagreements continue, but within a somewhat more stable framework. In particular, on December 12, 1993, a narrow referendum victory for Yeltsin and the reformers – mainly "centrists," but also "democrats" – retrospectively legitimized the President's suppression of the Congress of People's Deputies, the introduction of the new Constitution, and the election of the new Federal Assembly. For the first time ever, Russia has a democratically elected head of state and a democratically approved political structure, crucially including an upper house, the Council of the Federation, that reflects the ethnic and geographic diversity of the world's largest country.

Nevertheless, continuing economic problems have the potential to destabilize not only Russia but the whole CIS region. Near-total economic collapse in August 1998 led to another political crisis, and Yeltsin's government was at loggerheads once again with the legislature, this time with the lower house, the State Duma. The process of state-building is still very much in its formative stages. Democratic institutions have not yet matured, and the relationship between central government and the regional and local authorities remains ambiguous. Officially, Russia is committed to the development of a multiethnic, multicultural society, in which citizenship is associated with responsibility to the democratic institutions of state. This civic-institutional approach to statehood is the most inclusive form of nationalism, but it sits uneasily with the ethnicized forms of nationalism – albeit largely stopping short of separatism – that are still evident in some of the republics and regions, from the North Caucasus (Chechnya, Kabardino-Balkaria, and, to a lesser extent, Dagestan), to Tatarstan and Bashkortostan, to Karelia (where ethnic Karelians now form a small minority), to Tuva Ulus and Sakha (Yakutia). Civic-institutional nationalism also has little appeal to the more right-wing elements of the Russian patriotic movement. Given the fact that both the Federal Treaty and the Constitution legitimate ethnonational entities, there is a very delicate balance between inclusive and exclusive variants of nationalism. If it is upset, it has the potential to destroy Russia.

Belarus, Moldova, and Ukraine

The awkward geostrategic position of these three countries, located between Russia and the countries of central and eastern Europe, most of which are moving ever closer to structural integration with western Europe, has complicated their post-Soviet transitions. Russia's strong cultural affinity with Belarus and Ukraine, and the initial aspirations of some

Moldovan politicians to reunion with Romania, have also exacerbated internal social divisions and heightened international tensions. Russia's "loss" of Belarus and Ukraine was a bitter psychological blow. Ukraine in particular is of tremendous historical significance to Russia, for its capital, Kyiv – known as Kiev to Russians and, significantly, to most non-Russians too – is seen as the cradle of the Russian state. Russia continues to refer to both states as "little brothers" and has displayed a corresponding desire to influence their development.

Belarus

Among these three countries, social divisions are least marked in Belarus, a stable society despite economic hardship and limited political reform, which has led to international concern over human rights standards. In marked contrast to many other CIS countries, interethnic relations are remarkably harmonious. The population's weak sense of national identity is problematic for the enterprise of state-building, but it effectively excludes the key dynamic for ethnic conflict.

Ethnic Belarusians, around 78% of the population, are almost indistinguishable from Russians and invariably speak Russian too; and heavy dependence on Russian economic support also contributes to maintaining the close association between the two countries. Russia does not perceive its interests as being threatened by Belarusian diplomatic overtures to western Europe and has therefore resisted the temptation to stir interethnic animosities. Ironically, however, Russia has been less than enthralled by talk of reunification with Belarus, being fearful that the added burden of the ailing Belarusian economy would topple the shaky Russian economy. Russia and Belarus have signed agreements on monetary union, free trade, and a common ruble (April 1994), on a bilateral "Community of Sovereign Republics" (April 1996), and on several other joint enterprises (see Appendix 1), but all of these have been slow to produce any results. Meanwhile, Belarus has tied itself as closely as possible to Russia through the institutions of the CIS.

The combination of Belarusia's economic malaise with the lack of serious political reform may well be the most serious long-term threat to internal social stability. Interethnic relations remain excellent, but economic decline, coupled with the lack of democratic reform and concern over the long-term effect of close alliance with Russia on Belarusian sovereignty, may eventually lead to considerable instability.

Moldova

Interethnic relations in Moldova stand in marked contrast to those in Belarus. Unlike ethnic Belarusians, ethnic Moldovans are not closely akin to Russians, being of Romanian descent. During the Soviet period, Moscow asserted its authority over Moldova by suppressing indigenous culture, while simultaneously encouraging Russification, and giving ethnic Russians and Ukrainians a disproportionate amount of power within the republic's Communist Party. The political and cultural marginalization of the titular nationality inevitably led to interethnic friction. Russians and Ukrainians, primarily situated in Transnistria in the East, and the Gagauz people of the South, remained largely unintegrated with the indigenous community. Hence, the revival of Moldovan nationalism and the declaration of sovereignty by a newly elected, largely anti-Communist legislature in June 1990 were followed within months by the establishment of the Dnestr Moldavian Republic and the autonomous state of Gagauz-Yeri.

The Gagauz accepted a compromise with the Moldovan government in March 1992, but in Transnistria the confrontation turned violent and drew in Russian forces. A ceasefire in July 1992 established a special security zone around Transnistria, ceding effective political control of the region to the Dnestr Republic. Social divisions have been tempered since then by political moderation on the part of the Moldovan government and the prospect of unification with Romania, which had alarmed the ethnic minorities, was decisively rejected in a referendum in March 1994. It now appears that the major stumbling bloc to social stability is the radicalism of the ethnic minorities' leaderships, particularly in the Dnestr Republic.

Mark Webber is not the only observer to have concluded that the confrontational politics of the Transnistrian authorities reflects "either a lingering Communist nostalgia or a pronounced Russian nationalism, rather than justifiable fears concerning ethnic discrimination" (Webber 1996 p. 239). Igor Smirnov, the "President" of the Dnestr Republic, formally accepted autonomy within Moldova in June 1996, but this has never been ratified and anti-Moldovan sentiment lingers.

Clearly, until the issue of Transnistria has been permanently resolved, the potential for renewed social instability in Moldova remains. Moldova also shares common problems with many other CIS states. In particular, the potential for continued Russian interference in Moldovan politics, above all over Transnistria, is considerable, even though the Moldovan government has taken a pragmatic and conciliatory course toward Russia in recent years. As elsewhere, further economic and political reform is also necessary for any future stability.

Ukraine

The situation in Ukraine is potentially among the most explosive in any of the CIS countries. The process of nation-building since independence was declared on August 24, 1991, has been complicated by external relations with Russia. Russia's identity crisis during the early 1990s fueled interethnic animosity within Ukraine too. Ukrainian-Russian relations have gone through periodic bouts of high tension, further exacerbating divisions within both states. Ukraine's lack of experience of independent statehood and its huge economic problems have made the post-Soviet transition even more difficult.

Ethnic Russians form around 20% of the Ukrainian population and dominate the East and South of the country, as well as Crimea. However, Ukraine has not fractured along ethnic lines. With the exception of the Russians in Crimea, Ukraine's ethnic minorities have not mobilized in coherent opposition to Ukrainian independence or in favor of secession to Russia. The close cultural and ethnic ties between Ukrainians and Russians sustain generally peaceful and friendly personal relations.

The government's enlightened attitude toward minorities has further reduced tension. The 1989 Language Law established Ukrainian as the state language, but also recognized the right of national minorities to continue to use their own languages; the 1991 Law on Citizenship offered the vast majority of Ukraine's national minorities citizenship on the same terms as ethnic Ukrainians; and the 1992 Law on National Minorities made substantial provision for the protection of minority linguistic and religious rights. The 1996 Constitution is a liberal and inclusive document that leaves little scope for accusations of prejudice, although some grievances have been expressed over the refusal to allow dual citizenship or to grant Russian a status as a second state language. International organizations, such as the Council of Europe, the OSCE, and the UN, have consistently praised Ukraine for its minorities policies.

However, Russian separatism has presented problems in Crimea, where ethnic Russians amount to around 70% of the population. The region was granted full autonomy in February 1991, but the Crimean authorities, comprising a high proportion of Russian nationalists and Communists, continued to canvass support for secession. The subsequent confrontation with the Ukrainian authorities was complicated by the disputes with Russia over the Black Sea Fleet and Ukraine's nuclear arsenal. Crimea unilaterally declared itself a republic on February 26, 1992, and then declared independence on May 5, only to back down a few days later after the President of Ukraine, Leonid Kravchuk, ceded even greater autonomy to the region. A more serious confrontation developed during the course of 1994, after the pro-Russian Yuri Meshkov was elected President of Crimea in January and the "Russia Bloc" won 58 of the 97 seats in the Crimean legislature in March. Taking advantage of political inertia during Ukraine's presidential election campaign, Crimea voted to restore its 1992 Constitution. The new President, Leonid Kuchma, surprised those who saw him as pro-Russian by displaying as strong a commitment to Ukraine's territorial integrity as Kravchuk had. In March 1995, taking advantage of improved relations with Russia, and of Russia's

increasing distraction over Chechnya, Kuchma abolished the Crimean presidency and suspended the Crimean Constitution. The subsequent fall from power of the Russia Bloc and the reining in of Crimean autonomy (stopping short of abolishing it, however) signaled a respite in the power struggle, but not an end to separatist feeling.

Conflict between the Russian majority in Crimea and the returning Crimean Tatars also presents Ukraine with a potential source of serious social instability. After being deported to Central Asia in May 1944, on the pretext that they had allegedly collaborated with the Nazi invasion of the Soviet Union, the Crimean Tatars won the right to return home only in 1988. Around 185,000 of them have returned to Crimea, but find themselves socially isolated and politically and economically disadvantaged. Lingering ill will between the Crimean Tatars and Russians has exacerbated social tension on the peninsula and interethnic bloodshed, particularly between Crimean Tatar traders and local organized crime, is not unheard of. The Ukrainian government is keen to reintegrate the Crimean Tatars as quickly as possible but its uneasy relationship with the Crimean authorities is making this problematic.

The prospects for long-term Ukrainian social stability are mixed. Ukraine's ethnic groups display very few extremist tendencies and successive governments have been committed to democratic and inclusive state-building. Ukraine will continue to need determined yet moderate leadership, of the type that Presidents Kravchuk and Kuchma have provided so far, if it is to develop a strong and stable society. The separatist tendencies of many Crimean Russians and their fraught relations with the Crimean Tartars remain the most immediate threats to stability, but serious reform also needs to be undertaken if economic atrophy is not to undermine Ukrainian society.

Central Asia

As in the rest of the CIS, the Central Asian republics of Kazakhstan, Kyrgyzstan, Tajikistan, Turkmenistan, and Uzbekistan have experienced considerable problems since the collapse of the Soviet Union. However, only in Tajikistan did social and political divisions culminate in civil war (1992–93) in the wake of independence. The desperate need of the Central Asian states to retain their Slavic minorities, who represent a large proportion of the skilled labor force, has been a major factor mitigating the potential for interethnic conflict. All five states suffer from a weak sense of national identity and the difficulties of state-building are still manifest in the authoritarian nature of their governments, the large-scale emigration by ethnic minorities, the retention of somewhat arbitrary state and regional boundaries, and the continuance of widespread loyalty to family or regional groupings rather than states.

The imposition of centralized power structures and fixed boundaries by the Soviet authorities led to an increased awareness of the state, but local loyalties remained strong throughout the Soviet period (see Akiner in Ferdinand pp. 16–17). Traditionally dominant groups, such as the Senior Horde in Kazakhstan, the Khujand clan in Tajikistan, and the Tekke tribe in Uzbekistan, exploited Soviet power structures, to the extent of eliminating their rivals (Akiner p. 16.). When Soviet authority collapsed, clan competition emerged as a very influential factor in politics, and resentment of the Khujand clan was certainly a contributing factor in Tajikistan's civil war (see below). The elites of Central Asia generally regard tribal or interethnic rivalry as the most likely short-term threats to stability. Partly as a result, all five states have invested considerable authority in their presidents, to such a degree that they have been referred to by one analyst, Oleg Panfilov, as the "five royal presidents" (see Panfilov). In the short term, authoritarian rule may enhance stability, but the implications for future democratic development are grave. If any of the presidents begins to lose support, or even dies, central government may disintegrate rapidly.

Interethnic rivalries are potentially destabilizing factors not only within the five states, but between them, since some of their frontiers arbitrarily divide ethnic communities. For example, Bokhara and Samarkand are populated predominantly by ethnic Tajiks, yet both cities are in Uzbekistan, while the Fergana (or Farghona) Valley, which has a predominantly Uzbek population, is divided between Uzbekistan, Tajikistan, and Kyrgyzstan. Bloodshed in the Fergana Valley during 1989, mainly aimed at its Meskhetian population, demonstrated its volatility.

However, it is the relationships between the titular nationalities and ethnic minorities of European extraction that give most cause for concern. All five states have sizable Russian-speaking populations: between 6.7 and 8% of the total population in Tajikistan, Uzbekistan and Turkmenistan, around 19% in Kyrgyzstan, and around 31.4% in Kazakhstan. Maintaining the delicate balance between reviving the fortunes of titular nationalities and engendering interethnic harmony, in order to persuade ethnic minorities to stay, has not been easy. All five states have adopted inclusive citizenship laws, but other laws introduced during 1989 and 1990 made the five titular languages into state languages, undermining the previously privileged position of Russian. The perceived "nationalization" of the state *apparat* and demographic trends that favor the titular nationalities have also made many among the ethnic minorities feel increasingly marginalized. As elsewhere in the CIS, anti-Russian sentiment also increased after the collapse of the Soviet Union, although it is by no means endemic. The combination of these factors led to a dramatic exodus of Russian-speaking and other European settlers to their parent countries and to an increase in social tensions. In particular – although it should be noted that this was an extreme case – around 80% of the Slavic population of Tajikistan had left by mid-1993 (Anderson p. 151).

Tajikistan's civil war of 1992–93 offered an ominous glimpse of Central Asia's potential for social conflict. In essence, the war was a power struggle between the dominant clan from Khujand in the North and its main rival from Külob in the South, while other clans exploited the conflict to enhance their own positions, and ideological rivalry erupted among former Communists, committed democrats, and Islamists. Islam had been largely suppressed during the Soviet period, but since independence the Fergana Valley in particular has seen a religious revival. However, it was the prominent role played by the Islamic Renaissance Party in Tajikistan's civil war that revived fears about Islamist activism among many (while also, of course, reviving hopes among others). Even after the civil war officially ended, in 1993, Islamist forces continued to harass government forces from their bases in Afghanistan. Their links with Afghan fundamentalists heightened concern that revitalized Islamic sentiment could easily become politicized and destabilize the entire region. However, the material aid from elements of the Russian 201st Division to Tajik government forces had implications for the region's stability and independence that were at least as serious.

In any case, the potential for Islamic fundamentalism is only one element of a multifaceted situation and it is debatable whether it poses a real threat or merely provides a convenient image of enemy forces. In Tajikistan, Islamic activism only became a significant political factor in response to the anti-democratic nature of the regime and long-established regional rivalries: the Tajik population never showed any great interest in forming an Islamic state. Islamic revivalism could become a destabilizing factor, but only in the same way as interethnic tension or regional and tribal rivalries.

As elsewhere in the CIS, Central Asia's economic problems need to be resolved if there is to be long-term stability (Petersen p. 134). The region's abundant natural resources, primarily oil and natural gas, offer some hope that economic rehabilitation may be achieved, although it will take time. Finally, the authoritarian nature of all five regimes and the continued influence of Russia, both justified as maintaining stability, nevertheless have serious implications for the independent and democratic development of Central Asia.

Transcaucasia

Transcaucasia is the most conflict-ridden of all the regions in the CIS. Aside from the instability within Russia, discussed above, Armenia and Azerbaijan have been involved in a protracted dispute over the future of Nagorno-Karabakh, and Georgia has been plagued by a series of civil wars. The recent stabilization of Transcaucasia should not mask the fact that few of the underlying sources of conflict have been permanently resolved.

Armenia, Azerbaijan, and Nagorno-Karabakh

The region of Nagorno-Karabakh (which Armenians call Karabagh or Artsakh) was populated overwhelmingly by ethnic Armenians (more than 70% by 1988), but was governed as part of Azerbaijan from 1921 onward. Resentment of Azeri rule grew as Azerbaijan ignored Armenian cultural and economic needs, and encouraged large-scale Azeri immigration (Zverev in Coppieters pp. 17–19). Sporadic interethnic violence occurred under Soviet rule but became far more serious as Soviet authority began to slip in the late 1980s. In February 1988, around 80,000 Karabakh Armenians petitioned for union with Armenia, sparking protracted interethnic violence, and tension between Armenia and Azerbaijan. Anti-Armenian pogroms took place in Azerbaijan, anti-Soviet protests erupted in Armenia, Armenian paramilitary units mobilized in Karabakh, and on December 1, 1989, Armenia formally accepted the petition. The conflict was further confused by the revival of independence movements in both Armenia and Azerbaijan, which ruthlessly exploited nationalist sentiment. On September 2, 1991, the Karabakh authorities declared independence. Azeri forces suffered a series of embarrassing military defeats at the hands of the Karabakh defense forces, which effectively removed much of the region from Azeri control by the end of 1993.

The conflict over Karabakh has flared intermittently ever since. Direct conflict between Armenia and Azerbaijan has been averted by Armenia's refusal to commit government forces directly, although it has supplied the Karabakh forces and done nothing to prevent Armenian volunteers from engaging in combat. Meanwhile, Russia's assumption of the role of chief mediator has had mixed results, as ceasefires have been agreed but regularly broken. Other international efforts, particularly those of the OSCE's Minsk Group, have been severely circumscribed by Russia's determination to retain primacy, as well as by the intransigence of the combatants. Karabakh separatism remains extremely virulent and resolution of the conflict is still a distant prospect.

The effect on internal stability within Armenia and Azerbaijan has been considerable. Outside Karabakh itself, both states have a high degree of ethnic homogeneity (around 83% in the case of Azerbaijan and nearly 94% in the case of Armenia), which has prevented more widespread interethnic violence. However, Azerbaijan's inability to subdue Karabakh separatism has been a major factor in political instability, leading to the downfall of three successive presidents between 1992 and 1993 (Webber 1996 pp. 228–9). Similarly, Armenia has suffered considerable hardship because of the Azeri economic blockade and large-scale emigration. The softening of Armenia's approach to the dispute has helped in the revival of its fortunes since 1994, but the economy remains very weak.

Georgia

Georgia has experienced an even more tumultuous transition to independence (see Simonsen). At one point in 1992, the government found itself embroiled in three separate civil wars, with Abkhazia, South Ossetia and the "Zviadists," supporters of the deposed President, Zviad Gamsakhurdia. With the economy in free fall and organized crime flourishing, the total disintegration of the Georgian state appeared imminent. Since then, however, there has been an unsteady but significant recovery.

As elsewhere in the CIS, the loosening of centralized Soviet control during the late 1980s increasingly left a political vacuum in Georgia, which rival politicians attempted to fill. The ensuing power struggle fueled the revival of national self-awareness in Georgia and provided the backdrop for increasing interethnic tensions between the titular nation and some of the country's ethnic minorities, most notably the Abkhazians, a mainly Moslem Caucasian people; the Ossetians, a mainly Christian Iranian people; and the

Adzharians, who are often counted as ethnic Georgians but differ from other Georgians in being Moslem rather than Christian. The deaths of 20 pro-independence demonstrators in the capital, Tbilisi, at the hands of Soviet Army and Interior Ministry forces on April 9, 1989, radicalized Georgia's initially moderate and inclusive independence movement, which acquired a far more exclusive ethnic-religious character. The most popular advocate of independence, Zviad Gamsakhurdia, was a strictly Georgian Christian patriot who espoused an aggressive ethnic chauvinism that could do little else but alienate ethnic and/or religious minorities.

The period of Soviet domination had also done much to create a deep-seated animosity between ethnic Georgians, on the one hand, and Abkhazians and Ossetians, on the other. Moscow played skillfully upon political and cultural differences in Georgia, instituting complicated and divisive state structures that pitted Georgia's different ethnic groups against one another. The 1920s saw Abkhazia and Adzharia accorded the status of autonomous republics. This in itself was not a source of disharmony within Georgia because both had been accorded such status during Georgia's brief period of independence between 1918 and 1921. The Adzharians, who may account for around 4.9% of the Georgian population, are the largest minority in Georgia after the Russians, Armenians, and Azeris. They have managed to maintain their culture within their autonomous republic up to the present day. In contrast, the annihilation of the Abkhazian intelligentsia and forced migration under Stalin drastically reduced the ethnic Abkhazian element of their republic's population to around 18%, and permanently soured relations between them and the ethnic Georgians who had increasingly colonized the region. Meanwhile, ill will between Ossetians and Georgians over the bloody suppression of the Ossetian uprising of 1920 was exacerbated by the decision to create the South Ossetian Autonomous *Oblast* in 1922.

Soviet nationalities policy in Georgia followed a familiar pattern of divide and rule, exacerbating old tensions between the titular nation and its ethnic minorities, and creating new tensions as well. Thus, despite constituting only around 2% and 3% of Georgia's population, respectively, Abkhazians and Ossetians came to represent serious threats to its territorial integrity on the eve of independence. Decades of perceived suppression under Georgian rule had created severe interethnic animosity. Both Abkhazia and South Ossetia looked North to Russia for support.

By 1990, political radicalism in the Georgian independence movement and the close affiliation of Abkhazia and South Ossetia with Russia had inflamed interethnic relations to the point of serious violence. Both in Abkhazia and in South Ossetia, the local Soviets (legislatures) voiced separatist sentiments, and clashes between Georgian and Ossetian nationalists occurred during the winter of 1989–90. The Georgian Supreme Soviet, now firmly under the control of nationalists led by Gamsakhurdia, pursued increasingly divisive policies throughout 1990 that marginalized Georgia's ethnic minorities and resecured political, social and economic power for ethnic Georgians (Jones in Bremner and Taras p. 512). In response, the Abkhazian Soviet issued a declaration of sovereignty in August 1990, and a month later the South Ossetian Soviet proclaimed the region an autonomous republic. On December 11, 1990, the Georgian Supreme Soviet formally reduced South Ossetia to the status of an ordinary region. Serious conflict ensued between Georgian and Ossetian militias, and Georgia blockaded the region in an attempt to force compliance.

The election of Gamsakhurdia as President after Georgia declared independence in April 1991 led to an escalation of the conflict in South Ossetia and a further deterioration of relations with Abkhazia, which was now becoming more defiant under the leadership of Vladislav Ardzinba. On January 2, 1992, Gamsakhurdia was overthrown in a coup mounted by Georgia's most powerful paramilitary organizations, and was replaced first by the self-styled "Military Council", dominated by the paramilitary leaders Dzhaba Ioseliani and Tengiz Kitovani, and subsequently by Eduard Shevardnadze, formerly Foreign Minister of the Soviet Union. His return to Georgia, where he

had been leader of the Communist Party up to 1985, could not hide the fact that the new regime was essentially a military junta that had overthrown a democratically elected president. Gamsakhurdia, who had fled to Chechnya, was able to exploit its lack of legitimacy and raise considerable support in some of Georgia's regions, notably Mingrelia. Guerrilla war between the "Zviadists" and government forces swiftly followed.

Georgia teetered on the brink of total disintegration throughout 1992 and 1993. President Yeltsin of Russia successfully brokered the Sochi Agreement, securing a ceasefire between the Georgian government and South Ossetia, in June 1992, but hostilities erupted in Abkhazia in August. While Georgia's paramilitary forces enjoyed superior firepower, the lack of both a well-trained professional army and strategic awareness undermined its advantage. Ferocious Abkhazian defense was soon bolstered by Russian material aid and volunteer forces from the KGNK. Yeltsin brokered another ceasefire agreement in July 1993, but this was broken in September when Abkhazian forces launched a surprise offensive and expelled all Georgian troops from Abkhazia.

Stability only gradually returned to Georgia when a desperate Shevardnadze accepted the necessity of returning Georgia to an asymmetrical strategic relationship with Russia, joining the CIS in December 1993 and signing the bilateral Treaty on Friendship, Neighborliness, and Cooperation in February 1994. In return, Russia brokered a more lasting ceasefire with Abkhazia in May 1994 – although, as in South Ossetia, no final settlement has been reached – and Russia also aided government forces in defeating the Zviadists, who continued to oppose the Georgian government in Mingrelia.

With the cessation of hostilities in South Ossetia and Abkhazia, and the suppression of the Zviadist insurgents, Shevardnadze was able to turn his attention to Georgia's other social, economic, and political problems. In August 1995, a referendum majority in favor of the new, democratic Constitution symbolized the return of a semblance of political legitimacy to the government, while the Constitution itself invested the post of President with considerable executive power. Shevardnadze's subsequent election as President, in November, gave him the necessary authority to wrest power from the paramilitaries who had come to dominate Georgian politics, and to tackle the related problems of organized crime, lawlessness, and economic reform. Considerable progress has been made on all of these fronts, although the slow pace of economic recovery has hampered Shevardnadze's efforts. Shevardnadze's pursuit of far more inclusive policies than Gamsakhurdia ever envisaged has also reduced social division within Georgia.

Optimism about Georgia's future must be tempered by a realistic assessment of the problems that it must still surmount. Neither the Abkhazian nor the South Ossetian disputes has been permanently resolved. Similarly, despite Gamsakhurdia's death in November 1993, he remains a symbol of Georgian independence for a small but potentially rebellious part of the population (Aves 1996 p. 8). Festering Zviadist sentiment has been cited, for example, as a factor in the abortive military coup of October 1998 (*Transitions*, December 1998). The economy remains fragile, living standards for large segments of the population remain low, and organized crime is still a major problem. Georgian political and social life has always been marked by a high degree of regionalism, which continues to sit uneasily with any concept of centralized power and could be a source of future disharmony.

Finally, stability in Georgian politics remains heavily dependent on President Shevardnadze. Attempts on his life in August 1995 and February 1998 are indicative of the potential for renewed instability. While Shevardnadze must be given due credit for his central role in Georgia's political and social recovery, he also enjoys considerable personal power and has created a government largely in his own image. As elsewhere in the CIS, such a heavy emphasis on personal rule, while it provides short-term stability, leaves the future unsettled and could ultimately undermine the well-being of the state.

Conclusion

Social divisions remain sources of serious problems throughout much of the CIS, in large part arising from the process of transition from Soviet rule to national politics and national economic development. The difficulties of the transition have been exacerbated by the Soviet legacy of disunity and fragmentation, the result of a deliberate long-term strategy of divide and rule. The creation of national identities was consistently stifled by the Soviet authorities, which left religious, ethnic, tribal, and regional divisions unaddressed – and therefore available for exploitation in the successor states, for better and for worse, as they attempt to build stable modern societies.

Further, certain elements of the Russian elite are still struggling to come to terms with the demise of the Soviet Union. Russian interference, whether direct or indirect, in the domestic affairs of the other successor states has periodically exacerbated social divisions and political instability. Yet Russia is also undergoing a difficult transition to democracy as it struggles to overcome a Soviet legacy that was no less damaging to itself than to the other CIS states. This should be borne in mind whenever one is tempted to lay all the blame for the widespread instability in the CIS at Russia's doorstep, as should the fact that Russia has been at the forefront of efforts to resolve, or at least settle, many of the conflicts. Russia can be accused, with some justification, of exploiting and even inciting some of those conflicts, most notably in Georgia and Moldova, but it must also be acknowledged that Russia, more than any other state, has a vested interest in the long-term stability of the CIS region as a whole. Partly for this very reason, international efforts to play a role in the prevention, management, and resolution of conflicts in the CIS have been constrained by Russia's determination to retain primacy in any such processes. Nevertheless, several international organizations, notably the OSCE and the UN, are actively engaged, in a noncoercive, facilitative capacity, with many of the region's most intractable disputes, for example in Georgia, Moldova, Nagorno-Karabakh, and Tajikistan.

These and other ethnic and political disputes in CIS countries undoubtedly have their origins in the Soviet period – or even earlier – and many such disputes have been exploited by Russia to reassert some influence in the "near abroad." However, whether they take on religious, ethnic, tribal or regional forms, their immediate catalysts, more often than not, have been power struggles between rival local figures or elites, who have thought nothing of inciting nationalism and other divisive ideologies, in their most rabid and xenophobic forms, in pursuit of their own ambitions. Social divisions can generate lively local identities and beneficial cultural variety; it is when they are exploited for political ends that they become destabilizing.

Further Reading

Anderson, John, *The International Politics of Central Asia*, Manchester: Manchester University Press, 1997

An important guide to the politics of newly independent Central Asia

Aves, Jonathan, *Paths to National Independence in Georgia, 1987–1990*, London: University of London School of Slavonic and East European Studies, 1991

A detailed look at the complexities of Georgian politics in the years leading up to independence

Aves, Jonathan, *Georgia: From Chaos to Stability?*, London: Royal Institute of International Affairs, 1996

A concise examination of Georgia's post-Soviet transition period

Baev, Pavel, *Russia's Policies in the Caucasus*, London: Royal Institute of International Affairs, 1997

A concise account of Russian foreign policy in Transcaucasia

Bremner, Ian, and Ray Taras, editors, *New States, New Politics: Building the Post-Soviet Nations*, Cambridge and New York: Cambridge University Press, 1997

An excellent text looking at the broad sweep of post-Soviet transitions

Bukkvoll, Tor, *Ukraine and European Security*, London: Royal Institute of International Affairs, 1997

A detailed yet concise account of the post-Soviet development of Ukraine

Chayes, Abram, and Antonia Handler Chayes, editors, *Preventing Ethnic Conflict in the Post-Communist World: Mobilizing International and Regional Organizations*, Washington, DC: Brookings Institution, 1996

An important study of the actual and potential roles of international institutions in the prevention, management and resolution of ethnic conflict in the post-Soviet environment

Chervonnaya, Svetlana, *Conflict in the Caucasus: Georgia, Abkhazia and the Russian Shadow*, Glastonbury: Gothic Image Publications, 1994

A detailed account of the slide into civil war in Georgia

Coppieters, Bruno, editor, *Contested Borders in the Caucasus*, Brussels: Vubpress, 1996

An excellent overview of the problems faced in Transcaucasia

Croft, Stuart, John Redmond, G. Wyn Rees, and Mark Webber, *The Enlargement of Europe*, Manchester: Manchester University Press, 1999

An excellent new analysis of the development of Europe's principal international organizations since the end of the Cold War

Dawisha, Karen, and Bruce Parrott, *Russia and the New States of Eurasia: The Politics of Upheaval*, Cambridge and New York: Cambridge University Press, 1994

A good, although already dated, general overview of the transformation from Soviet to post-Soviet systems

Ferdinand, Peter, editor, *The New Central Asia and Its Neighbors*, London and New York: Pinter, 1994

A good early account of the problems faced by the five newly independent states of Central Asia

Henderson, Karen, and Robinson, Neil, *Post-Communist Politics: An Introduction*, London and New York: Prentice Hall, 1997

An excellent, wide-ranging introduction to the topic

Kolsto, Pal, *Russians in the Former Soviet Republics*, Bloomington: Indiana University Press, and London: Hurst, 1995

A thorough discussion of the role of ethnic Russians in the successor states

Kuzio, Taras, *Ukraine: Back from the Brink*, London: Institute for European Defence and Strategic Studies, 1995

A short but detailed examination of Ukraine's progress in the immediate aftermath of independence

Kuzio, Taras, *Ukrainian Security Policy*, Westport, CT: Praeger, 1995

Another study by a leading expert on the country, focused on defense and foreign policy

O'Ballance, Edgar, *Wars in the Caucasus, 1990–1995*, London: Macmillan, and New York: New York University Press, 1997

A useful and impressive attempt to provide an overview of these complex conflicts

Olcott, Martha Brill, *Central Asia's New States*, Washington, DC: United States Institute of Peace Press, 1996

A good overview of the politics of the five states in this crucial part of the CIS region

Panfilov, Oleg, "Five Royal Presidents Rule Their Kingdoms: Central Asia's Return to the Middle Ages", in *Transitions*, Volume 5, number 10, October 1998

An informative survey article, which is accompanied by pieces on Kyrgyzstan, Uzbekistan, and Turkmenistan by other writers

Saikal, Amin, and William Maley, editors, *Russia in Search of its Future*, Cambridge and New York: Cambridge University Press, 1995

A clear guide to the complexities of transformation in the Russian Federation. It concludes with T. H. Rigby's important and interesting paper, also entitled "Russia in Search of its Future," which is quoted in this chapter.

Sakwa, Richard, *Russian Politics and Society*, second edition, London and New York: Routledge, 1996

Among the most comprehensive studies of Russia's development since the collapse of the Soviet Union

Simonsen, Sven Gunnar, editor, *Conflicts in the OSCE Area*, Oslo: International Peace Research Institute, 1997

A concise guide to social divisions and conflicts in the countries that belong to the OSCE, including those in central and eastern Europe as well as members of the CIS

Suny, Ronald Grigor, editor, *Transcaucasia, Nationalism and Social Change: Essays in the History of Armenia, Azerbaijan, and Georgia*, second edition, Ann Arbor: University of Michigan Press, 1996

A collection of papers providing detailed background information on these countries

Taylor, Trevor, *European Security and the Former Soviet Union: Dangers, Opportunities and Gambles*, London: Royal Institute of International Affairs, 1994

An excellent early analysis, placing the problems of the ex-Soviet states in the context of European security

Webber, Mark, *The International Politics of Russia and the Successor States*, Manchester: Manchester University Press, 1996

An excellent guide to the main national and international issues concerning the successor states

Webber, Mark, *CIS Integration Trends: Russia and the Former Soviet South*, London: Royal Institute of International Affairs, 1997

A sharp-witted report on the limited progress of the CIS in its early years

White, Stephen, Alex Pravda, and Zvi Gitelman, *Developments in Russian Politics 4*, London: Macmillan, and Durham, NC: Duke University Press, 1997

One of the most comprehensive guides to post-Soviet politics in Russia and the successor states

White, Stephen, et al., *Religion and Political Activism in Post-Communist Europe*, Glasgow: University of Strathclyde Centre for the Study of Public Policy, 1998

A concise report highlighting the use and abuse of religious faith for political objectives

Periodicals

The following journals have been used extensively in the writing of this chapter: *Central Asian Survey, Diplomacy and International Relations, European Security, Helsinki Monitor, International Affairs* (London: Royal Institute of International Affairs), *International Affairs: A Russian Journal of World Politics, Journal of Peace Research, Orbis, Security Dialogue, SLOVO, Survival* (London: International Institute for Strategic Studies), and *Transition* (and other publications of the Open Media Research Institute and Radio Free Europe/Radio Liberty).

Dr Stuart Griffin is a Visiting Lecturer in the Department of Political Science and International Studies at the University of Birmingham in England.

International Relations

Chapter Fourteen

Russia and East Asia

Terence P. McNeill

Over the past three centuries, the importance of East Asia to Russia has revolved primarily around three geostrategic factors: Russia's territorial integrity, its naval access to the Pacific Ocean, and its sea lanes of communication. The Russian empire's desire for dominance was reflected, for example, in the naming of the city of Vladivostok, which means "ruler of the East." Political boundaries have been established and reversed on many occasions in the past 200 years, leaving a legacy of unfinished business. Meanwhile, the significance of East Asia has grown since World War II, as it has become the intersection for the interests of three key nuclear states – Russia, China, and the United States – and as it has undergone rapid economic development, most notably in Japan and, more recently, in China. By the 1980s, Pacific Rim countries accounted for around 60% of the world's aggregate GNP.

Against this background, the position and status of the Soviet Union were being gravely undermined in the 1980s. First, Soviet policies aroused deep antipathy and suspicion. Its armed forces were seen as posing potent nuclear and conventional threats to neighboring countries, and its invasion of Afghanistan, its support for Vietnam's intervention in Cambodia, and its establishment of military bases in Indochina all seemed intensely destabilizing. Second, and relatedly, the normalization of China's relations with Japan and the United States could only work to the detriment of the Soviet Union. Third, the progressive stagnation of the Soviet economy had led to an increasing need to tap into the abundant mineral and energy resources in Siberia and the Soviet (now Russian) Far East. Poor infrastructure and transportation, and a lack of financial resources, acted as obstacles to their development, at a time when the Soviet Union's eastern flank was perceived to be under threat from China, Japan, the United States, and South Korea. Yet it was not simply an economic imperative that dictated the protection and development of these remote regions. Nearly 23 million Soviet citizens lived in Siberia, and 8 million in the Far East; the Soviet armed forces had a high profile in both regions; and the Soviet Union's status as a superpower depended on a substantial presence there.

Gorbachev's Initiatives

Mikhail Gorbachev, who came to power in Moscow in March 1985, lost no time in launching a diplomatic offensive toward East Asia, aimed at projecting a more positive image for the Soviet Union. Foreign Ministry officials were dispatched on fence-mending missions to Japan, China, and the member states of the Association of Southeast Asian Nations (ASEAN). However, trust was undermined by continuing military activities. In 1985, for example, Russian aircraft were observed, for the first time, spying on the Chinese provinces of Jiangsu and Zhejiang from the Yellow Sea, and the Soviet Pacific Fleet conducted massive amphibious landing exercises in a simulated invasion of Hokkaido, Japan.

However, Gorbachev's Vladivostok initiatives, announced on July 28, 1986, did constitute a turning point in relations with East Asia. They consisted of:

- a comprehensive package of measures designed to boost the economic development of the Soviet Far East as a national priority;
- a strong plea for improved relations between the Soviet Union and the Asian states with coasts on the Pacific, as well as among those states themselves, notably China and Vietnam;
- a promise to withdraw six Soviet regiments from Afghanistan, coupled with a pledge to run down the numbers of Soviet troops deployed along the border between Mongolia and China;
- detailed proposals for improving Soviet relations with Japan and China, including suggestions for cooperation on developing commercial prospects and space exploration; and
- a proposal for a "Pacific Area Security Conference," aimed at averting military buildup and confrontation in the region, along the lines of the CSCE process in Europe.

These initiatives were soon followed up by Gorbachev's unilateral proposal to eliminate all medium-range missiles in the Asian part of the Soviet Union.

Thus, the main tenets of Gorbachev's East Asia policy were to revive political and economic relations with China, realize economic links with Japan, work behind the scenes for economic ties with South Korea and Taiwan, increase dialogue with the ASEAN states, and encourage the transfer of technology and investment from capitalist states in order to bolster Soviet economic fortunes, especially in the Soviet Far East. By the end of 1990, Moscow had closed its naval base at Cam Rhan Bay in Vietnam, withdrawn its forces from Afghanistan, forged diplomatic links with South Korea at the expense of its relationship with North Korea, achieved a rapprochement in its relations with China, advanced its discreet economic dealings with Taiwan, endeavored to promote regional cooperation and trade in its Far East territories through an "open door"

policy, and broken the ice in its efforts to improve relations with Japan.

The Development of Russian Policy since 1991

In the wake of the dissolution of the Soviet empire, the foreign policy of the new Russia was initially directed toward closer identification with western interests, as Russia officially aimed to focus on being a "Euro-Atlantic" power. However, conservative and nationalist elements were soon in the ascendant, condemning Boris Yeltsin's deferential approach to the United States and its allies, the country's dependence on western institutions, and its reverence for the western liberal democratic model of development. The failure of the West to provide adequate funds to rescue the country from its economic plight prompted these and other, more moderate "Eurasian" elements in Russian political circles to demand a turn to the East. Both groups shared, and exploited, the belief that Russia's geographic position as a vital bridge between Europe and Asia, and its historical and cultural links with the Asian continent, meant that Russia and East Asia in particular shared a common destiny. Many also concluded that the economic success of East Asia pointed to the wisdom of adopting a model of economic and political development that included a substantial state input, in keeping with Russia's own traditions.

Since the start of 1993, Russia's foreign policy has been set on an altered course, as its focus has shifted towards the Asia-Pacific region. The departure of the unpopular pro-western foreign minister, Andrei Kozyrev, and his replacement by Yevgeni Primakov in January 1996 strengthened this tendency. Particular emphasis has been given to nurturing and deepening Russia's core relationship with China, coupled with concerted efforts to repair ties with Japan, and to revive links with former client states such as North Korea and Vietnam. Attempts to promote overseas trade and investment in the Russian Far East have continued, but contradictions and weaknesses in central government policy have not helped to ease isolationist tendencies in the region.

The Russian Far East

The Russian Far East comprises 42% of Russian territory, stretching from the Bering Strait in the North to the Chinese frontier in the South, and from the Pacific Ocean in the East to the border with Siberia, East of Lake Baikal, in the West. The southern section of the Far East region, which incorporates Primorskii *krai* (district), Khabarovsk *krai*, Amur *oblast* (region) and the Jewish autonomous *oblast* of Birobidzhan, is where the bulk of the population is located. Here can be found more than 70% of the region's agricultural production, consumer goods manufacture, heavy industry, and food-processing plants. The northern section of the region includes the Northern Territories and islands in the Bering Strait, the Sakha Republic, and the Magadan and Kamchatka *oblasts*, and the two primary industries are fishing and nonferrous metals.

The Russian Far East is a borderland. Its history has brought it closer contacts and links with populations across the frontier than with those in the rest of Russia, above all with the 300 million people who live in Dongbei and other nearby Chinese provinces. Separated from Moscow by the vast Siberian wilderness, the distance of the Russian Far East from the center has long left it open to infiltration by Japanese and Chinese forces. Underpopulation has been an intractable problem, which has not been eased by the lack of investment in infrastructure, communications and transportation. After World War II, migration from elsewhere in the Soviet Union was given an impetus by wage incentives and generous state funding, dictated primarily by security considerations, and the wages paid to the military and those employed in associated enterprises were generally higher than average.

From 1988 onwards this relatively favorable state of affairs came to an end for a number of reasons. First, the restoration of diplomatic links between the Soviet Union and China, in 1988, led to the opening of the border and the entry of foreign workers. Second, Gorbachev's "non-market, non-plan" economic policy led to falls in production and escalating price rises followed by shortages, which drove regional enterprises to resort to barter trading with

Chinese and other crossborder merchants. Third, the collapse of the Soviet in 1991 left local authorities and enterprises in the Russian Far East with uncompetitive production, and a dearth of essential raw materials and consumer goods. The region's political leaders and enterprises had little option but to seek resources and investment from states nearer to hand. Fourth, the huge reduction in military activity in the region drastically reduced the incomes and jobs that it had generated in previous decades.

The changes that are taking place as a result of these developments are momentous and far-reaching. For example, according to an unofficial source, in 1994 an estimated 1 million Chinese were living along the Russo-Chinese border, around 200,000 of them inside the Russian Far East. At about the same time, there were thought to be up to 20,000 North Korean workers in the timber trade in the Khabarovsk *krai* and the Amur *oblast*. Since 1991, there has been a decline in the Russian population of the region, as vast numbers of professional and skilled Russians have returned home. Russians have also tended to avoid semi-skilled or unskilled work in timber, agriculture, construction, and light manufacturing, leaving these jobs open to workers from China and North Korea, who accept lower wages and tougher discipline, and do not expect to be housed by the enterprises. The growing trade with China is still largely based on barter. For example, it was reported that payment for Russian S-300 surface-to-air missiles to China was in the form of women's underwear and T-shirts, which arrived in two rail carriages.

This process of transformation cannot be regarded as altogether favorable to Russia's interests. Commercial activity between the Russian Far East and China, Japan, and South Korea now exceeds that with European Russia. The Chinese penetration of the region, and the simultaneous desertion of the Russian population, are major causes for concern. On the one hand, fragmenting links with the center, an ambiguous and inept defense conversion policy, chronic economic and political instability, and Russia's unwillingness to allow unrestricted commercial dealings with Asian neighbors, for fear of enhancing regional autonomy, pose formidable obstacles to healthy economic development in the Russian Far East. On the other hand, Chinese investment is directed chiefly towards establishing a strong economic foothold in the region, and especially a market for Chinese-made products; acquiring necessary energy and mineral resources, together with advanced technologies from Russian industry and scientific centers; and using the region as a means of relieving domestic demographic pressure by encouraging migration. The risks for Russia are being compounded by inadequate policing and border controls, which effectively permit both legal and illegal entry by Chinese nationals, as well as an influx of drug dealers, secret agents, assassins, and thieves. Criminal activities have escalated in a region that already had relatively high crime rates, fueling animosity toward the Chinese. There have also been reports of clashes between Chinese and Russian gangs. Bribery, corruption, money laundering, and the transfer of large amounts of hard currency abroad appear to be spreading, with virtual impunity, and local leaders have become implicated in corruption.

Russia's loss of control over its Far East has other serious implications. First, the military there are in a dilapidated state. There have been deaths from starvation and suicide among the rank and file, submarines are rusting, leakages of plutonium have occurred, and members of the Army and Navy hierarchies are alleged to be engaged in illegal trading with Japan and China. All this is in stark contrast to the growing might of the Chinese military across the border.

Second, the Russian inhabitants of the region are increasingly alienated from western Russia and the authorities in Moscow, and increasingly willing to tolerate the despotism of some of their regional leaders. For example, Yevgeny Nazdratenko, who won re-election as governor of Primorskii *krai* in December 1995, with 70% of the votes cast, has asserted his jurisdiction over matters that in principle are federal responsibilities, such as economic reform, the tax police, privatization, pensions, bankruptcy, and property. He was vehemently opposed to Moscow's decision, in 1993, to return to China around 1,500 hectares of territory adjacent to the Amur river, and in

April 1998, he announced that all foreigners would be banned from involvement in "strategic" sectors and enterprises. Elsewhere in the region, President Mikhail Nikolaev of the Sakha Republic has been more moderate but at least as decisive. His republic has huge but still largely untapped mineral and energy wealth, and has achieved the best economic performance of any of the units of the Russian Federation. It has taken to dealing directly with foreign companies, leading to lucrative contracts with states in East Asia and elsewhere, and its Constitution, adopted in 1992, reserves the right to leave the Federation. It may well do so if turmoil at the center becomes sufficient to provoke it.

The federal authorities have not exactly improved their image by their persistent failure to pay either the wages of workers in state employment or the bills for the energy consumption of state industries. On Sakhalin island, for example, the federal debt amounted to R200 million in August 1998. Unpaid miners went on strike, blocking the access routes to the Sakhalin power station.

China

Since the normalization of Sino-Soviet ties in 1988, relations with China have become close and stable. Both Russia and China have realized the potential gains of cooperation, as their economies have similar consumption practices and preferences, as well as similar structural and technological needs. Many industrial enterprises in China still use Soviet-made machinery that is now in need of renewal or upgrading, and Russia can also provide the full range of military systems, trucks, timber, machine tools, fertilizers, and energy equipment that China wants. Meanwhile, the Russian market can absorb the energy systems, engineering services, and consumer goods that China has to offer. Thus, from around US$4 billion in 1990, the value of bilateral trade increased to US$7.8 billion in 1993 and, although it dipped to US$5 billion in 1994, by 1996 it was around US$7.9 billion. Between December 1992, when Boris Yeltsin first visited Beijing, and mid-1997, the two countries had signed more than 200 trading and economic agreements, and Presidents Yeltsin and Jiang had met six times.

The military partnership is at least as extensive as the civilian one. The Joint Russian-Chinese Declaration About a Multi-polar World and the Formation of a New International Order, issued in February 1998, was aimed at producing a military-strategic partnership for the 21st century. In 1993, the two states signed a five-year Agreement on Military Cooperation, covering border demarcation and management, military exchanges and training, joint military ventures, and confidence-building measures. The extent of bilateral defense cooperation is widely believed to exceed that enjoyed by Moscow or by Beijing with any other country. It is the Russian transfer of weapons systems and other advanced technologies that constitutes the key element in this rapprochement.

These affordable and compatible military systems became available to China at a critical time. Trade sanctions had been imposed following the massacre in Tienanmen Square in June 1989, and the victory of the UN forces in the Gulf War in 1991 had made Chinese leaders aware of the need to upgrade the technological thrust and power of their armed forces. This coincided conveniently with Russia's desperate search for new markets, and its new foreign policy orientation. Since the end of 1993, China has purchased bombers, submarines, military transport aircraft, and surface-to-air missile systems. It has also begun to participate in the manufacture of advanced military hardware. There have also been reports that as many as 4,000 Russians are working in China's military industrial enterprises. All this activity is widely considered to be primarily responsible for the shift in China's military doctrine from "active defense" to high-tech "limited warfare."

Many leaders of neighboring countries have voiced serious misgivings about this new defense axis. The survival of the defense industry is now a driving force in Russian foreign policy, and many observers have argued that the Russian military could even be used to try to reconstruct the Soviet empire. Russia's arms and technology transfers to China are substantially augmenting that country's military power

and projection, destabilizing the region and fueling an arms race. Russia may have entered into something of a Faustian pact with China.

In any case, cooperation at all costs is already displaying signs of being counterproductive. First, Russia has allowed China to pursue its own interests in Central Asia virtually unhindered. For example, as no agreement has been achieved on the demarcation of the border between China and Kazakhstan, Chinese citizens have been able to enter through visa-free border crossings. Chinese merchants are reported to control nearly all market place retailing, and recently China won contracts to take over two key Kazakh oil companies, Uzenmunaigaz and Munai. There may be as many as 300,000 Chinese in Kazakhstan, and by 2000 there may be 500,000. If Russian leaders continue to be distracted by domestic political problems, they may find their influence in Central Asia increasingly marginalized.

Second, it can be argued that Russia needs China far more than the reverse, and that China is cynically using Russia as a temporary expedient to realize its principal aim of becoming a world power. For example, as discussed above, China is fostering the development of the Russian Far East in ways that may be to Russia's disadvantage; and the Chinese government has also failed to encourage Russian participation in decisions on the Korean peninsula. China may yet abandon Russia as its goals are realized, probably in favor of the United States, with which its trade is eight times greater.

Taiwan

Russia's commitment to its very close relationship with China inevitably has a significant impact on its relations with Taiwan. Russia officially opposes Taiwanese independence and membership of international organizations, it rejects the concept of "two Chinas," and in November 1998 it announced that it would not sell arms to Taiwan, even though Taiwan has never sought to buy Russian arms. Nevertheless, links between Russia and Taiwan have been growing over recent years, with China's unofficial blessing. (Indeed, China [including Hong Kong] has itself become

Taiwan's largest single trading partner.) In 1997, Taiwan imported US$1.2 billion-worth of goods from Russia, while its exports to Russia amounted to US$103 million. Although two-way trade fell slightly in the first six months of 1998, Russia has been very keen to create new business opportunities in Taiwan, and to earn hard currency there through the sale of advanced technology. During 1998, it offered 69 technologies to domestic industries in Taiwan.

Japan

Unlike the other wartime Allies, the Soviet Union never signed a peace treaty with Japan after World War II, partly because of a dispute over four islands, known in Japan as the Northern Territories, that Soviet forces seized in 1945. Russia has inherited these islands, which are now largely populated by Russian citizens, and has refused to return them to Japanese control. The development of stable relations has also been set back by the imbalance in the sources of power of the two states. Russia is militarily strong and economically weak, while Japan remains far stronger economically, despite its current problems, but is militarily relatively weak.

A visit to Tokyo by Eduard Shevardnadze, then Soviet Foreign Minister, in January 1986 was overshadowed by the reinforcement of the Soviet forces occupying the islands. However, when Uno Sosuke, then Japan's Foreign Minister, visited Moscow in May 1989 he initiated a new stage in relations, based on Japan's extending humanitarian, intellectual, technological and financial assistance to Russia, commensurate with the degree of progress on resolving the territorial dispute. During a visit to Tokyo in April 1991, Gorbachev announced that all Soviet troops would soon be withdrawn from the four islands. Later that year, in September, Yeltsin put forward a strategy for solving the dispute, again including the withdrawal of all troops except border guards. In October, the Japan Export-Import Bank furnished Russia with US$500 million in financing. By the end of 1992, Russia had halved the number of troops in its Far East region, which includes the islands, reduced its

Pacific Fleet, removed 30 MiG-23 fighters from the island of Etorofu, dramatically cut back on its naval activities in the area, and pledged to cease the construction of submarines for military use. Japan responded at first by citing Russia's redistribution of forces from central and eastern Europe to the Far East, and its expanded operations at its nuclear naval base at Kamchatka. However, in 1993 Japan announced cuts in its own land forces, and a redeployment of some of its troops away from Hokkaido, the closest to Russia among its four main islands. The Tokyo Declaration, signed by Russia and Japan in October 1993, set out the conditions for the normalization of their relationship, and included a pledge to resolve the territorial dispute on the basis of "law and justice."

However, bilateral relations then reached a nadir. The success of conservative and nationalist elements in the Russian elections of December 1993 shut the door on further negotiations and, when a terrible earthquake struck the disputed islands in October 1994, Yeltsin refused to accept Japan's initial offer of assistance. Russia's past failure to pay its debt to Japanese firms, and the gross instability in its markets, kept Japanese trade and investment in Russia to a minimum. Russia's fishing lobby was adamantly opposed to a settlement of the dispute, issuing stark warnings that up to US$2 billion a year would be forfeited if the islands were transferred to Japan. The military establishment was equally opposed to a settlement, and strenuously promoted a view of Japan as eager for military expansion.

Relations could not go on deteriorating. For Russia, Japan represented a strategic counterbalance both to China and to external intervention in Central Asia, as well as a potential source of investment in the Russian Far East and other regions. For Japan, improvements in the relationship with Russia would help to address the potentially dangerous clashes between Japanese fishing fleets and Russian border guards that resulted from the undefined boundaries. They would also promote the dismantling of Russian armaments in the Far East region and the Sea of Okhotsk, encourage Russia to stop dumping nuclear waste in the Sea of Japan, and help to prevent a repetition of the oil spill that occurred when a Russian tanker broke up in the Sea of Japan in 1996. Japanese business was also increasingly interested in gaining access to Russia's mineral and energy resources. Finally, for both countries an improvement in relations could provide an insurance policy if relations with the United States faltered.

In November 1996, Yevgeni Primakov, then Russia's Foreign Minister, visited Tokyo and announced the latest Russian policy on the disputed islands. The dispute was to be resolved on the basis of the Tokyo Declaration; the islands would continue to be demilitarized; non-visa exchange visits by Japanese nationals would be expanded; joint economic development would be promoted; and there would be a widening of all channels of contacts. Many Japanese decision-makers warned that Russia could change the policy at any time, putting any Japanese-funded facilities at risk, but the government has gone ahead with providing aid and assistance to the islands, notably for infrastructure projects. Security relations have also improved, as demilitarization of the disputed islands has continued, and Russia's Pacific Fleet has been charged with the exclusive mission of defending territorial waters. Full-scale joint naval exercises in the Sea of Japan have been held, to test means of cooperating in conducting search and rescue missions, and – in sharp contrast to China – Russia has indicated that it does not feel threatened by the expansion of the security relationship between Japan and the United States. There can be no doubting the new warmth in relations with Japan since 1996, symbolized by the numerous exchange visits by leading politicians from both countries.

The Two Koreas

After decades of mutual distrust, the Soviet Union and South Korea implemented mutual recognition in September 1990. This drew a deeply hostile response from North Korea, which was compounded in January 1991, when Russia demanded that North Korea pay for oil and other commodities in hard currency. President Yeltsin and his liberal advisers had nothing but contempt for Kim Il Sung's

Stalinist regime in North Korea, and by 1994 Russia had cut off supplies of aid, drastically reduced bilateral trading, and made it clear that the military provisions in the mutual friendship treaty signed by the Soviet Union and North Korea in 1961 would be renegotiated. A slight improvement in relations followed conciliatory overtures from North Korea in 1992, and this was welcomed by South Korea, which hoped that Russia could influence Kim Il Sung. However, a furious row broke out in 1993 over North Korea's failure to comply with the Nuclear Nonproliferation Treaty. Russia recalled the scientists who had been assisting North Korea's weapons development programs, accused loggers from North Korea who were working in the Russian Far East of operating concentration camps and peddling drugs, and demanded repayment of North Korea's debts, which amounted to US$3.5 billion. When Kim Il Sung died in July 1994, President Yeltsin refrained from sending condolences.

Meanwhile, Russia's burgeoning relationship with South Korea yielded a number of treaties and agreements on basic relations, military exchanges, and cultural exchanges, and companies from South Korea became active in the Russian markets. In 1992, South Korea reinstated a loan of US$3 billion that had been frozen in the aftermath of the collapse of the Soviet Union, and indicated its wish to be involved in Russia's defense conversion process. Joint ventures have since been announced in lasers, aerospace, advanced materials and electronics. In 1993, however, Russia abruptly decided to postpone payments owing on the loan, and South Korea froze the payment of the second half. South Korea also criticized Russia's dumping of nuclear waste in the Sea of Japan, its denial of responsibility for the Soviet Union's destruction of the KAL 007 airliner in 1983, and its prohibition on fishing in part of the Sea of Okhotsk.

By 1994, Russia had decided to pursue balanced ties with the two Koreas, and to put itself forward as a mediator, in the hope of offsetting the influence of the United States and its allies. Russia had been ignored in the negotiations over the ending of North Korea's nuclear weapons capability, in exchange for the provision of light-water reactors by the United States and Japan. In 1994, Russia complicated matters by offering nuclear reactors of its own and proposing an international conference on the future of the peninsula. Japan, the United States, China, and both Koreas rejected both proposals. It then emerged that Russia had not annulled the military provisions of the 1961 treaty and had not ceased its arms transfers to North Korea in 1992, as it had previously claimed. Since then, Russia has resumed supplying oil and renovating factories built during the Soviet period. It is also alleged to be supplying North Korea with satellite data, and Russian scientists are reported to have remained in North Korea, under altered names. The 1961 treaty expired in September 1996, but Russia stated that all its military provisions were still valid. By then, North Korea's unpaid debts to Russia totaled US$5 billion. In December 1996, Russia closed its trade representative's office in Pyongyang.

Meanwhile, Russia had informed South Korea that its debt would be repaid only in the form of military equipment, and that it would consider exporting weaponry to North Korea if this arrangement was rejected. In 1995 and 1996, Russia and South Korea agreed that part of the debt would be repaid with tanks, infantry fighting vehicles, missiles, ammunition and spare parts, raw materials and civilian helicopters. In December 1996, the signing of a memorandum on military cooperation initiated an increase in the transfer of military technology, the training of units from South Korea in Russia, and the exchange of military experts. Russia has since pressed South Korea to buy its submarines and S-300 surface-to-air missiles, using a combination of hard cash and redemption of the estimated US$1 billion still owed in unpaid debts. However, their bilateral relationship received a setback in July 1998, when one of South Korea's diplomats was expelled from Moscow for alleged espionage.

Russia's furtive dual diplomacy has not helped to engender trust in either of the two Koreas. Russia's abandonment of North Korea in the early 1990s has almost certainly contributed to that country's efforts to obtain nuclear weapons, and has therefore been counterproductive to its declared aim of enhancing peaceful and harmonious relations in the peninsula. While Russia's own economic crisis prevents it from doing much about North Korea's acute difficulties, North Korea itself seems far more interested in improving relations with the United States and Japan. Russia's relations with South Korea have been somewhat more successful, notably in the sphere of military transfers, which have helped Russia to reinstate itself on the Korean peninsula. In other respects, Russia's inability to implement a stable market economy, and its variable foreign policy, have generated not only mistrust, but a loss of patience in South Korea.

Vietnam

Russia's relations with Vietnam reached a low point in 1991, when Russia stopped all economic, military and technical assistance, and withdrew its defense forces from the naval base at Cam Ranh Bay. By 1998, however, relations appeared to have returned to the pattern of military and commercial cooperation established during the Soviet period.

Expanding military influence in Southeast Asia is considered a matter of priority by the Russian leadership, and Vietnam is the most obvious partner, given the past closeness of the two countries. Vietnam is also one of only four countries, out of 36 in the Soviet period, in which the state-owned Russian arms company, Rosvooruzheniye, has retained full representation, the others being China, India, and Iran. In October 1998, Vice-Admiral Nikolai Patrushev, Deputy Chief of the Russian Navy's Main Staff, declared during a visit to Vietnam that Russian warships and nuclear submarines need the Cam Ranh facilities to support crossings from the Pacific Ocean to the Indian Ocean, and to counter possible threats from the increase in US naval activity in the Asia-Pacific region following the creation of its Fifth Fleet in 1995. It was also in October 1998 that the two countries signed their first binding military agreements since the Soviet Union collapsed. Russia is not only supplying weaponry and other materials, but engaging with Vietnam in the joint construction of military facilities, and it has resumed its training of Vietnamese military personnel.

Russia has also restored its presence at Cam Ranh Bay. Under the terms of the original agreement on this base, signed in 1979, its dock complex, airfield, and logistical support center were transferred to Vietnamese ownership, free of charge, in return for Vietnam pledging to allow Russian warships unfettered and rent-free access. Now, however, Vietnam is seeking payment, in the form of advanced weapons, other military equipment, and spare parts.

Trade between Russia and Vietnam is worth only around US$300 million a year, although there is also extensive barter trade. Indeed, perhaps most trading between the two nations takes place on a barter basis. The fact that both countries are now suffering from economic crises accounts in large part for the renewed vigor with which they are pursuing the joint development of Vietnam's extensive resources of oil and natural gas, which is earning vital foreign currency reserves for both states. The Russian-Vietnamese enterprise Vietsovpetro is developing oilfields on the continental shelf of southern Vietnam; the Russian company Zarubezhneft and PetroVietnam are building Vietnam's first oil refinery, which is to produce diesel oil, fuel oil, liquefied petroleum and propylene from 2001 onward; Zarubezhneftegaz of Russia is negotiating to develop the natural gas fields on Vietnam's continental shelf; and other joint ventures are building hydroelectric and thermal power plants. Targeting energy investment in Vietnam, where labor is very cheap and there is good access to high-capacity regional markets, is a most attractive prospect for Russia.

ASEAN

The main thrust of Russia's policy in Southeast Asia has been to persuade ASEAN states – including Vietnam – to invest in the Russian Far East, to broaden bilateral trading and investment links, and to purchase Russian military hardware. Trade with ASEAN as a whole rose from US$1.6 billion in 1994 to US$5.2 billion in 1996. In particular, purchases of advanced Russian arms at affordable prices have been seen as providing a means to counter the threat that China is perceived to pose to

all the ASEAN states. Accordingly, Russia has sold weapons to Malaysia, Singapore, Vietnam, Burma, Laos, and, following US criticisms of Indonesia's human rights record, Indonesia as well.

Recent military cutbacks throughout the region have reduced these sales, and brought about some disagreements. For example, Russia has refused to accept Indonesia's offer of agricultural products in exchange for jets and helicopters. Russia's own extremely precarious internal problems have meant that ASEAN states are once again looking to the United States both for security cover against the Chinese threat, and for weapons systems that are reliable and that come with offset packages or deferred payment deals. Assiduous attempts by Russia to persuade Thailand and the Philippines to buy airplanes, submarines and tanks have been rebuffed, even though it has been prepared to accept rice or other commodities in payment.

Nevertheless, many in the ASEAN states continue to view Russia as a moderating voice among the major powers, and as a counterweight both to Chinese expansionism and to US domination of the global economy. The first meeting of a new forum, the ASEAN-Russian Dialogue, took place in June 1998, and Russia has allocated US$500,000 to set up a Russo-ASEAN Business Council, which is to promote private trade and investment. Russia is concentrating its efforts on areas such as biotechnology, new materials, microelectronics, meteorology, and geophysics, where it has the edge over ASEAN's other dialogue partners.

Conclusion

Russia's huge landmass and wealth of natural resources, and its vast arsenal of conventional and nuclear arms, guarantee a position of continuing importance on the world stage. However, its deepseated and intractable domestic difficulties have greatly diminished its ability to play a leading role in East Asia. Russia does not have the economic and political stability needed to exercise influence.

Russia's efforts to consolidate its partnership with China and offset US dominance have proved successful, to some extent, but Russia is likely to find itself beholden to China's national ambitions as a result. China has not abandoned its ambitions to recover territory, now in the Russian Far East and Central Asia, that its emperors once ruled, and for the time being Russia has little choice but to acquiesce in Chinese penetration into these areas. The normalization of relations with Japan would considerably enhance Russia's security interests and help to balance its links with China, but with Japan's attention being focused on its domestic economic problems, trade and investment are likely to be much more limited than either side had hoped in earlier years. Russia now has little influence on the Korean peninsula: its weapons sales to South Korea may be mutually beneficial, but Russia's economic weakness detracts from its capacity to gain real leverage there. In Southeast Asia Russia remains a largely peripheral player, outside the arms business. Indeed, Russia's practice of selling advanced weaponry to almost any country willing to pay the price is fraught with danger for the whole of East Asia. Not only are potential rivals being armed up to the hilt, but an arms race is being encouraged that is likely to take off once the economic crises that began in 1997 have run their course. Such an arms race would be in no country's interests, Russia's included.

Further Reading

Akaha Tsuneo, "Japanese Security Policy in Post-Cold War Asia," in Tae-Hwab Kwak and Edward A. Olsen, editors, *The Major Powers of Northeast Asia: Seeking Peace and Security*, Boulder, CO: Lynne Rienner, 1996

Bazhanov, Eugene, and Natasha Bazhanov, "The Evolution of Russian-Korean Relations," in *Asian Survey*, Volume 34, number 9, September 1994

Blank, Stephen, "Playing with Fire: Russian Sales in Asia," in *Jane's Intelligence Review*, Volume 9, number 4 (April 1997)

Blank, Stephen, "Which Way for Sino-Russian Relations?," in *Orbis*, Volume 42, number 3, Summer 1998

Bok, Georges Tan Eng, "The USSR in East Asia," in *Atlantic Papers*, number 59/60, Paris: Atlantic Institute for International Affairs, 1986

Brutents, Karen, "Russia and the East," in *International Affairs: A Russian Journal of World Politics*, numbers 1–2, January 1994

Chongkittavorn, Kavi, "Regional Perspective: Russia Gaining Asean's Trust," in *The Nation*, June 8, 1998

Dibb, Paul, "Soviet Capabilities, Interests and Strategies in East Asia in the 1980s," in *Survival*, Volume 24, number 4, July/August 1982

Dibb, Paul, "The Soviet Union's Security Outlook," in Donald Hugh McMillen, editor, *Asian Perspectives on International Security*, London: Macmillan, and New York: St Martin's Press, 1984

Galeotti, Mark, "Russia Looks East," in *Jane's Intelligence Review*, Volume 9, number 7, July 1997

Irguebaev, Amangueldy, "The Prospects of a Settlement in Korea and Russia's Approach: Beyond the US-North Korea Nuclear Accord," in *Korean Journal of Defense Analysis*, Volume 7, number 1, Summer 1995

Kanet, Roger E., and Susanne M. Birgerson, "The Domestic-Foreign Policy Linkage in Russian Politics: Nationalist Influences on Russian Foreign Policy," in *Communist and Post-Communist Studies*, Volume 30, number 4, 1997

Karaganov, Sergei A., "Russia: The New Foreign Policy and Security Agenda: A View from Moscow," in *London Defence Studies 1992*, Oxford: Brassey and Centre for Defence Studies, 1992

Kerr, David, "Opening and Closing the Sino-Russian Border: Trade, Regional Development and Political Interest in Northeast Asia," in *Europe-Asia Studies*, Volume 48, number 6, 1996

Kim Won Bae, "Sino-Russian Relations and Chinese Workers in the Russian Far East," in *Asian Survey*, Volume 34, number 12, December 1994

Kim Yong-ho, "Pyongyang's Foreign Relations," in *Korea Focus*, Volume 4, number 1, January-February 1996

Kim Young Rae, "The Soviet Union's Shifting Policy Toward East Asia," in Park Jae Kyu and Joseph M. Ha, editors, *The Soviet Union and East Asia in the 1980s*, Seoul: Kyungnan University Institute for Far Eastern Studies, 1983

Kim Yu-nam, "A Review of Seoul-Moscow

Relations," in *Korea Focus*, Volume 3, number 6, November-December 1995

Kimura Hiroshi, "Primakov's Offensive: A Catalyst in Stalemated Russo-Japanese Relations?" in *Communist and Post-Communist Studies*, Volume 30, number 4, 1997

Klintworth, Gary, "China: Status Quo Power or Regional Threat," in *Journal of East Asian Affairs*, Volume 12, number 2, Summer/Fall 1998

Kotkin, Stephen, and David Wolff, editors, *Rediscovering Russia in Asia: Siberia and the Russian Far East*, Armonk, NY: M. E. Sharpe, 1995

This valuable collection of scholarly papers includes pieces by Marjorie Mandelstam Balzer, on the Sakha Republic; by Viktor Larin, on the Chinese and the Russian Far East; by Pavel A. Minakir, also on the Russian Far East; by Gilbert Rozman, on the Russo-Chinese border; and by Elizabeth Wishnick, on forestry policy.

McNeill, T. P., "Soviet Policy in the Far East," in *Report on the USSR*, Volume 2, number 42, October 19, 1990

Malik, Hafeez, editor, *The Roles of the United States, Russia and China in the New World Order*, New York: St Martin's Press, and London: Macmillan, 1997

This collection includes a paper by Richard Thornton on Russo-Chinese detente and its implications for the emerging new world order.

Mandelbaum, Michael, editor, *The Strategic Quadrangle: Russia, China, Japan, and the United States in East Asia*, New York: Council on Foreign Relations Press, 1995

The papers in this wide-ranging volume include one on Russia, by Robert Legvold, and one on Japan, by Mike M. Mochizuki.

Meyer, P. F., "Moscow's Relations with Tokyo: Domestic Obstacles to a Territorial Agreement," in *Asian Survey*, Volume 33, number 10, 1993

Miasnikov, Vladimir S., "Russian-South Korean Security Cooperation," in *Korean Journal of Defense Analysis*, Volume 6, number 2, Winter 1994

Moody, R. Adam, "Armageddon for Hire," in *Jane's International Defense Review*, Volume 30, number 2, February 1997

Pierre, Andrew J., and Dmitri V. Trenin, editors, *Russia in the World Arms Trade*, Washington, DC: Carnegie Endowment for International Peace, 1997

Pipes, Richard, "Is Russia Still an Enemy?" in *Foreign Affairs*, Volume 76, number 5, September-October 1997

Randolph, Sean, "Pacific Overtures," in *Foreign Policy*, number 57, Winter 1984–85

Rozman, Gilbert, "Russian Populist Reactions in 1993–94 to the Coming of the Chinese," a paper presented at a Conference on Recent Demographic Trends in Eastern Siberia: The Question of Chinese Immigration, Atlanta, Georgia: Institute of Technology, December 12–13, 1994

Russian Far Eastern Economic Yearbook 1992, Khabarovsk: Economic Research Institute, 1993

Sakwa, Richard, *Gorbachev and His Reforms 1985–1990*, New York and London: Prentice Hall, 1991

Sarkisov, Konstantin, "The Northern Territories Issue after Yeltsin's Re-election: Obstacles to a Resolution from a Russian Perspective," in *Communist and Post-Communist Studies*, Volume 30, number 4, 1997

Shlapentokh, Vladimir, "Russia, China, and the Far East: Old Geopolitics or a New Peaceful Cooperation," in *Communist and Post-Communist Studies*, Volume 28, number 3, 1995

Simon, D. F., "Charting Taiwan's Technological Future: The Impact of Globalization and Regionalization," in *China Quarterly*, number 148, 1996

Solomon, Richard H., "East Asia and the Great Power Coalitions," in *Foreign Affairs*, Volume 60, number 3, Fall 1981

State Commission for Statistics, *Russian Statistical Yearbook*, Moscow: Goscomstat, 1992

Stockholm International Peace Research Institute, *SIPRI Yearbook of Armaments and Disarmaments*, Stockholm: Alqvist and Wiksell, annual publication

The 1997 edition of this book contains a useful survey of Asian security policies, while the 1998 edition has an interesting article by Siemon T. and Pieter D. Wezeman on the transfer of major conventional weapons among states.

Tkachenko, Vadim P., "The Transition of Russia-North Korea Relations and Their Impact on North and South Korea Relations," a paper presented at the 101st Seminar at Hanyang University, Seoul, May 24, 1993

Togo, K., *Approach Run to the New Era of Japan-Russian Relations*, Tokyo: Saimaru Shuppankai, 1993

Van Selm, Bert, "Economic Performance in Russia's Regions," in *Europe-Asia Studies*, Volume 50, number 4, 1998

Voskressenski, Alexei D., "The Perceptions of China by Russia's Foreign Policy Elite," in *Issues and Studies*, Volume 33, number 3, March 1997

Yakovlev, A. G., "Russia and China: The Current Stage and Prospects of Relations," in *China in the World and Regional Politics: History and Current Affairs*, Moscow: Institute for Far Eastern Studies, 1995

Yeo In Kon, "Russia's Policies Toward North Korea," in *East Asian Review*, Volume 6, number 2, Summer 1994

Yon, Hyon-Sik, "The Russian Security Interests in Northeast Asia," in *Korean Journal of Defense Analysis*, Volume 6, number 1, Summer 1994

Zagoria, Donald S., "The Soviet Quandary in Asia," in *Foreign Affairs*, Volume 56, number 2, January 1978

Zagoria, Donald S., editor, *Soviet Policy in East Asia*, New Haven, CT: Yale University Press, 1982

This book includes a particularly interesting paper by Robert A. Scalapino on the political influence of the Soviet Union in Asia.

Zagorski, A., "The Post-Cold War Security Agenda of Russia: Implications for Northeast Asia," in *Pacific Review*, Volume 8, number 1, 1995

Ziegler, Charles E., "Russian Politics and Foreign Policy after the Elections: Implications for Korea and East Asia," in *Korean Journal of Defense Analysis*, Volume 8, number 2, 1996

Periodicals

Daily newspapers, weekly magazines, and other non-academic periodicals can be useful sources of information and insight. English-language publications consulted for this chapter include the *Asian Defence Journal*, the *Asian Wall Street Journal*, the *Current Digest of the Post-Soviet Press*, *Defense News*, the *Far Eastern Economic Review*, the *Korea Times*, the *New York Times*, the *Washington Post*, the *Yomiuri Shimbun* (Tokyo), and the *Summary of World Broadcasts* compiled by the British Broadcasting Corporation. Russian-language periodicals consulted include *Izvestia*, *Krasnaya Zvezda*, *Nezavisimaya Gazeta*, *Noviye Izvestia*, and *Pravda*.

Professor Terence P. McNeill is Head of the Department of Politics and Asian Studies at the University of Hull in England. He is indebted to Dr Sally Harris, Research Fellow at the University of Hull, who provided invaluable assistance in the preparation of this chapter.

Chapter Fifteen

Relations with the United States

Laura Richards Cleary

The CIS was formed in December 1991 in order to achieve a degree of stability in the economic, political and military affairs of the republics of the former Soviet Union. Depending on one's point of view, it was either supposed to be a temporary measure, which would assist the members in their transitions from Soviet republics to independent states, or it was supposed to emulate the functions of the EU. It was never supposed to be, nor has it become, a direct replacement for the Soviet Union. Thus, it is impossible to speak of a CIS foreign policy directed at the United States. Nor is it possible to argue that the United States treats the members of the CIS in a uniform manner. Instead, Washington's policy has been to establish bilateral ties with all of the former Soviet republics. Some links are closer than others, and this has as much to do with the diaspora who have chosen to make the United States their home as with the strategic locations and assets of the republics themselves.

While it is not possible to outline a specific policy in relation to the CIS and the United States, it is possible to identify, for the purposes of discussion, a number of key issues that have generated a high degree of diplomatic activity: disarmament, the eastward expansion of NATO, and the provision of economic assistance. It is important to understand, however, that they all have a bearing on each other, and that in reality they are far less easy to disentangle. Further, while in diplomatic parlance the United States would argue that all members of the CIS are equal, this is not the case. The United States and the members of the CIS themselves recognize that Russia is of paramount importance to the security of the region. Thus, greater effort is made toward meeting Russia's needs, for a secure and stable Russia poses far less of a threat to its newly independent neighbors.

Securing the Peace

When Mikhail Gorbachev became the General Secretary of the Communist Party of the Soviet Union in 1985, he took control of a state that was on the brink of economic collapse and political stagnation. The one sector that was truly thriving was the military-industrial complex (see Chapter 11). The armed forces had experienced mixed fortunes under Josef Stalin and Nikita Khrushchev, but under the leadership of Leonid Brezhnev (from 1964 to 1982) they had benefited from an increase in size and the development of new technology. By 1985, the armed forces totaled around 5 million personnel, there were an estimated 10 million engineers and workers in the defense enterprises, and defense spending was in the region of 30% of Soviet GNP (Cleary pp. 47–51). The physical security of the state had been achieved at the expense of its political and economic security. Gorbachev quickly realized that if *perestroika*, his program for economic and political reform, was to succeed, it would have to occur in conjunction with a significant change in foreign policy. His program of "New Thinking" in foreign policy emphasized the need for a relaxation in tensions with the West, and a more cooperative approach to common problems. Gorbachev believed that actively promoting disarmament could help to reduce tension in international relations. The progress of disarmament was rapid. In 1987, the Soviet

Union and the United States signed the Intermediate Nuclear Forces (INF) Treaty, and in 1988 Gorbachev announced an initiative for unilateral disarmament at the UN. This latter proposal was implemented with the partial withdrawal of troops from central and eastern Europe in January 1990, and from Mongolia in February of the same year. Advances in disarmament in Europe were further supported by the Soviet Union's accession to the "2 + 4" Treaty on German unification in September, and the signing of the Conventional Forces in Europe (CFE) Treaty in November. During the late 1980s, headway was also made on the negotiation of the first Strategic Arms Reduction Treaty (START I), which was signed in 1992. Each of these acts contributed to bringing about the conclusion of the Cold War, and to creating the security environment that continues in Europe to date.

US reactions to these initiatives were initially skeptical, but as precedents were established, and the political climate on both sides of the Atlantic changed, relations became more cordial, and, one could argue, more friendly (see Palazachenko). President George Bush (1988–92) recognized that in attempting to reform the Soviet Union Gorbachev had set himself a task of Sisyphean proportions. Constrained by a Congress that was divided over the best approach to the Soviet Union, President Bush offered as much support as he could to Gorbachev's reforms, and attempted to dissuade the republics from their precipitous course of dismantling the Union in 1990–91.

Although a new phase in East-West relations officially began when the Soviet Union was dissolved on December 26, 1991, the policies initiated in the late Soviet period remained essentially unchanged. Diplomatic relations were established with the newly independent states during the course of 1992. Disarmament, however, remained the most pressing issue in US-CIS relations, and it continued apace with the signing of START II by George Bush and Boris Yeltsin, President of Russia, on January 3, 1993. This was, however, the last significant step in the disarmament process. Any further discussions have concerned the need to revise the CFE Treaty and to ratify the START II agreement.

Both these agreements reflected a security system that was no longer in existence. The CFE Treaty in particular had been negotiated on a "pact to pact" basis. The initial impetus for discussing such a treaty had come from the Soviet unilateral withdrawal from Europe. The general consensus was that, if the Soviet Union was willing to withdraw partially from Europe and restructure its remaining forces, then the western powers should do the same. The negotiations between the member states of NATO and the Warsaw Pact began in March 1989 in Vienna. The two main aims were, first, to follow on from unilateral action and achieve an even lower balance of forces deployed between the Atlantic and the Urals, and, second, to eliminate the ability to launch a surprise attack or to launch and sustain large-scale offensive operations. The two parties were beginning to reorganize their armies in terms of what they perceived to be "reasonably sufficient" force, considering the lower levels of international tension.

The CFE Treaty did not deal with specific limits on personnel, because it was assumed that there would be further unilateral reductions on both sides, and that a future "CFE II" agreement would establish appropriate guidelines. Instead, the Treaty, as signed on November 19, 1990, set a series of ceilings on weapons for the "collective holdings of each group of parties, for geographic regions and for individual member states." Each alliance would be limited to 20,000 tanks, 20,000 artillery pieces, 30,000 armored combat vehicles, 2,000 combat helicopters and 6,800 combat aircraft. A sufficiency limit had been set of 13,300 tanks and 13,700 artillery pieces for any one country; the Soviet Union, however, was forced to accept different totals because its allies wanted a greater share of the weapons. In the end the Soviet Union was limited to 13,150 tanks and 13,175 artillery pieces. The Warsaw Pact was forced to destroy 50,700 pieces of equipment; the Soviet Union's share of that total was 25,000.

Although the CFE Treaty went a considerable distance in limiting the forces of NATO and the Warsaw Pact, it was quickly outpaced by events. Following Gorbachev's lead, the member states of the Warsaw Pact began unilaterally reducing their own armed forces. On July 1, 1991, a treaty was signed which formally dissolved the Warsaw Pact, thus placing the structure of the CFE Treaty, with its "group of parties" and its "zonal sub-limits tied to geographic regions," into question. The breakup of the Soviet Union during the course of 1991 further hindered implementation. The former republics of the Soviet Union, as well as some states in central and eastern Europe, began to argue that the ceilings set by the CFE Treaty were no longer applicable. In January 1992, in an interview with this author, General Ivan Ivanovich, Commander of the Rostov-on-Don military district, expressed the opinion that much as both sides wanted to see ratification of the CFE Treaty, it might no longer be possible.

Ivanovich's pessimism in regard to the specific issue was, in the end, unfounded. As a result of a great deal of negotiation during the course of 1992, a solution was finally found to the problem of which states were responsible for the weapons of the former Soviet Union. In May 1992, at a summit meeting in Tashkent, Uzbekistan, the members of the CIS agreed that quotas would be set among them to apportion these weapons. In an initial proposal, Russia had argued that the share of weapons should be based on the total area of the state, the size of the population, and the length of the borders that had to be defended. Under this formula Russia would have held 54% of the total of the five categories of weapons, Ukraine 22% and Belarus 6.6%. The non-Slavic European republics (Armenia, Azerbaijan, Georgia, and Moldova) would have held 17.5% of the total inventory. In the end, this was not the formula that was adopted. Russia received 51%, Ukraine 27.5%, and Belarus 12%. Once the shares had been apportioned, it was necessary for each state to ratify the Treaty. On July 10, 1992, the revised CFE Treaty was signed by 29 states. The ratification process took nearly as long as the initial negotiations.

For Russia, the CFE issue has remained at the top of the domestic and international political agendas, since it views the Treaty as a threat to its security. At the domestic level, Colonel-General Yurii Baleuvsky, a member of

the Russian General Staff, is only one of many who have argued that, because of the continuing tensions in the North Caucasus, Russia cannot comply even with the revised version of the CFE Treaty. At the international level, the expansion of NATO to include former allies of Russia is of particular concern. One former Defense Minister, Pavel Grachev, argued that enlargement would invalidate the CFE Treaty, and as recently as December 1998 Foreign Minister Igor Ivanov stated that an updated version of the treaty must be ratified before NATO admits any former Warsaw Pact countries. The NATO-Russia Founding Act (1997) provides a framework for the adaptation of the Treaty, but in the stridency of their comments Grachev and Ivanov are playing to a particular gallery. Their views have received a great deal of support from those politicians who strongly believe in the great power status of Russia and promote a policy of "Russia First" (see Truscott).

Questions of status also have a bearing on nuclear disarmament. START I was a bilateral agreement between the two superpowers, holders of the largest nuclear stockpiles. Under that agreement, the two parties were limited to no more than 1,600 strategic nuclear delivery vehicles, comprising deployed intercontinental ballistic missiles (ICBMs), sea-launched ballistic missiles (SLBMs), and heavy bombers; 6,000 total accountable warheads; 4,900 accountable warheads deployed on ICBMs or SLBMs; 1,540 accountable warheads deployed on mobile ICBMs; and an aggregate throw-weight of deployed ICBMs and SLBMs equal to 3.6 billion metric tons.

These levels marked a significant reduction from those previously held. At the time of the August coup in 1991, it was believed that the Soviet Union held around 27,000 nuclear weapons of various classifications (air, land, and sea-launched; and tactical and strategic). Of this total, 80–85% were presumed to be located within the territory of Russia, leaving around 4,500 warheads in other locations. As the central command structure of the old state dissolved, the individual republics began to claim ownership of the weapons. They linked the possession of nuclear warheads with an increase in international recognition.

Of the four republics which held nuclear stockpiles, two, Belarus and Ukraine, declared their intention to become nuclear-free zones – on their own terms. The Ukrainians were most vociferous in their distrust of the Russians' ability to dispose of nuclear weapons-grade material. The government of then President Leonid Kravchuk also decried Russia's attempts to position itself as the leading state in the CIS. While Washington and Moscow wanted START I to remain bilateral, Kravchuk argued that all former Soviet republics holding nuclear weapons should be treated equally. Kravchuk won the argument in the end. On May 23, 1992, representatives from the United States, Russia, Ukraine, Belarus, and Kazakhstan met in Lisbon, Portugal, to sign a protocol to START I, which recognized the responsibility of each of the signatories for the disposal of the nuclear weapons positioned on its territory.

This did not, however, mark the end of the disagreement. Despite having announced its intention to become a nuclear-free state, in its Declaration of Sovereignty in 1990, Ukraine decided to retain nuclear weapons as a bargaining chip in its dealings with Russia and the United States. Specifically, Ukraine wanted guarantees that if it returned the weapons to Russia they would not be used against it. Further, the weapons were viewed as a means of achieving financial assistance. Ukraine's aims were achieved in January 1994 with the signing of a tripartite agreement in which it agreed to give up its nuclear weapons and the US Congress approved US$1.2 billion to cover the costs of dismantling them.

Kazakhstan and Belarus proved to be far more obliging, ratifying START I in 1992 and early 1993 respectively, and becoming signatories to the Nuclear Nonproliferation Treaty of 1968 during the course of 1993. In affirming their commitment to these treaties, both governments promised that all existing nuclear weapons would be transferred to Russia, with the aid of technical and financial resources from the United States. In the case of Kazakhstan, this task was accomplished by April 1995. Belarus encountered severe financial difficulties, which resulted in noncompliance on both START I and CFE, and in 1994 President Clinton found it necessary to increase

aid to US$100 million, most of which was related to disarmament.

Diplomatic momentum on disarmament continued, and Presidents Bush and Yeltsin initialed a proposal for START II on January 3, 1993. It was agreed that by the year 2000 each country would retain no more than 3,800 to 4,250 nuclear warheads on strategic missiles, while the Russians would be allowed to keep 6,000 warheads on heavy missiles. In the second stage, which would run until 2003, the total limit of weapons allowed to Russia would be 3,000 and to the United States 3,500.

This treaty was lauded by the international community for its attempt to bring about significant reductions in the nuclear arsenals of the two superpowers. Despite the fanfare, it has never been ratified. There are several reasons for this. The US Congress is reluctant to ratify the treaty when its co-signatory has no apparent desire to do so. Within the State Duma, the lower house of the Russian Federal Assembly, START II has become a hostage to fortune. The initial reaction among opponents to Yeltsin was that Russia had perhaps given too much away, and that Yeltsin was acting like Gorbachev in courting the West. As time has passed, the reasons for the obstruction have changed. First, the retention of nuclear weapons underlines Russia's "great power" status and gives it credibility in its dealings with NATO. Second, the Russian armed forces have, since 1991, effectively imploded. Conventional forces are undermanned and badly trained, and lack sufficient resources. Nuclear weapons are increasingly seen as being the only war-fighting capability the Russians have. Third, by avoiding or delaying ratification Russian politicians can express their dissatisfaction over other international issues. The events of December 1998 provide an appropriate example. It appeared that the Duma was finally going to ratify the treaty, or at least send the draft law to Yeltsin on December 15, later postponed to December 17. A concerted effort was made by the government and the Ministry of Defense to ensure its safe passage, but this was derailed by the bombing of Iraq by US and British forces. While First Deputy Prime Minister Yurii Maslyukov held out hope that the treaty could be ratified, he stated that this could not occur while the bombings continued to take place. Much the same happened in March 1999, when Prime Minister Yevgeni Primakov agreed with the State Duma not to go ahead with ratification of START II so long as NATO was launching air strikes on Yugoslavia. The fourth and final consideration is that, like Ukraine, Russia does not have the financial or technical wherewithal to dismantle the nuclear weapons. Implementation of both START I and START II is dependent upon the financial generosity or strategic foresight of the United States.

Despite the delayed implementation of these two treaties and the increasingly combative rhetoric emanating from Moscow, the US military is still keen to pursue a third START agreement. Representatives of the US Joint Chiefs of Staff have testified to Congress that they fully support further reductions in deployed strategic warheads. They have even proposed that levels be reduced below the limit of 6,000 warheads established by START I, even before START II is ratified by the Duma (Cirincione pp. 22–25). This proposal is in line with the strategic thinking outlined in the Bush administration's "Base Force" review and the Clinton administration's "Bottom Up Review." Both recognized that the security environment had been fundamentally altered. While they did not successfully define the role of the United States in a world of shifting alliances and relationships, the Department of Defense has attempted to confine its role. These attempts are in response to policy prescriptions as well as ever more restrictive defense budgets. It is believed that the United States would have to spend an additional US$1 billion each year to maintain its forces at START I levels: this money could be used for other, more vital missions (Cirincione p. 22). Despite these considerations, it is unlikely that Congressional and executive approval will be forthcoming until other obstacles in US-Russian relations have been overcome.

The Eastward Expansion of NATO

Proposals to expand NATO to the East have colored US-Russian relations and have seeped into US-CIS relations. While NATO's intentions are honorable, if not a little misguided (see Art, and also Perlmutter and Carpenter), this is not always the way they are portrayed in the East. From the western perspective, the reasons for expansion are straightforward. It was recognized that the disbanding of the Warsaw Pact and the dissolution of the Soviet Union marked the end not only of an institution and of a state, but of a larger European security order. A void was created, which needed to be filled rapidly if stability was to be maintained in Europe. NATO has attempted to do this by placing an increased emphasis on its political and social roles, and downplaying its military function. There has been a significant shift away from the static defense posture required to support a policy of nuclear deterrence, toward a more flexible and rapidly deployable force. The new Strategic Concept unveiled at NATO's summit meeting in Rome in 1991, which was being revised in advance of NATO's 50th anniversary in April 1999, clearly states that NATO no longer recognizes a specific enemy. The process of reform that began in 1991 has been necessary to make the institution more responsive to the types of threats that are likely to be encountered in the modern security environment: ethnic and religious conflict; transnational crime; and the problems associated with the transition to democracy, in central and eastern Europe as well as in the former Soviet republics. The Combined Joint Task Forces enables NATO to respond more rapidly to calls for collective defense, peace support and counterproliferation measures, while the North Atlantic Cooperation Council, established in 1991, and the Partnership for Peace program (PfP), started in 1994, have helped to tie post-Communist states into the NATO sphere. US Secretary of State Madeleine Albright has explained that through the process of reform and expansion it is intended that NATO should "do for Europe's East what [it] did 50 years ago for Europe's West: to integrate new democracies, defeat old hatreds, provide confidence in economic recovery, and deter conflict" (see Albright and Obey). Within the United States, those who favor NATO expansion stress that it is not "threat-driven," that it is part of an overall strategy to "project stability," and that it will benefit "Russian security and the security of other former Soviet states" (Perlmutter and Carpenter p. 3). Those who oppose expansion argue that it will achieve none of these things, and is likely only to destabilize the delicate balance in the CIS.

This is an opinion increasingly shared by politicians of all political hues in Russia. Between 1991 and 1993 Yeltsin and his then Foreign Minister, Andrei Kozyrev, pursued a pro-western foreign policy. Their reaction to calls for a new security regime in Europe was quite favorable and they stated that such a regime could not be achieved without Russia. Their views on what should be the cornerstone of that security architecture differed from those held in Washington. The CSCE (now the OSCE), rather than NATO, was the preferred choice. Nevertheless, Yeltsin was willing to concede the participation of former Warsaw Pact members in the political committee of NATO. Russia also took a fairly relaxed view of the PfP program when the concept was first tabled in late 1993. Both the political and military establishment believed that PfP would be a "waiting room" for post-Communist states, since it did not appear at that time that NATO was seriously considering expansion.

As the groundswell of opinion in favor of enlargement increased within the United States and Europe, the response in Moscow turned more bellicose. There are three specific reasons for this change. First, at the very moment when NATO was pushing ahead with PfP it was becoming increasingly apparent that the liberal agenda adopted by the Yeltsin team was not going to provide the remarkable transformation of society which had been promised in the time stated. The challenges to society's security in the economic, political and cultural spheres could not be met by the existing political institutions. Second, because the liberal agenda had been advocated by the United States and other members of the Group of Seven, politicians within Russia began to turn away from such prescriptions and promote a Russian or "Eurasian" antidote. As nationalist fervor increased among all political parties so too did more insular viewpoints. Finally, despite US and NATO

assurances that NATO expansion was not "threat-driven" and that Russia was viewed as a partner in, rather than an enemy of, security, Russian political and military elites continued to believe that the process of enlargement was aimed at Russia.

From a Russian perspective, NATO's deeds do not match its words. Successive invasions throughout the ages, by, among others, Mongol, Polish, Swedish, French, German, British, and US forces, have all left their mark on the Russian national psyche. Russia has always favored the creation of a buffer zone to ensure its security. With the inclusion of post-Communist states within NATO activities, Russia would effectively become encircled: it would be confronted by NATO on its western borders and on its eastern borders, since the United States is a mere 50 miles away. It is for this reason that Russia has been so vociferous in its objections to enlargement.

Of particular concern to the Russian establishment are the development of closer links between the Baltic states and NATO. Although Lithuania, Latvia, and Estonia refused to join the CIS, Russia continues to consider them within its sphere of influence. Despite the associated problems of disentangling the Communist economic network and dealing with sizable Russian populations, the Baltic states have made integration into the political, economic and security institutions of western Europe one of their main priorities (see Ferry and Kanet pp. 191–199). To this end, they were among the first post-Communist states to pursue closer ties with NATO, believing that the security guarantees offered by that institution would provide sufficient protection from a revanchist Russia. While forging new links with NATO generates a sense of security within the Baltic states, it creates the opposite feeling in Russia. If Lithuania, Latvia, and Estonia became full members of NATO, Russia might be denied the access to the Baltic Sea that it has struggled throughout history to maintain. For this reason, Deputy Defense Minister Nikolai Mikhailov announced on December 2, 1998, that troops in the Kaliningrad *oblast* (region) – the Russian enclave to the West of Lithuania – would act as the spearhead of Russia's deterrent against NATO.

Russia's reactions to the prospective inclusion of Ukraine in NATO are equally strong, but based on different motivations. Since the end of the Cold War and the collapse of the Soviet Union, Russia has experienced a crisis of identity. Within the Russian context, the state and its ideology essentially create the nation. There are three distinct layers to the state. There is, of course, an ethnic Russian core, but there is also an historic Russia, embracing Belarus and Ukraine, and an imperial Russia, incorporating other ethnic groups overcome during historically recent periods of expansion. When the Soviet Union dissolved in 1991, Russia was stripped of two of its mantles, leaving a federation that Aleksandr Tsipko, for example, has described as "an artificial entity, a kind of remainder after the subtraction of the rest of the Soviet republics" (Tsipko p. 187).

Russia is left feeling insecure, and that feeling is heightened by Ukrainian moves towards western institutions, particularly NATO. The member states of NATO view an independent, stable and democratic Ukraine as being of strategic importance for the development of the continent as a whole. Ukraine in turn views NATO as the most capable and reliable pillar of European security. It also views cooperation with, and integration into, the institutions of Europe as means by which it can assert its own identity and independence from Russia. Thus, Ukraine has been keen to participate in the PfP program, to participate in several joint exercises, and to provide peacekeepers for Bosnia-Herzegovina. While the Ukrainian government is working towards full-scale integration into European and transatlantic security structures, it realizes that it is not yet ready to achieve that goal: its political and military institutions must develop further. Continued involvement in a variety of regional associations should help to secure the reform process, while the establishment of closer relations with Poland provides it with a representative within western institutions (see Ferry and Kanet pp. 160–176). Ukraine is aware, however, that it is trying to perform a difficult balancing act. Closer integration with the West is necessary for its long-term security and prosperity, but too rapid pursuit of that course will jeopardize its security. At each step it must appease Russia.

Russia is not easily appeased. Since the collapse of Communism, members of the Russian elite have toyed with elements of liberalism, yet failure to apply these wholeheartedly or consistently has meant that reform has borne insufficient fruit. Liberalism, as a result, has been abandoned. In the absence of any clear program for transforming Russia, politicians have recreated an old "enemy" in order to unify society. That enemy is NATO.

Militarily, NATO is a US-led institution: the post of Supreme Allied Commander in Europe (SACEUR) is always filled by a US general. Yet all the member states have an input into the strategic outlook of the institution, and its political mission is defined by the Secretary General, who may be of any nationality, and by various committees, in which each member has an equal voice. Given the changed security environment, the end of ideological confrontation, and the increased emphasis on NATO as a support to European political security, it should be less easy to denounce NATO as a US-led institution. Nevertheless, it is frequently portrayed in Russia as underwriting US supremacy rather than European security.

This is a tactic used by politicians in an attempt to score cheap political points, despite the fact that the general populace has little interest in whether or not NATO expands. The military as an institution, elements of the Foreign Ministry, and some members of the Yeltsin government have recognized that a *modus vivendi* must be achieved if Russia is to avoid being pushed to the periphery. So, like the other members of the CIS, Russia has participated in the PfP program, and contributed to peacekeeping in Bosnia-Herzegovina. On May 27, 1997, the NATO-Russia Founding Act was signed. Russia, reflecting on past glory as a superpower, had long demanded a veto over NATO actions. This was a right which neither NATO nor the United States was ever likely to grant. The Founding Act does, however, establish the basis for a permanent security partnership. Crucial to this is the statement that NATO and Russia do not consider each other as adversaries. The mechanism for consultation and cooperation is a Permanent Joint Council that meets at three levels: foreign ministers, defense ministers, and ambassadors. In Russia, vested interests have a direct impact on international representations. Thus, varying degrees of cooperation can be noted at the different levels. The participation of Russian forces in peacekeeping in Bosnia-Herzegovina, the interaction of military personnel within NATO, and their attendance at various seminars on civil-military relations have led to the development of a stable working relationship with their US counterparts. Indeed, it has become apparent that they have much in common. Within the Supreme Headquarters Allied Powers Europe (SHAPE) there exists a reasonable, functioning relationship. At the ambassadorial level of the Permanent Joint Council, however, political posturing has limited effectiveness. This is indicative of Russian-US relations as a whole: political rhetoric does not provide an accurate representation of the day-to-day working relationship. This is apparent with respect to NATO and also with respect to economic relations.

Economic Relations

When the Soviet Union collapsed and its constituent parts began the difficult process of establishing separate economies, it was suggested that a "Marshall Plan Mark II" be offered. Yet the conditions in 1991 were dramatically different from those of 1947. At the time of the Marshall Plan, the United States was, to all intents and purposes, self-sufficient in natural, technological and financial resources. World War II had rejuvenated, rather than devastated, the US economy. Partly altruistic, partly an example of extreme strategic foresight, Marshall aid was intended to facilitate the reconstruction of the economic infrastructure, in order to dampen the rising tide of social discontent in Europe and to block growing Soviet influence. Assistance was available in the form of grants and technology transfers, so long as European states cooperated and organized themselves to facilitate the distribution of aid. The success of the Marshall Plan was such that not only did the United States recreate specific markets, it provided the impetus for a truly integrated global economy. While it remains a significant player within that

economy, it no longer has complete freedom to act. It is subject to sizable foreign investments, like any other country, and its currency no longer stands alone, being frequently propped up by the yen on the financial markets. As a result, the United States is no longer in a position to provide another Marshall Plan, but instead must act in concert with other members of the Group of Seven and the IMF.

Western financial assistance has been made available since 1991, but both its scale and composition have been called into question. The primary recipient has been Russia, which received US$24 billion in 1992, and a further US$43 billion in 1993 from the Group of Seven. In this instance the United States acted as Russia's advocate, since Japan wanted a resolution to the question of the Kurile Islands (which the Soviet Union took over from Japan in 1945) before any further aid was granted. By targeting Russia it was hoped that the benefits would "trickle down" to the rest of the CIS. Yet this was never likely to happen, given that a substantial portion of the total sum was in the form of debt relief, and that another large tranche was in the form of export credits. Very little aid was made up of grants. Another problem has been that foreign direct investment has remained comparatively small throughout the CIS. Western corporations and investors have been interested in two sectors, oil and natural gas, and defense, and the bulk of industry has not been considered worth the investment risk.

Direct aid from the US government has, generally, not been used to "pump prime" economic growth in the CIS. Instead, it has been linked to the reduction of strategic threats. For example, in the case of Belarus, by September 1995 the United States had provided around US$75 million in humanitarian aid shipments, US$229 million in Department of Agriculture food assistance, and US$19 million in technical assistance. Any additional aid was targeted for disarmament, with the United States providing more than US$75 million in Nunn-Lugar assistance. When economic crisis prevented Belarus from meeting its obligations in 1994, President Clinton increased US aid to US$100 million, most of which had to be spent on disarmament rather than the general economy. The United States and Germany eventually promised to provide US$230 million in aid to complete the arms reduction process. However, on other issues the United States finds itself unable to engage in normal relations with the government of President Alyaksandr Lukashenka, and is unwilling to provide economic assistance to support his authoritarian regime.

In the case of Uzbekistan, aid has been linked to an improvement in human rights. Under the leadership of President Islam Karimov, the situation has improved, and Uzbekistan has worked towards creating a measure of stability within Central Asia by engaging in peacekeeping operations and offering its diplomatic services in a number of situations. Its success in these fields has led the United States to consider it an "island of stability." Recognition and funding have been forthcoming, a US delegation visited in 1996, and President Clinton has submitted a bilateral investment treaty to the US Senate.

The United States will fund projects that are related to its specific security interests, but it is no longer in a position to oversee the complete overhaul of economic systems. That is a task that falls to the IMF. Its record has not been marked with success in Russia, but this has as much to do with inappropriate loans as with the Russian central bank undermining various financial reforms initiated by the government. In Georgia, where the government, exhausted by civil war, was desperate to have someone come in and manage the economy, the record has been better. Since 1994 hyperinflation has been cut, the national currency, the lari, has been stabilized and has ousted the ruble, and investment in the oil industry has increased, paving the way for western corporate investment.

Conclusion

Relations between the United States and the CIS continue to be determined by "great power" politics. As the sole remaining superpower, the United States exerts a degree of political, economic and military influence within international relations. It was predictable that the newly independent states would gravitate towards the hegemon, and that they would desire to be party to institutions and agreements sanctioned by that power. It was equally understandable that Russia, uncomfortable with the fact that its status has been revoked, would attempt to maintain some semblance of its former sphere of influence.

Aware of what a proud nation Russia is, the United States has been willing to overlook the hostile rhetoric and concentrate on shared concerns. In the absence of ideological confrontation, both the United States and Russia can focus on specifically national interests. These include continued cooperation on reducing the arsenals of weapons of mass destruction, the development of a European or Eurasian security system, the integration of Russia into the world economy, and the establishment of a working partnership to address various global problems (see Matlock). In order to secure a more compliant Russia, the United States has tried to avoid becoming involved in the various conflicts in the CIS, acknowledging instead a *de facto* Russian sphere of influence. Thus, for example, Russia has succeeded to the Soviet Union's seat on the UN Security Council; it plays a larger role in the OSCE; and it has been invited to sign the NATO-Russia Founding Act, as a basis for engaging in a special relationship with that institution. It has also been invited to participate in the IMF, the World Bank, the European Bank for Reconstruction and Development, and numerous commercial banks. Finally, having already been asked to contribute its diplomatic offices in the war in Bosnia-Herzegovina, it was closely involved in diplomatic activity over the crisis in Kosovo as this was being written (see Odom).

While these actions may go some way towards appeasing Russia, they place the other states of the CIS in a difficult position. Just as the Clinton administration has been accused of an unquestioning support of the Yeltsin regime, to the detriment of fostering relations with other viable politicians, so too can it be accused of overlooking, to a degree, the needs and assets of the other CIS countries. It is unarguable that Russia will remain the linchpin in any new security structure, yet it is also true that, if that new regime is to be of a truly pan-European or even Eurasian nature, the other members of the CIS must feel as if they are equal partners with Russia.

According to President Karimov of Uzbekistan, the central issues pertaining to the security of the CIS are maintaining territorial cohesion, continuing economic relations, retaining open borders, and creating a foreign policy that works for all the nations involved (see Kangas). That security is very much dependent upon the actions of its members. While the United States will remain for many a symbol of what a democratic, free-market state can become, each of the members of the CIS will have to devise its own means of achieving its goals. As has become apparent since 1991, that is likely to result in cooperation within the CIS, bilateral links between states, and regional alliances either with central and eastern Europe or with the Arab world. Given the global financial situation in 1998–99, there is very little that the United States can offer in the form of direct assistance. Nevertheless, the United States will continue to survey developments within the region, offering encouragement where it can, assuaging fears when required, and rebuking those who threaten to destabilize the larger security regime.

Further Reading

Albright, Madeleine, and Obey, D., "Does NATO Enlargement Serve US Interests?," in *CQ Researcher*, May 7, 1997

This article presents a useful insight into US policy in the late 1990s.

Art, Robert J., "Creating a Disaster: NATO's Open Door Policy," in *Political Science Quarterly*, Volume 113, number 3, 1998

This article is representative of the types of arguments posed by some US academics against NATO enlargement.

Cirincione, Joseph, "New Initiatives Towards a World With Fewer Nuclear Weapons," in *Disarmament: A Periodic Review by the United Nations*, Volume 20, numbers 2 and 3, 1997

Cirincione provides a concise overview of recent proposals made for the elimination or significant reduction of nuclear arsenals.

Cleary, Laura Richards, *Security Systems in Transition*, Aldershot and Brookfield, VT: Ashgate, 1998

A comparative study of the transformation of the US and Russian military-industrial complexes in the post-Cold War era, concentrating primarily on the political and social, rather than economic, repercussions.

Ferry, William E., and Roger E. Kanet, *Post-Communist States in the World Community*, London: Macmillan, and New York: St Martin's Press, 1998

Based on a series of papers presented at the Fifth World Congress of Central and East European Studies in Warsaw in 1995, the book is slightly dated, but it provides a useful basis for understanding foreign policy issues in the region.

Kangas, Roger D., "Taking the Lead in Central Asian Security," in *Transition*, Volume 2, number 9, 1996

Kangas provides a good historical overview of the development of Uzbekistan's role in the affairs of Central Asia.

Matlock, Jack, F., "Dealing With a Russia in Turmoil," in *Foreign Affairs*, Volume 75, number 3, 1996

Matlock, who was US Ambassador to the Soviet Union from 1987 to 1991, clearly outlines areas of shared interest and cooperation between the United States and Russia.

Odom, William E., "Russia's Several Seats at the Table," in *International Affairs*, Volume 74, number 4, 1998

In this article Odom advances the argument that NATO enlargement should be viewed in terms of maintaining US involvement in Europe in order to secure a greater level of stability and to prevent Russia from destabilizing that order.

Palazachenko, Pavel, *My Years with Gorbachev and Shevardnadze: the Memoir of a Soviet Interpreter*, University Park: Pennsylvania State University Press, 1997

Palazachenko provides an excellent firsthand account of the monumental changes that occurred in Soviet foreign and domestic policy during the Gorbachev years.

Perlmutter, Amos, and Ted Galen Carpenter, "NATO's Expensive Trip East: The Folly of Enlargement," in *Foreign Affairs*, Volume 77, number 1, 1998

Perlmutter and Carpenter argue that NATO's policy of enlargement has not been properly thought through and that as a result there is a risk that a still viable institution will be weakened.

Truscott, Peter, *Russia First: Breaking with the West*, London and New York: I. B. Tauris, 1997

The central argument of this book is that only by understanding Russian traditions can one understand the particular domestic and foreign policies that Russia has adopted. In advancing his argument, Truscott manages to provide a certain clarity to the welter of policies emanating from Yeltsin's governments.

Tsipko, Aleksandr, "Dialectics of the Ascent of a New Russian Statehood," in Osamu Ieda, editor, *New Order in Post-Communist Eurasia*, Sapporo: Slavic Research Center, Hokkaido University, 1993

Tsipko, who is clearly angered by the manner in which the Soviet Union disintegrated, provides an insightful account of Russian interpretations of statehood and nationality.

Dr Laura Richards Cleary is a Lecturer in International Relations at the University of Stirling in Scotland.

Chapter Sixteen

Relations with European Countries

Bogdan Szajkowski and
Nieves Pérez-Solórzano Borragán

The demise of the Soviet Union and the subsequent dissolution of the Warsaw Pact and Comecon have left the countries of the CIS in search of new political and economic arrangements with the rest of the world. What follows is an attempt to analyze the current state of relations between the CIS countries and European countries. However, since a full and comprehensive exploration of these relations would obviously require much greater space than is available here, we shall concentrate on the principal organizations and institutions that bring the two groups of countries together.

Attitudes to Europe

In the West between the end of World War II and the collapse of Communism, "Europe" tended to become synonymous with "western Europe," both in popular perception and in the vocabulary of politics. During the same period, the Soviet Union reinforced its isolationist policies through its entirely negative approach to the construction of European institutions, in particular the emerging European Communities. This hostility reflected, in part, some of the ambivalence, about belonging to Europe or to Asia, that has characterized the long history of the Russian empire, the Soviet Union, and their successor states – and that lingers on into the present. One particularly noticeable repercussion of this ambivalence is the lack of any comprehensive, cohesive, and long-term strategy for modernization among the CIS countries. Such a strategy would enable them to take advantage of western European

standards, experience, and expertise. It would thus assist them in dealing with the substantial problem of finding their own individual places, both within the CIS itself and within the new post-Communist international system.

Given its preponderant size and status, this is a problem for Russia above all. Throughout most of its history, Russia has been the center of an empire. The dissolution of the Soviet Union allowed the emergence of a new set of nations around Russia, the "near abroad," and Russia had to adjust to the idea that these nations were independent, as well as to the need to redefine Russia itself. In the words of Anatoly Chubais (see Prochazkova):

> "[Russia] was a country that was torn away from Europe and from its own roots. Communism was a form of outside-ism. We are now returning to Europe, but it won't be quick. At the moment, we know and understand the West better than we know ourselves, but unless we understand ourselves we will not be able to include ourselves anywhere or to communicate with anybody. There is also the danger that the search for a national idea can be abused. It can be used to isolate us. That is why we have to start answering the questions that are sleeping in people's souls. We have to express our citizenship. We cannot allow the vacuum to be filled by nationalists, Communists, fascists, [or] extremists."

Against this background, current attitudes to Europe, in Russia but also in other CIS countries, can be summarized as falling within one of three different perspectives: "Europeanist" or westernizing; conservative/nationalist or Slavophile; or "Eurasianist." The Europeanists argue that future prosperity lies in the absorption of western social, economic, political, and cultural norms and institutions. Leading Soviet and Russian politicians have repeatedly stressed their wish for Russia – and, by implication, at least some of the other CIS countries – to become part of Europe. The term "Common European Home" was used as far back as 1981 by Leonid Brezhnev and, in a speech in 1989, Mikhail Gorbachev called for the creation of a "Common European Home" as a

> "common legal space within which there is to be complete uniformity in the understanding and application by all states of the norms of international law . . . We envision Europe as a commonwealth of sovereign states with a high level of equitable interdependence and easily accessible borders, open to the exchange of products, technologies, and ideas, and wide-ranging contacts among people" (see Sakwa).

In contrast, Slavophiles, who trace their origins to the work of such 19th-century thinkers as Ivan Kireevsky, Aleksei Khomyakov or Konstantin Aksakov, believe that Russia (often seen in combination with the other Slavic states) possesses a unique civilization that must pursue its own path of development. It follows that secular western influences should be rejected in the name of Russian orthodoxy, and that political and economic isolationism should be maintained.

Finally, Eurasianists, starting with many thinkers among those who left Bolshevik Russia in the early 1920s, maintain that Russia is a bridge between Europe and Asia, and does not exclusively belong to either continent. There is a widely held view that Russia could play a unique role as a bridge between Europe and Asia, and could contribute towards extending the area of European cooperation, particularly in the economic field, from the Atlantic to the Pacific.

All three sets of attitudes continue to influence debates about national identity, political and economic reform, and international relations.

The Former Satellites of the Soviet Union

During the Cold War years, the Soviet regime exercised its dominance over most of central and eastern Europe through two institutions: the Warsaw Pact and Comecon (formally, the Council for Mutual Economic Assistance, or CMEA). Despite their nominally multilateral character, relations within the Soviet bloc were based upon a series of bilateral agreements. In the 1990s, however, looser groupings have been created, with specialized areas of concern and overlapping memberships, reflecting the much greater heterogeneity of central and eastern Europe following the breakup, not only of the Soviet Union, but of Czechoslovakia and Yugoslavia as well (see Hyde-Price).

For example, Russia, Ukraine, and Belarus now find themselves among the neighbors of the five countries in the Central European Free Trade Association (CEFTA) – Poland, the Czech Republic, Slovakia, Hungary, and Slovenia – which are setting them an example for voluntary and effective cooperation and harmonization on economic issues. Russia has also managed to maintain contact with its former area of influence through its membership of the Council of Baltic Sea States, created in March 1992, which brings it together with Sweden, Norway, Finland, Denmark, Iceland, Lithuania, Latvia, Estonia, Germany, and Poland. The areas of "informal" multilateral cooperation through the CBSS include environmental protection, energy, trade promotion around the Baltic, and transnational crime. Other new groupings have not been so effective, including, for example, the Black Sea Economic Cooperation (BSEC) group. This organization, founded in June 1992, has 11 members: six from the CIS (Armenia, Azerbaijan, Georgia, Moldova, Russia, and Ukraine), three other ex-Communist states (Albania, Bulgaria, and Romania), as well as Turkey and Greece. Turkey in particular has made attempts to enhance the role of the BSEC group, in order to foster its strategic relations with Russia and to show the EU that it is capable of providing leadership for the southeastern portion of the continent. Yet deeply-rooted historical animosities, combined

with the fragile political and economic conditions of most of its members, have continued
to hold it back from success.

Meanwhile, all the countries of central and
eastern Europe – with the obvious exception
of Yugoslavia – have made clear their strong
desire to follow Poland, the Czech Republic,
and Hungary in becoming full members of
NATO. Estonia, Latvia, and Lithuania in
particular, having experienced Soviet occupation and Russification for nearly 50 years, see
NATO membership as their guarantee against
any revival of Russian or "Soviet" imperialism.
The security anxieties of these states, as of their
neighbors, would be understandable even if
Russia did not pose a residual threat: as relatively small countries, they realise that they
cannot ensure their own security by themselves
(see Mihalka).

In addition, some CIS politicians have
voiced concern that the accession of countries
in central and eastern Europe to membership
of the EU could adversely affect those countries' economic ties with the CIS as a result of
the introduction of EU standards and trade
restrictions. Indeed, it has been estimated that
the Russian economy, for example, is losing
US$240 million a year because of present
obstacles to trade with the EU (see Danilov).
However, Russia and the other CIS countries
could also directly benefit from the accession
of new members to the EU. Given the differences between the EU economies and those of
central and eastern Europe, the Soviet Union's
former satellites may discover an interest in
rebuilding ties with CIS partners and modernizing plants built in the Communist period (see
Danilov). In particular, the Russian government would welcome the entry of the three
Baltic states into the EU, not least because this
seems likely to ensure better treatment for
Russian-speaking minorities in these countries.

Cooperation with the EU

As early as January 1992, just one month
after the Soviet Union collapsed, Andrei
Kozyrev, then Foreign Minister of Russia,
called for assistance to "set us on our feet and
become a normal member of the European
Community"; on January 29, 1994, Viktor

Chernomyrdin, then Prime Minister, expressed
Russia's desire to become a member of both
the EU and what is beginning to be known
as the Group of Eight (both cited in *Euro-East*).
Leading politicians in Russia, as well as in the
other CIS countries, are aware that their
country is not in a position to aspire to EU
membership at present, but even some western
experts have expressed their support for the
idea that at least some CIS countries must
join sooner rather than later. Jacques Attali,
the former head of the European Bank for
Reconstruction and Development, has gone so
far as argue that "in order to avoid the possible
isolation of Russia, negotiations on its membership in the EU should begin" immediately (as
cited by Danilov).

Nevertheless, there are differences of opinion
regarding the EU among the political and
economic elites of the CIS. Negative views of
the EU emanate, as one would expect, from
those with traditional anti-western ideologies;
but they are also expressed by those who regard
international relations as a zero-sum game. In
the case of Russia in particular, their view is
that an enlarged EU would only contribute to
the isolation of Russia in Europe, while
harming Russia's trade with those countries in
central and eastern Europe that acquire EU
membership (see Borko). More benign, "westernizing" observers see the EU as the main
source of stability in Europe and conclude
that the long-term success of the main EU
projects – the stabilization of the euro and
enlargement to the East – can only have beneficial effects, even if only indirectly. Faced with
their domestic preoccupations, most CIS citizens appear not to be very concerned about
cooperation with the EU, and the media tend
to pay much more attention to the issue of
NATO enlargement, leaving a general deficit
of information about the EU.

TACIS

EU assistance, first to the Soviet Union, and
then to the 12 CIS countries and Mongolia,
has been based on a recognition of the
need to support progress toward democracy
and market economies in these countries.
Significantly, it has consistently outweighed the

assistance provided by the United States or Japan (see Table 16.1). One EU program, now called Technical Assistance to the CIS (TACIS), is its major tool for facilitating cooperation. TACIS was conceived, even before the CIS itself, in December 1990, at a meeting in Rome of the European Council, the body comprising the heads of state and government of what was then the European Community. It was formally established by a Regulation adopted by the Community's Council of Ministers in July 1991, at a time when 400 million European currency units (Ecus) had been set aside for aid to the Soviet Union, the largest single amount provided for a single country by the Community at that time. Subsequent annual TACIS budgets brought the total funding for transfer of know-how to Ecu 3.3 billion during the period during 1991–97.

The latest TACIS Regulation was approved on July 4, 1996, and is valid until the end of 1999. On December 22, 1998, however, the EU's executive body, the Commission, adopted a proposal for overhauling the program. From 2000, its main focus will be on promoting democracy and stimulating investment in the CIS countries (and Mongolia), with up to 25% of the budget being used for the latter purpose. The EU will allocate approximately 4 billion euros to the 13 countries in question over the period 2000–06.

EU Partnership and Cooperation Agreements

In order to take account of the new political and economic realities, the EU has also negotiated new agreements with 10 countries among the CIS 12, replacing the trade and cooperation agreement signed with the Soviet Union in 1989 (Tajikistan and Turkmenistan being the exceptions – see Table 16.2). The new agreements are diverse, reflecting the differences among the partner countries themselves, but each agreement establishes a strong and comprehensive political and economic partnership with the EU, covering trade in goods, conditions for investment, and the strengthening of economic and political institutions. In addition, the agreement with Russia

envisaged an EU-Russia Cooperation Council, which met for the first time in January 1998 to adopt a program for implementing the agreement over the coming year (see Danilov). The agreements envisage wide-ranging and long-term cooperation, and more optimistic observers and decision-makers have already begun forecasting the establishment of a free trade area between the EU and the CIS, covering substantially all trade in goods, as well as the eventual securing of common standards for the establishment of companies, crossborder trade in services, and capital movements.

Security Issues

Many Russians believe that Germany's position on security issues will become more important as the US military presence in Europe is reduced over time (see Smith). Many also see France as their country's next most important partner in western Europe and welcome the Gaullist orientation in French foreign policy, primarily because of what can appear to be its anti-US overtones. Nevertheless, on a wide range of issues the EU countries and the CIS interact either through multilateral channels or through arrangements that give a special place to Russia, the largest of the CIS 12. It is therefore all the more puzzling and frustrating for at least some Russian politicians to find that the Western European Union (WEU), which became the "defense component" of the EU in 1991, has remained practically the only European organization that has not established formal and permanent structures for cooperation with Russia, let alone the other CIS countries or the CIS's own security-related institutions (see Chapter 2). Instead, the WEU's member states have preferred to rely exclusively on NATO, with which the WEU has close historical ties, in developing their security relationship with the ex-Soviet countries. These linkages between NATO, the WEU, and the EU offer potential for further misunderstandings in the future, especially in the absence of comparably effective mechanisms for formulating and executing security policies among the CIS countries themselves.

The Council of Europe

From its establishment in 1949 onward, the Council of Europe was compelled by the conditions of the Cold War to remain exclusively concerned with western Europe, where it first developed its monitoring of human rights, democracy, the treatment of minorities, and cultural issues. In 1985 the Council of Europe devoted an extraordinary session entirely to "East-West relations." A resolution of the Council passed in April the same year stressed the view that "unity in diversity" had long characterized European culture and that cultural cooperation between the two halves of the divided continent could benefit peoples and governments alike. In 1989, the year when Communism collapsed across central and eastern Europe, the Parliamentary Assembly established a special guest status for delegations from the legislatures of countries willing to apply the provisions of the Helsinki Final Act and the UN Covenant on Human Rights. This status was granted initially to the legislatures of Hungary, Poland, the Soviet Union, and Yugoslavia. Thus, the Council opened the way to the full accession of ex-Communist countries to membership, and declared its support for the trends towards democratization and marketization. Indeed, in relation to these countries the Council of Europe became a kind of antechamber for integration with the rest of Europe, as it had previously been for Spain and Portugal.

In the event, Moldova and Ukraine became the first CIS countries to join the Council of Europe, on July 13, 1995, and November 9, 1995, respectively. Russia had formally expressed its wish to become a member of the Council as early as May 6, 1992, but it was not admitted until February 23, 1996, and then only after considerable debate. The Council appears to have been reluctant to admit Russia as a full member primarily because of its poor record on human rights and the continuing war in Chechnya. Among the nine other CIS countries, Armenia and Azerbaijan have guest status at the Council of Europe; Belarus also has guest status, but this has been suspended since 1996 (see Chapter 5). Georgia, meanwhile, became the Council's 41st member state in 1999.

The principal mechanism that the Council of Europe uses in formulating and monitoring its policies is the drafting and circulation of conventions, which are binding agreements among the countries that have ratified them. By 1999, Moldova had ratified 23 of the main conventions of the Council, including the Convention for the Protection of Human Rights and Fundamental Freedoms, the European Cultural Convention, the European Convention on Extradition, and the Framework Convention on the Protection of National Minorities. Ukraine had ratified 29 of its conventions, including, in addition to those just mentioned, the European Convention on Mutual Assistance in Criminal Matters, the European Convention on the Prevention of Torture and Inhuman or Degrading Treatment or Punishment, and the Convention on Laundering, Search, Seizure, and Confiscation of the Proceeds from Crime. Russia had managed to ratify 32 of the main conventions, notably those already cited on human rights, culture, torture, and minorities. The ratification of the Council's conventions not only means that these countries have accepted western European legal standards, thus giving their citizens access to protection and assistance from beyond their national borders, but it has undoubtedly accelerated the assimilation of these countries' social and political structures with western standards as well.

The OSCE

With 55 participating states, the OSCE can claim to be the largest existing regional security organisation. Its area includes continental Europe, the Caucasus, Central Asia, and North America, and it also cooperates with Mediterranean and Asian partners. The OSCE thus brings together the "Euro-Atlantic" and the "Euro-Asian" communities, "from Vancouver to Vladivostok." The consensus among Russian decision-makers is that the OSCE is the perfect instrument for Russian involvement in the security of Europe as a whole, since Russia is not in NATO or the WEU.

Russia's call for a comprehensive system of collective security based on what was then the

CSCE was formally presented in July 1994. In response to the Russian proposals for change, a CSCE source stated:

> "What is needed is a system that would combine and strengthen all the existing mechanisms of the Conference on Security and Cooperation in Europe, the North Atlantic alliance, the European and Western European Unions, and the North Atlantic Cooperation Council . . . Moscow proceeds from the premise that the CSCE should play a central role among the combined international organisations operating on the European continent . . . Moscow is proposing far-reaching reforms and the creation of an executive body – a Security Council of sorts – within the framework of the all-European conference" (as cited in *Krasnaya Zvezda*, July 14, 1994).

Russia's proposal was aimed at halting NATO's eastward expansion and securing its own participation in Europe's defence and security strategies. Indeed, it would have had the effect of subordinating NATO to the OSCE. It seems likely, however, that the Russian government never seriously believed that the OSCE could become an effective pan-European security organization (see Sakwa) and, in any case, the Budapest summit meeting of the CSCE did not accept the proposal. Instead, it relaunched the CSCE as the OSCE, effective from 1995, declaring it to be "a primary instrument for early warning, conflict prevention and crisis management in the region."

The OSCE has been active in the area of arms control, under the terms of a new Vienna Convention adopted in 1994; in conflict prevention, preventive diplomacy, and conflict resolution; in establishing a comprehensive approach to European security; and in monitoring the rights of ethnic minorities and the conduct of elections. Within the CIS region, it has been active and influential in Georgia, Moldova, Tajikistan, Ukraine, and Nagorno-Karabakh (see Chapter 13); in central and eastern Europe, it has had missions in Kosovo, Sanjak, Vojvodina, Macedonia, Estonia, and Latvia, and is engaged in facilitating the Dayton Peace Plan for Bosnia-Herzegovina. Over and above these specific activities, the OSCE enjoys a political legitimacy in European security which is not shared by other security organizations, deriving from its uniquely broad membership and its consensus-based procedures. However, these assets have also proved to be the source of its weaknesses, chiefly its lack of any means to enforce its decisions or compel groups in conflict to stop fighting (as in Chechnya or Kosovo, to take two of the most outstanding examples).

Conclusion

For the countries of the CIS, the process of economic, political, and social transformation undertaken during the 1990s has been very complex and painful. While it has been relatively easy to accomplish structural change, the social change necessary for the effective functioning of new political and economic structures has not yet been achieved. Russia in particular epitomizes the difficulties, which have also been reflected in the search for new political and economic relations with the institutions and organizations that embody Europe and the West. The problems are compounded by a widespread lack of confidence in the internal processes of change and by the apparent absence of any long-term and comprehensive modernizing strategy on the part of the CIS countries. Such a strategy would clearly help to set out the paths and patterns of collaboration with the rest of Europe. The CIS countries are thus attempting to find their place in the international community in conditions of considerable internal and international weakness.

Placed alongside Russia, the other countries in the CIS find it difficult to extricate themselves from their traditional "client" relationships with their enormous neighbor. Russia itself, on the other hand, is still profoundly affected by the assumptions that it is a great power and should be recognized as such, and that it plays – and ought to play – the leading role in shaping the CIS region and its relations with the rest of the world. The scaling down of Russian perceptions to take account of new conditions has proved to be one of the most difficult aspects of relations within the CIS and beyond it; nor have these perceptions had entirely positive effects on relations between the wider Europe and the CIS as a whole. The considerable ambivalence of European organizations on the subject of Russia and the CIS stems from this complex set of misunderstandings, based on mistrust and dilemmas about identity.

Nevertheless, the countries of the CIS are being increasingly and relatively rapidly drawn into the domain of western structures and institutions. Involvement in extensive and complex dealings with the EU, the Council of Europe, NATO, and the OSCE – as well as other institutions that address international relations within the various regions of Europe – allows the CIS countries to participate actively in the functioning and policy-making of these very influential bodies. These developments constitute a two-way street: the countries of the CIS may well benefit, directly or indirectly, from sustained contact with the democratic standards and liberal experience of these institutions, while they in turn can work to secure stability, and the observance of civil rights and the rule of law, in the eastern reaches of the European continent. There is some encouraging evidence that these changes for the better are slowly taking place.

Further Reading

Borko, Y., "The New Intra-European Relations and Russia," in M. Maresceau, editor, *Enlarging the European Union: Relations Between the EU and Central and Eastern Europe*, London and New York: Longman, 1997

This is one of several outstanding papers in a remarkable volume that offers a thorough, multidisciplinary and up-to-date analysis of all aspects of relations between the EU and the ex-Communist countries.

Carr, F., editor, *Europe: The Cold Divide*, London: Macmillan, and New York: St Martin's Press, 1998

This volume constitutes a mixture of contributions on the changing environment facing the EU, central and eastern Europe, and the CIS as they address the gigantic challenge of reshaping relations within their continent.

Chinyaeya, E., "The Search For the 'Russian Idea'," in *Transitions*, June 1997

This very interesting article presents a clear and accurate picture of the perceptions that Russians have of themselves, both in relation to their national identity and as a mirror of their perceptions of the rest of Europe.

CSCE, *Budapest Summit Declaration*, Washington, DC: Commission on Security and Cooperation in Europe, 1994

The Summit Declaration endorses the institutional transformation of the CSCE into the OSCE, while rejecting Russian proposals to turn the CSCE into an international organization with a legally binding charter.

Danilov, D., "A Piece of the Partnership," in *Transitions*, April 1998

This article offers an excellent insight into Russian views on the enlargement of NATO and the EU. To illustrate the analysis, the author uses testimonies from Russia's main political actors.

Euro-East, number 19, February 21, 1994

This issue of a generally thorough and impressive series is focused on the new architecture of Europe.

George, B., "Forging the NATO-OSCE Partnership," in *OSCE Bulletin*, December 1998

This article investigates the framework for collaboration between these two major international organizations in the creation of a stable security structure for Europe. Issues such as conflict prevention, conflict resolution, and arms control and monitoring are thoroughly scrutinized.

Hyde-Price, A., "Patterns of International Politics," in S. White, J. Batt, and P. G. Lewis, editors, *Developments in Central and East European Politics 2*, London: Macmillan, and Durham, NC: Duke University Press, 1998

This volume groups together contributions from a number of specialists in post-Communist studies, addressing such issues as the working of the democratic systems in each country, the pattern of international relations in the region, the environment, and voting behavior.

Kugler, R. L., *Enlarging NATO: The Russian Factor*, Santa Monica, CA: RAND, 1996

One of the best and most thorough books on the role of NATO in the "New Europe," taking into consideration the need to avoid leaving Russia out of the process of change

Lapidus, G. W., editor, *The New Russia: Troubled Transformation*, Boulder, CO: Westview Press, 1995

A comprehensive volume on the transformation process that occurred in Russia during the 1990s

Mihalka, M., "The Emerging European Security Order," in *OMRI Analytical Briefs*, Volume 1, number 23, December 1995

As in other publications from the Open Media Research Institute, this article offers an in-depth analysis of the characteristics and implications of the new security map of Europe.

Pehe, J., "Paradoxes and Pragmatism," in *Transitions*, November 1996

This article covers the complexities that have traditionally characterized attempts to come to terms with the nature of Russia and its role in the world.

Prochazkova, Petra, "We Have To Return Home," in *Transitions*, June 1997

In a wideranging interview, Anatoly Chubais, a former Deputy Prime Minister of Russia, discusses the need to define a common ground for a clear definition of Russia, covering issues such as his country's role in the "New World Order" and the dangers of empty nationalist rhetoric.

Saikal, Amin, and William Maley, editors, *Russia in Search of its Future*, Cambridge and New York: Cambridge University Press, 1995

A collection of very interesting and useful material on what is likely to come next for Russia and its difficulties in adapting to its new role in the world

Sakwa, Richard, *Russian Politics and Society*, London and New York: Routledge, 1996

This is one of the most insightful accounts of the social, economic and political transformation that has occurred in Russia since the years of *glasnost* and *perestroika*.

Smith, M. A., "Russian Foreign Policy Towards the Near Abroad," Sandhurst: Royal Military Academy, Conflict Studies Research Centre, November 1997

A very useful analysis of Russian's complex approaches to the making of foreign policy, specifically in the case of its relations with other CIS countries

Szajkowski, Bogdan, editor, *Encyclopaedia of Conflicts, Disputes and Flashpoints in Eastern Europe, Russia and the Successor States*, Harlow: Longman, 1993

This reference text is intended to enhance understanding of actual and latent sources of conflict in these turbulent regions by providing a wealth of background data.

White, Stephen, Alex Pravda, and Zvi Gitelman, *Developments in Russian Politics 4*, London: Macmillan, and Durham, NC: Duke University Press, 1997

In this collection of analyses of the policy processes in Russia and other CIS countries since the demise of the Soviet Union, each contributor covers a specific aspect of these processes, such as political parties, parliamentary politics, the executive, and international relations.

Williams, C., and Sfikas, T. D., editors, *Ethnicity and Nationalism in Russia, the CIS and the Baltic States*, Aldershot and Brookfield, VT: Ashgate, 1999

Some of the papers contributed to this book by internationally established experts address theoretical aspects of the concepts of ethnicity and nationalism, while others illustrate the characteristics of both phenomena in the 15 countries in question.

Bogdan Szajkowski is Professor of Pan-European Politics and Director of the Centre for European Studies at the University of Exeter in England, and *Nieves Pérez-Solórzano Borragán* is a part-time Lecturer in the Centre and a doctoral candidate in the Department of Politics.

Table 16.1 Assistance to the Newly Independent States by Major Donors, September 30, 1990 to January 1, 1996[1]

	Value in billions of European currency units (Ecus)[2]	Proportion of total (%)
EU institutions	5.1	4.1
EU member states	67.6	54.9
United States	17.1	13.9
Japan	6.3	5.1
Subtotal (without IFI)	96.1	78.0
International Financial Instruments	27.1	22.0
Total	132.1	

Source: Services of the EU Commission

1 Includes Mongolia
2 On January 1, 1999, the euro replaced the Ecu-basket at the rate of one to one.

Table 16.2 Agreements Between the EU and 10 CIS Countries, 1994–98

	Partnership and Cooperation Agreements	Interim Agreements
Ukraine	signed June 14, 1994; entered into force March 1, 1998	entered into force February 1, 1996
Russia	signed June 24, 1994; entered into force December 1, 1997	entered into force February 1, 1996
Moldova	signed November 28, 1994; entered into force July 1, 1998	entered into force May 1, 1996
Kazakhstan	signed January 23, 1995	entered into force April 1, 1997
Kyrgyzstan	signed February 9, 1995	signed November 28, 1996
Belarus	signed March 6, 1995	signed March 25, 1996
Armenia	signed April, 22, 1996	entered into force December 1, 1997
Azerbaijan	signed April 22, 1996	signed October 8, 1997
Georgia	signed April 22, 1996	entered into force September 1, 1997
Uzbekistan	signed June 21, 1996	signed November 14, 1996

Source: Services of the EU Commission

Appendices

Appendix 1

Chronology

This listing is focused on political, economic and military events that continue to affect the CIS countries as the 20th century nears its end. However, this Chronology excludes many topics mentioned elsewhere in the appendices; and, inevitably, it overlaps with, but also accompanies, the Chronology in another volume in this series, *The Central and Eastern Europe Handbook*.

1939	**April**	The United Kingdom and France reject proposals from the Soviet government for an alliance that could defend central and eastern Europe against aggression by Nazi Germany.
	September	World War II begins in Europe with the signing of a nonaggression pact by Nazi Germany and the Soviet Union, their partition of Poland, and the declaration of war on Germany by Britain and France. Up to June 1941, around 750,000 Poles are killed, deported, or allowed to starve to death in the Soviet-occupied zone, which is incorporated into *Ukraine* and *Belarus* (see December 1943).
	October	Estonia, Latvia, and Lithuania acquiesce in the stationing of Soviet troops on their territories.
	November	The Soviet Union invades Finland.
1940	**March**	Finland and the Soviet Union make peace, and Finland loses 10% of its territory.
		Soviet forces murder and bury around 22,000 military officers, politicians, and other leading figures from Poland in a forest near Katyn; the massacre is uncovered in 1943, but not admitted until 1992.
	June	The Soviet Union occupies Estonia, Latvia, and Lithuania, and transfers Vilnius (Wilno) from occupied Poland to Lithuania; all three Baltic states are declared Soviet republics in August, a change in status never recognized by most other nations.
		Soviet forces invade Romania, seizing the province of Bukovina and incorporating it into *Ukraine*, where it remains today.
	August	The Soviet Union seizes the province of Bessarabia from Romania, incorporates part of it into *Ukraine*, and merges most of it with the Moldavian autonomous republic (previously inside Ukraine) to form a new Union Republic of Moldavia, now *Moldova*.
1941	**June**	Nazi Germany, Hungary, Romania, and Slovakia attack the Soviet Union, which then signs treaties with the western Allies. German forces eventually occupy Estonia, Latvia, Lithuania, *Ukraine*, *Belarus*, and parts of *Russia*, murdering Jews, Communists, gypsies, and other "enemies" in huge numbers. Romania seizes control of Bukovina

and *Moldova*, where around 250,000 Jews are murdered, by Romanian fascists and then by German forces, up to September 1944.

Nationalist rebels in *Belarus* begin attacks against both the invaders and the Soviet authorities, which continue into the early 1950s; other Belarusians collaborate with the Nazi occupation and take part in its extermination programs up to 1944.

July   Having already massacred hundreds of thousands of Jews, Poles, and other subject peoples, Nazi Germany begins construction of extermination camps, mainly in Poland (Maidanek, Auschwitz, Treblinka, Sobibor, Chelmno, and Belzec). By 1945, around 6 million Jews, at least 500,000 Roma, and tens of thousands of political opponents, homosexuals, and other victims have been deported from all over occupied Europe, including the western Soviet Union, and murdered.

August   The entire population of the Volga German republic in *Russia*, mainly settled by immigrants from Germany in the 18th century, is deported East of the Urals; they are "rehabilitated" in 1964. (They and their descendants mostly migrate to Germany in the 1990s.)

September   The German siege of Leningrad (St Petersburg) begins; it continues for 872 days until the Germans are routed in January 1944, the longest siege in 20th-century Europe until the encirclement of Sarajevo in 1992–95.

German forces capture Kyiv, the capital of *Ukraine*, and establish a collaborationist government, headed by Stepan Bandera. Up to 1944, it assists the Nazis by conscripting Ukrainian troops and participating in the extermination of almost all the Jews in the country, who numbered more than 1 million before the war.

1942 January   The Soviet Union persuades its western Allies to reject a proposal from the governments of Poland and Czechoslovakia, based in London, that their countries form a union after the war and invite neighboring countries to join it.

1943 January   The Soviet victory over the Germans in the Battle of Stalingrad marks "the turning of the tide" (as Winston Churchill put it) in World War II.

April   The Polish government in exile in London breaks off relations with the Soviet Union, accusing it (accurately) of having organized the Katyn massacre uncovered by German troops (see March 1940).

May   Stalin dissolves the Communist International (Comintern).

September   Stalin meets Sergei, Aleksei, and Nikolai, Metropolitans of the Russian Orthodox Church, who agree to support the war effort in return for a relaxation of repressive measures against religion.

December   At a conference in Tehran, Winston Churchill, Prime Minister of the United Kingdom, and US President Franklin D. Roosevelt accept the incorporation of the former eastern provinces of Poland into Soviet *Ukraine* and *Belarus* (resulting from the Nazi-Soviet Pact of 1939).

1944 January   The Soviet Army launches the first of the offensives that will extend Soviet control over central and eastern Europe by the end of the war.

June   The Soviet Union attacks Finland again and reoccupies Lithuania.

July The Soviet Union establishes a puppet government for Poland, at Lublin.

August The Soviet Army waits while Nazi troops suppress the uprising in Warsaw, the capital of Poland. It also retakes Riga, the capital of Latvia, from the Germans, then organizes the deportation of around 320,000 Latvians into *Russia*.

September The provisional government of Romania, which is largely controlled by the Soviet Army, makes peace with the Allies. The Communist Party in Bulgaria mounts a successful coup, with aid from the Soviet Army, and installs a "Fatherland Front" government. Finland makes peace with the Soviet Union, confirming the transfer of territory in 1940, and ceding Petsama and Porkkala as well. The Soviet Army retakes Estonia.

October At a meeting in Moscow, Churchill and Stalin reach agreement on the postwar division of influence in Romania (the Soviet Union 90%, the West 10%), Yugoslavia and Hungary (50/50), and Bulgaria (the Soviet Union 75%, the West 25%).

The western Allies begin to repatriate citizens of the Soviet Union, to a total of more than 5.4 million by the end of the war. Hundreds of thousands of these returnees are murdered or jailed in the following few years.

December The Communist Party in Hungary, aided by the Soviet troops occupying the eastern half of the country, establishes a provisional government, in coalition with other parties, at Debrecen.

1945 January The Soviet Army enters the ruins of Warsaw, the capital of Poland, destroyed by the Nazis after the suppression of the uprising in the city.

February At the Yalta Conference, Roosevelt, Churchill, and Stalin agree on the division of Germany, the holding of free elections in Poland, and a Soviet declaration of war on Japan, abandoning the neutrality agreed in 1941, in return for Soviet control of four Japanese islands. (These are still the subject of a territorial dispute between Japan and Russia.)

The Soviet Army takes control of Budapest, the capital of Hungary.

April A National Front government for Czechoslovakia, dominated by Communists and their allies, is created in Moscow.

May World War II, known in the Soviet Union as the "Great Patriotic War," ends in Europe. The Soviet Union has lost at least 26 million dead, but has taken extra territory and population, and has military control of Bulgaria, Czechoslovakia, Hungary, Poland, Romania, and eastern Germany, all future members of the Soviet bloc.

The region of Kaliningrad (formerly Königsberg) is transferred from Germany to the Soviet Union: it is now an enclave belonging to *Russia*, but separated from the rest of Russia by Lithuania.

Stalin's speech to Army commanders, praising the confidence of the "Great Russian" people in the government as the "decisive factor" in victory, initiates a further shift toward Russification throughout the Soviet Union.

June Subcarpathian Ruthenia, part of Czechoslovakia until its seizure by Hungary in 1939, becomes part of *Ukraine*, where it remains today.

August   At the Potsdam Conference, Stalin, US President Harry S Truman and Clement Attlee, Prime Minister of the United Kingdom, reach agreement on Czechoslovakia and Poland, but leave other issues to a general peace conference that never takes place.

September   The Soviet Union actively supports the formation of a short-lived "Azerbaijan Democratic Republic" in northern Iran, but withdraws its troops and officials after gaining oil concessions from the Iranian government. Azeri nationalists are also suppressed in *Azerbaijan* itself, and contacts across the frontier with Iran are prohibited.

October   The Soviet government announces the abolition of the Kalmyk, Crimean Tatar, and Chechen-Ingush republics, the Karachev region, and the Balkar area. This is the only official indication that most of the inhabitants of these territories number among more than 2 million people – mostly Moslems, but also Jews, Germans, Koreans, and Moldovans – deported to Siberia and Central Asia during the war, on the spurious grounds that they were actual or potential collaborators with the German occupation (see January 1957).

The Soviet "labor unions" join the new World Federation of Trade Unions, alongside their counterparts throughout Europe and the Americas (but see December 1949).

1946 February   Andrei Zhdanov, secretary of the Central Committee of the Soviet Communist Party and Stalin's leading ideologue, launches a major campaign against "bourgeois tendencies" in intellectual and cultural activities, reimposing Stalin's doctrine of "socialist realism," with effects lasting into the 1980s.

March   In a speech at Fulton, Missouri, Winston Churchill, former Prime Minister of the United Kingdom, denounces the "Iron Curtain" that separates the western democracies from the countries in central and eastern Europe that are coming increasingly under Soviet domination.

1947 February   In Paris, the wartime Allies (the United Kingdom, France, the Soviet Union, and the United States) sign peace treaties with five former enemy states: Bulgaria, Italy, Finland, Hungary, and Romania.

March   The Soviet Union's domination of central and eastern Europe, its intervention in the Greek civil war, and its withdrawal of cooperation in occupied Germany lead US President Truman to commit his country to the defense of "free peoples who are resisting subjugation by armed minorities or outside pressure" (the "Truman doctrine"). His adviser Bernard Baruch coins the term "the Cold War" soon after.

October   The Soviet Communist Party and eight other Communist Parties in Europe establish the Communist Information Bureau (Cominform), widely seen as the successor to the Communist International, a vehicle for Soviet control of other Communist parties that was dissolved in 1943 (but see April 1956).

1948 June   The growing hostility between the western Allies and the Soviet Union culminates in the breakdown of cooperation in occupied Germany, and the Soviet blockade of Berlin (to May 1949).

1949 January   Comecon is established in Moscow by the Soviet Union, Bulgaria, Czechoslovakia, Hungary, Poland, and Romania; Albania joins in February.

Pravda, the newspaper of the Soviet Communist Party, launches a campaign against "cosmopolitans" in cultural and intellectual life, reinforcing the emphasis on nationalism imposed during the war with a revival of anti-Semitism.

April The formation of NATO seals the western alliance against the Soviet bloc.

July Around 36,000 people accused of "nationalistic tendencies" are deported from *Moldova* to *Russia*.

August The Soviet Union becomes the world's second nuclear power by successfully testing an atomic bomb at Semipalatinsk (now Semey) in *Kazakhstan* (not made public until March 1950). This is the first of 470 nuclear tests at the site, including 118 in the atmosphere, up to its closure in 1989, leaving considerable radioactive contamination across the surrounding region of around 300,000 square kilometers.

September The Soviet Union denounces its treaty with Yugoslavia, which is viewed as insufficiently obedient to Stalin's wishes.

December Labor federations from western countries withdraw from the World Federation of Trade Unions, which becomes a Communist organization, and create the rival International Confederation of Free Trade Unions.

1950 February The Soviet Union and the People's Republic of China sign a 30-year Treaty of Friendship, Alliance, and Mutual Assistance (but see February 1964).

June The Communist regime in North Korea, advised by Soviet military officers, attacks the South, initiating the Korean War (to July 1953). In the course of the war, US and Soviet fighter planes take part in the only direct confrontations ever to occur between armed forces of the two "superpowers."

1953 January The anti-Semitic campaign culminates in allegations that Jewish doctors working in the Kremlin have murdered leading Soviet officials and are planning to murder more.

March The Soviet dictator Josef Stalin dies in Moscow, and is succeeded by a collective leadership, headed initially by Georgii Malenkov.

July An uprising at the Vorkuta labor camp is brutally suppressed, and information about it is kept secret up to the 1980s.

Lavrenti Beria and other Communists prominent in the security apparatus are arrested as the Party formally reasserts control over its activities. Beria is executed in December and the apparatus is renamed the KGB in 1954.

September Nikita Khrushchev is appointed First Secretary of the Communist Party of the Soviet Union.

1954 January Khrushchev launches the "Virgin Lands" campaign, a largely disastrous attempt to convert fallow land on the Volga River, in *Kazakhstan*, and elsewhere for grain production. The campaign, in which Leonid Brezhnev becomes prominent, is abandoned in 1956.

April Khrushchev commemorates the 300th anniversary of the absorption of eastern *Ukraine* into the Russian empire by transferring Crimea from *Russia* to Ukraine.

1955	**February**	Khrushchev arranges for Georgii Malenkov to take the blame for the problems in the Virgin Lands campaign and other policies in agriculture, and has him removed from the post of Prime Minister.
	May	The Warsaw Pact is created by the Soviet Union, Albania, Bulgaria, Czechoslovakia, Hungary, Poland, and Romania. East Germany joins in January 1956.
1956	**February**	At the 20th Congress of the Communist Party of the Soviet Union, Khrushchev delivers his "secret speech" in the absence of foreign Communists and all reporters, denouncing Stalin's crimes and the "cult of personality," but implicitly exonerating himself and other former aides of the dictator. The full text is suppressed in the Soviet Union until the 1980s.
	April	Cominform, the international organization of Communist parties, is abolished, although Soviet domination of the Communist parties in central and eastern Europe continues.
	May	A nationalist uprising in Tbilisi, the capital of *Georgia*, is brutally suppressed.
	August	The Supreme Soviet of *Azerbaijan* accedes to demands that Azeri become the sole official language of the republic, but nationalist movements are suppressed and the Communist Party is purged.
	October/ November	Soviet intervention to curb attempts to introduce reform and gain greater autonomy in Hungary and Poland indicate the strict limits on Khrushchev's "liberal" version of Stalinism.
1957	**January**	Most of the peoples deported to Siberia and Central Asia during World War II (see October 1945) are "rehabilitated" and permitted to return to their homelands, apart from the Volga Germans, the Crimean Tatars, and the Meskhetians. These three groups are rehabilitated in 1964, 1967, and 1968 respectively, but up to the 1990s the Crimean Tatars are prevented from returning to *Ukraine* and the Meskhetians are prevented from returning to *Georgia*.
	February	Andrei Gromyko begins his 28-year career as Soviet Foreign Minister.
	June	Khrushchev claims that Georgii Malenkov, Lazar Kaganovich, and others have formed an "anti-Party group," and has them removed from their posts.
	October	The launch of the world's first artificial satellite, Sputnik, inaugurates the "space race" with the United States.
1958	**March**	Khrushchev replaces Nikolai Bulganin as Prime Minister, while continuing as First Secretary of the Communist Party.
	December	A major legal reform abolishes the "principle of analogy" (which had allowed undefined "antisocial" acts to be punished as crimes), the security service's special courts, the criminal responsibility of children, unlimited prison sentences, and other features of Soviet law introduced by Stalin.
1959	**December**	The member states of Comecon – the Soviet Union, East Germany, Albania, Bulgaria, Czechoslovakia, Hungary, Poland, and Romania – sign a treaty on economic specialization, under which each country will seek to direct investment into certain designated industries as part of a common plan for the bloc; the scheme is never fully implemented.

1960 August The deteriorating relationship between the Soviet Union and the People's Republic of China leads to the withdrawal of Soviet technicians sent to advise Chinese industry.

1961 April Yuri Gagarin becomes the first person to leave the Earth's atmosphere, and returns to the Soviet Union to become a national hero up to his mysterious death in 1968.

October At its 22nd Congress, the Communist Party of the Soviet Union launches its first new program since 1919, forecasting parity with the United States by 1980 and completion of Communism by 1981. It also accepts the doctrine of "polycentrism," formally abandoning attempts to dictate policy to other Communist Parties.

Stalin's remains are removed from Lenin's Mausoleum in Red Square, and cities named for him and his collaborators revert to their original names.

December The Soviet Union breaks off relations with Albania over its support for China.

1962 January Cuba, subjected to an economic blockade by the United States, signs a trade pact with the Soviet Union, beginning a dependence that will last until 1991.

June Protests over increases in food prices erupt throughout the Soviet Union; in Novocherkassk in *Ukraine*, a still uncertain number of protesters are killed by machine gun fire as police clear the streets.

August The Soviet Union, the United States, and the United Kingdom sign the Nuclear Test Ban Treaty.

October The crisis over the stationing of Soviet missiles in Cuba ends with their removal in response to assurances from the United States that its forces will not invade Cuba.

1964 February Mao Zedong, paramount leader of Communist China, denounces the Soviet Union as "fascist," confirming the complete breakdown of relations between the world's two largest Communist states.

October Khrushchev is removed from power and replaced, by Leonid Brezhnev as First Secretary of the Communist Party and by Aleksei Kosygin as Prime Minister.

1965 September The Party announces a program of economic reforms, based on proposals by the economist Evsei Liberman, which emphasizes reduced control of enterprises and greater use of market-like incentives. The program is only partially implemented and is abandoned by 1968.

1966 February The cultural "thaw" started by Khrushchev ends with the trial and imprisonment of Andrei Sinyavsky and Yulii Daniel for publishing "anti-Soviet" writings in the West.

1968 August Soviet troops lead the Warsaw Pact invasion of Czechoslovakia.

November At a summit meeting in Warsaw, Leonid Brezhnev announces that the Warsaw Pact will continue "the defense of socialist gains" (the "Brezhnev doctrine"; but see October 1989).

1969 March Soviet and Chinese troops clash on a disputed section of their common frontier but further conflict between Asia's last remaining empires is averted.

	November	The United States and the Soviet Union become the first countries to sign the Nuclear Nonproliferation Treaty.
1970	**August**	A treaty signed by the Soviet Union and West Germany recognizes the Polish-German border as decided in 1945, signaling the beginning of a period of *détente* between the West and the Soviet bloc.
1972	**May**	US President Nixon and the Soviet leader Leonid Brezhnev sign the first Strategic Arms Limitation Treaty (SALT 1).
1973	**October**	The main petroleum-exporting countries raise prices and cut output, boosting the foreign earnings of the Soviet Union, which accelerates the extension of its diplomatic and military contacts outside Europe.
1974	**February**	The dissident writer and Nobel laureate Aleksandr Solzhenitsyn becomes the first person to be forcibly deported from the Soviet Union since Leon Trotsky in 1929.
1975	**July**	The Soviet Union buys US wheat, corn, and barley for the first time.
	August	The United States, Canada, and 33 European states sign the Helsinki Accords on international frontiers and human rights at the first CSCE, but its provisions under the latter heading continue to be widely disregarded in the Soviet Union and the countries allied to it.
1977	**June**	Leonid Brezhnev is appointed Chairman of the Presidium of the Supreme Soviet, effectively Soviet head of state.
	October	The Soviet Union adopts its third and last Constitution (following those of 1924 and 1936). It declares that the country is now a "developed socialist society," a term unknown to Marxism.
1978	**July**	As part of a renewed campaign against dissidents, in particular Jews seeking to emigrate to Israel, Anatoli (now Natan) Shcharansky, Yuri Orlov, and Aleksandr Ginzburg are jailed for "anti-Soviet agitation."
1979	**June**	The United States and the Soviet Union sign the second Strategic Arms Limitation Treaty (SALT 2), which is eventually rejected by the US Senate.
	December	The Soviet invasion of Afghanistan, in support of Babrak Karmal's faction of the Afghan Communist Party, causes the collapse of *détente* with the West (see April 1988).
1981	**December**	The United States and some other western countries impose sanctions on the Soviet Union in response to the imposition of martial law in Poland.
1982	**November**	Following the death of Leonid Brezhnev, Yuri Andropov is appointed General Secretary of the Communist Party (becoming Chairman of the Presidium in June 1983).
1984	**February**	Following the death of Yuri Andropov, Konstantin Chernenko becomes General Secretary of the Communist Party (becoming Chairman of the Presidium in April).
1985	**March**	Following the death of Konstantin Chernenko, Mikhail Gorbachev becomes General Secretary of the Communist Party.
	April	Gorbachev launches his program of *perestroika* ("restructuring") and *glasnost* ("openness").

July   Andrei Gromyko, replaced by Eduard Shevardnadze as Foreign Minister after 28 years in the post, is appointed as Chairman of the Presidium in succession to Chernenko.

1986 April   An explosion at the Chernobyl' nuclear power plant in *Ukraine* results in an increase in radiation around the world, and poisons organisms across large areas of Ukraine and *Belarus*, damaging their economies, killing thousands of people over the following decades, and undermining the reputation of the nuclear power industry.

May   Mikhail Gorbachev indicates the limits of his policy of *glasnost* by waiting a month before revealing any information about the Chernobyl' disaster; and what he reveals is minimal and misleading anyway.

1987 October   Boris Yeltsin, a Communist Party official as yet little-known to the general public, loses his post as secretary of the Moscow committee of the Party after criticizing Gorbachev's caution and inconsistency at a meeting of the All-Union Party Central Committee.

December   US President Ronald Reagan and Mikhail Gorbachev sign the Intermediate Nuclear Forces (INF) Treaty: their countries are to reduce their stockpiles of inter-mediate nuclear weapons, thus reducing the number of nuclear warheads each country holds by around 4%.

1988 February   The legislature of Nagorno-Karabakh, a region within *Azerbaijan* inhabited by around 120,000 Armenians and 40,000 Azeris, responds favorably to a petition signed by around 80,000 people and proclaims its adherence to *Armenia*. At least 32 Armenians are killed during riots in the city of Sumgait (Sumqayit) in Azerbaijan.

April   The Soviet Union begins to withdraw troops from Afghanistan.

May   Gorbachev leads the official celebrations of the millennium of Christianity at Kyiv, the capital of *Ukraine*, interpreting the event as an expression of Soviet unity.

                          US President Ronald Reagan visits the Soviet Union for the signing of the Intermediate Nuclear Forces (INF) Treaty.

                          In *Belarus*, the discovery of the mass burial of around 200,000 people at Kurpaty, followed by confirmation that they were murdered by Soviet security forces between 1937 and 1941 (not by the German invaders later), fuels the revival of anti-Communist and nationalist opinion.

                          The Popular Front of *Moldova* holds its first congress.

June   The European Community (now the EU) signs an agreement on trade with Comecon, which is followed by agreements with the Soviet Union (in 1989) and other Comecon members.

                          Gorbachev sends troops to Nagorno-Karabakh and to Yerevan, the capital of *Armenia*.

September   The arrest on corruption charges of Yuri Churbanov, son in law of the late Leonid Brezhnev, marks another stage in the exposure of the crimes and inefficiencies at the heart of the Soviet system.

October   Gorbachev succeeds Gromyko as Chairman of the Presidium.

December
A major earthquake in *Armenia* destroys the cities of Gumry and Spitak, leaving at least 55,000 people dead. In response to fears over its safety in another earthquake, Armenia's only nuclear power plant, at Medzamor (30 miles from the capital, Yerevan, and 60 miles from the epicenter of the December earthquake), is closed down early in 1989, plunging the country into a severe energy shortage and economic crisis (see June 1995).

Following the earthquake in *Armenia*, leading nationalists from the Karabakh Committee, which has criticized the government's relief efforts, are briefly detained on charges of "slandering the Soviet state." After their release, they establish the Armenian National Movement.

In an address to the UN General Assembly, Gorbachev announces the unilateral withdrawal of Soviet troops from central and eastern Europe, and from the Soviet Far East, as well as a reduction in the size of the armed forces by 500,000.

1989 January
After months of unrest, the majority-Armenian region of Nagorno-Karabakh in *Azerbaijan* is placed under the direct control of the Soviet government.

Nationalists begin a series of demonstrations in Chişinău (Kishinev), the capital of *Moldova*.

March
Elections to a new Congress of People's Deputies are contested among several candidates in most areas of the Soviet Union, but largely boycotted in *Armenia*. Non-Communists are prevented from organizing political parties, there is extensive manipulation of nomination and election procedures, and one third of seats are reserved for Party organizations. Boris Yeltsin, Andrei Sakharov, and other dissidents win huge personal votes, but the proportion of Party members in the Congress (80%) is actually higher than in the former Supreme Soviet.

April
Army units are used to disperse demonstrations in favor of greater autonomy in Tbilisi, the capital of *Georgia*.

May
Gorbachev visits Beijing for the first Sino-Soviet summit meeting in 30 years.

June
Army units are sent to quell unrest in *Uzbekistan*, where Uzbeks have rioted and attacked members of the Meskhetian minority.

The Popular Front for independence – also known as Adradzhenne (Renaissance) – is launched in *Belarus*.

July
More than 100,000 miners, in Vorkutka, *Kazakhstan*, Siberia, and *Ukraine*, strike for better pay and conditions, in contrast to the generally low level of labor militancy throughout the Soviet Union and its successor states.

August
The Popular Front in *Azerbaijan* calls a general strike in support of its demands for separation from the Soviet Union and reoccupation of the disputed region of Nagorno-Karabakh. Over the following months, its followers collaborate with state officials in a blockade of *Armenia*.

In *Moldova*, Moldovan is declared the state language and plans are announced to restrict the use of Russian in government services (but see March 1994).

September
The Popular Movement for Restructuring (Rukh), a national democratic movement, is founded in *Ukraine*.

October   Gorbachev formally renounces the "Brezhnev doctrine" (see November 1968), thus abandoning the Communist regimes of central and eastern Europe to collapse over the following months.

November   Renewed protests against the Soviet regime in Chişinău (Kishinev), the capital of *Moldova*, end in riots, military repression, and the dismissal of the republic's Communist leader, Semyon Grossu.

1990 January   The Soviet Union begins full-scale withdrawal of its military forces from central and eastern Europe.

Interethnic violence in *Georgia* leads to military intervention by the Soviet government.

In *Azerbaijan*, the Popular Front seizes power and declares independence, but Soviet forces restore President Ayaz Mutalibov to power after just one day. Azerbaijan and *Armenia* then go to war over the disputed region of Nagorno-Karabakh.

The Supreme Soviet of *Belarus* makes Belarusian the official language of the republic instead of Russian.

In *Ukraine*, Rukh organizes a "human chain," composed of thousands of supporters of independence holding hands, across 325 miles between Kyiv and L'viv.

February   The Communist Party of the Soviet Union formally surrenders its monopoly of political power; the Soviet Constitution is amended accordingly in March.

March   Gorbachev is reelected President of the Soviet Union, with enhanced powers.

In elections for the Supreme Soviet of *Ukraine*, Rukh and allied national democratic groups win one quarter of the seats.

The new nationalist majority in the Supreme Soviet of *Georgia* denounces the treaty that created the Soviet Union in 1922.

Elections in other republics, where the Communist Party retains its control of the electoral system, result in little change.

April   The Soviet government imposes sanctions on Lithuania, following its declaration of independence in March.

In *Kazakhstan*, Nursultan Nazarbayev is appointed by the Supreme Soviet (legislature) to the new post of President (confirmed by a direct election in December 1991, in which he secures 98.8% of the votes cast with no opponents running).

May   Boris Yeltsin becomes Chairman of the Supreme Soviet of *Russia*.

June   *Russia* and *Moldova* declare themselves sovereign states.

Uzbekistan also declares sovereignty, but in a "renewed Soviet federation," under its Communist President Islam Karimov (appointed by the Supreme Soviet in March 1990, and directly elected in December 1991).

Army units are sent to quell unrest in *Kyrgyzstan*, where interethnic violence has broken out between Kyrgyz and Uzbeks in the cities of Osh and Uzgen.

July   Boris Yeltsin resigns from the Communist Party but remains Chairman of the Supreme Soviet of *Russia*.

                    The Supreme Soviet in *Ukraine* declares sovereignty and chooses the ex-Communist Leonid Kravchuk as President.

August   The Supreme Soviet in *Armenia* elects the nationalist Levon Ter-Petrosian as President (see October 1991) and issues a declaration of sovereignty.

                    The Gagauz region of *Moldova* declares itself an autonomous republic, under the name Gagauz-Yeri.

                    The republic of Abkhazia in *Georgia* issues a declaration of sovereignty (see August 1992).

September   The Transnistria region of *Moldova* declares itself an autonomous republic.

                    The South Ossetia region of *Georgia* declares itself an autonomous republic (see December).

                    The Allied occupation powers (the Soviet Union, France, the United Kingdom, and the United States) join West and East Germany in signing a treaty on German unification known as the "2+4" Treaty.

                    Belarus declares sovereignty.

                    The Supreme Soviet of *Azerbaijan* issues a declaration of sovereignty. The Communists win the subsequent elections and their leader, Ayaz Mutalibov, becomes President after an election in which he is the only candidate.

October   Following the unification of Germany, the repatriation of former Soviet troops and their dependents from former Warsaw Pact countries accelerates, while increasing numbers of ethnic Germans from CIS countries emigrate to Germany.

                    A new law is enacted by the All-Union Supreme Soviet to permit freedom of worship, the opening of church schools, and the ownership of property by religious bodies, provided that they are registered with the state.

                    Saparmurat Niyazov, the leader of the Communist Party in *Turkmenistan*, is elected President, unopposed, with 98.3% of the votes cast.

November   The Soviet Union joins with other members of the CSCE (now the OSCE) to sign the Charter of Paris for a New Europe, which includes commitments to multiparty democracy, market-based economies, the rule of law, and respect for human rights. The CSCE also agrees to begin monitoring human rights, thus abandoning the principle of nonintervention in the internal affairs of sovereign states.

                    The member states of the Warsaw Pact and NATO sign the first version of a treaty on reducing conventional forces in Europe (the CFE Treaty).

                    In *Georgia*, following the victory of the nationalist coalition Round Table/Free Georgia in elections in October, its leader, Zviad Gamsakhurdia, takes office as Chairman of the republic's Supreme Soviet (see May 1991).

                    A state of emergency is declared in the mainly ethnic-Russian Transnistria region of *Moldova*, following weeks of interethnic unrest.

December   *Russia* legalizes the private ownership of land under strict conditions.

Georgia formally denounces South Ossetia's aspirations to autonomous status: war erupts between Georgian troops and South Ossetian forces, the latter reinforced with paramilitary groups from the North Caucasus republics inside *Russia* (see June 1992).

1991 January   The member states of Comecon agree to dissolve it.

Following Soviet military intervention in Lithuania, Boris Yeltsin, Chairman of the Supreme Soviet of *Russia*, signs mutual security agreements with all three Baltic states.

March   In a referendum held in most of the constituent republics of the Soviet Union, around 60% of eligible voters endorse Gorbachev's proposal for a "renewed federation of equal sovereign republics." However, in *Georgia*, *Armenia*, and the occupied Baltic states separate referendums on independence show large majorities in favor, as does another referendum in *Moldova* in May.

The prices of most foodstuffs and clothes are tripled or quadrupled by decree.

April   The Soviet government signs a treaty with all the republics except *Georgia* and *Kyrgyzstan* (and the Baltic states) on a new form of union.

A general strike takes place in Minsk, the capital of *Belarus*, to demand further reform.

Georgia becomes the first Union Republic to declare independence.

May   Zviad Gamsakhurdia, Chairman of the Supreme Soviet of *Georgia*, wins the country's first election for the post of President, with 86% of the votes cast.

Soviet troops join forces raised by the government of *Azerbaijan* in operations on the border with *Armenia*, forcing thousands of Armenians to leave Azerbaijan.

June   Boris Yeltsin is directly elected as President of *Russia*, the first head of a Russian state ever to be chosen in this way.

July   The Warsaw Pact is formally dissolved. The Soviet Union and the United States sign the first Strategic Arms Reduction Treaty (START I), committing them to hold no more than 6,000 nuclear warheads each.

The Supreme Soviet of *Belarus* approves a declaration of independence from the Soviet Union.

August   Political and military leaders opposed to reform launch a coup while Gorbachev is away from Moscow, two days before the new union treaty is to take effect. Boris Yeltsin, President of *Russia*, places himself at the head of the popular protests that defeat it.

After the defeat of the coup attempt, Gorbachev resigns as General Secretary of the Communist Party, which is suspended or banned in *Russia*, *Belarus*, *Kyrgyzstan*, and *Moldova*.

Russia, *Kyrgyzstan*, *Moldova*, *Ukraine*, and *Uzbekistan* declare independence; the Supreme Soviet in *Azerbaijan* also votes in favor of independence; and *Belarus* activates the declaration of independence passed in July.

September   The Transnistria region in *Moldova* declares itself independent as the "Dnestr Moldavian Republic."

President Gamsakhurdia of *Georgia* responds to demonstrations against his rule by imposing a state of emergency.

The Soviet Union recognizes the independence of the Baltic states, 51 years after the Soviet occupation began, but insists that the occupation was both legal and necessary.

Tajikistan declares independence under the leadership of its new President, Rakhmon Nabiyev, head of the Communist Party (renamed the Socialist Party), as the country plunges into civil war between his supporters and his opponents, who are led by Islamist and democratic parties.

Armenia also declares independence, following a 94% vote in favor in a referendum.

October   President Akayev of *Kyrgyzstan*, appointed to the office in October 1990, becomes the country's first directly elected leader, with 95% of the votes cast.

President Ter-Petrosian of *Armenia* becomes the country's first directly elected leader, winning 87% of the votes cast.

Turkmenistan and *Azerbaijan* declare independence.

November   *Azerbaijan* initiates an official blockade on movement of oil and other supplies into *Armenia*.

Chechnya, part of the Chechen-Ingush republic within *Russia*, unilaterally declares independence under Dzhokhar Dudayev, elected its President in October through a voting process of dubious fairness and legality.

December   More than 90% of voters in *Ukraine* endorse independence in a referendum and more than 60% elect Leonid Kravchuk as President.

Russia, *Belarus* and *Ukraine* create the CIS; eight other ex-Soviet republics join later in the month, with only *Georgia* remaining outside (see also Appendix 4).

Kazakhstan becomes the last Soviet republic to declare independence.

Mikhail Gorbachev resigns as President of the Soviet Union.

The Congress of People's Deputies abolishes the Soviet Union, 69 years after it was founded, and then dissolves itself.

1992 January   Price liberalization for most commodities except oil takes effect in *Russia*, fueling inflation (the domestic price of oil is liberalized in September).

Russia ceases to target its nuclear warheads at cities in the United States.

Armenia introduces a "shock therapy" program of economic reforms.

President Gamsakhurdia of *Georgia* flees into exile, initially in *Armenia*, while his opponents take power.

March	The leaders of the CIS countries agree on a division of responsibility for the repayment of the Soviet Union's foreign debt.

In *Russia*, 18 of the (then) 20 autonomous republics agree to remain within the country under the terms of a new Federation Treaty. Tatarstan and Chechen-Ingushetia reassert their claims to independence, but the former accepts autonomy within Russia (in February 1994), and the latter is effectively split into Chechnya and Ingushetia as war starts in Chechnya (in September 1994).

The IMF begins lending US$4 billion to *Russia* to support economic reform.

Ukraine begins the privatization of state-owned enterprises.

In *Georgia*, Eduard Shevardnadze, former Foreign Minister of the Soviet Union, becomes Chairman of the State Council created by the opponents of President Gamsakhurdia, who remains in exile (mainly in Chechnya) until September.

President Mircea Snegur of *Moldova* declares a state of emergency in the Transnistria region, where an independence movement has been fighting government forces since December 1991, while the leaders of Gagauz-Yeri accept autonomy within Moldova.

May   Six states sign a treaty on CIS collective security. The transfer of all tactical nuclear weapons to *Russia* from other ex-Soviet states is completed. *Russia, Ukraine, Belarus,* and *Kazakhstan* sign START I with the United States, under which Russia is to reduce its strategic nuclear arsenal and the other three countries are to eliminate theirs.

The region of Crimea declares independence from *Ukraine*.

Armenia conquers a "land bridge" through the territory of *Azerbaijan* to the disputed region of Nagorno-Karabakh.

June   After leading an uprising against the Communist government of *Azerbaijan* in May, Abulfaz Elchibey, leader of the Popular Front, is elected President.

Under a ceasefire agreement brokered by President Yeltsin of *Russia*, South Ossetia remains *de jure* a republic within *Georgia* but obtains extensive *de facto* autonomy.

July   The revised CFE Treaty is signed by 29 states.

Russia and other CIS states create a peacekeeping force, which is deployed to monitor a ceasefire in the Transnistria region of *Moldova*, where ethnic Russians have declared an independent "Dnestr Moldavian Republic."

Russia abolishes all state controls on the exchange of the ruble, then still the common currency of the 12 Soviet successor states, as well as of Estonia, Latvia, and Lithuania (see also May 1996).

August   An independence movement in the republic of Abkhazia begins an uprising against the government of *Georgia*. Georgian government forces take control of the republic's capital city, Sukhumi (Sukhum in Abkhazian) but the uprising continues, with some support from paramilitary forces recruited in the North Caucasus republics of *Russia* (see September 1993).

Azerbaijan introduces its own currency, the manat, as a parallel means of exchange to the Russian ruble, but remains within the ruble zone until November 1993.

September   Civil war continues in *Tajikistan* between supporters of President Rakhmon Nabiyev, deposed this month, and the United Tajik Opposition, led by Akbasho Iskandrov, who is made "interim head of state" in place of Nabiyev.

Ex-President Gamsakhurdia of *Georgia* returns from exile to lead a rising against his successors.

October   A program of voucher privatization begins in *Russia*.

Azerbaijan leaves the CIS (but rejoins in September 1993).

November   In *Tajikistan*, the ex-Communist supporters of former President Nabiyev seize control of the government and appoint Imamali Rakhmonov, Chairman of its Supreme Soviet, as head of state; he imposes restrictions on opposition groups and the media.

December   President Islam Karimov of *Uzbekistan* introduces a new constitution, and bans three opposition parties – Birlik (Unity), the Erk (Freedom) Democratic Party, and the Islamic Rebirth Party. Abdullah Utayev, leader of the last-named party, disappears.

1993 January   Seven states sign the CIS Charter.

US President George Bush and President Yeltsin of *Russia* sign the second Strategic Arms Reduction Treaty (START II), confirming previous announcements that by 2003 the number of US nuclear warheads would be cut to 3,500, while the number of Russian nuclear warheads would be cut to 3,000. The treaty has not been ratified.

Diphtheria becomes epidemic in many parts of *Russia* and *Ukraine*.

February   In *Belarus*, the Supreme Soviet ratifies the Nuclear Nonproliferation Treaty and START I, and lifts the ban on the Communist Party.

March   *Belarus* adopts a new Constitution with a strong presidency (see July 1994).

A CIS peacekeeping force seeks to intervene in the civil war in *Tajikistan*.

April   A referendum in *Russia* shows a majority of those voting in support of President Yeltsin and his program of economic reform. The Group of Seven leading industrialized economies lend US$43 billion to Russia.

The IMF introduces a "Systemic Transformation Facility" for post-Communist economies, offering credit of various amounts in return for economic reforms, including limits on central bank financing of budget deficits, reduced subsidies for production, full liberalization of prices, and privatization.

May   *Kyrgyzstan* becomes the first CIS country to leave the ruble zone by introducing a new currency, the som; it also promulgates a new constitution, committing the state to support for Islam.

June   In *Azerbaijan*, the Popular Front government of President Abulfaz Elchibey is overthrown by ex-Communists, led by Heydar Aliyev. (June 15, the day when Aliyev took power, has been officially celebrated as "National Salvation Day" since 1997.)

July   *Russia* withdraws all rubles issued before 1993 without warning the governments of the other CIS countries still using the ruble.

September   In *Russia*, the Congress of People's Deputies, led by its Chairman, Ruslan Khasbulatov, rejects President Yeltsin's decree aimed at dissolving it and replacing it with a new bicameral Federal Assembly (the State Duma and the Council of the Federation). The Congress then votes to impeach Yeltsin and replace him with Vice President Aleksandr Rutskoi.

                  Azerbaijan, now ruled by ex-Communists, rejoins the CIS.

                  In *Georgia*, forces seeking independence for Abkhazia take control of the republic in fierce fighting, leaving around 10,000 people dead and around 250,000 displaced. Sporadic conflict continues (see July 1994).

October   President Yeltsin of *Russia* orders the bombardment of the White House, the Moscow building where the Congress of People's Deputies meets, and secures the dissolution of the Congress.

                  Heydar Aliyev, who seized power in *Azerbaijan* in June, is sworn in as President after an election marked by ballot-rigging, repression of opponents of his regime, and state control over most media.

November   *Russia* and the other member states of the CIS agree to abandon the ruble zone, in which all but *Kyrgyzstan* had continued using the Russian ruble, in favor of establishing a national currency for each state. *Armenia, Kazakhstan, Moldova, Turkmenistan,* and *Uzbekistan* introduce new currencies immediately; *Azerbaijan* makes its currency, the manat, fully convertible.

                  A revolt in *Georgia*, led by supporters of ex-President Gamsakhurdia, ends in victory for the government and the death of Gamsakhurdia himself.

December   In *Russia*, a majority in a referendum approves the new Constitution, which, among other changes, abolishes the post of Vice President, and establishes a new legislature. Elections result in significant gains for Communist and nationalist groups in the State Duma, the lower house of the new Federal Assembly, which together outnumber the supporters of President Yeltsin.

                  Georgia joins the CIS.

1994 January A referendum in *Kyrgyzstan* confirms President Akayev in office, apparently with 96% of the votes cast.

                  Tajikistan enters a monetary union with *Russia* (to May 1995).

                  President Saparmurat Niyazov of *Turkmenistan*, in power since 1990, has his term of office extended to 2002 as a result of a referendum reportedly showing 99.99% support for the proposal.

March   The first multiparty elections are held in *Kazakhstan*, but several seats in the legislature are reserved for nominees of President Nursultan Nazarbayev and some opposition parties are banned; the Constitutional Court invalidates the elections (see August 1995).

                  An overwhelming majority in a referendum in *Moldova* rejects a proposal for union with Romania.

April   The Prime Ministers of *Russia* and *Belarus* sign an agreement on monetary union, free trade, and a common ruble zone.

                   The Parliament of *Moldova* ratifies the country's membership of the CIS.

May   The Parliament of *Moldova* repeals the law passed in August 1989 that gave Moldovan exclusive status as an official language.

June   *Russia* becomes the first CIS country to join NATO's Partnership for Peace program, launched in January.

                   Russia and *Ukraine* sign partnership and cooperation agreements with the EU (effective from December 1997 and March 1998, respectively).

July   Alyaksandr Lukashenka wins the first presidential election to be held in *Belarus* under the new Constitution promulgated in March 1993.

                   Azerbaijan and *Armenia* agree a ceasefire in their war over the disputed region of Nagorno-Karabakh.

                   A CIS peacekeeping force is deployed in the breakaway republic of Abkhazia in *Georgia*, following the signing of a ceasefire in April (see May 1998).

August   The last ex-Soviet troops and their dependants are withdrawn from Germany – bringing the totals withdrawn to 340,000 and 210,000, respectively, since 1990 – and return to *Russia*, *Ukraine*, and *Belarus*; the last Russian combat troops in Latvia and Estonia also depart.

September   Martial law is declared by Dzhokhar Dudayev, President of the republic of Chechnya (a part of the Chechen-Ingush republic, inside *Russia*, that has unilaterally declared independence), as his opponents, who are receiving Russian aid, launch a concerted military offensive against his supporters.

                   BP, Statoil, and seven other western oil companies sign agreements with the state oil company of *Azerbaijan* and Lukoil of *Russia* on joint exploration and development of oil fields near the Caspian Sea.

October   *Russia* undergoes economic crisis following the collapse of the ruble on the foreign exchange markets.

                   Leonid Kuchma, elected President of *Ukraine* in July, announces a radical economic reform program and begins to court western support.

November   Following a ceasefire in the civil war in *Tajikistan* (signed in September), a presidential election is organized, but it is boycotted by the United Tajik Opposition. Imamali Rakhmonov, effective head of state since November 1992, becomes President after defeating Abdulmalik Abdullodzhonov in an election process extensively manipulated by the government.

                   Ukraine ratifies the Nuclear Nonproliferation Treaty and receives security guarantees from the nuclear powers.

                   Moldova signs a partnership and cooperation agreement with the EU.

                   The government of *Armenia* launches a program of economic reforms supported by the IMF.

December	The government of *Russia* sends troops to intervene in the civil war in Chechnya.
	In elections in *Turkmenistan*, 50 candidates approved by President Niyazov run for the 50 seats in the Assembly (the Majlis), and it is claimed that 98% of voters take part in the elections.
1995 January	The IMF grants loans to *Uzbekistan*, which starts to implement economic reforms.
	Kazakhstan signs a partnership and cooperation agreement with the EU, and forms a customs union with *Russia* and *Belarus*.
February	In *Tajikistan*, legislative elections boycotted by the United Tajik Opposition result in victory for supporters of President Rakhmonov, but they are condemned as unfair by the OSCE.
	Kyrgyzstan signs a partnership and cooperation agreement with the EU.
March	*Russia* signs an agreement with the IMF on a stabilization program that mandates, among other changes, independence for the Bank of Russia (from April), and the imposition of strict monetary targets.
	Ukraine annuls the independence of Crimea (declared in May 1992), abolishes its presidency, and imposes direct presidential rule (to August).
	Belarus signs a partnership and cooperation agreement with the EU.
	Georgia arranges a loan from the IMF, and introduces a privatization program.
	President Karimov of *Uzbekistan* wins a referendum extending his term of office to 2000.
April	President Nazarbayev of *Kazakhstan* wins a referendum extending his term of office to 2000 (but see January 1999).
	Deputies belonging to opposition parties in the Parliament of *Belarus* are beaten and arrested inside the Parliament building, signaling a renewed campaign by President Lukashenka against dissenters.
May	President Lukashenka of *Belarus* wins support in a referendum for his proposals to restore Russian as an official language, revive Soviet-style state symbols, pursue closer integration with Russia, and enhance the powers of his office.
	Tajikistan abandons use of the Russian ruble in favor of its own Tajik ruble.
June	In *Armenia*, which has few domestic sources of energy, one of two units at the Medzamor nuclear power plant serving the capital, Yerevan, closed down after the earthquake in December 1988, is restarted.
July	*Armenia* promulgates a new Constitution, and a new National Assembly is elected, in which the majority of seats are held by the Pan-Armenian National Movement and its allies.
August	A majority in a referendum in *Kazakhstan* approves a new constitution, extending the powers of President Nazarbayev, making Kazakh the official language, and abolishing the Constitutional Court.

With the support of the UN, *Kyrgyzstan* celebrates the millennium of its national epic, the *Manas*, which had been banned by the Soviet government from 1952 to 1989.

September   *Georgia* introduces its national currency, the lari.

November   In *Azerbaijan*, the New Azerbaijani Party, which supports the regime of President Aliyev, wins a majority in the National Assembly, in elections that are condemned by the OSCE as unfair. President Aliyev's powers are extended under a new Constitution.

December   Following elections in *Russia*, the Communist Party becomes the largest group in the State Duma, giving the combined opposition to President Yeltsin and to thorough economic reform an even larger majority than before.

The Group of Seven leading industrialized countries and the International Atomic Energy Agency grant funds to *Ukraine* to assist in the closure of the Chernobyl' nuclear power plant by 2000.

A referendum in the Transnistria region of *Moldova* shows a majority in favor of independence for the "Dnestr Moldavian Republic."

1996 March   The IMF initiates a loan of US$10 billion to *Russia*, to be paid out up to 1999 on condition that economic reforms proceed as planned.

The Presidents of *Russia*, *Belarus*, *Kazakhstan*, and *Kyrgyzstan* sign the Quadrilateral Treaty, aiming to create a common market, a customs union, and joint transportation, energy and information systems; *Tajikistan* joins the group later.

The Constitution of *Kyrgyzstan* is amended to allow the use of Russian as an official language in districts and places of work that have Russian majorities.

In Chechnya, rebel forces demanding full independence from *Russia* (instead of autonomy within it) attack and occupy the capital city, Grozny.

April   The Paris Club of western governments reschedules payment of *Russia*'s external debt, which amounts to around US$40 billion.

Presidents Yeltsin of *Russia* and Lukashenka of *Belarus* sign a treaty on a Community of Sovereign Republics, providing for closer integration and eventual confederation; this is followed by an Act of Union, signed in April 1997, and a Declaration of Intent on economic and security issues in December 1998.

In *Russia*, Dzhokhar Dudayev, President of the breakaway republic of Chechnya since October 1991, is killed in battle.

Armenia, *Azerbaijan*, and *Georgia* sign partnership and cooperation agreements with the EU.

May   In *Russia*, the central bank abandons floating exchange rates for the ruble and starts to set rates within a "crawling peg" linked to western currencies.

Moldova becomes the first CIS country to bring its law into line with Council of Europe standards by abolishing the death penalty.

June	Boris Yeltsin wins reelection as President of *Russia*, with 35% of votes cast in the first round (against five other candidates) and 53.7% in the second round (against the Communist leader Gennadi Zyuganov).
	The Transnistria region agrees to become an autonomous republic within *Moldova*; the agreement remains unratified.
August	General Aleksandr Lebed, head of the Security Council in *Russia*, negotiates the withdrawal of Russian federal forces from the breakaway republic of Chechnya (completed in January 1997). The two sides also agree to defer the final decision on autonomy or independence to 2001.
	Ukraine introduces its new national currency, the hrivna.
September	President Levon Ter-Petrosian of *Armenia* is reelected amid allegations that voting procedures have been manipulated, as well as reports that police have detained and beaten supporters of opposition parties.
November	President Lukashenka of *Belarus* is given extensive powers under a new Constitution apparently approved by referendum, following a campaign in which 90% of television reports, and most other media coverage, favored his plans to postpone the next presidential election from 1999 to 2001 and to retain the death penalty. In response, the Council of Europe suspends Belarus's guest status in January 1997.
	President Yeltsin of *Russia* issues a decree designating November 7 – the anniversary of the Bolshevik Revolution in 1917 – as an annual "Day of Accord and Reconciliation."
December	The governments of *Kazakhstan* and *Russia* sign an agreement with a number of oil companies on a Caspian Pipeline, to be completed by 2001, linking the Tengiz oil field in Kazakhstan to the Black Sea port of Novorossisk in Russia.
1997 March	President Yeltsin of *Russia* appoints a new government headed again by the relatively cautious Viktor Chernomyrdin, but also including Anatoly Chubais, Boris Nemtsov, and others seeking radical reform.
April	*Russia, Kazakhstan, Kyrgyzstan,* and *Tajikistan* reach agreement with China on the demarcation of frontiers, after decades of disputes.
	The World Bank lends US$6 billion to *Russia*, to be disbursed over two years.
	Opponents of President Lukashenka of *Belarus*, including his two predecessors and other politicians, are beaten and arrested during a demonstration in the capital, Minsk, while police squads clear streets by attacking people at random.
May	A Treaty of Friendship, Cooperation, and Partnership is signed by *Russia* and *Ukraine* (see also February 1999).
	Presidents Yeltsin of *Russia* and Clinton of the United States sign the Founding Act on Mutual Relations, Cooperation, and Security between NATO and Russia, establishing a Permanent Joint Council for mutual consultations (but see March 1999).
	President Lukashenka of *Belarus* dissolves Parliament and creates a "National Assembly" packed with his supporters.

June An agreement on "peace and national reconciliation" in *Tajikistan* is signed (in Moscow) by the Tajik government and the United Tajik Opposition, formally ending their civil war, which has caused the displacement of around 1 million people and the killing of around 50,000 since September 1992.

July A Charter on a Distinctive NATO-*Ukraine* Partnership is signed.

President Yeltsin of *Russia* decrees a reduction in the armed forces from 1.8 million to 1.2 million personnel by 2000.

September A law is enacted in *Russia* banning any religious group that did not exist in the country before 1982 from seeking converts.

November The government of *Belarus* bans the main opposition newspaper, *Svaboda*.

Georgia becomes the second CIS country (after Moldova in May 1996) to bring its law into line with Council of Europe standards by abolishing the death penalty, but remains unable to enforce this and other reforms of Soviet laws in Abkhazia and South Ossetia.

The IMF suspends its extended loan facility for *Moldova*, on the grounds that the government has failed to bring the budget deficit and the money supply under control.

The government of *Azerbaijan* allows the production of oil to begin from the Caspian Sea, despite the protests of *Turkmenistan* and other states in the region, and in the absence of an international agreement on the division of the Caspian reserves of oil and natural gas.

December US officials are prevented from inspecting military bases in *Belarus* under the terms of the CFE Treaty; the US Defense Department withdraws cooperation on dismantling the bases.

1998 January *Russia* issues new rubles, each worth one thousandth of the old ruble, in an attempt to restore domestic and international confidence in the currency.

February President Ter-Petrosian of *Armenia* resigns, following the collapse of a coalition government in a dispute over Ter-Petrosian's attempts to make peace with *Azerbaijan*.

March In *Russia*, President Boris Yeltsin dismisses Prime Minister Viktor Chernomyrdin and his government, replacing them with a new administration headed by Sergei Kiriyenko.

Elections in *Moldova* are won by a center-right coalition led by Ion Ciubuk, who becomes Prime Minister of the country's first wholly non-Communist government (although only for 11 months).

In *Armenia*, Robert Kocharian (formerly President of the disputed region of Nagorno-Karabakh and Prime Minister of Armenia itself) becomes President, after winning an election that, according to the OSCE, was marked by "widespread irregularities."

April Boris Berezovsky, a leading member of the business elite in *Russia*, is appointed Executive Secretary of the CIS, replacing Ivan Korotchenya (to March 1999).

In a new wave of repression in *Belarus*, police attack opposition groups protesting against the proposed union with *Russia*, six political parties are dissolved by the authorities, and food rationing is reimposed.

May   Coalminers blockade the Trans-Siberian Railway in *Russia* in a protest over unpaid wages.

The government of *Georgia* arranges yet another ceasefire with the leaders of the breakaway republic of Abkhazia, who accept autonomy within a federalized Georgia.

June   Diplomats representing the United States, the 15 members of the EU, and six other countries depart from *Belarus* after President Alyaksandr Lukashenka closes their residences, which are said to be in need of repair (but see January 1999).

President Nursultan Nazarbayev of *Kazakhstan* inaugurates Astana, the new capital city in the North of the country.

The IMF releases a further tranche of its loan to *Russia* (worth US$670 million), but criticizes the government's failure to collect sufficient tax revenues.

July   The IMF and other international lenders provide US$4.8 billion to support economic reform in *Russia*.

August   *Russia*, facing a severe economic crisis and the collapse of several financial institutions, devalues the ruble and announces (but then postpones) a 90-day moratorium on repaying some of its international debts. President Yeltsin dismisses Sergei Kiriyenko's government and attempts to reappoint Viktor Chernomyrdin as Prime Minister, but the State Duma rejects him twice. Yevgeni Primakov becomes Prime Minister instead.

October   In the wake of the financial crisis that has spread from *Russia* since August, the economy of *Ukraine* is badly hit by inflation at 12.8% a month and a fall of 50% in the value of its currency, the hrivna, against the US dollar. The IMF provides the first installment of a US$2.2 billion credit to the country.

The government of *Georgia*, facing an expanding trade deficit and economic recession, floats its currency, the lari, on the foreign exchange markets.

Heydar Aliyev, President of *Azerbaijan*, claims to have won 76% of the votes cast in the presidential election, but opposition groups and some foreign observers allege fraud.

The government of *Kyrgyzstan* bans the Kyrgyz Committee for Human Rights two weeks before a referendum on amendments to the Constitution, which the government then claims to have won.

November   In *Tajikistan*, the government and the United Tajik Opposition join in suppressing a revolt in the Leninobod region, led by Mahmud Khudaberdiev, and in accusing *Uzbekistan* of supporting the rebels. Uzbekistan responds by withdrawing its troops from the CIS peacekeeping force in Tajikistan.

December   In Ulyanovsk in *Russia*, Aleksandr Motorin, a schoolteacher, dies while on hunger strike in protest over the nonpayment of wages. Thousands of other teachers and medical workers continue similar hunger strikes and other protests across the country.

Pavlo Lazarenko, a former Prime Minister of *Ukraine*, is charged with fraud and money-laundering in Switzerland.

As the economy of *Kazakhstan* suffers from the effects of declining foreign currency reserves and export prices, the IMF provides the first installment of a US$433 million credit.

President Akayev of *Kyrgyzstan* dismisses the government, which he holds responsible for failing to resolve the economic crisis and combat corruption, and obtains aid from *Russia* to pay for natural gas supplied by *Uzbekistan*.

1999 January
President Nursultan Nazarbayev of *Kazakhstan* is reelected with a large majority, but opposition parties have been banned or intimidated and there is evidence of electoral fraud in some areas. Nazarbayev then imposes temporary import controls on goods from *Russia*, which have become much cheaper as a result of the devaluation of the ruble.

In *Belarus*, President Lukashenka decrees the renewed registration of all political parties but instructs the courts to refuse registration to "radical or extremist" groups. The ambassadors of EU countries (but not of the United States) return to the country.

Georgia becomes the first CIS country to abolish registration of ethnicity in identity papers and other official documents.

February
Several explosions in Tashkent, the capital of *Uzbekistan*, kill at least 15 people; 30 people, most of them supporters of the Islamist opposition to President Karimov, are arrested.

In *Russia*, the Council of the Federation, the upper house of the Federal Assembly, ratifies a treaty with *Ukraine*, signed in May 1997, permitting Russia to lease the Black Sea port of Sevastopol from Ukraine for 20 years. However, the Council attaches a requirement that Ukraine must ratify agreements on the Black Sea Fleet, which is to be based in the port.

President Aslan Maskhadov of Chechnya suspends the legislature and decrees the introduction of Moslem (Sharia) law.

President Niyazov of *Turkmenistan* signs a contract with a consortium of US companies on the building of a natural gas pipeline under the Caspian Sea to Turkey.

Workers in the five nuclear power plants that provide nearly half the electricity in *Ukraine* start a series of protests over arrears in their wages and a decline in safety standards.

March
President Yeltsin of *Russia* seeks the support of other CIS leaders for his dismissal of Boris Berezovsky, Executive Secretary of the CIS, on the grounds that he has exceeded his powers; Presidents Aliyev of *Azerbaijan*, Shevardnadze of *Georgia*, and Karimov of *Uzbekistan* protest.

The *Washington Post* reports that, since 1993, the Bank of *Russia* has secretly transferred billions of US dollars-worth of foreign currency reserves to Jersey, an offshore tax haven, and that in 1996 it illicitly directed some of the money into Russia's government bond market.

More than 50 people are killed when a bomb explodes in a marketplace in Vladikavkaz, the capital of North Ossetia in *Russia*.

Azerbaijan intercepts and halts an illicit shipment of MiG fighter planes apparently en route from *Russia* to Yugoslavia. *Kazakhstan* supports Russia's explanation that the planes were en route from Kazakhstan to Slovakia, but they are impounded as smuggled goods anyway.

Denouncing NATO's air strikes on targets throughout Yugoslavia, President Yeltsin of *Russia* withdraws his country from NATO's Partnership for Peace program, expels NATO representatives, and arranges the postponement of ratification of the START II treaty. At the UN Security Council in New York, a Russian motion calling for the ending of the NATO campaign receives support only from Namibia.

The government of *Belarus* charges a former Prime Minister, Mikhail Chigir, with corruption during his earlier career as a banker; opposition groups that support Chigir's candidacy in the presidential election due in May protest that the charges are false and have been brought to prevent him from campaigning.

In *Tajikistan*, Safarali Kendzhayev, leader of the Socialist Party and Chairman of the Human Rights Committee in the legislature, is shot dead by persons unknown.

April   *Uzbekistan* and *Azerbaijan* withdraw from the CIS Collective Security Treaty, but it is formally renewed by its other signatories.

A summit meeting of CIS leaders in Moscow endorses the dismissal of Boris Berezovsky as Executive Secretary of the organization, and replaces him with Yuri Yarov. Berezovsky and the financier Aleksandr Smolensky, the head of SBS-Agrobank, are then charged with corruption on the initiative of Yuri Skuratov, Procurator General of *Russia*, who is himself at the center of a scandal over videotapes reportedly showing sexual misdeeds by Skuratov and other prominent individuals.

As the economic and financial crisis that started in August 1998 intensifies throughout the CIS, *Kazakhstan* abandons its attempt to manage the exchange rate for its currency, the tenge.

President Lukashenka of *Belarus* joins President Yeltsin of *Russia* in rejecting Yugoslavia's application to join the "union" between their two countries, then visits Belgrade to offer his services as a go-between with NATO.

Georgia and *Azerbaijan* celebrate the opening of a new oil pipeline, running 830 kilometers between Supsa, a Georgian port on the Black Sea, and Baku, the capital of Azerbaijan. It is intended as a substitute for an existing pipeline through the unstable republic of Chechnya in *Russia*, which has been inoperative.

The IMF agrees to lend *Russia* up to US$4.5 billion over 18 months, based on achieving a primary budget surplus of 2% of GDP and repayment of previous loans. This would permit Russia to begin restructuring its debts to the World Bank, the Paris Club of governments and the London Club of commercial banks.

May   President Shevardnadze of *Georgia*, the only CIS head of state to support NATO's attacks on Yugoslavia and denounce "ethnic cleansing" in Kosovo, announces that he hopes his country, which has just joined the Council of Europe, will also soon join NATO.

In *Kazakhstan*, Akezhan Kazhegeldin, a former Prime Minister banned from running in the presidential election in January, is charged with tax evasion and money-laundering. Many observers see the charges as politically motivated rather than legally sound.

President Yeltsin of *Russia* suddenly dismisses Prime Minister Yevgeni Primakov and the rest of his government for "procrastination" over economic reform, and appoints Sergei Stepashin in Primakov's place. The majority in the State Duma proceeds to vote on proposals to impeach Yeltsin, all of which are defeated.

In *Belarus*, around 52% of voters take part in a presidential election organized by opposition groups, despite harassment by government officials. Of the two candidates in the election, Zenon Poznyak, in exile in Poland, has withdrawn his candidacy, while Mikhail Chigir is in prison.

The government of *Russia* revokes the license of one of the country's largest banks, Bank Menatep, as well as the licenses of 11 minor banks, as the first step in a reorganization of the banking industry recommended by the IMF and the World Bank.

Appendix 2

Glossary

apparat: the apparatus of political and economic institutions that controlled the command economies of the Stalinist regimes, including the Communist Party, the various branches of government, and the official organizations referred to as "labor unions." The term *apparatchik*, referring to a member of the *apparat*, came to have some of the pejorative connotations that "bureaucrat" has acquired in English. Since the early 1990s, *apparat* itself has increasingly been used to describe the interlocking elites that control much of public life, both in the CIS countries, and in central and eastern Europe.

basmachi: the name given to a variety of Moslem and nationalist groups in Central Asia that took up arms against the Soviet government during the 1920s and 1930s. The first *basmachi* were organized in support of an Islamic fundamentalist movement in the Fergana Valley (now divided among Kyrgyzstan, Tajikistan, and Uzbekistan) in 1918. Similar forces were raised by or on behalf of the traditional rulers of the cities and principalities of Central Asia, notably the Emir of Bokhara, whose supporters continued to wage guerilla campaigns against Soviet rule for several years after he was overthrown and exiled to Afghanistan (in 1921).

demokratizatsia: "democratization," a term designed to characterize growing citizen participation in the Soviet Union during the Gorbachev era.

glasnost: "openness" – increased communication, discussion and participation by the population of the Soviet Union in the Gorbachev era.

kulak: literally meaning "fist," a pejorative term for the prosperous peasants who were first heavily taxed, and then "liquidated," in the Soviet Union under Stalin, and in the Communist states of central and eastern Europe after World War II.

nomenklatura: originally, the lists of approved candidates for important political and economic posts in the Communist system; later used more broadly and negatively to refer to the ruling elites also known as the *apparat*.

perestroika: "restructuring," the term adopted by Mikhail Gorbachev to summarize his policy of liberalizing political and economic activities, while retaining the dominant role of the Communist Party and the unity of the Soviet Union. It is now used broadly to characterize the period 1985–90, when Gorbachev was generally able to have his policies implemented.

propiska: the system of registration introduced in the Soviet Union in 1932. The registration papers of Soviet citizens, sometimes referred to in English as "internal passports," indicated personal name, place of residence, marital status, employment, and "nationality" (officially defined ethnic group). Most citizens were required to carry these papers at all times, and to ensure that they were up to date, but the papers of workers in defense industries, coal mines, transportation, and banks were held by their employers. Certain groups were excluded from the system: military personnel and most agricultural workers, to prevent absence without leave; domestic servants of the *nomenklatura*, to conceal the nature of their employment; and people in prisons, labor camps, and other forms of detention, to conceal their locations.

soviet: "council." The first *soviets* were committees of workers' representatives established during the abortive Russian revolution of 1905. They reappeared, as councils representing workers, soldiers, and peasants, during the revolution of February 1917 that overthrew the Romanov dynasty. Following the

Bolshevik (Communist) revolution in October/November 1917, these *soviets* rapidly became party organs and the word also appeared in territorial names, starting with the Russian Soviet Federative Socialist Republic (1918) and the Union of Soviet Socialist Republics (1922). Eventually, *soviet* came to mean the main organ of the Communist Party dictatorship at every level, from the All-Union Supreme Soviet (or legislature) to village soviets. It is also used to refer to a nationality ("Soviet citizens"), an ideology ("Soviet Communism"), and a geopolitical unit ("the Soviet Union" and, after World War II, "the Soviet bloc"). Its meaning has clearly moved a long way from its revolutionary origins.

talon: consumer vouchers used as instruments of rationing in the Soviet Union, where they were introduced in 1989, and remained in use up to 1991.

trudovaja knizhka: the "labor record book" introduced for industrial and transportation workers in the Soviet Union in 1931, and for all other workers in 1938. Every individual beginning employment was required to provide this document to his or her employer, which retained it while that person's employment lasted. The system was intended to monitor, and discourage, individuals seeking to change employment, but managers and workers frequently colluded in falsifying the record, especially where labor was scarce.

uskorenie: "accelerating," a term that came into wider use during the years when Mikhail Gorbachev was attempting to reform the Soviet economy. Speeding up the rate of change was seen as essential both for economic growth in general (for which the Russian term is *rost*), and in relation to productivity, technological innovation, decentralization of decision-making, and so on.

Appendix 3

Personalities

Paramount Leaders of the Soviet Union After World War II

The (First or General) Secretary was the highest official in the Communist Party; the Chairman of the Presidium of the Supreme Soviet was effectively the head of state; the Chairman of the Council of Ministers was the head of government.

To 1953	Josef Stalin	General Secretary (1922–34), Secretary (1934–53), Chairman of the Council of Ministers (1941–53)
1953–55	Georgii Malenkov	First Secretary (1953), Chairman of the Council of Ministers (1953–55)
1955–64	Nikita Khrushchev	First Secretary (1953–64), Chairman of the Council of Ministers (1958–64)
1964–82	Leonid Brezhnev	First Secretary (1964–66), General Secretary (1966–82), Chairman of the Presidium (1977–82)
1982–84	Yuri Andropov	General Secretary (1982–84), Chairman of the Presidium (1983–84)
1984–85	Konstantin Chernenko	General Secretary and Chairman of the Presidium
1985–91	Mikhail Gorbachev	General Secretary (1985–91), Chairman of the Presidium (1988–89), President (1989–91)

Presidents of the Successor States

Armenia	Levon Ter-Petrosian (1990–98), Robert Kocharian (1998–)
Azerbaijan	Ayaz Mutalibov (1991–92), Albulfaz Elchibey (1992–93), Heydar Aliyev (1993–)
Belarus	Stanislau Shushkevich (1991–94), Myacheslau Gryb (1994), Alyaksandr Lukashenka (1994–)
Georgia	Zviad Gamsakhurdia (1990–92), Eduard Shevardnadze (1992–)
Kazakhstan	Nursultan Nazarbayev (1990–)
Kyrgyzstan	Askar Akayev (1990–)
Moldova	Mircea Snegur (1991–97), Petru Lucinschi (1997–)
Russia	Boris Yeltsin (1991–)
Tajikistan	Kakhar Makkhamov (1990–91), Rakhmon Nabiyev (1991–92), Imamali Rakhmonov (Chairman of the Supreme Soviet 1992–94; President 1994–)
Turkmenistan	Saparmurat Niyazov "Turkmenbashi" (1991–)
Ukraine	Leonid Kravchuk (1991–94), Leonid Kuchma (1994–)
Uzbekistan	Islam Karimov (1990–)

Akayev, Askar (1944–): President of Kyrgyzstan since 1990. Akayev trained and worked as a physicist during the Soviet period, and joined the Communist Party as a matter of course. By 1989, he was Chairman of the Academy of Sciences in his native Kyrgyzstan. He was able to use this influential post as a launchpad for his rapid elevation to head of the Kyrgyz state, initially through selection by the legislature, then by direct elections in 1991 and 1995. Akayev's years in office have been marked by assertions of national identity, such as making Kyrgyzstan the first CIS country to leave the ruble zone (in 1993). There have also been struggles over the division of powers between the presidency and the legislature, culminating in referendums in 1994 and 1996 that gave Akayev greater influence.

Aliyev, Heydar (1923–): NKVD and KGB officer from 1941, Communist leader of Azerbaijan from 1969 to 1983, Deputy Prime Minister of the Soviet Union from 1983 to 1987, President of Azerbaijan since 1993. Aliyev was born in Nakhichevan – an enclave of Azerbaijan surrounded by Iranian and Armenian territory – and has frequently been accused of favoring individuals and groups from that enclave over other Azerbaijanis. He entered the Soviet security apparatus, then called the NKVD, after leaving school, and joined the Communist Party in 1945. By 1966, he was a major-general and Chairman of the KGB of Azerbaijan. He used this powerful position to discredit Veli Akhundov, then Secretary of the republic's Communist Party, whom he succeeded in 1969. His 14 years in power were characterized by extensive corruption and by repression of the Armenians in the Nagorno-Karabakh region, then ruled by Azerbaijan. In 1983, the Soviet leader Leonid Brezhnev called Aliyev to Moscow, where he became a Deputy Prime Minister, while retaining control of Azerbaijan through his protégé and nominal successor Kyamran Bagirov. Dismissed from office by Mikhail Gorbachev in 1987, Aliyev returned to Nakhichevan, where he left the Comunist Party and became Chairman of the regional assembly in September 1991. After the collapse of the Soviet Union, he also became a member of the new Milli Mejlis (National Assembly) of Azerbaijan. Another native of Nakhichevan, Abulfaz Elchibey, leader of the anti-Communist Popular Front, seized power in May 1992 and was elected President in June. One year later, Aliyev was elected Chairman of the Milli Mejlis. After Colonel Surat Huseinov overthrew President Elchibey later that month, the Milli Mejlis appointed Aliyev acting President and Huseinov Prime Minister. Aliyev's position was endorsed in a hastily organized and doubtfully democratic referendum. It was then strengthened by his victory in an election in October in which he was the only candidate, supported by the state media and local election officials. Together with Huseinov, Aliyev directed the continuing war with Armenia over the disputed region of Nagorno-Karabakh, which resulted in Azerbaijan losing large swathes of territory before Russia arranged a ceasefire in 1994. In September 1994, Aliyev signed an agreement with a consortium of international corporations to exploit oil under the Caspian Sea. In August 1995, he used the pretext of continuing tension with Armenia to extend the existing state of emergency and ban several opposition parties, including the Popular Front. This alone rendered the results of legislative elections in November extremely dubious, quite apart from the irregularities in the election process itself. Aliyev was re-elected President in 1998, with the opposition boycotting yet another flawed election process.

Andropov, Yuri (1914–84): General Secretary of the Soviet Communist Party from 1982, and Chairman of the Presidium of the Supreme Soviet from 1983, up to his death. Andropov took part in resisting the German occupation during World War II, then rose rapidly through the Party to become Ambassador to Hungary in 1954. Two years later, he ensured the defeat of the uprising there by coordinating the efforts of Hungarian Stalinists with the operations of the Soviet Army. His reward was to be placed in charge of Soviet relations with foreign Communist Parties up to 1962. In 1967, he was made head of the Committee for State Security (KGB), and spent 15 years loyally carrying out Brezhnev's orders to suppress all forms of dissent. His chief innovation was to detain dissidents in psychiatric hospitals, as well as in camps and jails. As General Secretary, he was promoted abroad as a reformer who allegedly loved jazz; but he achieved little. His main contribution to the history of the Soviet Union may turn out to have been his patronage of Mikhail Gorbachev.

Berezovsky, Boris (1946–): Russian business magnate, Executive Secretary of the CIS from 1998 to 1999. Berezovsky, a professor of mathematics during the Soviet period, made his fortune in the 1990s, initially through the Logovaz car dealership, and then by building up shareholdings in Russian Public Television (ORT), other media companies, the oil company Sibeneft, and Aeroflot, the airline that Russia inherited from the Soviet Union. He became openly involved in politics in 1996, when he led fundraising efforts on behalf of President Yeltsin's reelection campaign. Berezovsky is perhaps the most prominent among the business leaders, often referred to as "the oligarchs," who have consistently opposed plans for more rapid and far-reaching economic reforms. His approach is uncomplicated: "if something is advantageous to capital, it goes without saying that it is advantageous to the nation." However, by 1999 he was out of favor with the Russian government. It was Yeltsin who engineered Berezovsky's dismissal from his CIS post.

Brezhnev, Leonid (1906–82): Chairman of the Presidium of the Supreme Soviet from 1960 to 1964, and from 1977–82, First Secretary of the Communist Party, then General Secretary, from 1964 until his death. After leading the group of Politburo members that overthrew Khrushchev in 1964, Brezhnev became the dominant figure in Soviet politics for almost two decades. His place in history is chiefly due to developments in economic and foreign policy. There was a gradual but irreversible decline in the Soviet economy during his period in power, often referred to as an age of stagnation. Soviet foreign policy, meanwhile, went through three phases: assertiveness, typified in the invasion of Czechoslovakia, and the announcement of the "Brezhnev Doctrine" of defending "socialist gains," both in 1968; *détente*, with agreements on arms reductions, and an extension of Soviet involvement in developing countries; and then, after the Soviet invasion of Afghanistan in 1978, the development of what has been called "the second Cold War."

Chernomyrdin, Viktor (1938–): Russian politician, in charge of the Soviet oil and natural gas industries from 1985 to 1992, Prime Minister from 1992 to 1998. Chernomyrdin started his career as an engineer in the oil industry in Siberia. In 1985, Mikhail Gorbachev appointed him to run the Ministry for the Oil and Natural Gas Industries, which was reorganized as the Concern Gazprom in 1989. Chernomyrdin was its chief executive until 1992, when he became Deputy Prime Minister and, shortly after, Prime Minister. His relatively long service in that post provided him with valuable contacts and standing among western states and international agencies, but also exposed him to unrelenting opposition from the State Duma, the Communist-dominated lower house of the legislature, which distrusted him as a reformer and a "westernizer." In 1999, he returned to prominence in Russian affairs, first as an advocate of further credits in discussions with the IMF and the US government, then as President Yeltsin's special representative on the unfolding crisis in Yugoslavia. Throughout his post-Communist career, Chernomyrdin has been both praised and derided for preferring compromise to confrontation.

Chornovil, Viacheslav (1937–99): Ukrainian nationalist politician, leader of the Popular Movement for Restructuring (Rukh) from 1989 to 1999. Chornovil was trained as a journalist, and began dissident activity in defense of human rights in 1966, publishing a pamphlet available in English as *Chornovil's Papers*. He was first jailed in 1967, and spent many years in and out of prison. He helped found the Ukrainian Helsinki Union in 1988 and Rukh in 1989. He was a leading figure in the independence movement, and was elected Chairman of the L'viv Oblast Council in 1990, but was the main loser in the presidential election in 1991 and one of the losers in the presidential election in 1994. He remained a prominent member of the legislature throughout. In February 1999, Rukh was split into two parties, as opponents of Chornovil's leadership took control and Chornovil himself established a separate group, Rukh Number One. In March, he was killed in a road accident.

Chubais, Anatoly (1955–): Russian reformist politician. During the closing years of the Soviet period Chubais actively participated in the pro-democracy movement in Leningrad (now St Petersburg), and he served as Deputy Mayor of that city, in charge of the economy, from 1990 to 1991. Since then, he has worked closely with Yegor Gaidar, both in the Democratic Choice party and in government, notably as the main proponent of Russia's privatization program. He served, at different times, as Deputy Prime Minister and as the head of President Yeltsin's staff, but he left government after the economic crisis in the summer of 1998.

Gaidar, Yegor (1956–): Russian reformist politician, Prime Minister during the second half of 1992. After graduating from Moscow University, Gaidar worked as an economist at the Academy of Sciences, and was then a journalist from 1987 to 1990. He followed Boris Yeltsin in resigning from the Party in 1990. Two years later, he was chosen to spearhead Yeltsin's first attempt at rapid liberalization of the economy. In November 1992, however, Yeltsin, faced with mounting opposition to Gaidar's proposals, dismissed him from the government. Gaidar was briefly back in office, as First Deputy Prime Minister and Minister of the Economy, from 1993 to 1994. In December 1993, Democratic Choice, the party he leads, became the largest single group in the new State Duma, but was far outnumbered by his opponents. He resigned from the government following policy disagreements with his more cautious colleagues and in December 1994 he broke with Yeltsin, condemning the government's intervention in Chechnya. While Gaidar has won the respect of many western politicians and economists, he has perhaps been better at working out theories than at putting them into practice. He came to international prominence once more in 1999, when he led a Russian delegation to Serbia during the NATO bombardment of that country, only to be denounced as "scum and trash" by its state-controlled media.

Gorbachev, Mikhail (1931–): General Secretary of the Communist Party of the Soviet Union from 1985 to 1991, Chairman of the Presidium from 1988 to 1989, President from 1989 to 1991, and winner of the Nobel Peace Prize in 1990. After joining the Party in 1952, Gorbachev made rapid progress through its ranks to become the youngest member of its highest body, the Politburo, in 1980. His attempts, as General Secretary, to secure "restructuring" (*perestroika*) and "openness" (*glasnost*) attracted interest, and even excitement, around the world. However, his hostility to nationalist movements in the Soviet republics, and his reluctance to surrender the Communist Party's monopoly of power, made him increasingly unpopular with democrats and liberals, while his promotion of greater freedom of speech and of economic liberalization frightened many Communists. His greatest achievements may have been in foreign policy. These include the signing of the Intermediate Nuclear Forces (INF) Treaty in 1987; the explicit abandonment of the Brezhnev Doctrine in 1989, which left the Communist regimes of central and eastern Europe unable to turn to the Soviet Union for help; and the acceptance of German unification in 1990. After the failure of a coup led by former colleagues in August 1991, Gorbachev was forced to acquiesce in the effective dissolution of the Party and of the Soviet Union itself. In the election for the Russian presidency in 1996, he won only 0.5% of the votes cast. At the end of 1998, it was revealed that he and his charitable foundation had been bankrupted during the financial crisis of that year.

Karimov, Islam (1938–): Communist leader of Uzbekistan from 1989 to 1990, President since then. Karimov worked as an aviation engineer in Tashkent, while taking evening classes in economics, from 1960 to 1966, when he joined the All-Union State Planning Commission (Gosplan). In 1983, he returned to Uzbekistan to become Minister of Finance there. Three years later, following a purge of the Uzbek elites, he became a Deputy Chairman of the republic's Council of Ministers and joined the Central Committee of its Communist Party. In 1989, he became First Secretary of the Party in the midst of interethnic rioting. He was appointed President in 1990, resigned his Party membership following the attempted coup in Moscow in 1991 and was confirmed as President by popular vote later that year. He has faced down protests over price rises and cuts in social benefits, in 1992, and ensured his continuance in power by taking control of appointments to regional leaderships and other posts, and by repressing parties urging fundamentalist Islamic policies. He has favored close ties with other states in Central Asia, but has been reluctant to concede any real powers to the CIS. In 1995, his term was extended to 2000 by referendum, reportedly with the backing of 99.9% of those voting.

Khrushchev, Nikita (1894–1970): First Secretary of the Communist Party of the Soviet Union from 1953, and Chairman of the Council of Ministers from 1958, until his removal in 1964. Khrushchev began his adult life as a coalminer in the Donbas region of Ukraine, but became active in the Bolshevik Party as a soldier in World War I. He continued soldiering during the Bolshevik Revolution of 1917 and the subsequent Civil War, and was rewarded with the post of Party secretary in Kharkov in 1925. Under Stalin's dictatorship, he became Moscow Party leader in 1935 and then Ukraine Party leader in 1938, and was a political commissar in the Soviet Army during the Battle of Stalingrad (1942–43). Throughout these years, he was a loyal and assiduous follower of Stalin. After the dictator's death in 1953, he allied with Georgii Malenkov against the security chief, Lavrenti Beria, who was executed, and then removed Malenkov from office too. Having secured control of the Party, he proceeded to denounce the "cult of personality" around Stalin, in 1956. As paramount leader, he launched the disastrous "Virgin Lands" campaign, tried to reorganize industry and agriculture, which were already perceptibly failing, repressed uprisings in central and eastern Europe, and stage-managed a cultural "Thaw" that saw the publication of some previously banned books, but had little lasting effect on Soviet society. He was removed from office by the majority in the Politburo, led by Brezhnev (see above), and was allowed to retire into obscurity. Khrushchev has been variously represented as an opportunistic peasant, a liberalizing Marxist, and a ruthless dictator who denounced Stalin chiefly to improve his own image: the controversy continues.

Kravchuk, Leonid (1934–): head of state in Ukraine from 1989 to 1994, as Chairman of the Supreme Soviet to 1991 and then as President. A graduate of Kyiv University and the Academy of Social Sciences in Moscow, Kravchuk worked in the Communist Party bureaucracy, rising to the Politburo of the Ukrainian Party and serving as Chairman of the Supreme Soviet. On December 1, 1991, he was elected the first President of independent Ukraine. He was one of the founders of the CIS. He is credited with helping to safeguard Ukrainian independence, but was unable to push through measures to revive the economy and lost the presidency in 1994. He is now a leading member of the United Social Democratic Party in the legislature, the People's Council, and is also head of the International Union of Ukrainian Entrepreneurs.

Kuchma, Leonid (1938–): Prime Minister of Ukraine from 1992 to 1993, President since 1994. Trained as an engineer, Kuchma became director of the Pivenmash plant in Dnipropetrovs'k, the world's largest single maker of nuclear missiles. He was Prime Minister for only 11 months, resigning to become leader of the Ukrainian Union of Industrialists and Entrepreneurs. He also helped to found a new political party, the Interregional Bloc for Reform. As President, he has pushed through some economic reforms, and improved relations with Russia as well as with the West, although in 1999 he made his opposition to NATO's bombing of Yugoslavia very clear. He is to run for reelection in October 1999.

Lazarenko, Pavlo (1953–): Prime Minister of Ukraine 1996–97. Lazarenko was the director of a collective farm and a member of the Supreme Soviet of Ukraine during the Communist period. He was appointed Governor of Dnipropetrovs'k in 1992, became President Kuchma's regional representative in 1995 and then served as a Deputy Prime Minister, in charge of energy, before becoming Prime Minister in May 1996. After a dispute with Kuchma and amid allegations of corruption, he resigned, forming the Hromada party in 1997. He was widely expected to be a leading contender for the presidency in 1999, but his arrest in Switzerland in December 1998 has made his political future very cloudy.

Lebed, Aleksandr (1950–): Russian military officer and politician, Governor of Krasnoyarsk since 1998. As a boy, Lebed lost his father to the Gulag and witnessed the police killing protesters in his native city of Novocherkassk. After some years fighting in Afghanistan, he returned to the Soviet Union. From 1988 to 1989, he commanded the special military district in Baku, the capital of Azerbaijan, during the anti-Armenian unrest and the state of emergency. In 1991, when he was commander of the Airborne Division in Tula, he refused orders from the leaders of the coup against President Gorbachev to attack Russian government buildings. In 1992, he was appointed commander of the 14th Army in Moldova, which was engaged in supporting the breakaway Dnestr Moldavian Republic, but in 1995 he was dismissed. President Yeltsin appointed him head of the Security Council in June 1996 and he reached a peace agreement with the leaders of the breakaway republic of Chechnya. Lebed was one of the losing candidates in the presidential election in 1996; in 1998, however, he was elected Governor of the Krasnoyarsk region.

Lukashenka, Alyaksandr (1955–): President of Belarus since 1994. Formerly a director of a state farm, Lukashenka became a deputy in the Supreme Soviet of Belarus before the collapse of the Communist system and chaired its commission on corruption. He played a crucial role in ousting Stanislau Shushkevich, the former Chairman of the Supreme Soviet, ostensibly over business improprieties. He won the presidential election in 1994, receiving significant popular support for his campaign against corruption, his advocacy of closer ties with Russia, and his plans for strong state control of the economy. Since taking office, he has replaced the Parliament elected in 1995 with an assembly packed with his own supporters, overhauled the Constitutional Court to remove judges opposed to his decrees, and taken extensive powers for himself through two referendums, both manipulated in his favor. Lukashenka's control of the media and his use of the security forces to suppress opposition were sufficient to indicate that he had become a dictator, even before he began isolating Belarus from western governments and international agencies, expressing solidarity with the rulers of Iraq and Yugoslavia, and calling for the recreation of the Soviet Union.

Luzhkov, Yuri (1936–): Russian politician, Mayor of Moscow since 1992. In 1987, Luzhkov was appointed Deputy Chairman of the city *soviet*'s Executive Committee, and in 1990 he became its Chairman. Thus, ever since 1987 he has been in a position to control business in the metropolitan region, both through issuing or withholding licenses, and through the city's investments, believed to be worth around US$25 billion, in real estate, broadcasting, retailing, banking, oil, and other ventures. These assets have been acquired, or retained, to a greater extent than in most Russian cities. Luzhkov regarded the privatization program devised by Anatoly Chubais as an attempt to destroy the economy and managed to exclude Moscow from its provisions. He has also spent the city's money freely on such projects as the rebuilding of Christ the Savior Cathedral (to be opened in 2000), the erection of a statue of Peter the Great, and, in September 1997, the celebrations of Moscow's 850th anniversary.

Nazarbayev, Nursultan (1940–): Communist leader of Kazakhstan from 1989 to 1990, President since then. A loyal Communist for many years, Nazarbayev became Chairman of the Kazakh Council of Ministers in 1984 and First Secretary of the republic's Communist Party in 1989. He was appointed President in 1990 and was confirmed in the post in a popular election, in which he was the only candidate, in 1991. Favoring close ties with the other ex-Soviet republics, Nazarbayev ensured that Kazakhstan was the last Union Republic to declare independence and the first to join the CIS after its three founding members. He has also led the country into the Central Asian Union, in 1994, and a Customs Union with Russia and other states, in 1995. In 1999, he won a second term as President, defeating rival candidates in an election criticized by the OSCE and other observers, and is not due to run for a third term until 2006.

Niyazov, Saparmurat (1940–): Communist leader of Turkmenistan from 1984 to 1990, President since then. Born into the dominant Tekke tribe of Turkmenistan but orphaned as a child, Niyazov was educated in Leningrad (now St Petersburg) in Russia. He joined the Communist Party at the age of 22 and rose rapidly through the system, became First Secretary of the Party in Turkmenistan in 1984 and head of the republic's government in 1985. He was elected unopposed as President in 1990, retaining the post after independence through a direct election in 1992 and a referendum in 1994, both strongly manipulated in his favor. In 1991, he relaunched the Communists as "Democrats"; in 1993, he took the surname "Turkmenbashi," Leader of the Turkmen. Little else has changed. Niyazov still appoints all government ministers, higher officials, and judges, and selects candidates to run unopposed in legislative "elections." Censorship of the media is extensive and opposition groups have been harassed throughout his years in power. The economy is still focused on extracting and transporting hydrocarbons, with foreign investors and aid agencies replacing Moscow's planners.

Primakov, Yevgeni (1929–): Russian politician, Prime Minister and frequently Acting President from September 1998 to May 1999. When Primakov was born, in Kyiv, the capital of Ukraine, his father, whose family name appears to have been Kirshinblat, was probably in jail, one of the millions of victims of Stalinism. Primakov was brought up by his mother in Georgia and went on to study at the Moscow Institute of Oriental Studies. He then worked for 14 years as a journalist, specializing in Arab affairs. From 1970 to 1989, he was Director of the Institute for International Relations in Moscow. He moved from advising the government to taking part in it after Mikhail Gorbachev came to power, becoming a candidate member of the Communist Party Politburo; and he served as Chairman of the Congress of People's Deputies from 1989 to 1990. In 1991, Gorbachev appointed him to head the SVR, the foreign intelligence service established in place of the KGB's exterior branch. In 1996, President Yeltsin appointed Primakov Foreign Minister; two years later, he was made Prime Minister after the rejection of Yeltsin's first nominee, Viktor Chernomyrdin, by the State Duma. Primakov saw himself as a builder of bridges between the Yeltsin regime and its opponents in the State Duma, but he had little opportunity to achieve much change in government policy before Yeltsin, blaming him for "procrastination," suddenly dismissed him from office. Debate continues over the extent to which Primakov, or any other Russian ex-Communist, retains or has moved on from the Stalinist and nationalist ideals that he spent most of his career promoting.

Rakhmonov, Imamali (1952–): head of state in Tajikistan since 1992, as Chairman of the Supreme Soviet to 1994, then as President. Rakhmonov first made his mark on Tajik affairs during the country's civil war, as a politican and military leader loyal to the ex-Communist President Rakhmon Nabiyev. Once Nabiyev had been deposed and the presidency abolished, Rakhmonov took power and renewed his links with the Russian military in order to continue the conflict. His subsequent election to the presidency was made easier by his opponents' decision to boycott the proceedings, as well as by ballot-rigging in his favor. The latest in a series of ceasefires was signed in 1997 and has not yet been broken. Rakhmonov has thus had a free hand to go on controlling the media, interfering in legislative elections, and managing the economy in the interests of his networks of associates and clients.

Sakharov, Andrei (1921–89): Soviet nuclear physicist and dissident, winner of the Nobel Peace Prize in 1975. At one point the youngest member of the Soviet Academy of Sciences, Sakharov became known as the "father" of the Soviet hydrogen bomb in the 1950s, but as early as 1961 he was protesting publicly against nuclear weapons tests. With his wife, Yelena Bonner, he became a leading dissident, but, unlike the writer and fellow Nobel laureate, Aleksandr Solzhenitsyn, he could not be exiled because of his knowledge of nuclear secrets. From 1980 to 1986, Sakharov was required to live in Gorky (now, as before, Nizhnii Novgorod), and subjected to police harassment. He was elected to the Congress of People's Deputies with a huge personal vote, but was not able to make much impact on politics, partly because of illness, but partly also because his humanist idealism was decidedly out of fashion.

Shevardnadze, Eduard (1928–): Foreign Minister of the Soviet Union from 1985 to 1991, President of Georgia since 1992. By 1985, Shevardnadze had risen through the ranks of the Georgian Communist Party to become its head. He was invited to Moscow by Mikhail Gorbachev to replace the aged Andrei Gromyko and assist in revising Soviet foreign policy. Controversy still continues over whether Shevardnadze was fully committed to reform and democratization at that stage, or went along with the process of change for opportunistic reasons. There is also still debate over the extent to which Gorbachev, Shevardnadze or other decision-makers should be credited with allowing, or even encouraging, the Soviet bloc to break up and Germany to be unified relatively smoothly and peacefully. Indeed, many commentators have argued that events moved so fast and so unpredictably as to be beyond any politician's control. After the collapse of the Soviet Union, Shevardnadze returned to Georgia to take over as head of state there. He has survived several assassination attempts, as well as repeated accusations that he uses authoritarian methods, to steer the country toward somewhat closer relations with the West. He has been unable, however, to resolve the disputes over the autonomy, or independence, of Abkhazia and Adzharia.

Shushkevich, Stanislau (1934–): President of Belarus from 1991 to 1994. A physicist by profession, Shushkevich became a founding member of the Popular Front movement and was elected to the Supreme Soviet of Belarus in 1990. As its Chairman, he became *de facto* head of state after the failure of the Moscow coup in 1991. One of the founders of the CIS, he led Belarus through its first three years of independence, but lost the support of the majority in the legislature because of his preference for a parliamentary democracy, rather than a strong presidency, and his opposition to closer security ties with Russia. Since leaving office, Shushkevich has been an active opponent of President Lukashenka.

Snegur, Mircea (1940–): head of state in Moldova from 1989 to 1997, as Chairman of the Supreme Soviet to 1991, then as President. From 1961 onward, Snegur combined a professional career as an agronomist with a series of promotions through the hierarchy of the Moldavian Communist Party. He became its General Secretary in 1985 and Chairman of the republic's Supreme Soviet in 1989. In the latter capacity, he led Moldova through the collapse of the Soviet Union and the disintegration of the party that had given him his career. As head of a new Agrarian Party, and with a new legitimacy conferred by victory in an uncontested direct election in December 1991, Snegur led a campaign against union with Romania to victory in a referendum in 1994 and reached agreement on autonomy for the Gagauz people. He also took Moldova into NATO's Partnership for Peace program and signed an association agreement with the EU. However, he failed to prevent the *de facto* secession of the Transnistria region, where the majority of the population are ethnic Russians and Ukrainians. In June 1995, Snegur left the Agrarian Party to create the Party of Revival and Accord. In December 1996, he was defeated in Moldova's second presidential election by Petru Lucinschi. Since then, Snegur has been active in Parliament as the leading politician in the Alliance for Democracy and Reforms (formerly the Democratic Convention of Moldova), formed by his own party and the Christian Democratic Popular Front in June 1997.

Stalin, Josef (1879–1953): General Secretary of the Communist Party of the Soviet Union from 1922 to 1934, then its Secretary until his death; also Chairman of the Council of Ministers from 1941. Born Josef Djugashvili in Georgia, Stalin ("man of steel," his Party name) was educated in an Orthodox seminary, but after his expulsion from it, in 1899, he joined the revolutionary Social Democrats. After their split in 1903, he became a prominent organizer in the Bolshevik faction, but, unlike other Bolshevik leaders, he showed little interest in Marxist theory. In the Bolshevik (Communist) government that came to power in 1917, he antagonized Lenin, Trotsky, and others by opposing any extension of the rights of nationalities and was moved to the Party Secretariat. Once again, he clashed with Lenin, who regarded him as excessively ambitious, but after Lenin's death in 1924 he used his power over appointments to party posts to maneuver himself into supreme power. By 1929, he had defeated his principal rivals, Trotsky, Zinoviev, and Kamenev, and proceeded to launch the first Five-year Plan, forcing rapid industrialization at the cost of millions of lives. During the 1930s, millions more died as Stalin and his collaborators repeatedly purged the Party, removing almost all those who had led the Bolshevik Revolution, and terrorized the population. Stalin collaborated with Nazi Germany in the partition of Poland from 1939, only to be forced to flee East as the Nazis invaded in 1941. By the end of World War II, however, he was one of the "Big Three" world leaders, alongside the US President and the British Prime Minister, and had expanded the Soviet Union to include the occupied Baltic states, as well as territories seized from Poland, Romania, Finland, and Germany. During and after the war, he directed the Communist coups in central and eastern Europe, while giving free rein to his paranoia by deporting whole peoples to Central Asia and Siberia, and launching a repressive campaign against "rootless cosmopolitans" (Jews and western-oriented intellectuals). Stalin was the longest-lasting Soviet leader by far and his "cult of personality" has had a lasting impact on the countries he once ruled. He was among the most murderous dictators of the 20th century, but he made the Soviet Union into a superpower.

Stepashin, Sergei (1952–): Russian security officer and politician, Prime Minister since May 1999. Stepashin, a loyal supporter of President Yeltsin, first came to prominence in 1993, when he assisted in planning and executing the violent dispersal of the Congress of People's Deputies after it attempted to impeach the President. He was head of the FSB, the Russian counterintelligence agency, until 1995, when he was dismissed for failing to predict and prevent the renewal of fighting between Russia and the breakaway republic of Chechnya. In 1997, however, he returned to power as Minister of Justice. He was promoted to the Interior Ministry in 1998 and was then made a Deputy Prime Minister shortly before Yeltsin suddenly appointed him Prime Minister, in place of Yevgeni Primakov. Stepashin's appointment was rapidly confirmed by the State Duma, despite the opposition of the majority in that body to the economic reforms that Stepashin advocates (along with the IMF). If he remains in office, he will preside over the next elections to the Duma, in December 1999, and will then be in a position either to influence the presidential election in 2000 or even to take part in it himself.

Ter-Petrosian, Levon (1945–): head of state of Armenia from 1990 to 1998, as Chairman of the Supreme Soviet to 1991, then as President. Like a strikingly large number of other nationalist leaders throughout history, Ter-Petrosian was not born in the country he would eventually lead. He started life as a member of the Armenian minority in Syria, but went on to be educated in Yerevan, the Armenian capital, and in Leningrad (now, as before, St Petersburg). In 1988, he helped to found the nationalist Karabakh Committee, which called for reunion between Armenia and the majority-Armenian region of Nagorno-Karabakh in Azerbaijan, and spent six months in prison after publicly criticizing Soviet relief efforts following the major earthquake of December 1988. He then rose to power as leader of the Armenian National Movement formed by the Karabakh Committee after his release. Throughout his years in power, Ter-Petrosian tried to balance the demands of his nationalist supporters with his perception of the need to make peace with Azerbaijan over Nagorno-Karabakh. Criticism of his authoritarian methods mounted during and after legislative elections in 1995, which were manipulated in favor of his supporters, and by 1998 the legislature itself had also turned against him. Its rejection of his latest plan for peace with Azerbaijan left him no option but to resign. Within Armenia and beyond, opinions still differ widely about Ter-Petrosian's motives and achievements.

Yeltsin, Boris (1931–): head of state in Russia since 1990, as Chairman of the Supreme Soviet to 1991, then as President. An engineer by training, Yeltsin was also an active Communist, rising to become secretary of the Party in the Sverdlovsk region in 1976. In 1985, he was appointed by Mikhail Gorbachev to run the Communist Party in Moscow. He later fell out with Gorbachev over the slow pace of reform and resigned from his post in 1987. Two years later, he was elected to the Congress of People's Deputies and to the Russian Supreme Soviet. He was Chairman of the latter body from 1990 to 1991, and was then directly elected President. His popularity was probably enhanced by his widely publicized involvement in protests against the attempted coup in August 1991, but declined as living standards fell. Yeltsin won reelection in 1996. The economic crisis of 1998 and his increasing ill health seemed to have rendered him increasingly ineffective in the shaping of Russian policy until May 1999, when he suddenly replaced Prime Minister Yevgeni Primakov with a loyal supporter, Sergei Stepashin. It remains unclear to what extent Yeltsin is a free agent and to what extent others in his circle are acting in his name.

Zyuganov, Gennadi (1944–): leader of the Communist Party of Russia since 1993. Like Boris Yeltsin, whom he now bitterly opposes, Zyuganov had a successful career as a Communist Party official in the Soviet period; again like Yeltsin, he was appointed to its highest body, the Politburo, in 1990. In 1991, however, he supported the attempted coup against President Gorbachev. He returned to prominence following the lifting of the ban on the Communist Party in Russia, but was defeated by Yeltsin in the presidential election in 1996. Zyuganov remains prominent as a deputy in the State Duma and is likely to run for the presidency once again.

Appendix 4

Political and Economic Institutions

Political Systems

The Soviet system: During the Soviet period, the Communist Party monopolized political power, under the leadership of the First (or General) Secretary, the small, powerful group known as the Politburo (but as the Presidium from 1952 to 1966), and the larger, generally ineffective Central Committee. The Party used the *nomenklatura* system (see Glossary) to dominate such formal institutions of government as the Council of Ministers (Council of People's Commissars to 1946); the All-Union Supreme Soviet (established in 1936), which comprised the Soviet of the Union and the Soviet of Nationalities; and the Supreme Soviets of the Union Republics, which each had one chamber.

The Party also made extensive use of state security organs, although it can be argued that, at least for some parts of the Soviet period, these organs, which usually had direct links with the leadership, were more powerful than the bulk of the Party itself. They were successively reorganized and renamed as the Extraordinary Commission (Cheka, 1917–22), the (Unified) State Political Administration (GPU or OGPU, 1922–34), the People's Commissariat of Internal Affairs (NKVD, 1934–46), the People's Commissariat for State Security (NKGB, jointly with the NKVD, 1943–46), the Ministry of State Security (MGB, 1946–53), and the Committee of State Security (KGB, 1953–91).

The only major structural changes to this interlocking system of Party, government and security organs came in 1989, as Mikhail Gorbachev sought to revitalize the government by way of an executive presidency; a new legislature, the Congress of People's Deputies, based on a complex system of multi-candidate elections and government appointments; and the limited devolution of powers to republics and regions. It was the Congress that formally dissolved the Union, and itself, in 1991.

Presidencies since 1991: All 12 countries in the CIS have adopted new constitutions broadly based on the French model of mixed presidential/parliamentary democracy. Although several of the Presidents now in office started their presidencies after being elected by legislatures, all have now been directly elected by their respective populations. Each enjoys extensive powers, notably over defense and foreign policy, which have been of special significance in dealing with the secessionist movements, or other forms of civil unrest, that most of the CIS countries have experienced. However, there are some important variations among these countries, notably in respect of the President's powers of appointment. In Russia, Moldova, and Kyrgyzstan, for example, the legislature must approve the President's nominee as Prime Minister, but in the other four states of Central Asia, as well as in Belarus, the Presidents need not refer appointments to the legislatures at all. In addition, in most of the CIS countries Presidents have used referendums or other devices to take extra powers or extend their terms of office, and have exerted control or influence over the mass media, raising serious doubts about their commitment to pluralism and constitutional rule.

Post-Soviet legislatures: Under their new constitutions, seven CIS countries have established unicameral legislatures. Four of these are elected for maximum terms of four years: the National Assembly (Azgayin Joghov) of Armenia, the Parliament (Parlamenti) of Georgia, the Parliament (Parlamentul) of Moldova, and the legislature of Ukraine, known as the Supreme Council (Verkhovna Rada) until 1996, but now called the People's Council (Narodna Rada). The other three unicameral legislatures are elected for maximum terms of five years: the National Assembly (Milli Mejlis) of Azerbaijan, the Supreme Assembly (Majlisi Oli) of Tajikistan, and the Supreme Assembly (Oliy Majlis) of Uzbekistan.

Four of the remaining five countries have functioning bicameral legislatures. In Kazakhstan, Parliament (Parlament) comprises the Senate (Senat), with several members appointed by the President and others directly elected every four years, and the Majilis, elected every four years. In Kyrgyzstan, the Supreme Council (Zhogorku Kenesh) comprises the Assembly of People's Representatives and the Legislative Assembly, both elected every five years. In Russia, the Federal Assembly (Federal'noye Sobraniye) comprises the Council of the Federation (Soviet Federatsii), with delegations from the 89 units of the federation serving four-year terms, and the State Duma (Gosudarstvennaya Duma) elected every four years. In Turkmenistan, there is a People's Council (Halk Maslahaty), combining elected and appointed representatives, which meets only occasionally, and an Assembly (Majlis), which is elected every five years from among candidates approved by the President.

Belarus constitutes a special case. Under the Constitution of 1994, the National Parliament (Natsionalnoye Sobranie) comprises the Council of the Republic (Soviet Republiki), one eighth appointed by the President and seven eighths elected by local councils every four years, and the Chamber of Representatives (Palata Pretsaviteley), elected every five years. However, Parliament has been replaced by a "National Assembly," controlled by the President's supporters, since 1997.

Local government: The major subnational unit in most of the former Soviet republics is the region or province (*oblast, kray* or *okrug* in Russia, *voblasts'* in Belarus, *oblys* in Kazakhstan, *oblast* in Kyrgyzstan, *rayon* in Moldova, *viloyat* in Tajikistan, *welayat* in Turkmenistan, *oblast'* in Ukraine, *wiloyat* in Uzbekistan). These nine countries also have separate local governments for their capital cities and, in some cases, other major cities. Elsewhere, local government is based on a division into relatively smaller units, each of which is either a city or a county (respectively, *kaghak* and *marz* in Armenia, *sahar* and *rayon* in Azerbaijan, *kalaki* and *rayon* in Georgia).

Alongside these divisions, in some CIS countries, there are units now known as republics, but referred to as "autonomous republics" under Communism. These generally have a greater number and range of powers, and a greater degree of fiscal autonomy. There are 21 republics in Russia, among which 15 were autonomous republics during at least part of the Soviet period (Bashkortostan, Buryatia, Chavashia, Dagestan, Kabardino-Balkaria, Kalmykia, Karelia, Komi, Mari-El, Mordvinia, North Ossetia, Sakha, Tatarstan, Tuva Ulus, and Udmurtia); four were accorded republican status only after the collapse of the Soviet Union (Adygei, Altai, Karachai-Circassia, and Khakassia); and two were previously parts of one republic (Chechnya and Ingushetia). There are also two republics in Georgia (Abkhazia and Adzharia); two in Moldova (Gagauz-Yeri and, although only formally, the Dnestr Republic); and one each in Azerbaijan (Nakhichevan), Ukraine (Crimea), and Uzbekistan (Karakalpakstan). There are also a number of smaller and less powerful units, in Russia only, called "autonomous *okrugs*." Despite the attribution of autonomy, the republics were under strict control until the late 1980s, and could be created, redefined, or abolished at the whim of the central government. They were originally based on the homelands of minority nationalities, but in some cases they are now mainly inhabited by members of the majority nationalities.

Subnational government in most CIS countries has been subject to change and uncertainty. In Russia in particular, many regions and republics, starting with Tatarstan in August 1990, have defied the federal government by nullifying or amending laws made in Moscow, notably on citizenship, allocation of tax revenues, restrictions on exports from their territories, and price controls. Many have also retained, or even extended, government ownership and control in banking, the mass media, and other areas. Some continue to be affected by internal unrest or even armed conflict. Others have made agreements with the federal government on additional powers over state property, land, and revenues, either through the overall Federation Treaty of March 1992, or through additional bilateral agreements, such as the protocols signed by Russia and Tatarstan in March 1999. Across the CIS, various arrangements have also been made, or are being planned, for the administration of smaller units within the regions, counties or republics, modifying or replacing the local councils (*soviets*) inherited from the Communist regime.

Economic Institutions

Planning: During the Soviet period, the entire economy was organized, at least formally, under Five-year Plans prepared and monitored by the All-Union ministries in collaboration with the State Planning Commission (Gosplan), which was founded in 1921 and frequently reorganized. Gosplan was deprived of much of its influence under Gorbachev and was wound up in 1991.

Banking: During the Soviet period, banking was monopolized by the State Bank (Gosbank), until Mikhail Gorbachev broke it up into four separate institutions: Sberbank, a monopoly savings bank; Promstroybank, providing corporate services; Vnesheconombank, responsible for foreign exchange and borrowing transactions; and Vneshtorgbank, which financed foreign trade. By 1992, when Vnesheconombank closed its doors, all four had been overtaken by newly founded private sector competitors, and their various component units have since been transformed into national state banks or privatized. Many smaller banks appeared, some with links to organized crime, but most of them collapsed in 1995–96. In contrast to central and eastern Europe, relatively few foreign financial institutions have entered Russia or the other CIS states. Whatever the hopes and fears of 1991, banking in the CIS states has generally ended up in the hands of small groups of very powerful institutions, usually collaborating closely with the politicians in power.

Stock exchanges: Several small exchanges appeared, mainly in Russia, in the late 1980s and early 1990s. The electronic Russian Trading System, established in June 1995 and linked to a National Registry Company, rapidly became the most important exchange in the region. However, trading on all the stock exchanges is very limited in comparison to their counterparts in western Europe or North America.

Labor unions: The institutions known as "labor unions" under the Soviet regime ceased to have any degree of autonomy after 1929, when "one-man management" was imposed on all Soviet enterprises and the state began to penalize any attempt to strike as an act of "counterrevolutionary sabotage." As a result, labor unions became associated with state repression of economic and political freedoms. There has been some union activity since 1991, notably among coalminers and some public sector workers, and chiefly in Russia and Ukraine, but across the CIS attempts to revive labor unions have generally met with apathy among workers and hostility among managers. Except in Georgia and Moldova, major unions in the region have retained their membership of the World Federation of Trade Unions.

The CIS

The CIS is known as the SNG in Russian (an abbreviation of "Sodruzhestvo Nezavisimykh Gosudartsv"). It was established under an agreement signed by the Presidents of Russia, Belarus, and Ukraine, at Belovezha, near Minsk, the capital of Belarus, on December 8, 1991. Thirteen days later, at a meeting in Almaty, then the capital of Kazakhstan, Armenia, Azerbaijan, Kazakhstan, Kyrgyzstan, Moldova, Tajikistan, Turkmenistan, and Uzbekistan also agreed to join, although Azerbaijan's membership was not ratified by its Parliament until September 1993, and Moldova's was not ratified until April 1994. Georgia became the 12th member state of the CIS in December 1993. The CIS comprises a number of institutions, established at different dates, and with varying permutations of participating member states, broadly depending on whether they are concerned with political, economic or security issues. Only the more important are mentioned below (see also Chapters 2 and 3).

All 12 members participate in the Executive Secretariat, in Minsk; the regular meetings of the Council of Heads of State (presidents), the Council of Heads of Government (prime ministers), and the Interparliamentary Assembly; and the operations of the Railway Council. All five of these bodies were established in the early months of 1992. In addition, an Economic Court was established in July 1992, and the Council of Foreign Ministers was established in December 1993.

Eleven members – all except Georgia – participate in the Interstate Bank, created in December 1991, and the Economic Union, established by treaty in September 1993, although Ukraine and Turkmenistan are associate members of the Union rather than full members. In addition, 11 members – all except Tajikistan – created an Interstate Economic Council and a Payments Union in October 1994. Initial expectations that these four economic institutions would allow the CIS to play an important role, similar to that of the EU, have not been fulfilled.

Ten members – all except Ukraine and Moldova – have signed the Treaty on Collective Security since May 1992. Under its terms, they have made arrangements for a joint peacekeeping force, and established a Council of Heads of Collective Security (Defense Ministers), as well as a Joint Staff for Coordinating Military Cooperation. The 10 also agreed in November 1995 on the re-establishment of a joint air defense system.

Ten members – aside from Ukraine and Tajikistan – have ratified the CIS Charter since January 1993, creating the Coordinating and Consultative Committee, and a Court of Justice. These institutions, too, have been significantly less effective than their proponents hoped.

Other International Organizations

Worldwide: All 12 member states of the CIS were admitted to the UN and its agencies in 1992. Russia took over the Soviet Union's permanent seat in the UN Security Council and succeeded it in other institutions. Ukraine and Belarus inherited the seats given to the Ukrainian and Belarusian Soviet Socialist Republics, on Josef Stalin's insistence, at the foundation of the UN in 1945. Two UN bodies have special responsibilities for monitoring ceasefires in countries within the CIS: the UN Observer Mission in Georgia (UNOMIG), established in August 1993, and the UN Mission of Observers in Tajikistan (UNMOT), established in December 1994.

Since 1947, almost all European countries, as well as states in North America and Central Asia, have taken part in the activities of the UN Economic Commission on Europe (UNECE). Even during the Cold War, it had some success in promoting consensus and standardization in trade, transportation, science and technology, and the environment, and since 1989 it has also undertaken research and training in support of the transition to market practices in the post-Communist countries.

Since the World Trade Organization began operations in 1995, Azerbaijan, Tajikistan, and Turkmenistan have obtained observer status at its meetings, while the other nine CIS countries have all applied for membership.

During the Soviet Period: There was intensive liaison between the Soviet security service and its counterparts in the satellite countries, and over the years relatively informal political and economic deals also became increasingly important. However, the formal, overt framework of the Soviet bloc comprised three international organizations: Cominform, Comecon, and the Warsaw Pact.

Cominform (the Communist Information Bureau) was founded in Warsaw in 1947 and dissolved in Moscow in 1956. It had only nine members at the outset: the ruling parties of the Soviet Union, Bulgaria, Czechoslovakia, Hungary, Poland, Romania, and Yugoslavia, together with their sister parties in France and Italy. This was in marked contrast to the worldwide membership of the Communist International (the Comintern), established by Lenin in 1919 but dissolved by Stalin in 1943. The Yugoslav Party was expelled in 1948, following Tito's rejection of Stalin's hegemony; and it was mainly in the hope of a rapprochement with Yugoslavia that the Soviet leader Nikita Khrushchev abolished Cominform only eight years later.

Comecon was formally known as the Council for Mutual Economic Assistance (CMEA): the term "Comecon" appears to have been coined in the West. The organization, which had its headquarters in Moscow, was established in 1949 by the Soviet Union, along with Bulgaria, Czechoslovakia, Hungary, Poland, and Romania. Albania, admitted one month after the other members, was expelled in 1961. East Germany joined in 1950, Mongolia in 1962, Cuba in 1972, and Vietnam in 1978; Yugoslavia became an associate member in 1964. Trade agreements were made with a number of countries and organizations, notably the European Community (in 1988), and Comecon regulated trade among its members. For most of the period, around two thirds of the international trade of each member was with the other members. Comecon also played an important role in the system of economic planning: under an agreement signed in 1959, each member state was directed to specialize in selected industries. Comecon was dissolved in 1991. Its International Bank for Economic Cooperation, founded in 1963, and its International Investment Bank, founded in 1970, have become Russian commercial banks.

The Warsaw Pact alliance was established under a Treaty of Friendship, Cooperation, and Mutual Assistance signed in the capital of Poland in 1955 by Albania, Bulgaria, Czechoslovakia, East Germany, Hungary, Poland, Romania, and the Soviet Union. Albania was excluded from alliance meetings from 1961, and formally denounced the Pact in 1968. Despite its name, the political and military bodies that coordinated the Warsaw Pact's activities were based in Moscow, and its supreme commander was always a Soviet officer. The Pact took joint action only once, when the forces of its member states, except those of Albania and Romania, invaded Czechoslovakia. Its last formal act, before its dissolution in 1991, was to assist in representing its member states in talks on the Treaty on Conventional Forces in Europe, signed in 1990.

Links with Europe and North America: All 12 CIS countries are members of the OSCE (which began as the CSCE in 1975, but changed its name in 1995), alongside other European countries, the United States, and Canada. The OSCE addresses issues of security, economic cooperation, science and technology, the environment, and human rights. In particular, it is responsible for monitoring the observance of the 1990 Treaty on Conventional Forces in Europe (the CFE Treaty); it appointed its first High Commissioner on National Minorities in 1992; and it frequently monitors elections, ceasefire agreements, and other potential sources of conflict or crisis. Within the CIS region, the OSCE has missions in Georgia, Moldova, Ukraine, and Tajikistan, groups in Chechnya and Belarus, and a liaison office for Central Asia, based in Tashkent, the capital of Uzbekistan; and it also participates in the Minsk Group, which is working toward resolving the conflict over Nagorno-Karabakh.

All the CIS countries except Tajikistan have become associated with NATO, its 19 member states, and 13 other European states through the North Atlantic Cooperation Council (1991–97), and now the Euro-Atlantic Partnership Council (since 1997), the framework for NATO's Partnership for Peace program, which started in 1994.

Nine CIS countries have signed partnership and cooperation agreements with the EU (as the European Community has been known since November 1993), giving them access to the EU's single market, but to a much smaller extent than the EU's associates in central and eastern Europe. Most of these agreements have not yet been ratified. However, all 12 CIS countries, as well as Mongolia, have benefited from bilateral aid and advice delivered through an EU program known as TACIS (Technical Assistance to the CIS), which was established in 1990.

Belarus, Moldova, and Ukraine are members of the Central European Initiative (which began as the Pentagonale in July 1990), alongside Austria, Italy, and 11 countries in Central and Eastern Europe.

Moldova and Ukraine joined the Council of Europe in 1995, Russia joined it in 1996, and Georgia became its 41st member state in 1999. Armenia and Azerbaijan have guest status; Belarus also has guest status, but this has been suspended since 1997. The Council of Europe has monitored human rights, democracy, the treatment of minorities, and cultural issues since its establishment by 10 western European countries in 1949. (It should perhaps be mentioned that the Council of Europe and the European Court of Human Rights associated with it have no connection with the EU, its European Council or its European Court of Justice.)

All 12 CIS states have joined the European Bank for Reconstruction and Development (EBRD), which grew out of the meetings of the Group of 24 western nations during 1989–90. It began operations in 1991. Its other members include almost all the countries of Europe, as well as Australia, Canada, Egypt, Israel, Japan, South Korea, Morocco, New Zealand, the EU, and the European Investment Bank (an organ of the EU). In practice, most of the EBRD's activities have been in central and eastern Europe, where it has provided loans in support of economic reform, and taken shareholdings in privatized banks and other institutions.

Russia and Ukraine are now members of the Danube Commission, which supervises navigation on the river, while Moldova has observer status.

Among the CIS countries, Russia alone has joined the Council of Baltic Sea States, established in 1992, alongside Denmark, Estonia, Finland, Germany, Iceland, Latvia, Lithuania, Norway, Poland, and Sweden. The purpose of this "informal" body is to promote cooperation on the transition to free markets, as well as on energy and the environment, culture, crime, and communications.

Other: Soon after gaining independence, Turkmenistan and Uzbekistan became members of the Nonaligned Movement, established in 1961. Armenia and Azerbaijan have obtained observer status at its meetings.

In 1992, Azerbaijan and the five states of Central Asia (as well as Afghanistan) joined the Economic Cooperation Organization (ECO), established by Turkey, Iran, and Pakistan in 1985. The ECO has agreed on a system of preferential tariffs among member states, and is pursuing cooperation on trade and transportation.

The Declaration on Black Sea Economic and Environmental Cooperation was signed in 1992 by six CIS countries – Armenia, Azerbaijan, Georgia, Moldova, Russia, and Ukraine – along with Albania, Bulgaria, Romania, Turkey, and Greece. Together, these 11 countries are often referred to as the Black Sea Economic Cooperation (BSEC) group.

In 1994, Kazakhstan, Kyrgyzstan, and Uzbekistan established a Central Asian Economic Union. It was expanded to include Tajikistan in 1998.

In 1996, Moldova became the only CIS country to join with Greece, Turkey, and eight countries in central and eastern Europe in the Southeast Europe Cooperation Initiative (SECI). In close consultation with UNECE (see above), SECI works to promote cooperation on economic and environmental problems, and to encourage the private sector to collaborate in resolving them. In the same year, Moldova also became the only CIS country to join the Agence de la Francophonie, the international organization of countries and other territories that use the French language.

Russia and Ukraine have both joined the Nuclear Suppliers Group, which monitors exports of nuclear weapons materials and information. Finally, Russia is alone among the CIS countries in being a full member of the Asia-Pacific Economic Cooperation (APEC) forum, the Missile Technology Control Regime, and the Zangger Committee on guidelines for exports of nuclear weapons technology. It is also an observer at the European Organization for Nuclear Research (CERN), and a consultative partner of the Association of Southeast Asian Nations.

Appendix 5

Ethnic Groups

The Ethnic Composition of National Populations

The total populations and percentages set out below are all estimates, except where the taking of a census is indicated. All the figures, including those based on census returns, should be treated with caution. Some may be unreliable because of events since the estimates were made, such as civil wars or transfers of population between states. Others may be affected by tendencies to underestimate the social presence of disfavored groups and exaggerate the numbers of those in favored groups.

Armenia (1996): 3.4 million; Armenians 93.8%, Kurds 1.7%, Russians 1.6%, as well as Azeris, Roma, Ukrainians, Greeks, Assyrians, Belarusians

Azerbaijan (1992): 7.9 million; Azeris 83%, Russians 6%, Armenians 6%, as well as Kurds, Jews, Georgians, Turks, Avars, Belarusians, Lezgins, Ukrainians, Talysh, and Tatars

Belarus (1998): 10.4 million; Belarusians 78%, Russians 13%, Poles 4%, Ukrainians 3%, as well as Roma, Jews, Tatars, Lithuanians, and Latvians

Georgia (1995): 5.1 million; Georgians 70%, Armenians 8%, Russians 6%, Azeris 6%, Ossetians 3%, Greeks 2%, Abkhazians 2%, as well as Meskhetians, Adzharians, Ukrainians, Jews, Belarusians, Tatars, and Kurds

Kazakhstan (1994): 16.8 million; Kazakhs 45.1%, Russians 31.4%, Ukrainians 5.1%, Germans 4.7%, Tatars 2.3%, Uzbeks and Karakalpaks 2.1%, Uighurs 1.7%, Belarusians 1% as well as Koreans, Azeris, Poles, Chechens, Turks, Greeks, and around 100 other groups

Kyrgyzstan (1994): 4.5 million; Kyrgyz 54.4%, Russians 19.5%, Uzbeks 12.9%, as well as Ukrainians, Germans, Tatars, Kazakhs, Tajiks, Koreans, Azeris, and around 40 other groups

Moldova (1996): 4.5 million; Moldovans 65%, Ukrainians 14.2%, Russians 13%, Gagauz 4%, as well as Roma, Bulgarians, Jews, Germans, Belarusians, Tatars, Poles, and Greeks

Russia (1996): 147 million; Russians 77.9%, Tatars 4.5%, Ukrainians 2.9%, Bashkort 1.6%, Chavash 1.5%, Mordvins 1.2%, Belarusians 0.7%, as well as Udmurt, Chechens, Germans, Jews, Mari, Kazakhs, Avars, Armenians, Sakha, Ossetians, Buryat, Kabardins, Komi, and more than 150 other ethnic groups

Tajikistan (1989 census): 6 million; Tajiks 62%, Uzbeks 23%, Russians 8%, as well as Tatars, Kyrgyz, Germans, and Ukrainians, and other groups

Turkmenistan (1996 census): 4.3 million; Turkmen 77%, Uzbeks 9.2%, Russians 6.7%, Kazakhs 3.1%, Tatars 1.8%, Ukrainians 1.1%, as well as Azeris, Armenians, Lezgins, Belarusians, Mordvins, Koreans, Kurds, and others

Ukraine (1989 census): 50 million; Ukrainians 73%, Russians 22%, Belarusians 1%, Jews 1%, as well as Moldovans, Tatars, Poles, Hungarians, and Greeks

Uzbekistan (1995): 23.8 million; Uzbeks 71%, Russians 8%, Tajiks 5%, Kazakhs 4%, Karakalpaks 2.5%, as well as Tatars, Turkmen, Koreans, Kyrgyz, Ukrainians, and others

Nationalities in the CIS

There is not enough space here to examine all the ethnic groups in the CIS, or even to examine all the larger groups one by one. Accordingly, many have been grouped by reference to their linguistic and cultural affinities. This should not be taken to indicate any judgment on the relative importance or claims to recognition of any minority mentioned.

As with the percentages above, great care should be taken over all the figures set out below. They are all estimates, based on official sources and standard reference texts. They all fail to take account of intermarriage, religious conversion, and other forms of intermingling between groups and cultures: in the CIS, as elsewhere, claims to ethnic "purity" hardly ever have any basis in fact. References to a minority in a specific country do not necessarily indicate its absence from other countries in the region.

Abkhazians: This Caucasian people, whose name for themselves is Apsua, form the majority (numbering around 110,000) in Abkhazia, a republic in Georgia. Most are Moslems, but there is also an Orthodox Christian minority. A secessionist war that began in 1992 ended in 1994 with Abkhazia effectively defended by Russia.

Adzharians: Around 275,000 Adzharians live in the republic of Adzharia in Georgia. They share much of the Georgian linguistic and cultural heritage, and have long been counted as Georgians in censuses and for other purposes. However, the Sunni form of Islam practiced by most Adzharians has set them apart from other Georgians. Adzharia now has a degree of autonomy within Georgia.

Armenians: Of the 3.5 million people in the Republic of Armenia, 3.3 million are ethnic Armenians. There are also hundreds of thousands of Armenians in Russia, Georgia, Azerbaijan, Kyrgyzstan, Tajikistan, Turkmenistan, Ukraine, Uzbekistan, and Turkey; and there are probably even more people in the Armenian "diaspora," in the United States and other western countries, than in Armenia itself. The wide geographic dispersal of this people, whose traditional culture centers on their unique language and alphabet, and on one of the oldest forms of Christianity in the world, reflects their history of persecution under the Turkish and Russian empires up to the end of World War I. In the 1990s, most Armenians living in Azerbaijan, whether in the disputed region of Nagorno-Karabakh or elsewhere, left for Armenia during the conflict between the two countries over that region.

Assyrians: This ethnic group came into the North Caucasus and other parts of the space now occupied by the CIS both in the 19th century and after World War II. Assyrians originate from Turkey and other majority-Moslem countries in the Middle East, where they had long preserved Chaldean, Nestorian, and other ancient eastern forms of Christianity. Now numbering 50,000 or more, they form minorities in Armenia, Georgia, and Russia.

Azeris: There are around 6.7 million Azeris in Azerbaijan, but at least 15 million in neighboring Iran, in addition to Azeri minorities in Armenia (around 10,000, or one third of the number before the war over Nagorno-Karabakh), Georgia (360,000), Kazakhstan (100,000), Russia (340,000), and other CIS countries. The Azeris are a Turkic people, traditionally organized in pastoral clans, and most are Shi'a Moslems.

Baltic peoples (Latvians and Lithuanians): The 27,000 Latvians and 64,000 Lithuanians in Russia, and the 10,000 Lithuanians in Kazakhstan, are mostly descendants of individuals exiled to Siberia or Central Asia during the Soviet occupation of their home countries. However, the 11,000 Lithuanians and 5,000 Latvians in Belarus share with the Poles in that country a history of continuous settlement that goes back to the Middle Ages, when the Commonwealth of Poland-Lithuania, then a major European power, included large parts of modern Belarus and Latvia alike. (Estonians, who are linguistically and culturally very distinct from Latvians and Lithuanians, are listed under Finns below.)

Bashkort: Most of the 2.4 million members of this Turkic group, known as Bashkirs in Russian, live in the republic of Bashkortostan, west of the Ural Mountains, where they constitute around 22% of the population, or in other parts of Russia. There are also Bashkort communities in all five states in Central Asia, as well as in Ukraine. The Bashkort resemble the Tatars in some respects – their languages are closely related, and they both underwent mass conversion to Islam in the Middle Ages – but the Bashkort formed a military caste, modeled on the Cossacks, under the Russian empire, and resisted assimilation with the much larger Tatar people.

Belarusians: see under Russians

Bulgarians: Around 224,000 Bulgarians live in Ukraine, and around 85,000 in Moldova. Most of them are descendants of migrants given aid by the Russian government in the 19th century to settle and farm in undeveloped areas.

Buryat: The 455,000 Buryat, a Mongol people who have lived for centuries on the shores of Lake Baikal in eastern Siberia, are mostly Buddhists, although some have retained their original shamanistic religion, while others are Orthodox Christians. They live not only in Buryatia, a Russian republic, but also in two Russian regions, Agüt Buryatia and Ust-Ordün Buryatia, as well as elsewhere in eastern Siberia. However, they no longer form a majority in any of the territories named for them.

Caucasian peoples: In this context, "Caucasian" refers to a family of languages, not to the Caucasus region for which the family is named. All the Caucasian peoples of Russia and Georgia have lived in or near the region, which has also long been home to other peoples speaking unrelated languages, such as the Ossetians. Another common characteristic of the peoples who use Caucasian languages is that, with the notable exception of the Georgians, all have traditionally been Sunni Moslems, reflecting their history of conquest by the Mongols and Tatars in the Middle Ages.

In addition to the Abkhazians, Adzharians, Chechens, and Georgians, listed separately, there are at least 25 other Caucasian peoples in the CIS, concentrated mainly in five republics within Russia. To begin with, the 290,000 Ingush, whose own name for themselves is Galgai, form the majority in the Russian republic of Ingushetia, which was separated from Chechnya in 1992. Like the Chechens, they too were exiled to Kazakhstan in 1944, but most returned after 1957. In the meantime, however, part of their republic, the Prigorodnyi district, had been transferred to North Ossetia; this district became a focus of violent conflict in the early 1990s, when most of its Ingush population fled into Ingushetia.

The 440,000 Kabardins share the Russian republic of Kabardino-Balkaria with the 91,000 Balkars (a Turkic people); together they comprise 58% of its population. Most of the 130,000 Adygei live in the Russian republic that bears their name, although they constitute only 22% of its population. The 76,000 Circassians, who also call themselves Adygei, as well as 40,000 Abaza, share Karachai-Circassia with the 160,000 Karachai (another Turkic people).

There are 34 recognized nationalities in Dagestan, a Russian republic in the northeastern Caucasus that has a total population of around 1.9 million. Twenty of these speak Caucasian languages: 570,000 Avars, 370,000 Dargin, 260,000 Lezgins, 110,000 Tabasaran, 107,000 Laks, 76,000 Adzhai, 24,000 Agul, 23,000 Rutul, 13,000 Karata, 13,000 Chamalal, and smaller numbers of Tat, Botlikh, Tsakhur, Andi, Dido, Tindi, Akhvakh, Ghodoberi, Bezhta, and Hunzib. There are also Lezgins, Avars, and Tsakhur in Azerbaijan, and Lezgins in Turkmenistan, many as a result of deportation in World War II. The Kumyks and Nogai, who also live in Dagestan, are Turkic peoples – see below – and there are also Russians, Azerbaijanis, Chechens, and Jews in the republic.

Chavash: The 2.4 million Chavash, known to Russians as Chuvash, speak a language that is probably Turkic, but they differ from other Turkic-speaking peoples in being partly Finnic in ethnic origin, and in being mainly Orthodox Christians rather than Moslems. Fewer than half their number now live in the republic of Chavashia in European Russia, although they remain a majority within it. Most others live elsewhere in Russia, but there are also Chavash minorities in Uzbekistan and other states in Central Asia.

Chechens: Around 930,000 Chechens, a Sunni Moslem group who are the largest of the North Caucasian peoples, inhabit the republic of Chechnya, where they form around 58% of the population, and other areas in the Caucasus. Following deportations during World War II, mainly in 1944, there are also around 55,000 Chechens in Kazakhstan. During the Soviet period, their homeland was part of a single republic of Chechen-Ingushetia (up to 1944 and again from 1957), but it has now passed through war with Russia to *de facto* independence.

Crimean Tatars: see under Tatars

Czechs and Slovaks: The 42,000 Czechs and Slovaks in Ukraine descend from settlers who migrated into Transcarpathia (a region that Ukraine shares with Slovakia and Hungary today), either when it was part of the Kingdom of Hungary, under the Habsburg dual monarchy with Austria up to 1918, or between the world wars, when it was part of the former Czechoslovakia.

Finns, Estonians, and other Finnic peoples: In addition to the Mordvins and the Mari, both listed separately, the eight Finnic peoples in Russia comprise around 250,000 Karelians, around 105,000 Finns, 85,000 Ingrians (or Inkeri), 55,000 Estonians, 17,000 Veps, and 2,000 Sami, the nomadic reindeer herders often called Lapps by their neighbors. All are concentrated in the republic of Karelia, St Petersburg, and other parts of northwestern Russia, which their ancestors inhabited before the Russians entered the region. However, there are also some Finns in Central Asia, descendants of larger groups deported there in 1942. There was briefly a Karelo-Finnish Union Republic (1940–56), but during the Soviet period the cultures and languages of all these peoples were generally discouraged, and Russians now outnumber them in their homelands.

Gagauz: The 215,000 Gagauz live mainly in Gagauz-Yeri, a wine-producing region that was wholly within Moldova until 1945, when portions were transferred to Ukraine. (There are also some Gagauz in Bulgaria.) The Gagauz are probably of Slav origin and are still mostly Orthodox Christians, but they speak a Russian-influenced Turkic language. Having declared an autonomous republic within Moldova in 1990, their leaders made peace with the Moldovan government in 1992.

Georgians: This Caucasian people, numbering nearly 4 million among the 5.6 million people in their homeland, has also formed minorities in the neighboring states of Armenia, Azerbaijan, Russia, and Turkey; in Ukraine, across the Black Sea from Georgia; and, as deportees in World War II, in Kazakhstan and Uzbekistan. Georgians are divided, chiefly by dialect and ascribed home region, into Kartalians, Imeritians, Gurians, Mingrelians, and Svanetians, but most are united by adherence to the ancient Georgian Church and use of the Georgian alphabet. See also Adzharians.

Germans: Almost all the Germans in the CIS are descendants of those invited by Empress Catherine II to settle in the Volga basin and on the Black Sea in the 18th century. Around 900,000 remain in Russia, around 38,000 in Ukraine, and around 7,000 in Moldova. During World War II, however, thousands were deported to Central Asia on Stalin's orders: today, more than 900,000 live in Kazakhstan, Kyrgyzstan, and Uzbekistan. Some Germans from CIS countries have migrated to Germany during the 1990s.

Greeks: There are small numbers of Greeks in Russia descended from Communists who left Greece in the 1940s, during and after that country's civil war. However, most Greeks in the region are Pontian Greeks, tracing their ancestry to ancient settlements on the shores of the Black Sea. Although many of those who lived in Ukraine were deported into Russia during World War II, there are still 226,000 in Ukraine, as well as 112,000 in Georgia, 105,000 in Russia, 50,000 in Kazakhstan, and smaller numbers in other CIS countries. In recent years, many have received aid from the Greek government to migrate to their ancestral homeland, but thousands remain in Armenia, Georgia, Kazakhstan, Russia, and Ukraine.

Hungarians: Most of the 178,000 Hungarians in Ukraine descend from settlers who migrated into Transcarpathia (a region that Ukraine shares with Slovakia and Hungary today) when it was part of the Kingdom of Hungary, under the Habsburg dual monarchy with Austria, up to 1918.

Jews: Like the Roma, the Jews have suffered varying degrees of persecution and discrimination throughout Christian Europe. In the Soviet Union, where they were registered as a nationality, assimilation was encouraged and traditional anti-Semitism was occasionally unleashed, notably under Stalin in the 1940s and again under Brezhnev in the 1970s. It has been estimated that by the end of World War II, during which hundreds of thousands of Soviet Jews were murdered by the Nazi invaders and their collaborators, there were around 1.5 million Jews in the Soviet Union. Since then, however, emigration has reduced their numbers, following a trend that sharply accelerated after the breakup of the Soviet system. Between 1990 and 1997, for example, 822,000 Jews emigrated to Israel from Russia and other CIS countries, and thousands more went to North America and western Europe.

Today, there are significant Jewish minorities in Azerbaijan (around 6,000 people, some of whom still speak an Iranian language called Tat), in Belarus (112,000), in Georgia (18,000, some of whom still speak Judeo-Georgian), Kazakhstan (20,000, mostly descendants of deportees in World War II and participants in the "Virgin Lands" campaign in the 1950s), Moldova (35,000), Russia (around 840,000, among them 8,000 living in the Jewish Autonomous Oblast in the Russian Far East), Tajikistan (11,000, mostly descended from wartime deportees), Ukraine (265,000), and Uzbekistan (100,000, some of whom still speak Bukharic).

Kalmyks: The 210,000 Kalmyks (or Khal'mg) are a Mongol people, descendants of groups in Central Asia that joined the Golden Horde during its conquests of Russia and neighboring countries. Nowadays, most Kalmyks live in the Russian republic of Kalmykia, on the shores of the Caspian Sea, although they form only 45% of its population. They have retained their Buddhist heritage even though they have been neighbors to Moslems and Christians for centuries. They were subject to persecution during the Soviet period, when they were forced to abandon nomadism. Many were deported to Central Asia and Siberia in January 1944, and their republic was not reestablished until 1957.

Karakalpaks: The ethnic identity of the 840,000 Karakalpaks of Uzbekistan, most of whom live in the autonomous republic that bears their name, has been a subject of scholarly dispute and occasional nonscholarly conflict. They are sometimes regarded as a subgroup of the Uzbeks, while others regard them as a Kazakh clan separated from the other clans.

Kazakhs: The 7.7 million Kazakhs in their home state, the 840,000 in Uzbekistan, and the 850,000 in the other states of Central Asia, in Russia, and in Ukraine, speak a Turkic language and have largely retained their traditional clan structure, derived from the Mongol-Tatar Hordes that conquered much of what is now the CIS in the Middle Ages. Most Kazakhs are Sunni Moslems.

Komi and Komi-Permyak: These two related Permian peoples, who share many cultural traits with the Udmurt, inhabit adjacent territories to the west of the Ural Mountains in Russia. The 430,000 Komi mostly live in the republic that bears their name, while the 175,000 Komi-Permyak inhabit the Komi-Permyak region to the South. However, both these territories now have Russian majorities, partly as a result of the creation of labor camps by the Soviet regime. The Komi and Komi-Permyak are mainly Russian Orthodox, and have lost much of their traditional cultures.

Koreans: There have been Korean communities in what is now the CIS for centuries, engaging in trading, fishing, and farming. Today, there are two main concentrations of Koreans in the region. Those in Central Asia, now numbering around 320,000, first arrived there from 1937 onward, as the first ethnic group to be deported *en masse* from one part of the Soviet Union to another, in their case on the absurd grounds that they were spying for imperial Japan (which ruled Korea itself from 1910 to 1945). The 312,000 Koreans living on Sakhalin Island and elsewhere in the Russian Far East are mostly the remnants of a larger slave labor force taken from their homeland to Sakhalin by the Japanese when they ruled the island before World War II. Most members of both groups have retained their language and Buddhist religion, despite considerable discrimination against them during the Soviet period.

Kurds: Of the more than 25 million Kurds around the world, widely recognized as the world's largest nation without a state of their own, most live in Turkey, Iraq, and Iran. Perhaps fewer than 500,000 live in CIS countries. As a recognized minority in each of these countries, they have been able to maintain their traditions and languages, and there has not been any Kurdish militancy on the scale seen in their main countries of residence.

Kyrgyz: The 2.4 million Kyrgyz form only a little more than half the population of Kyrgyzstan itself. They are a Turkic people, largely Sunni Moslem, who were forcibly transformed from nomads into settled farmers during the Soviet period. There are Kyrgyz minorities in the other three mainly Turkic, Sunni Moslem states of Central Asia – 183,000 in Uzbekistan, 98,000 in Tajikistan, and 15,000 in Kazakhstan – and much smaller numbers in other CIS countries.

Mari: The Mari, along with the Mordvins, were the original Finnic inhabitants of the Volga basin. Most are now Orthodox Christians, but their traditional culture, based on a blend of shamanism, Islam, and Christianity, has survived in the Russian republic of Mari-El, where most of the 770,000 Mari live. They comprise around 43% of its population. There are also small Mari communities in Kazakhstan.

Meskhetians: This was a Soviet term for a variety of mainly Moslem peoples deported from Georgia to Siberia and Central Asia in 1944, and "rehabilitated" in 1968. By then, they had become a distinct national group, using a dialect of Georgian as their common language. However, they have not been allowed to return to Georgia, and their mistreatment in exile culminated in murderous riots against them in Uzbekistan in 1989. Most of the 270,000 Meskhetians now live in Azerbaijan and Russia.

Moldovans and Romanians: The 2.8 million Moldovans in Moldova itself include more than 130,000 people who describe themselves as Romanians. The two peoples are very closely related, and the degree of difference between their languages and cultures is still disputed. Little or no distinction is made between the two peoples in Russia, where around 180,000 Moldovans and Romanians live, or in Kazakhstan, where the 33,000 Moldovans and Romanians are descendants of World War II deportees. In Ukraine, however, the 310,000 Moldovans are counted separately from the 152,000 Romanians. The presence of the former group in Ukraine, notably in North Bukovina and Eastern Bessarabia, has given rise to claims by some Moldovan nationalists that these areas should be incorporated into Moldova.

Mordvins: The Mordvins are a Finnic people that inhabited the Volga basin, alongside the Mari, before the Slav ancestors of the Russians arrived there. They have traditionally been Orthodox Christians. Most of the 1.8 million Mordvins live in Russia, although they are now a minority (around 33% of the total population) in the republic of Mordvinia itself. There are also around 60,000 Mordvins in Central Asia and 21,000 in Ukraine.

Ossetians: Members of this group, who call themselves Iristi, have lived in the Caucasus for centuries but are not ethnically "Caucasian." They belong to the Iranian family of peoples and were known to western Europe in the Dark Ages as Alans. The Ossetians were divided into two groups in the 13th century, when some were conquered by the Mongols and others fled South. Today, Ossetians form the majority of the population in two republics: North Ossetia in Russia, where around 500,000 mainly Orthodox Christian Ossetians live; and, on the other side of the Caucasus Mountains, South Ossetia in Georgia, home to around 170,000 mostly Sunni Moslem Ossetians. Many Ossetians in both republics have sought reunion over the centuries and again in the 1990s, when war broke out between South Ossetia and Georgia. There is also an Ossetian minority in Kabardino-Balkaria, a Russian republic bordering North Ossetia. Most of the 20,000 Moslem Ossetians in Central Asia arrived there as deportees from their homelands during World War II.

Paleo-Asiatic peoples: This anthropological term refers to three ethnic groups comprising the longest-established inhabitants of northern Russia and the Russian Far East. They are ethnically and culturally close to the native peoples of North America. Traditionally, the 36,000 Chukot (or Chukchi) have hunted reindeer, seals and whales, the 12,000 Koryak have herded cattle or fished, and the 3,000 Itel'men have been hunters on the Kamchatka Peninsula. However, all three peoples have been Russified to some extent and most Itel'men now work in fish canneries.

Poles: There are three major groups of Poles in the CIS. Those resident in western Ukraine and Belarus, numbering around 1.3 million and 430,000 respectively, belong to communities long established in those countries, parts of which were in Poland in the 16th and 17th centuries, and again from 1918 to World War II. The 97,000 Poles in Russia are descendants of eastward migrants or deportees from Ukraine and Belarus. Finally, those in Kazakhstan (around 65,000) are the descendants of deportees from Russia, sent into exile from the 19th century onward.

Roma: This has become the preferred term for the formerly nomadic people who are sometimes still called "gypsies" in reference to their supposed origins in Egypt. In fact, they originated in the Indian subcontinent, arriving in southeastern Europe in the 14th century and then spreading around the world. Like the Jews, the Roma were subjected to prejudice and discrimination throughout Christian Europe, culminating in the campaign of genocide by the Nazis and their collaborators during World War II. At least 500,000 Roma were murdered in what they call *O Porraimos*, "the Devouring."

    In the Soviet Union, Roma traditions were officially discouraged and occasional efforts were made to compel them to abandon nomadism. The situation of the Roma has not improved since Communism collapsed. There are now significant Roma minorities in Armenia (around 8,000 people), Belarus (115,000), Moldova (138,000), Russia (345,000), and Ukraine (258,000).

Romanians: see Moldovans

Russians, Belarusians, and Ukrainians: For centuries, these peoples were designated respectively as Great Russians, White Russians, and Little Russians. The growth of separate national identities, and the uncovering of Belarusian and Ukrainian history in particular, have been complex processes, hampered by the sheer size of the Russian people, and by the political and economic power of its successive elites.

During the Soviet period, many individuals from these three peoples were sent to the other Soviet republics as administrators, academics, or members of other professions. However, most of the Russians, Belarusians, and Ukrainians living outside their respective homelands today migrated after World War II to work in factories or on farms. Thus, in addition to the 115 million Russians in Russia itself, up to 25 million live outside it. The equivalent figures for Belarusians are around 8 million and roughly 4 million, and for Ukrainians 38 million and around 12 million. In addition, however, there are many other individuals who identify themselves as Russian or have mixed heritage. All three peoples form minorities in each other's countries, as well as in every other CIS country. In central and eastern Europe, where their presence generally goes back centuries, all three form minorities in Estonia, Latvia, and Lithuania; Russians and Ukrainians can also be found in the Czech Republic, Slovakia, and Yugoslavia; there are Belarusians and Ukrainians in Poland; and there are Ukrainians in Croatia. In some of these countries, all three peoples have been excluded from state posts or suffered other forms of discrimination, and many have returned or migrated to Russia, Belarus, and Ukraine.

It should be noted that a minority within the groups designated as Ukrainians in most of these countries regard themselves as a separate people, the Ruthenes or Rusyns. Their original homeland was in the Carpathian Mountains. They may now number around 1.5 million in Ukraine, with around 75,000 living in Slovakia, and 35,000 in Yugoslavia. Another factor that has complicated discussion of Ukrainian identity is the adherence of most Ukrainians to one of three rival forms of Christianity: the Ukrainian Orthodox Church, which is in communion with the Russian Orthodox Church); the Ukrainian Autocephalous Orthodox Church, which was persecuted under Communism but revived in 1992; and the Uniate Church, which uses Orthodox rites but is in communion with Rome.

Sakha: The 520,000 Sakha, known to the Russians as Yakut, constitute around one third of the population of the republic of Sakha (or Yakutia) in the Russian Far East, which they share with the descendants of Russian settlers and political exiles. Formerly nomads, with a complex culture combining Mongol, Turkic and Paleo-Asiatic elements, the Sakha are now mostly farmers and members of the Russian Orthodox Church. Their language is largely Turkic.

Samoyed peoples: The 38,000 Nenets, who were traditionally reindeer herders, and the 2,000 hunting and fishing Selkup are scattered across large areas of northwestern Siberia. Most members of both groups now use the Russian language and adhere to Orthodox Christianity, but their shamanistic traditions and their original languages have survived.

Tajiks: The Tajik people, numbering 4 million or more in Tajikistan, 1.2 million in Uzbekistan, 30,000 in Kazakhstan, 39,000 in Kyrgyzstan, and 42,000 in Russia, differ from the other peoples who have given their names to states in Central Asia in being linguistically and culturally Iranian, not Turkic. Most share the Sunni form of Islam that is dominant throughout the region. They also share a history of nomadism, which was abandoned only in the 20th century. The word "Tajik" also refers to the largest of the three subdivisions of this people. The other two are the Yagnobi, who were originally mountain dwellers, and the Badakhshoni (or Pamiri), who are mostly Ismaili Moslems and have their own autonomous region within Tajikistan.

Talysh: This Shi'a Moslem people of Iranian stock lives in southern Azerbaijan and northern Iran. A movement for local autonomy appeared in both these countries during the 1990s. Their numbers are disputed, but there may around 140,000 in Azerbaijan and a larger number in Iran.

Tatars and Crimean Tatars: The mainly Sunni Moslem Tatars are a Turkic people descended from the Mongol-Tatar Golden Horde that occupied large parts of Russia and neighboring countries between 1223 and 1480. They formed the largest single ethnic minority in the Russian empire, after the Russians themselves, and in the 19th century many Tatars were sent to majority-Moslem regions of that empire as officials and soldiers. Today, there are around 650,000 Tatars in Central Asia and Azerbaijan. In 1920, the Tatars' main area of concentrated settlement in Russia, in the Volga region, was designated the Tatarstan republic. Around 1.9 million Tatars live there today, comprising around 49% of the republic's population, but around 4.7 million others now live all over Russia. There are also 72,000 Tatars in Belarus, 5,000 in Georgia, and 2,000 in Moldova.

The Tatars are generally regarded as distinct from the much smaller minority known as the Crimean Tatars, most of whom were deported from Crimea to Uzbekistan and other states in Central Asia in May 1944. They were "rehabilitated" in 1967, but prevented from even trying to return to Crimea until 1988. There are now around 185,000 Crimean Tatars in Ukraine, 167,000 in Uzbekistan, and smaller numbers in Russia and Kyrgyzstan, but these numbers are changing as more and more return to Crimea. This mainly Moslem people includes a Jewish minority, the Karaim.

Turkic peoples: "Turkic" here refers to a language family: the peoples who use these languages have various and usually mixed ethnic origins, reflecting centuries of intermingling among Turkic tribes, Mongol hordes, and other peoples.

In addition to the Azeris, Bashkort, Chavàsh, Kazakhs, Kyrgyz, Sakha, Tatars, Turkmen, and Uzbeks, all listed separately, there are several other Turkic peoples in the CIS, almost all of them living in republics within Russia. Around 267,000 Kumyks and 81,000 Nogai share Dagestan with 20 Caucasian peoples (see above), and have developed secessionist movements during the 1990s. Around 245,000 Tuvin (or Uriankhai) inhabit Tuvà Ulus, which was part of China until 1914, and where they now constitute around two thirds of the population; they are mostly Buddhists, loyal to the Dalai Lama of Tibet. Around 160,000 Karachai (or Krachailyla) share Karachai-Circassia with 76,000 Circassians and 40,000 Abaza (both Caucasian peoples), as well as a large Russian population. Most of the Karachai were deported to Central Asia in December 1943 and prevented from returning until 1957. They are closely related to the 91,000 Balkar (or Malkar), who share Kabardino-Balkaria with another Caucasian people, the 440,000 Kabardins. The Balkars were deported to Central Asia in 1944, but most returned after 1957. Around 87,000 Khakas are now a minority (around 11% of the total population) in their homeland, the Russian republic of Khakassia, which lies in southern Siberia. Around 73,000 Altai are concentrated in the Russian republic that bears their name, in which they form around one third of the population. In 1904, the Russian empire suppressed an Altai rebellion, which had centered on defense of their religion, Burkhanism, a blend of shamanism and Buddhism; this has been revived in the 1990s.

In addition, there are 300,000 Uighurs in Kazakhstan, descendants of refugees from their homeland inside China, and around 90,000 elsewhere in Central Asia. Finally, the Turks in Azerbaijan and Central Asia, who have been settled there since the 17th century, if not earlier, now number at least 150,000.

Turkmen: The Turkmen, who number around 3.2 million in Turkmenistan itself, 229,000 in Uzbekistan, 18,000 in Tajikistan, and 3,000 in Kazakhstan, are former nomads who have maintained their traditional divisions into around 30 tribes and more than 100 clans. Most Turkmen are Sunni Moslems, but there is a Shi'a minority, mostly living near the borders with Iran and Afghanistan.

Udmurt: The Udmurt are the largest of the peoples speaking various Permian languages, and have much in common with the Komi and Komi-Permyak peoples in particular. Most of the 1.2 million Udmurt still live in the republic of Udmurtia, on the western side of the Ural Mountains, but there are many others elsewhere in Russia, and in Kazakhstan.

Ukrainians: see under Russians

Uzbeks: The Uzbeks are the largest ethnic group in Central Asia, comprising 16.7 million in Uzbekistan, 1.5 million in Tajikistan, 560,000 in Kyrgyzstan, 440,000 in Turkmenistan, and 360,000 in Kazakhstan (as well as 10,000 in Ukraine). Like the Kazakhs, Kyrgyz, and Turkmen, they are a mainly Sunni Moslem Turkic people.

Appendix 6

Bibliography

This bibliography is intended to draw the attention of readers to some of the most useful and stimulating English-language books on the CIS and its various member states available in the late 1990s. It therefore excludes periodicals and websites, as well as publications in other languages. It should be seen as a supplement to the suggestions for further reading at the end of each chapter.

Reference

Brown, Archie, Michael Kaser, and Gerald S. Smith, editors, *The Cambridge Encyclopedia of Russia and the Former Soviet Union*, Cambridge and New York: Cambridge University Press, 1994

This comprehensive and reliable text, edited and written by some of the leading experts on Soviet and CIS affairs, can be found in all good university and reference libraries.

Channon, John, *The Penguin Historical Atlas of Russia*, London and New York: Viking, 1995

An outstanding example of cartographic presentation of data, this volume provides comprehensive coverage of Russian history as well as contemporary issues.

Croucher, Murlin, editor, *Slavic Studies: A Guide to Bibliographies, Encyclopedias, and Handbooks*, in two volumes, Wilmington, DE: Scholarly Resources, 1993

This impressive work offers guidance to further research in several languages, not only on the Soviet Union, Russia, and other CIS countries but also on the Slavic nations in central and eastern Europe.

Eastern Europe and the Commonwealth of Independent States 1999, London: Europa Publications, 1999

This is the fourth edition of a reference work dealing with 27 post-Communist countries (12 in the CIS, 15 in central and eastern Europe). Prefaced by 12 introductory essays, each country survey has standardized entries on geography, history and economy, as well as chronologies, statistics, and data on public institutions.

Ference, Gregory C., editor, *Chronology of 20th-century Eastern European History*, Detroit, MI and London: Gale Research, 1994

An invaluable collection of historical data on what are now 27 ex-Communist countries, as well as the former East Germany, spanning the years up to the end of 1993. Its nine chapters are arranged country by country: the chapter on the Soviet Union and the post-Soviet states begins in 1917. The chronologies are accompanied with maps, photographs, biographies of prominent individuals, and a useful bibliography.

Modern Encyclopedia of Russian and Soviet History, in 55 volumes, Gulf Breeze, FL: Academic International Press, 1976–1993; *Modern Encyclopedia of Russian, Soviet, and Eurasian History*, in several volumes, Gulf Breeze, FL: Academic International Press, 1994 onward

This enormous, wide-ranging, and generally authoritative encyclopedia is divided into three parts: Volumes 1 to 46, the original work completed in 1987; Volumes 47 to 55, forming a supplement that addresses the collapse of the Soviet Union and its aftermath; and subsequent volumes, under a new title, continuing the project into the 21st century.

White, Stephen, editor, *Political and Economic Encyclopedia of the Soviet Union and Eastern Europe*, Harlow: Longman, 1990

This comprehensive reference text was already being overtaken by events as it was prepared and published, but it is still worth seeking out for data on the region in the Soviet period.

The Soviet Union

Brada, Josef C., and Michael P. Claudon, editors, *The Emerging Russian Bear: Integrating the Soviet Union into the World Economy*, New York: New York University Press, 1991

This book provides an in-depth analysis of Soviet economic policy from 1986 to 1991, focusing particularly on commercial law and commercial policy.

Cliff, Tony, *State Capitalism in Russia*, fifth edition, London: Bookmarks, 1988

An account of the creation and maintenance of the Stalinist system, with a long postscript on the period 1945–88. The author writes from an independent Marxist perspective, but the book will be of interest even to readers who do not share his views, perhaps especially to those who imagine that Marxism and Stalinism are one and the same.

Daniels, Robert V., editor, *A Documentary History of Communism*, Volume 1, *Communism in Russia*, and Volume 2, *Communism and the World*, revised and updated editions, Hanover, NH: University Press of New England, 1988 (Volume 1), 1994 (Volume 2)

A very useful collection of manifestos, laws, and other documents in English translation. Most of the items included are official in nature, but there are also some samples of dissident literature in the first volume.

Davies, R. W., *Soviet Economic Development from Lenin to Khrushchev*, Cambridge and New York: Cambridge University Press, 1998

A brief and very readable tour through the basic issues pertaining to the early years of the administrative command system

Ellman, Michael, and Vladimir Kontorovich, editors, *The Disintegration of the Soviet Economic System*, London and New York: Routledge, 1992

An in-depth analysis of the economic, social and political processes resulted in the collapse of the Soviet economy and the disintegration of the Soviet Union

Gregory, Paul R., and Robert C. Stuart, *Russian and Soviet Economic Performance and Structure*, sixth edition, Reading, MA and Harlow: Addison-Wesley, 1998

This standard text provides a thorough examination of the Russian imperial and Soviet economy from 1860 to 1991, then follows the latest stages of the Russian economic experience during the 1990s.

Hosking, Geoffrey, *A History of the Soviet Union*, second edition, London and New York: HarperCollins, 1991

Still an authoritative text, particularly for its focus on long-term developments within Soviet society.

Kochan, Lionel, and John Keep, *The Making of Modern Russia*, third edition, London: Penguin Books, 1997

The latest edition of a standard one-volume history, first published in 1962, which begins in prehistory and ends with the collapse of the Soviet Union and the triumph of Boris Yeltsin. For the Soviet period, the authors make use of a great deal of material that was not available until the 1990s, integrating it into a thoughtful and accessible account of the system's development and decline.

LaFeber, Walter, *America, Russia, and the Cold War, 1945–1996*, New York and London: McGraw-Hill, 1997

An important single-volume survey of the period, usefully recast to take account of new data and insights that became available after the Soviet Union collapsed

Lewin, Moshe, *The Gorbachev Phenomenon: A Historical Interpretation*, Berkeley: University of California Press, 1991

Lewin's predictions have not been fulfilled and some of his arguments are questionable, but at the heart of this short book is a thoughtful and impressive attempt to provide a sociology of the postwar Soviet Union, stressing urbanization as the motor of social change.

McAuley, Mary, *Soviet Politics 1917–1991*, Oxford and New York: Oxford University Press, 1992

With its judicious balance of political and economic narrative and sociological reflection, this is perhaps the best short overview of the subject.

Medvedev, Roy, *All Stalin's Men*, translated by Harold Shukman, Oxford: Basil Blackwell, and Garden City, NY: Anchor Press/Doubleday, 1983

This is perhaps the most distinctive of several books on Soviet history by this leading Russian scholar. By profiling six individuals – Voroshilov, Mikoyan, Suslov, Molotov, Kaganovich, and Malenkov – who often appear elsewhere as little more than names, Medvedev brings the complexities of the Soviet regime to life and implicitly challenges interpretations of that regime as either a personal dictatorship or an impersonal and unchanging political machine.

Newby, Eric, *The Big Red Train Ride*, London: Weidenfeld and Nicolson, and New York: St Martin's Press, 1978

This entertaining and insightful account of a journey through Siberia by a distinguished British travel writer is not a scholarly text, but it has probably done more than most books in English to awaken interest in the Soviet Union, even among many who have since become specialists.

Nove, Alec, *The Soviet Economic System*, London and Boston: Allen and Unwin, 1986

A classic text by a pioneer analyst of the Soviet economy

Nove, Alec, *An Economic History of the USSR 1917–1991*, London and New York: Penguin, 1992

This most recent edition of a readable, authoritative and highly informative analysis of the development of the Soviet economy has been supplemented but not yet surpassed.

Nove, Alec, *Alec Nove on Communist and Post-Communist Countries*, edited by Ian Thatcher, Cheltenham: Edward Elgar, 1998

This volume of pieces by the late Professor Nove provides a unique insight into developments from the late 1960s to mid-1990.

Palazachenko, Pavel, *My Years with Gorbachev and Shevardnadze: the Memoir of a Soviet Interpreter*, University Park: Pennsylvania State University Press, 1997

Palazachenko provides an excellent first-hand account of the monumental changes that occurred in Soviet foreign and domestic policy during the Gorbachev years.

Service, Robert, *A History of 20th-century Russia*, London and New York: Allen Lane, 1997; Cambridge, MA: Harvard University Press, 1998

This highly readable book has benefited from the author's access to recently released Soviet archives. It may well become a standard source for the subject, as its coverage of the whole century is thorough and insightful, but it is perhaps especially strong on the continuing controversies over the nature of Lenin's and Stalin's regimes.

Yeltsin, Boris [Valentin Yumashev, ghostwriter], *Against the Grain: An Autobiography*, translated by Michael Glenny, London: Jonathan Cape, and New York: Summit Books, 1990

Whatever Yumashev intended, the result of his labors on Yeltsin's behalf is a revealing account of life in the closing years of the Soviet Union, apparently from the point of view of a politician convinced of his own greatness and strikingly lacking in any principles.

Post-Soviet Developments Across the Region

Amsden, Alice H., Jacek Kochanowicz, and Lance Taylor, *The Market Meets its Match: Restructuring the Economies of Eastern Europe*, Cambridge, MA: Harvard University Press, 1994

The authors describe and explain the failure of the simplistic market medicine administered in the first five years of transition, in a major critique of the economic policies adopted in the CIS, as well as in central and eastern Europe.

Anderson, Ronald W., and Chantal Kegels, *Transition Banking: Financial Development of Central and Eastern Europe*, Oxford: Clarendon Press, and New York: Oxford University Press, 1998

Anderson and Kegels examine the evidence that has begun to emerge on the development of the financial sectors in the transition countries.

Bonin, John P., Kalman Mizsei, Istvan P. Szkely, and P. Wachtel, *Banking in Transition Economies: Developing Market-oriented Banking Sectors in Eastern Europe*, Cheltenham and Northampton, MA: Edward Elgar, 1998

Selected issues of financial reform are considered through in-depth comparative evaluations of the different approaches adopted in the post-Communist countries.

Bremmer, Ian, and Ray Taras, editors, *New States, New Politics: Building the Post-Soviet Nations*, Cambridge and New York: Cambridge University Press, 1997

This book contains 20 papers on political developments in post-Soviet states and various regions of Russia. Of particular interest are interethnic relations and the various state-building projects. Taken together, the essays provide a useful review of major developments in the initial post-Soviet period.

Colton, Tim, and Robert Legvold, editors, *After the Soviet Union: From Empire to Nations*, New York and London: Norton, 1992

This collection provides a somewhat dated but still valuable summary of events and processes before, during and after the collapse of the Soviet system.

Colton, Tim, and Robert Tucker, editors, *Patterns in Post-Soviet Leadership*, Boulder, CO: Westview Press, 1995

A collection of papers covering all of the Soviet Union's successor states in some depth, usefully tracing the impact of the Soviet legacy and the rise of new nationalisms

Fernández-Armesto, Felipe, editor, *The Times Guide to the Peoples of Europe*, revised edition, London: Times Books, 1997

This impressive survey of all the ethnic groups that share the continent is focused on contemporary conditions, but it also includes summaries of each group's history in relation to the state or states that they have inhabited. Its coverage extends to seven of the CIS countries, including the whole of Russia, but it excludes the five ex-Soviet states of Central Asia. By presenting a wealth of information from what is still an unusual angle, it provides a thought-provoking supplement to studies of states and national economies.

Gray, Gavin, *Eastern Europe*, London: Euromoney Publications, 1996

Despite its title, a study of the economic and financial aspects of the transition from Communism in 27 countries, not only in central and eastern Europe, but also in the CIS. The author packs a great deal of information into a text which is more thoughtful, and enduring, than most in the genre of business reportage.

Helmenstein, Christian, *Capital Markets in Central and Eastern Europe*, Cheltenham: Edward Elgar, 1998

This collection of comparative assessments of the emerging capital markets and related financial developments in the former command economies covers both CIS and non-CIS countries.

Henderson, Karen, and Neil Robinson, *Post-Communist Politics*, London and New York: Prentice Hall, 1997

A wide-ranging study that provides detailed political histories of the main CIS states since 1989, as well as analysis of the problems common to post-Communist states

Kaminski, Bartolomiej, editor, *Economic Transition in Russia and the New Independent States of Eurasia*, Armonk, NY: M. E. Sharpe, 1996

A comprehensive treatment of the economic conditions and policies of the former Soviet republics

Michelman, I. S., *The March to Capitalism in the Transition Countries*, Aldershot and Brookfield, VT: Ashgate, 1998

The author, a former adviser to the US Federal Reserve Board and Department of Commerce, presents an independent comparative analysis of Russia and other post-Communist countries, which will be interesting and useful for both specialists and non-expert readers.

Segbers, Klaus, and Stephan De Spiegeleire, editors, *Post-Soviet Puzzles: Mapping the Political Economy of the Former Soviet Union*, Baden-Baden: Nomos, 1995

This collection outlines a theoretical framework and provides empirical evidence for transition in the former Soviet Union, covering such issues as emerging geopolitical and territorial units; emerging economic, social, and political interests; and ethnopolitical conflicts.

Shaw, Denis J. B., editor, *The Post-Soviet Republics: A Systematic Geography*, Harlow: Longman, and New York: John Wiley, 1995

A comprehensive handbook on the CIS countries, with useful references

Skagen, Ottar, *Caspian Gas*, London: Royal Institute of International Affairs, Washington, DC: Brookings Institution, 1997

This study discusses projects started and proposals being discussed for the exploitation of natural gas deposits under the Caspian Sea, as well as other topics, including pipelines for export to Europe through Azerbaijan, Armenia, and Georgia.

UN Development Program, *The Shrinking State: Governance and Human Development in Eastern Europe and the Commonwealth of Independent States*, New York: UN Development Program, 1997

This is an important and timely study of the grave social effects of the withdrawal of the state from a wide range of activities, notably education, health, and other social services. It has had strikingly little impact on policy-making either within the post-Communist countries or beyond them.

World Bank, *From Plan to Market: World Development Report 1996*, Oxford and New York: Oxford University Press, 1996

This is a wide-ranging treatment of the opportunities and problems of the transition, not only in the CIS but also in central and eastern Europe. Readers can decide for themselves whether its conclusions remain valid – and whether the World Bank is exerting its influence (and spending our money) wisely.

Specific Countries

Ahdieh, Robert B., *Russia's Constitutional Revolution: Legal Consciousness and the Transition to Democracy, 1985–1996*, University Park: Pennsylvania State University Press, 1997

A relatively accessible analysis of a fascinating but somewhat forbidding topic, relating changes in legal forms and practices to wider changes in politics and the economy

Aves, Jonathan, *Georgia: From Chaos to Stability?*, London: Royal Institute of International Affairs, 1996

Aves describes the progress of Georgia from civil war to a fragile peace among secessionist provinces, and the dubious and varying Russian support for President Shevardnadze.

Blasi, Joseph R., Maya Kroumova, and Douglas Kruse, *Kremlin Capitalism: The Privatization of the Russian Economy*, Ithaca, NY: ILR Press, 1997

This insightful volume discusses the history, problems, and results of the privatization process in Russia, with an emphasis on the extent and impact of "insider" privatization.

Dawisha, Karen, and Bruce Parrott, editors, *Conflict, Cleavage and Change in Central Asia and the Caucasus*, Cambridge and New York: Cambridge University Press, 1997

Eight contributors and the editors survey trends towards and away from democratization and political stability in these two complex regions.

Eisenhower, Susan, and Roald Sagdeev, editors, *Central Asia: Conflict, Resolution, and Change*, Chevy Chase, MD: Center for Post-Soviet Studies, n.d.

A collection of numerous essays, many by citizens of the five states, on developments in Central Asia since independence. Topics covered include interethnic relations, foreign policy and regional integration, the creation of political institutions, and economic development.

Gachechiladze, Reva, *The New Georgia: Space, Society, Politics*, London, UCL Press, 1995

A comprehensive survey of the social and political geography of Georgia by a professor at Tbilisi State University

Hiro, Dilap, *Between Marx and Muhammad: The Changing Face of Central Asia*, London: HarperCollins, 1994

This is an interpretive history of Moslem-majority countries with Turkic and Farsi roots: six ex-Soviet republics (those in Central Asia, and Azerbaijan), as well as Afghanistan, Iran, and Turkey. Hiro assesses their geopolitical relations with Russia and the West, analyzing, among other topics, the influence of Turkey and of secularized Islam on Azerbaijan, and the conflict over Nagorno-Karabakh.

Kalyuzhnova, Yelena, *The Kazakhstani Economy: Independence and Transition*, London: Macmillan, New York: St Martin's Press, 1998

A thorough analysis of the development of the economy in the Soviet period, its legacies of trade dependence and environmental problems, and the effects of the influx of foreign investment

Kotkin, Stephen, and David Wolff, editors, *Rediscovering Russia in Asia: Siberia and the Russian Far East*, Armonk, NY: M. E. Sharpe, 1995

This valuable collection of scholarly papers usefully draws attention to the vast regions of Asian Russia that remain largely unknown to outsiders but hold great potential for the country's development in the 21st century.

Kuzio, Taras, *Ukraine: State and Nation Building*, London and New York: Routledge, 1998

This book reviews many of the most important issues in contemporary Ukrainian politics, focusing on the tasks of building a political community that will unite a population divided along ethnic and regional lines.

Kuzio, Taras, and Andrew Wilson, *Ukraine: Perestroika to Independence*, New York: St Martin's Press, and London: Macmillan, 1998

This work traces how the push for sovereignty and independence in Ukraine developed and gained political momentum through the last years of the Soviet Union. It is an important resource for those interested in this period.

Lazear, Edward P., *Economic Transition in Eastern Europe and Russia: Realities of Reform*, Stanford, CA: Hoover Institution Press, 1995

This book analyzes the economic aspects of post-Communist countries, comparing and contrasting economic policies in central and eastern Europe with those of Russia.

Olcott, M. B., *The Kazakhs*, second edition, Stanford, CA: Hoover Institution Press, 1995

An authoritative study of the history, geography, and economy of Kazakhstan, focusing on the Soviet period and the early stages of transition

Roche, A., *Children of Chernobyl*, London: HarperCollins, 1996

A very moving book, rich in detail, describing the dramatic impact of the Chernobyl' disaster on Belarus

Saikal, Amin, and William Maley, editors, *Russia in Search of its Future*, Cambridge and New York: Cambridge University Press, 1995

A clear guide to the complexities of transformation in the Russian Federation, combining surveys of recent events with analysis of long-term trends and prospects

Sakwa, Richard, *Russian Politics and Society*, London and New York: Routledge, 1996

A comprehensive and thought-provoking survey of developments after the collapse of the Soviet Union

Schleifer, Andrei, and Daniel Treisman, *The Economics of Politics and Transition to an Open Market Economy: Russia*, Paris: OECD, 1998

This monograph addresses the problems and prospects of the economic transition in Russia, with special reference to privatization and the development of capital markets.

Truscott, Peter, *Russia First: Breaking with the West*, London and New York: I. B. Tauris, 1997

The central argument of this book is that only by understanding Russian traditions can one understand the particular domestic and foreign policies that Russia has adopted. In advancing his argument, Truscott manages to provide a certain clarity to the welter of policies emanating from Yeltsin's governments.

Wilson, Andrew, *Ukrainian Nationalism in the 1990s: A Minority Faith*, Cambridge and New York: Cambridge University Press, 1996

A thorough review of the historical background and the most recent manifestation of Ukrainian nationalism. It reviews the various parties and elections in post-Soviet Ukraine. As the title suggests, it finds that nationalism has not taken root among most Ukrainians, but is instead confined to the western regions of the country.

International Relations

Allison, Roy, and Christoph Bluth, editors, *Security Dilemmas in Russia and Eurasia*, London: Royal Institute of International Affairs, 1998

The product of British and German research undertaken from 1994 to 1997, this collection comprises chapters by specialists on national, regional and global aspects of security in Russia, Central Asia, and the CIS as a whole. The civil war in Tajikistan is treated in some depth, as a regional security problem.

Baranovsky, Vladimir, editor, *Russia and Europe: The Emerging Security Agenda*, Stockholm: Sipri, and Oxford and New York: Oxford University Press, 1997

A collection of scholarly papers, including comprehensive reviews of Russia's relations with Ukraine, Belarus, and Moldova

Buszynski, Leszek, *Russian Foreign Policy after the Cold War*, Westport, CT: Praeger, 1996

A thorough account of the development of Russian foreign policy since 1991, including a description of the formation of the CIS and its early years

Cleary, Laura Richards, *Security Systems in Transition*, Aldershot and Brookfield, VT: Ashgate, 1998

A comparative study of the transformation of the US and Russian military-industrial complexes in the post-Cold War era, concentrating primarily on the political and social, rather than economic, repercussions

Ferdinand, Peter, editor, *The New Central Asia and Its Neighbours*, London: Pinter, 1994

Five papers by specialists on the international relations of the five ex-Soviet states in Central Asia, surveying particularly relations with Russia, the Middle East, and China

Jonson, Lena, and Clive Archer, *Peacekeeping and the Role of Russia in Eurasia*, Boulder, CO: Westview Press, 1996

A detailed analysis of regional conflicts in the CIS and Russian peacekeeping activities

Odom, William E., and Robert Dujarric, *Commonwealth or Empire? Russia, Central Asia, and the Transcaucasus*, Indianapolis, IN: Hudson Institute, 1995

A review of Russia's relations with the non-European CIS states and their concerns

Ra'anan, Uri, and Kate Martin, editors, *Russia: A Return to Imperialism?*, London: Macmillan, and New York: St. Martin's Press, 1996

A collection of essays focusing on Russia's relations with various post-Soviet and post-Communist countries. The overall thrust of the book is skeptical of Russian intentions in many areas.

Webber, Mark, *The International Politics of Russia and the Successor States*, Manchester: Manchester University Press, 1996

A good introduction to the foreign relations of Russia and other former Soviet states, including sections on the formation and development of the CIS, and on economic relations among CIS states

Index

Index

Index

National Frontiers and Capital Cities in the CIS